1983 1st ed OP 2500

1700

85 X

Skidmore, Owings & Merrill   Architecture and Urbanism   1973–1983

Skidmore, Owings & Merrill
Architecture and Urbanism
1973–1983

Introduction and Regional Prefaces by Albert Bush-Brown

Verlag Gerd Hatje
Van Nostrand Reinhold Company

Editorial review of commentaries and captions
and German translation: Oswald W. Grube

Firmwide book coordination and production for
Skidmore, Owings & Merrill:
Kathrin Moore in collaboration with
Debra Curtin, Sally Draht and Maureen O'Brien

Bearbeitung der Projekttexte und Bildkommentare
sowie Übersetzung ins Deutsche: Oswald W. Grube

Firmeninterne Buchkoordination und Betreuung für
Skidmore, Owings & Merrill:
Kathrin Moore in Zusammenarbeit mit
Debra Curtin, Sally Draht und Maureen O'Brien

Skidmore, Owings & Merrill

Partners 1973–1983

Nathaniel A. Owings
Gordon Bunshaft
J. Walter Severinghaus
William E. Hartmann
Walter A. Netsch
John O. Merrill, Jr.
Roy O. Allen
Edward C. Bassett
Bruce J. Graham
David A. Pugh
Myron Goldsmith
Albert Lockett
Walter H. Costa
Donald C. Smith
Marc E. Goldstein
Fazlur R. Khan
Whitson M. Overcash
James R. DeStefano
Robert Diamant
Thomas J. Eyerman
Richard E. Lenke
Michael A. McCarthy
Leon Moed
John K. Turley
Gordon Wildermuth
David M. Childs
Srinivasa Iyengar
Walter W. Arensberg
Richard H. Ciceri
Lawrence S. Doane
Parambir S. Gujral
Raul de Armas
William M. Drake
Richard C. Keating
John H. Winkler
James W. Christensen
Peter Hopkinson
Robert A. Hutchins
Roger M. Seitz
Adrian D. Smith
Kenneth A. Soldan
Robert P. Holmes
Maris Peika
Robert Armsby
Richard C. Foster
Richard A. Giegengack
Diane Legge Lohan

Contents · Inhalt

Einführung

Dieses Buch beschäftigt sich mit der Entwicklung der Architektur von Skidmore, Owings & Merrill in einem Jahrzehnt tiefgreifender gesellschaftlicher Veränderungen in den USA. Während den beiden früheren Bänden zu entnehmen ist, daß SOM damals einen breiten Kreis öffentlicher und privater Auftraggeber hatte, zeigt der vorliegende Band, daß sich inzwischen dieser Kreis in Amerika erheblich verengte.

Viele der Bauten der Jahre von 1973–1983 wurden von Bauträgern in Auftrag gegeben, die ausländisches oder amerikanisches Spekulationskapital verwalten, was Beschränkungen der architektonischen Ausdrucksmöglichkeiten nach sich zog, wie sie sie SOM bei den früheren Projekten für Firmenhauptverwaltungen selten erlebt hatte.

Um 1973 waren in den USA trotz der eindrucksvollen industriellen und verwaltungstechnischen Struktur des Landes die Städte heruntergekommen und harrten dringend der Erneuerung. Die Vororte konnten hingegen ihren fünfzigjährigen Aufschwung fortsetzen, und die Investitionen flossen dorthin statt in die Innenstädte. Ansätze zur Stadterneuerung wurden von politischen und wirtschaftlichen Ereignissen behindert: Der Watergateskandal beendete die Präsidentschaft von Richard Nixon und begrub zugleich dessen Sanierungsprogramm; mit dem Ende des Vietnamkriegs stiegen zwar die Hoffnungen auf Investitionen in den Städten, aber 1973 verursachte das arabische Erdölembargo eine Verknappung der Energie, in deren Gefolge höhere Ölpreise, eine allgemeine Inflation und Zinssätze um 20 Prozent wiederum Investitionen in den Innenstädten erheblich beeinträchtigten.

Von der darniederliegenden Wirtschaft im eigenen Land nicht ausgelastet, bemühte sich die technische und unternehmerische Elite der USA um Projekte im Ausland. Führende kanadische Bauträger vermittelten SOM Aufträge in Calgary und Edmonton. 1974 wurde SOM eingeladen, Architekten und Stadtplaner nach Algerien, Ägypten und dem Iran zu entsenden, und 1975 beauftragte Saudi-Arabien SOM mit der Planung des internationalen Flughafens und des Haj Terminal in Dschidda. Die Projekte in Algerien und Saudi-Arabien halfen SOM über die mageren Jahre von 1975 bis 1977 hinweg.

Nach 1976, als sich ausländische und amerikanische Investoren dem Bürohausbau in den amerikanischen Innenstädten zuwandten, trug SOM durch bemerkenswerte Bürotürme mit abwechslungsreichen Formen vielerorts zur Bereicherung der Stadtsilhouette bei. Das Jahr 1983 brachte für SOM einen Höhepunkt in dieser Entwicklung: Das Crocker Center in San Francisco, die dortige Federal Reserve Bank, das Crocker Center in Los Angeles [1], das Gebäude Allied Bank Plaza in Houston, das Gebäude One Magnificent Mile in Chicago [2], das Georgia-Pacific Center in Atlanta, das Southeast Financial Center in Miami, das Irving Trust Operations Center in New York [3] und das dortige Gebäude 780 Third Avenue – alle diese Bauten näherten sich um diese Zeit der Fertigstellung.

Im Vergleich mit dem Lever House in New York [4] oder dem Inland Steel Building in Chicago [5], beide entstanden in den fünfziger Jahren, fällt auf, daß SOM mit diesen neuen Projekten oft Schwierigkeiten zu meistern hatte, die von ungleichmäßig geschnittenen Grundstücken, Mischnutzungen oder der Forderung nach einem Höchstmaß an Nutzfläche bei möglichst geringen Kosten herrührten. Die sich daraus ergebenden Bauformen führten von dem früheren, technologisch begründeten Formenkanon weg. Mehr als zwei Jahrzehnte hatten das Lever House und das Inland Steel Building als Vorbilder für Architekten in aller Welt gedient. Führende Konzerne wie die Chase Manhattan Bank und die Connecticut General Life Insurance Company hatten mit ihren luxuriösen, oft mit Kunstwerken ausgestatteten Prestigebauten so etwas wie einen »Corporate style« geschaffen [6, 7]. Beim Lever House und dem Inland Steel Building wurden schmale, scheibenförmige Baukörper mit guter natürlicher Belichtung so an die Grundstücksgrenzen gerückt, daß vor dem Gebäude ein großer freier Raum mit einer platzartigen Erweiterung des Gehsteigs vor der verglasten Eingangshalle entstand. Heute wirken solche Gebäude bei all ihrer Eleganz naiv: unberührt von Fragen der Finanzierung und Vermietung, bescheiden in der Bauhöhe und Grundstücksausnutzung, indifferent gegenüber Parkplätzen oder vermietbaren Ladenflächen, sorglos gegenüber dem historischen Umfeld und nahezu blind gegenüber der Forderung nach Energieeinsparung. Mit Beginn der achtziger Jahre geriet diese Art des Bauens ins Kreuzfeuer der Kritik. Der vorgebliche Funktionalismus wurde in Frage gestellt, die durch Metallprofile gegliederte Glasfassade und die orthogonale Ordnung verfielen der Geringschätzung, und die isolierten, homogen genutzten Türme stießen als städtebauliches Modell auf Ablehnung. Die Anklage gipfelte schließlich darin, das technologische Symbol als abstrakt, kalt und leer zu verdammen.

Ganz offensichtlich ist diese scharfe Kritik Ausdruck veränderter ästhetischer Wertvorstellungen. Das SOM-Büro in San Francisco entwickelte in Zusammenarbeit mit anderen Architekturbüros schon vor 1970 das Projekt der Bank of America. 1980 sind dann das Büro in Chicago mit dem Gebäude One Magnificent Mile in Chicago und das Büro in San Francisco mit dem Gebäude Interfirst Plaza in Houston zu einer ganz neuen Vorstellungswelt vorgedrungen. Diese Bauten haben prismatische Formen und sind im Vergleich zu den flächigen und vordergründigen Gebäuden von früher schwer zu fassen. Zugleich nehmen sie Rücksicht auf umliegende Straßen, auf Nachbargebäude und Blickbeziehungen. An die Stelle einer übertriebenen Betonung des Trag-

1

2

3

Introduction

"SOM 1973–1983" reveals the architectural response of Skidmore, Owings & Merrill to a decade that greatly changed American society. Whereas its two earlier histories had recorded SOM's dramatic designs for a broad array of public and private clients, this book reveals a marked narrowing in America's sponsorship. Both federal and state governments slowed their construction programs, and, except for the ascendant pharmaceutical, energy and electronics industries, few manufacturing corporations commissioned new buildings. Like the industrial corporation, the university was no longer expanding, and although a few notable museums added large wings, America's enormous postwar expansion of its cultural institutions came to a pause. The decade 1973–1983 belonged to the urban office tower. Supplying rental office space, many towers were built by developers who, managing investments made by foreign and American speculators, set architectural constraints SOM had seldom known in earlier work for corporate patrons.

With its industrial and institutional structure in place, America in 1973 still needed to renew its worn cities, but, continuing a half-century surge, the suburbs rather than inner cities attracted investment, and urban renewal was deflected by political and economic events: Watergate ended Nixon's presidency and any chance for its urban program; withdrawal from the Vietnam War raised hopes for urban investment, but the 1973 Arab oil embargo caused an energy shortage, followed by increased oil prices, general inflation, twenty percent interest rates, and reduced urban investment. Before the pace of urban reform slackened, SOM completed important urban designs for Sacramento, Chicago and San Antonio, but, by 1975, impoverished Detroit and Cleveland, like other Northern industrial cities, could not finance their own renewal, and New York City barely avoided default on its borrowings.

4

5

Frustrated by a barren domestic economy, America's technical and organizational talent sought work abroad. Some of Canada's great developers called SOM to Calgary and Edmonton. In 1974, SOM was invited to send architects and planners to Algeria, Egypt and Iran, and, in 1975, Saudi Arabia asked SOM to design Jeddah's International Airport and Haj Terminal. The Algerian and Saudi Arabian projects helped carry SOM through the bleak years 1975–1977 when oil shifted the locus of economic power and the American economy sagged.

When, after 1976, foreign and American developers began to invest in office construction in American cities, SOM designed distinctive towers that lofted rich and often splendid forms into America's skylines. Thus, the year 1983 brought SOM to an architectural pinnacle: San Francisco's Crocker Center and Federal Reserve Bank, Los Angeles' Crocker Center [1], Houston's Allied Bank, Chicago's One Magnificent Mile [2], Atlanta's Georgia-Pacific, Miami's Southeast Financial Center, and New York City's Irving Trust [3] and 780 Third Avenue – all neared completion as 1983 approached.

In comparison with New York's Lever House [4] or Chicago's Inland Steel [5] of the 1950's, SOM's new buildings often resolve complexities imposed by irregular sites, mixed functions, and struggles to supply maximum rentable space at least cost. The resulting forms depart from the earlier technological imagery. For more than two decades, Lever House and Inland Steel had inspired the architectural profession. Elite corporate clients, such as Chase Manhattan Bank and Connecticut General, had set the corporate style by giving their own companies luxurious, prestigious, often art-filled occupancy [6, 7]. Lever House and Inland Steel confined narrow sunlighted slabs to the edges of their sites and offered air space, sidewalk plazas and glazed lobbies. Today, their elegance looks innocent: naive about those expediencies prompted by borrowed dollars and rental occupancies, modest in height and land coverage, indifferent about garages or concessionary services, cavalier about historic context, and almost oblivious to energy conservation. As the 1980's neared, their form came under attack. Its alleged functionalism was disputed; its glazed, mullioned expression and orthogonal order were demeaned; and its isolation and singular occupancy were rejected as an urban planning model. In the ultimate accusation, the technological symbol was maligned for being abstract, metallic and empty.

Clearly, that ultimate criticism springs from changed aesthetic values. SOM partners in the 1970's were less and less wedded to Lever House or Inland Steel. In collaboration with other architectural firms, SOM/San Francisco designed the Bank of America before 1970. By 1980, SOM/Chicago at Chicago's One Magnificent Mile and SOM/San Francisco at Houston's InterFirst Plaza modelled remarkably fresh images. Their form is prismatic and elusive where, before, it was planear and literal; it is attentive to adjoining streets, buildings and vistas, and it relies on faceted mass, rhythms, textures and color, without exaggerating structural systems to gain formal impact. Incorporating public spaces and circulation, the new buildings often combine retail, office and, sometimes, residential space, revealing a change in urban goals as well as aesthetic form.

Still, SOM's buildings of 1973–1983 continue SOM's commitment to originate beautiful form from technology and to perfect each building's total performance. Those hallmarks are not easily maintained. With thirty-three partners located in nine regional offices, SOM works hard at an ideal: vibrant design developed by coordinated experts bringing each project from client's stated need to completed building on scheduled date, at projected cost, and to satisfied occupancy. One SOM partner speaks of the "total integrity of completed projects". Another claims that SOM is a

werks treten als Ausdrucksmittel facettenreiche Massen, Materialien und Farben. Zu diesen Änderungen der Erscheinungsform kommen neue städtebauliche Ziele: Unter Einbeziehung von öffentlichen Funktionen und Verkehrswegen werden vielfach Läden, Büros und manchmal auch Wohnungen in einem Projekt zusammengefaßt.

Von der Gründung im Jahr 1936 an fühlte sich die Firma moderner Formgebung ohne geschichtliche Bindungen verpflichtet. Der im Ruhestand lebende Partner William Hartmann gliedert die Entwicklung von SOM in drei Phasen: 1936 bis 1946, als die Firma im Gefolge von Projekten für die Weltausstellung in Chicago und Neubauten für die H.J. Heinz Company [8] im Zweiten Weltkrieg mit den Laborbauten in Oak Ridge beauftragt wurde; 1946 bis 1973, als SOM im Rahmen der Umstellung der Wirtschaft auf zivile Aufgaben sich mit Krankenhäusern, Universitäten und Bürogebäuden – verkörpert im John Hancock Center in Chicago [9] und dem dortigen Sears Tower [10] – befaßte; sowie die Zeit seit 1973, in der die Firma vorwiegend Bürohochhäuser baute und gleichzeitig darauf wartete, daß die amerikanische Gesellschaft ihre seit langem aufgeschobenen Aufgaben bei der Sanierung von Industriegebieten und Wohnvierteln sowie des öffentlichen Nahverkehrs wahrnehmen würde.

Dem ersten Büro, das 1936 in Chicago gegründet wurde, folgte bald ein Büro in New York, an das sich weitere Büros in San Francisco und Portland anschlossen. In den siebziger Jahren entstanden schließlich vollausgestattete, von Partnern geleitete Büros in Washington, Houston, Los Angeles, Denver und Boston. Ende 1981 waren in den neun Büros mehr als 2100 Mitarbeiter tätig. Von den 33 leitenden Partnern, die SOM 1980 hatte, waren 75 Prozent seit 1960 als junge Architekten zu SOM gekommen, 80 Prozent waren nach 1970 – und der erfreulich hohe Prozentsatz von 55 Prozent sogar erst nach 1975 – in die Firmenspitze aufgestiegen.

Dieser Vormarsch junger Partner fiel mit dem Ausscheiden vieler älterer Partner zusammen. Im Jahrzehnt von 1973 bis 1983 zogen sich neben dem Gründungspartner Nathaniel Owings in New York Gordon Bunshaft, Walter Severinghaus und Roy Allen, in Chicago Walter Netsch und Myron Goldsmith und in San Francisco Edward Bassett zurück. Die hervorragenden Bauten dieser Männer hatten das Ansehen der Firma begründet. Wer würde nun die Nachfolge von Bunshaft in New York antreten, wo eine vollständige Ablösung der Führungsmannschaft erfolgte? Wer sollte die genialen baukonstruktiven Ideen des Chicagoer Partners Fazlur Khan fortführen, der 1982 überraschend einem Herzinfarkt erlag? Im Vertrauen auf ihre Selbsterneuerungskräfte entschloß sich die Firma, junge Partner aus dem Entwurfsbereich mit der Leitung neuer Regionalbüros und großer Projekte zu betrauen. Man hoffte, daß das partnerschaftliche Organisationsprinzip die jungen Partner in ihrer Entwicklung unterstützen würde, so wie es Bassett mit besonderem Gespür gelungen war, hervorragende Entwerfer in das SOM-Büro in San Francisco zu ziehen und sie dort zu fördern. Das Problem bestand darin, daß die jungen und an weit voneinander entfernten Orten tätigen Partner zwar die äußeren Erscheinungsformen der modernen Architektur erlernt hatten, ihnen jedoch diese Architektur als Triebkraft für den sozialen Fortschritt – und damit als ausdrucksvollstes Modell der gesellschaftlichen Ordnung seit der Renaissance – unbekannt geblieben war. Aus dieser Lücke erwuchs die Gefahr, daß die verjüngte Firma die sozialen und ästhetischen Grundsätze der modernen Architektur verleugnen würde, wie es einige kleinere, in Mode gekommene Architekturbüros Anfang der achtziger Jahre propagierten. Es ist einer Reihe von jungen Partnern mit ihren erfindungsreichen, zugleich von sozialem Bewußtsein und von gestalterischer Kraft geprägten Arbeiten zu verdanken, daß es dazu nicht kam.

Zu gleicher Zeit, als SOM Sorgen um Kontinuität und Nachfolge hatte, schwand auch das Vertrauen in die amerikanische Regierung, und als Folge gab die Architektenschaft ihre utopischen Zielvorstellungen auf. Ausschreitungen bei Bürgerrechtsdemonstrationen und Kundgebungen gegen die amerikanische Verwicklung in Vietnam und Kambodscha, die die Innenstädte schwer in Mitleidenschaft zogen, führten während der Regierungszeit Johnsons Ende der sechziger Jahre und Nixons Anfang der siebziger Jahre zu einer Flucht aus den großen Städten in die Vororte. Mitte der siebziger Jahre lehnte Präsident Ford Hilfe für die in Not geratene Stadt New York ab, und Präsident Carter versprach 1980 nur zögernd den Wiederaufbau des niedergebrannten New Yorker Stadtteils Bronx, die Rettung New Yorks vor dem finanziellen Zusammenbruch und eine Verbesserung des innerstädtischen Wohnungsbaus, des öffentlichen Nahverkehrs sowie der Beschäftigungslage. Dann wurde in Kalifornien und Massachusetts gegen Steuererhöhungen gestimmt, und das amerikanische Volk wählte Ronald Reagan, der versprach, die Staatsausgaben drastisch einzuschränken, zum Präsidenten.

Wenn Amerika 1982 so sehr um seine militärische Verteidigung und seine schlechte wirtschaftliche Lage besorgt war – und gleichzeitig Architekten nur noch für Bürohochhäuser und Luxuseigentumswohnungen brauchen konnte –, wo blieben dann die drängenden sozialen Probleme, die die moderne Architektur doch lösen sollte? Unter solchen Umständen nahm SOM die einzige soziale Aufgabe wahr, die gelöst werden konnte: gut zu bauen – so gut, hoffte man sogar, daß die Hochhäuser selbst eine Wiederbelebung der Innenstädte einleiten würden. Was nachgelassen hatte, war weder der formale Wagemut der Architekten noch deren soziales Bewußtsein, sondern der gesellschaftliche Idealismus des Landes. Nachdem sich die Firma während des Krieges bei den Oak Ridge Laboratories und nach dem Krieg bei der Siedlung Lake Meadows und der Air Force Academy [11] einen großen Erfahrungsschatz angeeignet hatte, suchte sie in den siebziger Jahren

6

7

8

9

10

"precision instrument". What is steadily impressive is SOM's drive to perfect artistic expression of technology through spatial and sculptural order.

SOM's growth as a partnership began almost 50 years ago. Founded in 1936, SOM started with a commitment to modern design, without traditional antecedents. Looking back, retired partner William Hartmann outlines SOM's development in three stages: 1936 through 1946, when, following the World's Fair projects and buildings for the H.J. Heinz Company [8], SOM designed the Oak Ridge Laboratories during World War II; 1946 through 1973, when SOM advanced the postwar conversion to a civilian economy by meeting needs for hospitals, universities, and office buildings, epitomized by Chicago's John Hancock Building [9] and Sears Tower [10]; and 1973 forward, when SOM built chiefly office towers while awaiting America's long-deferred decision to renew its industries, housing, and transit systems. Now, according to Hartmann, SOM and other American architectural firms are constrained from applying their enormous talents because the American economy has retreated from such investments.

Laments about America's neglect of its great architectural talent rose at a time when SOM's partnership was changing. Starting with an office in Chicago in 1936 and soon thereafter opening in New York, followed by offices in San Francisco and Portland, SOM in the 1970's established fully staffed, partner-led offices in Washington, Houston, Los Angeles, Denver and Boston. By late 1981, the 9 offices had more than 2,100 members. Of 33 General Partners in 1980, 75 percent had entered the firm as young professionals since 1960, 80 percent had become General Partners since 1970, and, of all 33, a promising 55 percent had become General Partners since 1975.

The young partners' ascendancy coincided with the retirement of many partners who had led SOM through the three stages Hartmann outlined. The decade 1973–1983 brought the retirement of founding partner Nathaniel Owings; New York's Gordon Bunshaft, Walter Severinghaus and Roy Allen; Chicago's Walter Netsch and Myron Goldsmith; and San Francisco's Edward C. Bassett. Their eminent buildings had created SOM's reputation. Who would succeed Bunshaft in SOM/New York, which had a complete turnover? Who would continue the deft structural insights lost when Chicago partner Fazlur Khan died of a heart attack in 1982? Unlike law firms, no previous American architectural partnership had survived with distinction into a third or fourth generation. Had SOM's retired leaders nurtured continuity and succession? Viewing SOM's future from his Chicago office General Partner Thomas Eyerman expected SOM's leadership to emerge through "creative dissidence". Willing to test their faith in self-renewal, SOM chose to spawn great artists by placing promising young design partners in charge of new regional offices and large projects. Hope lay in the belief that SOM's partnership would help the young partners grow, as Bassett's special vision had assembled and nurtured artists in SOM's San Francisco office. Still, the young and regionally dispersed partners had inherited modern architecture as sculptural form without knowing it as an agency of social reform, the most eloquent image for organizing society since the Renaissance. In that gap lay the great risk that the new SOM would renege on modern architecture's social and aesthetic demands, as some small, fashionable architectural firms urged in the early 1980's. That SOM did not do so is a tribute to several young partners who carried SOM into new acts of innovative art charged with social dedication and formal power.

Worry over SOM's continuity and succession rose at a time when faith in American government was unsettled and architects had abandoned utopian aspirations. Badly torn by riots during demonstrations over civil rights and American presence in Vietnam and Cambodia, American cities in Johnson's late 1960's and Nixon's early 1970's saw violence propel flight from city to suburb. At mid-decade, President Ford refused to aid distressed New York City, and President Carter in 1980 reluctantly promised to rebuild the burned-out Bronx, rescue New York City from insolvency, and improve urban housing, transportation and employment. But California and Massachusetts voted against rising taxes, and the nation elected President Reagan, who promised to reduce governmental functions. In 1982, he defended a multibillion dollar deficit and sharp reductions in urban programs. Americans then did not rally to voices urging better urban dwellings, hospitals or schools. The four conditions SOM had found essential for architectural patronage rarely converged: a society with idealistic objectives; clients who are cultured and altruistic; a respect for craftsmanship; and a reliable economy. As important urban projects were deferred or abandoned, the question was raised: "What is the national agenda? What programs are needed? Where is the demand for architecture?"

If, in 1982, America was anxious about military defense and a recessive domestic economy, and called architects only to design office towers and luxury condominiums, then where was the social urgency modern architecture was born to meet? In those circumstances, SOM accepted the only social obligation it was given: to build well, so well, one hoped, that the towers themselves might inspire an urban renaissance. What had eroded was neither modern architects' formal prowess nor their social dedications but society's domestic idealism. Even SOM was limited in how far it might lead a developer towards artistic patronage or press his office tower to benefit an urban neighborhood. Artistic integrity as a way to profit had to be demonstrated every day. Having sharpened their competence on urgent needs at the wartime Oak Ridge Laboratories and postwar Lake Meadows Housing and Air Force Academy [11], SOM sought comparable scope in the 1970's. Early in the decade, SOM addressed important urban problems in plans for Chicago 21, Sacra-

6. Chase Manhattan Bank, New York, New York.
7. Connecticut General Life Insurance Headquarters, Bloomfield, Connecticut.
8. Vinegar plant of the H.J. Heinz Company, Pittsburgh, Pennsylvania.
9. John Hancock Center, Chicago, Illinois.
10. Sears Tower, Chicago, Illinois.

nach vergleichbaren Aufgaben. Zu Beginn des Jahrzehnts wandte sich SOM mit dem Chicago 21 Plan, dem Sacramento Capitol Area Plan, einem Energieversorgungsgutachten für Oregon sowie den Studien für den San Antonio River Corridor und den Northeast Railroad Corridor wichtigen städtebaulichen Problemen zu, aber alle diese Vorschläge wurden nicht von ausdrücklichen Forderungen der Öffentlichkeit getragen.

Diese im Amerika der siebziger Jahre fehlende Willensbildung fand sich glücklicherweise gelegentlich in Nordafrika, dem Nahen Osten und Südostasien. Von 1974 bis 1978 bearbeitete SOM Projekte für Universitäten, neue Städte, Flughafengebäude und Geschäftsbauten in Algerien, Ägypten, dem Iran, Saudi-Arabien, Malaysia, Hongkong und Peking. Stellvertretend für diese internationalen Projekte steht der Haj Terminal in Dschidda. Oft allerdings folgte der Begeisterung bei der Planung lebenswichtiger Einrichtungen im Ausland die Enttäuschung über eine unvollkommene Bauausführung oder gar die Einstellung der Projekte. Als SOM den Entwurf für die Universität in Heluan bei Kairo [12] ausarbeitete, führte weder amerikanische Finanzhilfe noch der ägyptisch-israelische Vertrag von 1979 zu weiteren Aufträgen in Ägypten. Mit größtem Bedauern blickt SOM auf die Planungen für Städte im Iran aus den Jahren 1974 bis 1977 zurück.

Trotz alledem sprechen viele Partner von SOM positiv über die Erfahrungen, die sie in Nordafrika und dem Nahen Osten sammeln konnten. Ein Partner in San Francisco erinnert sich daran, wie Stadtplanungsprojekte im Iran sein Team mit dringenden sozialen Problemen konfrontierten und zu Grundlagenuntersuchungen über einheimische Bauformen anregten. In Chicago weist ein Partner auf Universitätsprojekte in Algerien hin, die »zu einer Feinfühligkeit gegenüber kulturellen Voraussetzungen führten«, und Fazlur Khan in Chicago meinte: »Die Beschäftigung mit anderen Kulturen – wie sie bei der Planung des Haj Terminal und der Universität in Mekka erforderlich wurde – veranlaßte uns zur Schaffung einer reichhaltigen und ihren lokalen Wurzeln fest verhafteten Formensprache.« In den Jahren 1975 bis 1977 vereinte das Projekt des Haj Terminal die SOM-Büros in New York und Chicago in der Suche nach kulturellen Sinnbildern, wobei neue Technologien und Computerberechnungen als Hilfen eingesetzt wurden. Wenn Khomeinis Iran die Pläne des SOM-Büros in San Francisco für die Neue Stadt Bandar Shapur verbrannt hat, hat das iranische Volk die Vision einer zwar modernen, aber doch auf der islamischen Tradition gegründeten Stadt verloren.

Bei ihrer Rückkehr zu Projekten in den Vereinigten Staaten in den Jahren 1976 und 1977 stellten die Partner von SOM vier wesentliche Grundlagen des Wachstums in den amerikanischen Städten fest: Erstens steckten kanadische und andere ausländische Investoren ihr Geld in Bauten in amerikanischen Großstädten. Zweitens dehnten die amerikanischen Städte ihre Funktionen als Finanzplätze aus, wobei durch wachsende Bankhäuser, Immobilienbüros, Rentenanstalten, Versicherungsgesellschaften und Börsenmaklerbüros ein Bedarf an Bürohochhäusern entstand. Drittens bereitete die Finanzkraft der Städte den Nährboden für Investitionen der Erziehungs- und Unterhaltungsbranche mit reichhaltigem Angebot an kulturellen Einrichtungen. Die Stadt San Francisco eröffnete die von SOM entworfene Louise M. Davies Symphony Hall [13], und in Chicago wurden die ebenfalls von SOM entworfenen Erweiterungsbauten des Art Institute [14] der Öffentlichkeit übergeben. Als vierter Wachstumsimpuls entwickelten sich in vielen älteren amerikanischen Städten Wohnviertel in der Nähe der auf dem Finanzsektor tätigen Firmen, in denen ein mehr und mehr an Universitäten ausgebildeter Nachwuchs Arbeit fand. Seit 1970 hatte sich die Zahl der 18- bis 25-jährigen um 30 Prozent erhöht und war 1980 auf 66 Millionen angewachsen. Zur Hälfte leben diese Altersjahrgänge in Ein- und Zweipersonenhaushalten in den städtischen Ballungsräumen, wo sie zunächst einen Bedarf an Mietwohnungen, später an Eigentumswohnungen hervorriefen. Wenn auch einerseits der Städtebaubericht des amerikanischen Präsidenten im Jahr 1978 123 in Not geratene Städte aufzählte, zeigten doch andererseits diejenigen Städte, die ein Wachstum ihrer Finanz- und Kultureinrichtungen zu verzeichnen hatten, einen deutlichen Aufschwung.

Ein Aufschwung der Innenstädte hatte sich schon 1976 angebahnt. Man hätte meinen sollen, daß es im Amerika der Jahre nach Vietnam und Watergate nicht viel zu feiern gab – die sich über das ganze Jahr 1976 hinziehenden Zweihundertjahrfeiern der USA widerlegten das jedoch. Völlig unerwartet setzte sich Amerika mit diesen Feiern über die Enttäuschungen mit Nixon und in Vietnam, über die Hilflosigkeit angesichts der Schwierigkeiten in den Städten und über die Apathie gegenüber nationalen Idealen hinweg. Plötzlich war auch das geschichtliche Erbe wieder von Bedeutung. Das SOM-Büro in Washington stellte die Washington Mall wieder her und plante die Constitution Gardens. Zunehmendes Interesse am Denkmalschutz brachte SOM die Aufträge, das Paramount Theater in Oakland [15] und die Orchestra Hall in Chicago [16] zu restaurieren. Am Metropolitan Square in Washington bezog das dortige SOM-Büro bei der Schließung einer Baulücke zwei sanierte Altbauten in eine neue Ladenanlage ein. Der Börsensaal von Louis Sullivans abgerissener Börse in Chicago wurde in die Erweiterung des Art Institute integriert, und beim Neubau des Crocker Center in San Francisco blieb die alte Bankhalle erhalten.

Während die Bauten von SOM in früheren Jahren oft technisches und ästhetisches Neuland beschritten, verlangte die Denkmalpflege geschichtliche Kontinuität und Respekt vor dem Bestand. Beim Anbau an das Opernhaus in San Francisco ging SOM so weit, die klassischen Mauerwerksformen in Stahlbeton fortzusetzen. Ältere Bauten beidseits des Neubaus der Federal Reserve Bank in San Francisco bildeten auch die Grundlage für die Gestaltung der zur Market Street weisenden

11

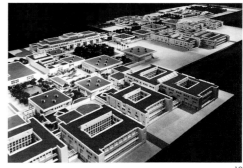

12

11. U.S. Air Force Academy, Colorado Springs, Colorado.
12. Helwan University, Helwan, Egypt.
13. Louise M. Davies Symphony Hall, San Francisco, California.
14. Art Institute of Chicago, Chicago, Illinois.
15. Paramount Theater, Oakland, California.
16. Orchestra Hall, Chicago, Illinois.

13

14

15

16

mento's Capitol Area Plan, Oregon's energy studies, the San Antonio River Corridor and the Northeast Railroad Corridor, but the proposals were not sustained by a national imperative. Fortunately, the imperative lacking in the American 1970's emerged sporadically in North Africa, the Middle East and Southeast Asia. In 1974–1978, SOM designed universities, new towns, airport terminals, and commercial buildings in Algeria, Egypt, Iran, Saudi Arabia, Malaysia, Hong Kong and Peking. Those international projects are epitomized in SOM's Haj Terminal at Jeddah. The exhilaration inherent in planning vital foreign institutions was often accompanied by disappointment over crude construction and cancelled projects. After SOM designed Cairo's Helwan University [12], additional Egyptian work was not stimulated by American investment or the 1979 Egyptian-Israeli treaty. Perhaps the greatest regret surrounds SOM's plans for Iranian cities in 1974–1977. After the Shah fled, Khomeini returned and the American Embassy was seized, a religious nationalism halted the Shah's urban and industrial plans. Seeing the Iranian reversal, cautious about fragile foreign economies, suspicious of Soviet Russia's global intentions, and still stung by the disastrous battles in Vietnam and Cambodia, Americans in 1982 watched successive South American, African and Middle Eastern conflicts and debated how much economic or architectural involvement they should risk in foreign causes.

Regrets aside, many SOM partners speak positively of their North African and Middle Eastern experience in 1975. A San Francisco partner recalls that Iranian town planning projects introduced his team to social urgency and primary research into indigenous form. A Chicago partner says that the Algerian university projects "produced a sensitivity to cultural impact". According to Chicago partner Fazlur Khan, "the process of getting into other cultures for the Haj Terminal and University at Makkah made us determined to create form that is rich and sure in its regional origin". In 1975–1977, the Haj Terminal drew SOM's New York and Chicago offices together in a search for cultural metaphor, assisted by new technology and computer analysis. If Khomeini's Iran has burned the plans SOM/San Francisco drew for Bandar Shapour, that nation has lost a sensitive vision of a modern city that preserves Islamic tradition.

When they returned to work in the United States in 1976 and 1977, the SOM partners found that American cities were responding to four sources of vitality. First, Canadian and other foreign investors began to build in American cities. Second, American cities were expanding as financial centers, with burgeoning banking houses, real estate firms, pension funds, insurance companies and brokerage houses, all creating demand for office towers. Third, the financial vitality made cities become places of education and spectacle, with lively markets and cultural institutions. Assisted by small but essential Federal subsidies, theaters, universities, museums, and symphony orchestras now flourished. New York's Metropolitan Museum of Art, later joined by Washington's National Gallery of Art, staged colossal exhibitions that toured nationally. San Francisco opened SOM's Louise M. Davies Symphony Hall [13]; Chicago dedicated SOM's additions to the Art Institute [14]. Then, in a fourth source of urban vitality, many older American cities offered residence close to the financial and professional firms where a now more largely college-educated youth found employment. By 1980, there were 66 million young adults aged 18 to 25, an increase of 30 percent since 1970, and half of them lived in one- or two-person households in metropolitan areas. They increased the demand for rental and later condominium apartments. Although the President's National Urban Policy Report in 1978 identified 123 distressed American cities, those cities that harbored growing financial industries and strong cultural institutions showed a resurgence and now offered a more diversified and extensive range of architectural commissions.

The new urban spirit was intimated as early as 1976. Although America in its post-Vietnam and Watergate years did not then seem to have much to celebrate, its year-long Bicentennial celebration proved otherwise. Far beyond anyone's expectation, the national spectacle cut through disappointment with Nixon and Vietnam, helplessness about cities, and apathy about America's ideals. Suddenly, heritage seemed important. SOM/Washington restored Washington's Mall and designed Constitution Gardens. A rising demand for architectural preservation urged SOM to undertake important restorations: the Paramount Theater in Oakland [15] and Orchestra Hall in Chicago [16]. In Washington, SOM/Washington incorporated two preserved buildings in a new mid-block store at Metropolitan Square. Louis Sullivan's Stock Exchange Trading Room was rebuilt inside SOM's additions to the Chicago Art Institute, and SOM/San Francisco's Crocker Center preserved a classical banking lobby.

Whereas SOM's earlier buildings often declared technological and aesthetic emancipations, preservationism encouraged historic continuities and welcomed context. At the San Francisco Opera House, SOM went so far as to repeat classical masonry forms in reinforced concrete. The classical buildings on either side of San Francisco's new Federal Reserve Building suggested themes that SOM/San Francisco interpreted in the Reserve's Market Street elevation, and SOM/New York's Park Avenue Plaza [17] turns its mass, chamfers its corners, and proportions its bays to accommodate the abutting Racquet and Tennis Club. At 1777 F Street, SOM/Washington incorporated nineteenth-century residential bays in a base for offices terraced above them, and SOM/Chicago's Three First National Plaza adjusts its form to preserved lower buildings. Bassett captured themes in San Francisco's classical Civic Center and banks; SOM/Washington admires Washington's L'Enfant plan and Beaux Arts buildings; and Chicago's Graham proudly empha-

Front dieses Gebäudes. Das Gebäude Park Avenue Plaza [17] des New Yorker Büros richtet sich mit seiner Massengliederung, den abgeschrägten Ecken und der Proportionierung seiner Stützenfelder nach dem unmittelbar davorliegenden Racquet and Tennis Club. Bei dem Projekt 1777 E Street bezog das Büro in Washington Teile einer vorhandenen Wohnbebauung aus dem 19. Jahrhundert in ein Podium ein, über dem sich terrassenförmig Bürogeschosse erheben. Auch der Baukomplex Three First National Plaza des Chicagoer Büros paßt sich an erhalten gebliebene, niedrige Bauten an. Bassett griff Motive aus dem neoklassizistischen Civic Center in San Francisco und von Bankgebäuden derselben Zeit auf, das Büro in Washington bewundert L'Enfants Plan für diese Stadt und Bauten der Beaux-Arts-Epoche, Graham in Chicago schließlich betont mit Stolz die Treue der Firma gegenüber dem Erbe von Louis Sullivan und John Welborn Root.

Die Bauten, die SOM zwischen 1973 und 1983 errichtete, spiegeln auch die Auseinandersetzung mit weiteren Veränderungen in der amerikanischen Gesellschaft. Da ist einmal das Problem der Bevölkerungsverteilung und des Landverbrauchs. Von 203 Millionen Menschen im Jahr 1970 wuchs die Bevölkerung der USA bis 1980 auf 226 Millionen an. Etwa 85 Prozent dieses Wachstums vollzog sich im Westen und Südwesten des Landes. Anfang 1973 arbeitete SOM an einer Planung, die den gesamten Staat Kalifornien umfaßte, und wenig später entstand die Planstudie für die Stadtregion von San Antonio in Texas. Mehr als 400.000 Hektar Freiland wurden jährlich verbaut, und 1975 lebten bereits 73 Prozent der Bevölkerung in den 272 städtischen Ballungsräumen der USA. SOM stellte mit einer Reihe von wesentlichen Stadtplanungsarbeiten und Bauprojekten fünf allgemein als Leitbilder angesehene Regeln dieser Siedlungstätigkeit in Frage: Die erste Regel schreibt die Trennung von Wohn- und Arbeitsbereichen vor. Als Produkt der frühen Industriestadt hält sich diese Vorstellung an Planungsrichtlinien, die eine Mischbebauung aus Büros und Wohnungen verbieten. Gerade in dieser Mischung bestand jedoch die Pioniertat des John Hancock Center in Chicago, und bei den neuen SOM-Bauten Olympic Centre [18] und One Magnificent Mile wurden weitere Mischnutzungen realisiert. Die zweite Regel sagt aus, daß das Leben in den Vororten dem Leben in der Stadt vorzuziehen sei. Ungefähr die Hälfte der Arbeitnehmer lebt heute dort, aber nur ein Viertel hat dort auch seinen Arbeitsplatz. Im Chicago 21 Plan bietet SOM eine innerstädtische Alternative zum Leben in den Vororten an. Die dritte Regel legt die Lebensart und das Streben der Amerikaner auf den Besitz eines frei stehenden Einfamilienhauses fest. Demgegenüber wird mit den Apartments des Dearborn Village aus dem Chicago 21 Plan eine verdichtete Bebauung in parkartiger Umgebung angeboten. Die vierte Regel geht vom durchgehenden Autoverkehr in Wohnvierteln aus. Dieser Planungsansatz wird durch die grundlegenden Untersuchungen in Frage gestellt, die SOM für das Irvine Center, den San Antonio River Corridor und Chicago – dort insbesondere mit dem Vorschlag der State Street Mall – durchführte. Eine fünfte und entscheidende Planungsannahme liegt in Amerikas Vorliebe für den Privatwagen und den Güterverkehr auf der Straße. SOM plante demgegenüber in Portland, Oregon eine Nahverkehrszone für Omnibusse und Fußgänger und schlug für die nordöstliche Eisenbahnstrecke von Boston im Norden bis Washington, D.C. im Süden, eine umfassende Modernisierung vor.

In einer Reihe von weiteren Untersuchungen widmeten sich Planer von SOM der Erhaltung von Landschaftsräumen. Naturschutzvereine wie der Sierra Club setzten sich zunehmend durch und wurden von neuen Verfechtern dieser Idee unterstützt, denen es gelang, die kalifornische Pazifikküste nördlich von San Francisco sowie den Küstenstreifen um Big Sur zwischen San Francisco und Los Angeles zu retten, wobei Nathaniel Owings, einer der Gründer von SOM, eine führende Rolle spielte. Das SOM-Büro in Portland schlug die Erhaltung von Inseln und Wasserläufen in städtischen Bereichen vor, die an den Willamette River grenzen. Als SOM 1973 mit dem California Tomorrow Plan an die Öffentlichkeit trat, wurde auf Drängen der Naturschutzbehörde zur Rettung von Waldgebieten, Sümpfen und Wiesenland der Trust for Public Land ins Leben gerufen. Die Notwendigkeit der Regionalplanung wird auch in der Studie für den San Antonio River Corridor von SOM deutlich, in der die Erhaltung des Flußlaufs als ein Mittel zur Verbesserung der städtischen Erholungsanlagen sowie der Geschäfts- und Wohngebiete vorgeschlagen wurde.

Als nächstes wandte sich SOM den schwierigen Problemen zu, die bei unmittelbar an Schnellstraßen angrenzender Bebauung auftreten. Bis SOM in den fünfziger Jahren das Gebäude der Connecticut General Life Insurance und im Anschluß daran eine Reihe von weiteren Firmenhauptverwaltungen auf dem Land entwarf, gab es nur wenige gute Lösungen für dieses Problem. Das SOM-Büro in San Francisco plante auf einem bewaldeten Areal an einem See in der Nähe von Tacoma, Washington für die Weyerhaeuser Company ein terrassiertes Bürogebäude [19], das internationale Beachtung fand. In den siebziger Jahren entstanden als beispielhafte Lösungen der Komplex 70/90 Universal City Plaza in Los Angeles [20], der sich in seiner Gliederung einem Hanggrundstück an einer Schnellstraße anpaßt, sowie als weitere Firmensitze an Schnellstraßen die Komplexe für Texaco, General Electric und Westinghouse. Das Southern California Operations Center der Wells Fargo Bank in El Monte, Kalifornien stellte als Gebäude für die Datenverarbeitungsanlagen einer Bank einen neuen Bautyp dar. Mit dem Irvine Center in Irvine, Kalifornien schlug SOM auch einen neuen regionalen Prototyp für zusammengelegte Bürogebäude vor.

Mit der Energiekrise kamen weitere Herausforderungen. Das Büro in Portland entwickelte schon frühzeitig ein etwa 125 Quadratmeter großes Versuchshaus und eignete sich damit Kenntnisse über den Energieverbrauch an. Solche Experimente erregten Aufmerksamkeit, als klar wurde, daß

17

17. Park Avenue Plaza, New York, New York.
18. Olympia Centre, Chicago, Illinois.
19. Weyerhaeuser Headquarters, Tacoma, Washington.
20. 70/90 Universal City Plaza, Universal City, California.
21. 33 West Monroe Street, Chicago, Illinois.

18

19

20

21

sizes SOM's faithfulness to the legacy left by Louis H. Sullivan and John Welborn Root. Still, although they are now more willing to seek coherence, even if it means suppressing structural display, SOM did not resort to historical quotation or eclectic reference; they accepted the contextual obligation as part of their more urgent quest for strong modern architecture.

SOM's architecture in 1973–1983 also reveals the partnership's response to other changes that swept American society. One was the problem of population dispersal and land consumption. The American population grew from 203 million in 1970 to 226 million in 1980, with about 85 percent of the increase occurring in the West and Southwest. Early in 1973, SOM worked on a statewide plan for California and, later, designed a plan for metropolitan San Antonio in Texas. Open land was being converted to buildings at the rate of one million acres a year, and in 1975, 73 percent of the American people lived in 272 metropolitan regions. Five national preferences guiding such settlements were challenged by SOM in important urban designs and buildings. One preference orders separation of residence from work. A product of early industrial cities, that idea persists in zoning regulations forbidding mixtures of offices and apartments. Such a mixture was pioneered by Chicago's John Hancock Tower, and SOM's new Olympia Centre [18] and One Magnificent Mile offer new combinations. A second idea is that suburban life is preferable, and almost 50 percent of Americans now live in suburbs, with perhaps half of them employed there. SOM's Chicago 21 Plan offers an urban alternative. A third goal establishes the style and scope of American ambition: ownership of the single-family, free-standing house. The apartments in Chicago 21's Dearborn Village offer densities in parklike settings. The fourth preference is the neighborhood vehicular street. That planning premise is challenged in SOM's seminal studies for Irvine Center, San Antonio River Corridor, and Chicago 21, notably its State Street Mall. A fifth and crucial urban premise lies in America's preference for the automobile and truck. SOM planned the bus-pedestrian mall in Portland, Oregon, and proposed an extensive modernization of the Northeast Rail Corridor, starting in Boston and ending in Washington, D.C. SOM also designed subway stations for Cambridge and San Francisco and incorporated transit stations in Minneapolis' Pillsbury Center and Miami's Southeast Financial Center.

Another series of studies directed SOM's talents to conservation of open land and forest. Becoming increasingly effective, older conservationist groups, such as the Sierra Club, were now joined by new advocates who saved California's coast north of San Francisco and the Big Sur, where SOM's Nathaniel Owings was a leader. SOM/Portland proposed conservation of islands and waterways in metropolitan areas bordering Oregon's Willamette River. In 1973, when SOM published The California Tomorrow Plan, the Trust for Public Land, urged by the Nature Conservancy, was established to save woodlands, swamps and meadows. The requisite regional planning is demonstrated in SOM's San Antonio River Corridor Study, which proposed water conservation as a means for improving that City's recreational lands and commercial and residential areas.

Next, SOM addressed the vexatious problems of buildings bordering highways. Until road construction slowed in the late 1970's, America was making 40,000 miles of road a year and opened much of rural America to development. Consuming land at the rate of 42 acres, each mile of the new Federal highways exposed an additional 2,500 acres to a potential 2,400 houses occupied by 8,500 people in dispersed residential settlements bordered by industry and offices. Until the 1950's, when SOM designed Connecticut General, followed by many fine rural administrative headquarters, builders had few distinguished models. Now in the 1970's, for the Weyerhaeuser Company, on a wooded lakeside outside Tacoma, Washington, SOM/San Francisco designed an internationally admired tier of terraced office floors [19]. 70/90 Universal City Plaza [20] was modelled to ride a slope adjacent to a Los Angeles freeway, and highway-related headquarters were designed for Texaco, General Electric and Westinghouse. A new building type, an office building for a bank's computers, was demonstrated at the Southern California Operations Center for Wells Fargo Bank in El Monte, California. Now SOM also proposed a new regional model for clustered office buildings: Irvine Center, California.

The energy crisis brought still other challenges. Beginning with an experimental 1,280-square-foot house in Oregon, SOM/Portland early developed expertise in energy analysis. Such experiments drew attention when even the Alaskan oil flowing from Prudhoe Bay beginning in June 1977 could not meet energy needs if consumption was not curtailed. Seeking a State policy for alternates to oil for producing electricity, Oregon's Governor in 1973 commissioned SOM/Portland to study nuclear and hydroelectric power. SOM's study showed that strong conservation measures could reduce reliance on oil and nuclear generation. Failure in Pennsylvania's Three Mile Island nuclear plant prompted the antinuclear demonstration at Washington in 1979, and coal still remained the primary source of electricity in 1982. By then, oil was plentiful again, as supplies increased and America stabilized its rate of consumption. Meanwhile, energy economies sparked four architectural responses: compact massing that reduces exposed surfaces; improved insulation and cladding; lessened dependence on lamps and motors; and improved cycling of cooled or heated air. The first response led to the cubic massing and internal atria in SOM/Chicago's 33 West Monroe Street in Chicago [21] and Pan American Life Center in New Orleans [22]. The second response brought smaller panes of thermal glass and larger use of masonry walls, after Italian

sogar das ab Juni 1977 aus der Prudhoe Bay in Alaska kommende Erdöl den Energiebedarf nicht ohne Verbrauchseinschränkungen würde decken können. Der Gouverneur von Oregon suchte 1973 nach Alternativen zum Erdöl bei der Stromerzeugung und beauftragte das Büro in Portland mit einer Untersuchung über die Stromgewinnung aus Kernenergie und Wasserkraft. Das Ergebnis war, daß weitgehende Maßnahmen zur Energieeinsparung die Abhängigkeit vom Öl und von der Kernenergie verringern könnten.

Inzwischen hatte die Energiesparwelle zu vier Reaktionen auf dem Gebiet der Architektur geführt: zur Schaffung kompakter Baumassen mit reduzierten Außenflächen, zur Verbesserung der Wärmedämmung und der Außenverkleidungen, zur Verringerung der Abhängigkeit von Kunstlicht und mechanischen Anlagen sowie zu Verbesserungen bei der Wiederverwendung von gekühlter oder aufgeheizter Luft. Die erste Reaktion führte zu den kubischen Baumassen und den innenliegenden Atrien bei den vom Chicagoer Büro entworfenen Gebäuden 33 West Monroe Street in Chicago [21] und Pan American Life Center in New Orleans [22]. Die zweite Reaktion führte zu kleineren Fensterflächen mit Scheiben aus Wärmeschutzglas und einem größeren Anteil massiver Wände, nachdem in den italienischen Steinbrüchen die Technik des Sägens und Polierens von sehr dünnen Granittafeln vervollkommnet worden war. Man sieht die Auswirkungen dieser Faktoren am Gebäude InterFirst Plaza in Houston [23] und am Crocker Center in San Francisco, die beide vom Büro in San Francisco entworfen wurden. Die dritte Reaktion tritt wiederum bei den Atrien sowie den doppelgeschossigen Aufzügen und der Arbeitsplatzbeleuchtung des Gebäudes 33 West Monroe Street in Chicago zutage. Die vierte Reaktion schließlich war die entscheidende Entwurfsgrundlage für die vom Büro in Denver entworfenen Gebäude der Gulf Mineral Resources Company [24]. Bei dem vom New Yorker Büro entworfenen Bau der Prudential Insurance Company in der Nähe von Princeton, New Jersey [25] werden als Experiment alle vier Aspekte miteinander kombiniert.

Zu den steigenden Energiekosten kamen die negativen Einflüsse der Inflation auf das Bauwesen. Seit 1960 hatten sich die Baukosten mehr als verdreifacht, und die Inflationsrate begünstigte den Bau von Bürohochhäusern, die hohe Mieteinnahmen versprachen. Die gestiegenen Kosten hatten auch zur Folge, daß unbebaute oder baulich gering genutzte Grundstücke in den Städten – wie beispielsweise Parkplätze – liegenblieben, da private Geldanleger auf ein Ansteigen der Rendite spekulierten. Oft führten Schwierigkeiten bei der Kapitalbeschaffung zu langen Verzögerungen zwischen der Planung eines Gebäudes und seiner Realisierung. Nachdem das Büro in San Francisco 1973 die Pläne für das Bürogebäude 444 Market Street fertiggestellt hatte, geriet das Projekt in die Rezession der Jahre 1974 und 1975, und mit dem Bau konnte erst begonnen werden, als die Shaklee Company als Hauptmieter auftrat. Die Entwurfsarbeiten mußten allgemein beschleunigt werden, um die Mittel der Geldanleger zu mobilisieren und so schnell wie möglich Mieteinnahmen zur Deckung der hohen Kosten des am Kapitalmarkt aufgenommenen Geldes zu erzielen. Die steigenden Kosten führten zu flexiblen und wirtschaftlichen Konstruktionssystemen bei Hochhäusern, insbesondere zu der sogenannten Rohrbauweise. SOM nahm bei dieser Entwicklung eine führende Rolle ein. Entscheidend für die Wahl zwischen Profilstahl oder Stahlbeton für das Tragwerk waren nicht die Materialkosten, sondern – in Abhängigkeit vom Ort und vom Zeitpunkt der Bauausführung – ebenso die Fertigstellungszeiten. 1981 mußten die tiefen Fensterlaibungen aus Granit, die das Büro in New York für ein Hochhaus in Kanada vorgeschlagen hatte, aus Kostengründen entfallen. Den Luxus plastisch gestalteter Fassaden mit tiefen Rücksprüngen, wie sie in früheren Jahren beim Tenneco Building in Houston oder beim Alcoa Building in San Francisco [26] möglich gewesen waren, konnte sich SOM nun kaum mehr erlauben.

Trotz des Einflusses der Inflation und der Energiekosten auf die Architektur machte die Bautechnik gegenüber den sechziger Jahren nur unwesentliche Fortschritte. Variationen der Rohrbauweise ermöglichten flexiblere und leichtere Tragwerkskonstruktionen bei Hochhäusern, erleichterten die Anpassung der Baumasse an unregelmäßig geschnittene Grundstücke und erlaubten die Kombination von Büro-, Laden- und Wohnnutzungen. Verbesserte getönte und reflektierende Gläser eröffneten neue Gestaltungsmöglichkeiten für durchsichtige und undurchsichtige Fassadenflächen – oftmals in Verbindung miteinander.

Die Möglichkeiten der Datenverarbeitung wurden von SOM frühzeitig erkannt. 1963 installierte die Firma eine IBM 1620 zur Berechnung statischer Systeme. Das ehrgeizige Unternehmen gewann immer mehr an Bedeutung; es wurden nun nicht nur Daten über Personalstunden und Kosten, Baustoffe sowie Inneneinrichtungen mit der Datenverarbeitung erfaßt, sondern SOM entwickelte auch die Möglichkeiten weiter, die der Computer zur graphischen Aufzeichnung besitzt. 1976 gelang mit weiterentwickelten Geräten die Vervielfältigung von Grundrissen mit genauen Angaben über konstruktive Details, Kanalführungen, elektrische Leitungen, Rohre und Möblierung. Darauf folgte die schnelle und exakte Untersuchung von Alternativen bei der Gebäudeform, dem Konstruktionssystem und dem Energieverbrauch sowie der Materialverwendung. 1980 versetzten dann graphische Computerausdrucke die Architekten von SOM in die Lage, perspektivische Darstellungen des Irving Trust Operations Center in New York und Querschnitte des Gebäudes 33 West Monroe Street in Chicago zu untersuchen. 1981 wurden dreidimensionale Schemazeichnungen der Innenstädte von Denver, Chicago, New York und Los Angeles in den Datenverarbeitungsgeräten der Firma gespeichert, so daß von SOM geplante Neubauten maßstäblich in diese Ansichten hin-

22

22. Pan American Life Center, New Orleans, Louisiana.
23. InterFirst Plaza, Houston, Texas.
24. Gulf Mineral Resources Headquarters, Denver, Colorado.
25. Prudential at Princeton, Plainsboro, New Jersey.
26. Alcoa Building, San Francisco, California.

23

24

25

quarriers perfected their sawing and polishing of thin granite slabs. Those features are visible in SOM/San Francisco's InterFirst Plaza in Houston [23] and Crocker Center in San Francisco. The third response is evident in the atria, double-story elevators and task lighting of 33 West Monroe Street. The fourth is essential to SOM/Denver's Gulf Mineral Resources Company buildings outside Denver [24]. An experiment combining aspects of all four responses is the office building SOM/New York designed for the Prudential Insurance Company outside Princeton, New Jersey [25].

As energy costs rose, inflation itself directly affected architecture. With construction costs more than tripled since 1960, inflation favored office towers that promised rental income. Costs also decreed that a city's open or underutilized land, including its parking lots, would remain vacant until private investors could gamble on a building's profitable return. Difficulties in assembling capital often caused long delays between a building's conception and erection. With plans completed in 1973, SOM/San Francisco's 444 Market Street ran against the economic slump of 1974 and 1975 and only after the Shaklee Company became its prime tenant could construction start towards 444's opening in 1981.

Rapid design was required to attract investors' funds, gain approval for plans, erect buildings, and realize rental income to carry the high cost of borrowed funds. Few architectural firms were ready to respond to clients' need for alternative schemes and speedy cost analysis. When capital was ready, construction drawings were wanted quickly, and rising costs demanded flexible, economical structural systems, notably the perimetal columnar, or tube, structures in high-rise towers, where SOM led the way. Steel might be more costly than concrete but quicker to erect, or the reverse, depending on the time and place. In 1981, the deep granite window frames SOM/New York proposed for a tall building in Canada were eliminated to save costs. Rarely did SOM now have the luxury of modelled surfaces and deep reveals, as in Houston's earlier Tenneco Building or San Francisco's Alcoa Building [26]. Instead, graphic composition in flamed and polished granite appears in San Francisco's Crocker Center, and a pattern of white and black granites ornaments Miami's Southeast Financial Center.

Although general inflation and energy costs affected architecture, technology itself was not greatly advanced beyond what was current in the late 1960's. Versatile structural tubes gave more flexible, lighter construction in tall buildings, eased the fitting of buildings to irregular sites, and accommodated combinations of office, commercial and residential spaces. Improved tinted and mirrored glass introduced varieties of translucency and opaqueness, often in combination. Where manufacturers could not eliminate ripples from double glazed windows, architects might choose to seek overall shimmering surfaces, as in SOM/New York's Park Avenue Plaza. Although the astronautical explorations stimulated invention, direct architectural dividends were minimal, limited to miniaturized electronic equipment, new alloys and new fabrics, but, indirectly, space exploration hastened the development of computer analysis, which held much architectural promise.

SOM early saw its potential. Installing an IBM 1620 in 1963, SOM set it to analyzing structural design. That ambitious goal became increasingly important, and while administrative data about man-hours and costs, materials, and furnishings were being computerized, SOM developed the computer's graphic potential. Duplicating floor plans, with detailed structure, ducts, wiring, pipes and furniture, was achieved with improved computers and staff by 1976. Next came rapid and accurate computer analysis of alternate building configurations, structural systems, energy demands, and building materials. By 1980, computerized graphic representations enabled SOM's architects to analyze multiple perspectives of New York's Irving Trust Operations Center and transverse sections through Chicago's 33 West Monroe Street. In 1981, SOM's computers could display downtown Denver, Chicago, New York and Los Angeles in three-dimensional views, and buildings SOM proposed could be inserted in scale and studied from many angles. The computer showed the tower of Chicago's Three First National Plaza [27] in its urban setting, documented year-round hourly incidence of sun on its nine-story atrium, and drew its structure and atrium trusses. Computer graphics revealed the shadows to be cast by Chicago's One Magnificent Mile [28, 29], helped with the analysis of the tubular frame carrying Houston's Allied Bank [30], and drew the complexly curved form of Jeddah's Haj tents [31, 32]. For Denver's Gulf Mineral Resources buildings, a computer solved 72 equations simultaneously on an hour-by-hour basis to predict energy efficiencies. SOM's adventurous and costly development of computerized representations is a signal and growing contribution to architects and clients.

Central to its technical and social response to the currents affecting American society was SOM's concern for aesthetic quality. Beyond the decisions needed daily in studio discussions of a building's form, there was rising inquiry into modern architecture's premises. In 1981, a conference in New York City confronted SOM/New York's design partners with challenges made by architects who, claiming to be "post-modernists", criticized SOM's attitudes about functionalism, structural expression and technological imagery. Critics often cited directions SOM had taken in the 1960's, like SOM/Chicago's John Hancock Tower, but neglected new directions in SOM/Houston's Allied Bank, SOM/New York's Park Avenue Plaza, SOM/Chicago's One Magnificent Mile, or the even more dramatic departures in SOM/San Francisco's California First Bank and Federal Reserve Building. Some SOM partners themselves held reservations about isolated, tall office towers and

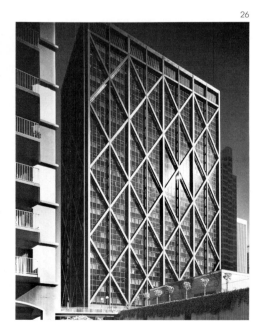

26

einkopiert und aus verschiedenen Blickwinkeln untersucht werden konnten. Ein Computer stellte auch das Hochhaus Three First National Plaza in Chicago [27] im innerstädtischen Kontext dar, belegte im Jahresverlauf den stündlichen Sonneneinfall in das neun Geschosse hohe Atrium der Anlage und zeichnete Tragwerk und Dachträger des Atriums auf. Mit Hilfe von Computeruntersuchungen wurde auch die Beschattung festgestellt, die von dem neuen Hochhaus One Magnificent Mile in Chicago [28, 29] ausgehen wird, sowie eine Berechnung des Rohrtragwerks der Allied Bank in Houston angefertigt [30] und die mehrfach gekrümmte Form der Zeltdachkonstruktion für den Haj Terminal in Dschidda aufgezeichnet [31, 32]. Ein Computer löste für die Gebäude der Gulf Mineral Resources in Denver gleichzeitig 72 Gleichungen, um für jede Stunde des Tages den Energieverbrauch feststellen zu können.

An zentraler Stelle bei den Lösungen, die SOM in technischer und sozialer Hinsicht für die Fragen der amerikanischen Gesellschaft bietet, steht das Bemühen um ästhetische Qualität. Über die alltägliche Arbeit im Büro hinaus läßt sich eine zunehmende Beschäftigung mit den Voraussetzungen der modernen Architektur überhaupt feststellen. 1981 sahen sich auf einer Konferenz in New York die Entwurfspartner des dortigen SOM-Büros mit Vorwürfen anderer Architekten konfrontiert, die sich »Postmoderne« nannten und die die Haltung von SOM gegenüber dem Funktionalismus, der Zurschaustellung der Konstruktion und der technologischen Formenwelt kritisierten. Allzuoft führten die Kritiker SOM-Arbeiten aus den sechziger Jahren an – wie etwa den John Hancock Tower des Chicagoer Büros –, ließen aber neue Richtungen außer acht, wie sie bei vielen Arbeiten der jüngsten Zeit zutage treten, so bei der Allied Bank des Büros in Houston, dem Gebäude One Magnificent Mile des Chicagoer Büros oder bei der California First Bank und dem Federal Reserve Building des Büros in San Francisco – die sich noch weiter von der früheren Formensprache entfernen.

So unterhaltsam diese Diskussionen auch waren, sie konnten SOM nicht von ihrem ästhetischen Erbe abbringen. Obgleich die Mannigfaltigkeit der Projekte, die SOM zu Beginn der achtziger Jahre bearbeitete, kaum ein gemeinsames Grundmotiv erkennen ließ, pflichten wahrscheinlich die meisten Partner immer noch dem verstorbenen Fazlur Khan und seiner Ansicht bei: »Unsere Kunstform ist die Technologie.« Voll Stolz über den Haj Terminal in Dschidda forderte Khan, das technische Tragwerk, die plastische Form und die räumliche Folge so zu verquicken, daß am Ende eine einfache und selbstverständliche Einheit daraus würde. Nach seiner Ansicht sollte sich die Form eines Hochhauses aus dem Raum ergeben, den eine ganz von der Technik bestimmte Konstruktion erzeugt. Er war begeistert von der Idee des Hochhauses: »Das Hochhaus schafft Arbeits- und Wohnraum, wann und wo es am notwendigsten ist.« Seine Größe und hohe Dichte faszinierten ihn: »Das Hochhaus ist ein beachtlicher Erfolg, sowohl in wirtschaftlicher als auch in symbolischer Hinsicht.« Khan sah die Technik als große Stütze des Städtebaus an und rief die Geschichte der Konstruktionssysteme für Hochhäuser ins Gedächtnis – vom einfachen Stahlskelett aus Balken und Stützen zu Konstruktionen mit aussteifenden Wänden, dann weiter zum einfachen Rohrskelett, zur Rohr-in-Rohr-Konstruktion und schließlich zur Konstruktion aus gebündelten Rohren, wie beim Sears Tower in Chicago. So macht die Anwendung der Rohrbauweise bei Hochhäusern wie One Magnificent Mile und Olympia Centre in Chicago erst die bewundernswerte soziale Leistung der Kombination von gewerblichen Räumen und Wohnungen möglich. Das ist die eine Seite der Tradition von SOM: Der funktionale Zweck der Konstruktion ist gesellschaftlicher Art.

Für SOM hat konstruktiver Ausdruck nach Fazlur Khan aber noch eine andere Bedeutung. SOM ist nicht zufrieden mit den rein technischen oder sozialen Leistungen einer Form, sondern möchte der Konstruktion darüber hinaus symbolhaften Charakter verleihen. In diesem Sinn erinnern die Arkade vor der Federal Reserve Bank in San Francisco und die Turmgruppen des Gebäudes One Magnificent Mile in Chicago an die baukonstruktiven Ursprünge großer historischer Sinnbilder wie des ägyptischen Hypostylons, des griechischen Säulengangs, der römischen Basilika und der gotischen Kathedrale. Dort werden überall konstruktive Elemente mit symbolischer Bedeutung verwendet: Die dorische Säule wird zur griechischen Ordnung an sich und der mittelalterliche Strebepfeiler zum gotischen Joch. Im Gegensatz zu Wright und Sullivan, für die die Natur Quelle organischer Metaphern war, sieht SOM in der Natur Ordnung und Sinnhaftigkeit in der Art einer gut funktionierenden Maschine. Weil diese Maschine Befreiung von der Abhängigkeit vom buchstabengetreuen Ausdruck der Funktion bietet, erhoben sich die modernen mechanistischen Formen sehr schnell über die Funktion und bildeten sich zu einem Ausdruck des Mechanismus als Symbol heraus. Dank der Elektrizität konnte bei Hochhäusern auf natürliche Belüftung und Belichtung sowie auf eine enge räumliche Beziehung unter den Nutzern verzichtet werden. Die Maschinen entließen die mechanistische Form aus der Treue zur Funktion. So konnte sich die Form die ihr gemäße geometrische Perfektion suchen sowie die Präzision, Wirtschaftlichkeit und Schönheit der Technik rühmen. Die gebrauchstüchtige und schlanke Form wurde zu einem Symbol, das für Wirtschaftlichkeit, Logik, Verläßlichkeit und Fortschritt steht. Der neue Typ des unternehmungslustigen Bauträgers eiferte den früheren Auftraggebern, den Firmenhauptverwaltungen, nach und wollte gerade diese Wertvorstellungen ausgedrückt sehen.

Umfeld für das Bestreben der Bauträger, Gebäude mit Prestigecharakter zu errichten, war die zunehmende Begeisterung für das Bauen in den Finanz- und Geschäftsvierteln der Städte. Ausländische Investoren erkannten die günstigen Gelegenheiten frühzeitig – wie das Beispiel der Firma

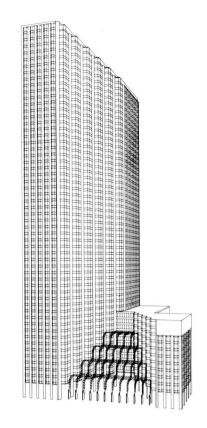

27

27. Three First National Plaza, Chicago, Illinois.
28, 29. One Magnificent Mile, Chicago, Illinois.
30. Allied Bank Plaza, Houston, Texas.
31, 32. Haj Terminal, Jeddah, Saudi Arabia.

28

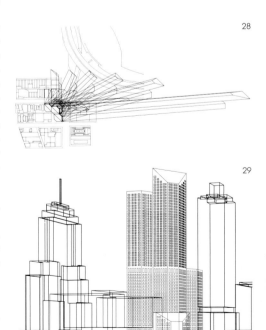

29

20

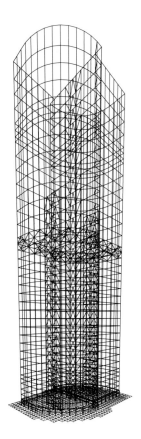

30

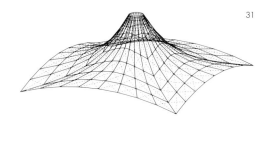

31

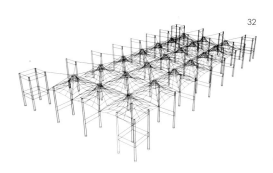

32

doubted that Chicago's 4.5-million-square-foot Sears Tower should enter 25,000 people through a mere revolving door. SOM's recent buildings were neither abstractions nor uncaring about urban and historic context, but SOM's critics wanted more. Many rejected early modern architecture's measures of efficiency, economy and mechanism. One writer blamed the liberal social goals of Walter Gropius, conveniently omitting the Saarinens and Bunshafts who did not share them but were modernists none the less. What the post-modernists wanted was never clear. Sometimes they fashioned shiny worlds of exposed machinery, ornamented facades with whimsical stylistic quotations, and manipulated masses and voids to butt contrasted scales. Their debates were not nearly as profound as those that ushered modern architecture into the American 1930's, an earlier decade when building slackened and theorists flourished.

However entertaining, those discussions did not deflect SOM from its aesthetic heritage. Even though the diversity of SOM's buildings in the early 1980's made it increasingly difficult to define any unifying theme, perhaps most partners still agree with the late Fazlur Khan's statement, "Technology is our art form". Proud of the Haj Terminal, Khan urged the marriage of technical support, sculptural form and spatial sequence so that their unity looks simple and inevitable. A tower's form, he believed, should originate from spaces formed by a structure that integrates all technology. He was enthusiastic about the tall building: "It gives work and residential space when and where most needed." Its scale and density excited him: "The tall building is a remarkable economic and symbolic success." When he recited the history of structure, how the steel beam and column frame led to shear wall construction, then to framed tubes, next to tubes within tubes, and ultimately to a cluster of tubes, as in the Sears Tower, Khan presented technology as a great urban service. Thus, the tube structures enabling One Magnificent Mile and the Olympia Centre to combine work space with residential space are admirable for their social service. That is one part of SOM's heritage: Structure's functional purpose is social.

For SOM structural expression has a further meaning, as Khan also insisted. Not satisfied by a form's sheerly mechanical or social performance, SOM has sought to make structure symbolic. Here the arcade at San Francisco's Federal Reserve Bank and the towers grouped at Chicago's One Magnificent Mile suggest the structural origins of great historic symbols, such as the Egyptian hypostyle hall, the Grecian colonnade, the Roman basilica, and the Gothic cathedral. There, the structural element is organized for symbolic intent: Doric column becomes Grecian order and mediaeval pier becomes Gothic bay. Unlike Wright and Sullivan who adopted organic metaphors, SOM premises order and meaning on nature conceived as a well-working machine. Since the machine itself provides escape from servitude to utility's literal expression, modern mechanistic forms soon subordinated function and organized themselves to express mechanism as symbol. Electric motors freed tall buildings to disregard natural ventilation, illumination, and contiguities among occupants. Machines released mechanistic form from functional fidelity. Form could seek its own geometric perfection and celebrate technology's precision, economy and luster. The efficient or funicular shape became symbolic, a mechanism denoting economy, logic, even reliability and progress, which, in emulation of earlier corporate patrons, the aggressive developer-client now wanted to declare.

Surrounding developers' zeal to build prestigious buildings was a rising fervor to build in urban financial and commercial districts. Foreign investors saw opportunity early, as highlighted in the 1976 purchase by Toronto's Olympia & York of eight New York City skyscrapers for $350 million, said to be worth over $1 billion in 1982. Pleased to encourage such private investors, cities awarded tax abatements, extra floor areas and other relief from zoning restrictions, in exchange for public gardens, retail lobbies and enclosed entries to subways. Given a location at a major transit interchange and allowed maximum net floor area, the rentable office tower was profitable in a rising market, and foreign and, then later, American speculative builders risked expensive capital. Their bold decisions to invest in American high-rise office buildings beginning in 1976 resulted in energetic construction during 1979–1983. As their buildings rose, the American economy was still depressed in the three influential sectors of housing, automobiles, and heavy manufacturing. Thus, although 1982 and 1983 saw the completion of many of SOM's finest office towers, a lessening demand for office space slowed new investments. Some foreign developers encountered reverses and sold the American properties they had avidly bought or financed in 1976, and the sporadic opportunities for new tall office towers in 1982 and early 1983 did not match those boldly offered in 1976–1981, when developers in that five-year span quickened the vitality of American cities.

SOM had enjoyed early successes in gaining admirable architecture through developers. As early as the 1960's, with Harry Helmsley in association with Morse-Diesel, SOM had designed the lower Manhattan tower that Helmsley later partly leased to Marine Midland Bank, and, in Buffalo, SOM had designed the Marine Midland Center for a developer, Cabot, Cabot and Forbes, and a banking group led by Seymour Knox. Even the best developers demanded adherence to restrictive confines. Building sites were apt to be irregular, and parcels were won or lost as design proceeded. Chicago's Three First National Plaza reflects the need to preserve views and an historic Chicago building. New York's Irving Trust, Atlanta's Georgia-Pacific [33] and Washington's Metro Center had to adjust their forms to suit special sites. Programs that required mixing rental offices, retail stores, and banking floors, sometimes adding residential apartments, tended to be

Olympia & York aus Toronto zeigt, die 1976 acht Hochhäuser in New York für 350 Millionen Dollar erwarb. Die Stadtverwaltungen unterstützten die privaten Bauträger gern und gewährten ihnen Steuernachlässe, Geschoßflächenzuschläge und andere Planungserleichterungen, um dafür öffentliche Grünflächen, Hallen mit Ladengeschäften oder überdachte Eingänge zur Untergrundbahn einzutauschen. Als Mietbürohochhäuser auf Bauplätzen in verkehrsgünstiger Lage und mit höchstmöglichen Nutzflächenzahlen sich zu rentieren begannen, zogen sie zunächst ausländisches und später auch teures amerikanisches Risikokapital von Bauspekulanten an. Die ab 1976 gefällten Entscheidungen dieser Bauherren, ihr Geld in amerikanischen Bürohochhäusern anzulegen, lösten in den Jahren 1979 bis 1983 eine kräftige Bauwelle aus. Zugleich befand sich allerdings die amerikanische Wirtschaft in den drei einflußreichen Sektoren Wohnungsbau, Automobilbau und schwerindustrielle Fertigung noch in einer Depression. Obgleich also in den Jahren 1982 und 1983 eine große Zahl bemerkenswerter Bürohochhäuser von SOM fertiggestellt wurde, verlangsamte daher gleichzeitig eine sinkende Nachfrage nach Büroraum neue Investitionen. Die gelegentlich auftauchenden Marktchancen für neue Bürotürme im Jahr 1982 und Anfang 1983 waren nicht vergleichbar mit den kühnen Möglichkeiten der Jahre 1976 bis 1981, als in diesem Zeitraum von fünf Jahren Bauträger die Lebensfähigkeit der amerikanischen Städte wesentlich erhöht hatten.

SOM war es frühzeitig gelungen, Erfolge mit guter Architektur in der Zusammenarbeit mit Bauträgern zu erzielen. Schon in den sechziger Jahren hatte SOM zusammen mit Harry Helmsley – und in Verbindung mit Morse-Diesel – im unteren Manhattan ein Bürohochhaus gebaut, das Helmsley später teilweise an die Marine Midland Bank verpachtete. In Buffalo hatte SOM das Marine Midland Center für die Bauträger-Firma Cabot, Cabot and Forbes und eine Gruppe von Bankiers unter Führung von Seymour Knox errichtet. Aber auch die aufgeschlossensten Bauträger erwarteten die Befolgung einschränkender Bedingungen. Das Irving Trust Operations Center in New York, das Georgia-Pacific Center in Atlanta [33] und das Metro Center in Washington mußten in ihren Baumassen besonders geformten Grundstücken angepaßt werden. Bauprogramme, die Mischnutzungen von Mietbüros, Läden, Banketagen – und gelegentlich dazu noch Wohnungen – vorsahen, waren meist kompliziert und voller Widersprüche: Man erwartete ein Höchstmaß an vermietbarer Fläche, kleinstmögliche Kernzonen, aber gleichzeitig kurze Wartezeiten an den Aufzügen, Übersichtlichkeit und Sicherheit in den Büroetagen, aber für die Öffentlichkeit gut zugängliche Ladenbereiche. Außerdem stellten die Bürohochhäuser jedes für sich ein Anlagekapital von mindestens 100 Millionen Dollar dar – wozu noch die Finanzierungskosten kamen –, und die Investoren forderten deshalb eine möglichst rasche Beziehbarkeit. Da die Anleger oft Banken, Versicherungen und Rentenfonds waren, sprachen sie nicht mit einer Zunge, was sich nachteilig auf das Bauprogramm und die Qualität der Hochhäuser auswirken konnte.

Trotz alledem schuf SOM für Bauträger oft Gebäude von bemerkenswerter Qualität. Das Gebäude Park Avenue Plaza für die Fisher Brothers hat die Anerkennung der New Yorker nicht nur wegen des gelungenen Spannungsverhältnisses zwischen dem Neubau und dem historischen Racquet and Tennis Club gefunden, sondern auch wegen der Öffnung der Park Avenue gegenüber der maßstäblich weiteren Bebauung in Blockmitte. Nicht minder qualitätsvoll als das herausragende Tenneco Building sind die jüngst von SOM für Bauträger entworfenen Hochhäuser InterFirst Plaza und Allied Bank Plaza in Houston. Möglicherweise wird diese Gruppe noch durch den Campeau Tower und das Four Houston Center ergänzt werden. Die schon klassischen Chicagoer SOM-Bauten – das Inland Steel Building, das Brunswick Building, das John Hancock Center und der Sears Tower – haben in den Gebäuden Three First National Plaza und One Magnificent Mile gleichwertige Nachbarn. Neue Akzente in Kalifornien sind die Crocker-Bauten in San Francisco [34] und Los Angeles.

Die Architektur von SOM läßt sich in verschiedener Art und Weise darstellen: nach Gebäudetypen, in zeitlicher Abfolge, nach den verschiedenen Büros oder nach Regionen. Bei dem vorliegenden Band entschied man sich für die Gliederung nach geographischen Gesichtspunkten, weil damit das Wirken von SOM in den verschiedenen Regionen herausgestellt wird. Entsprechend dieser Ordnung werden in vier Abschnitten die Bauten von SOM in Amerika und in einem fünften die ausländischen Arbeiten gezeigt. Den Einführungen zu den einzelnen Abschnitten liegen die volkswirtschaftlichen, sozialen und gestalterischen Probleme zugrunde, welche die architektonischen Lösungen von SOM in dem schwierigen, oft widrigen und manchmal auch höchst erfolgreichen Jahrzehnt von 1973 bis 1983 beeinflußt haben.

33

33. Georgia-Pacific Center, Atlanta, Georgia.

34. Crocker Center and Galleria, San Francisco, California.

complex and conflicting: maximum rental area but ample windows and views; slender mechanical cores but speedy elevator service; privacy and security in office floors but easy public access to retail areas. Then, too, each tall office tower represented an investment of $100 million or more, plus the costs of financing, and its investors wanted rapid occupancy. Since they often represented banks, insurance companies and pension funds, the investors' multiple voices could affect a tower's program and quality. Nor were they the final hazard: rental occupants at Park Avenue Plaza introduced alien ceiling lights, furniture and partitions, in marked contrast to SOM's experience at Lever House and Inland Steel.

Still, SOM's developer buildings often achieve architectural distinction. Fisher Brothers' Park Avenue Plaza has won New Yorkers' admiration not only for its counterpoint to the classic Racquet and Tennis Club but for opening Park Avenue to the wider midblock scale. Into the class of its signal Tenneco Building, SOM now introduced two developer's buildings: Houston's InterFirst Plaza and Allied Bank, with the possibility of Campeau Tower and Four Houston Center ahead. Chicago's masterpieces – Inland Steel, Brunswick, John Hancock and Sears Tower – now had allies in Three First National Plaza and One Magnificent Mile. California gained the two Crocker Centers in San Francisco [34] and Los Angeles. Their artistic merit disguises the persistence needed in urging perfected detail, even where a contest came down to a quarter-inch recess or almost imperceptible subtleties within a palette of granite, glass and metal.

SOM's architecture might be displayed in any of several sequences: by building type, by chronology, by individual offices, or by regional folios. The regional sequence has been chosen for this book because it reflects SOM's geographic presence. Accordingly, SOM's American buildings are presented in four folios; a fifth shows the international work. Underlying the prefatory themes introducing each folio are the national economic, social and aesthetic issues that affected SOM's architectural response in the difficult, often adverse and sometimes triumphant decade, 1973–1983.

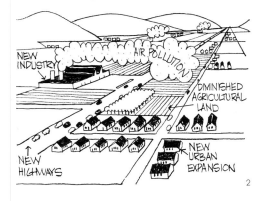

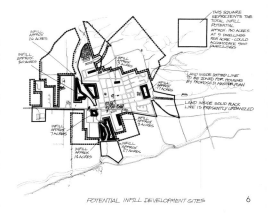

FOTENTIAL INFILL DEVELOPMENT SITES 6

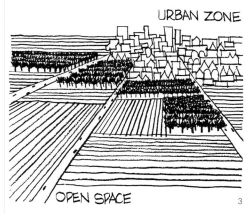

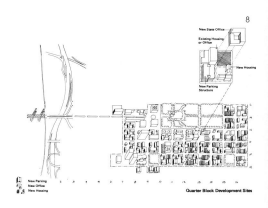

NEW ISOLATED SUB-
DIVISIONS TEND TO
FRAGMENT THE CITY
INTO SEPERATE
DISTRICTS AND FORCES
MORE USE OF THE
CAR. 7

1. Skyline of San Francisco, California.
2, 3. The California Tomorrow Plan.
4. Carmel Valley Manor, Carmel Valley, California.
5. Mauna Kea Beach Hotel, Kamuela, Hawaii.
6, 7. Plan for Saint Helena, California.
8, 9. Plan for Sacramento, California.

Die Westküste

Gibt es wirklich eine eigenständige Denkweise im amerikanischen Westen, einen spezifischen Charakter im Bereich der Bay von San Francisco oder des Puget Sound im Bundesstaat Washington, der eine besondere Architektur hervorbringt? Noch im Jahr 1960 hätte das bloße Stellen dieser Frage Erstaunen hervorgerufen. Lange zuvor hatte allerdings der Regionalismus des Westens den Architekten Winsor Soule zur Idee eines spanischen Stils für Santa Barbara angeregt, und bis in die sechziger Jahre – als die Westküste ihre typische Erscheinung und ihre Landschaftsformen verlor – interessierten sich Architekten für die Formenwelt landesüblicher Wohnhäuser aus Holz. Dann überschwemmten Ladenzentren, Industrieanlagen und Wohnsiedlungen die Täler und Hänge der Berge.

Das SOM-Büro in San Francisco wurde zur treibenden Kraft für eine planvolle Regionalentwicklung, und die Anerkennung dafür ist noch im Steigen begriffen. Auf Anregung des Gründungspartners Nathaniel Owings schuf SOM im Jahr 1971 ein ganz Kalifornien umfassendes Landschaftsschutzmodell, das als California Tomorrow Plan veröffentlicht wurde [2, 3]. Mit der verdichteten ländlichen Wohnsiedlung Carmel Valley Manor in Kalifornien [4] und dem anmutig an der Küste Hawaiis gelegenen Mauna Kea Hotel [5] hatte SOM schon vorher sein Können unter Beweis gestellt.

Das Büro in San Francisco entwickelte seine Planungskonzepte dann in drei grundlegenden Studien weiter. Als beispielhafte Lösung für die von ausufernden Wohnsiedlungen bedrohten Weinberge im Napa Valley in Kalifornien entwickelte SOM 1974 einen Generalplan für die Stadt Saint Helena [6, 7], der aufzeigt, wie die Stadtzufahrten, das Verkehrssystem, die Baugrundstücke und die Hauptstraße verbessert werden könnten. 1977 wurde der Stadt Sacramento von SOM eine Entwurfsstudie für ein Gebiet von etwa 30 Hektar besten innerstädtischen Bodens unterbreitet, das in den sechziger Jahren von Bauwerken freigemacht und in Parkplätze verwandelt worden war [8, 9]. Auf einem dreieckigen Areal im Kreuzungsbereich von drei Autobahnen in Irvine plante SOM 1981 ein urbanes Zentrum mit Bürohochhäusern, öffentlichen Plätzen und Gartenanlagen [10].

Das Büro in Portland, Oregon, das von den Partnern David Pugh und James Christensen geleitet wird und von dem das Portland Center [11] stammt, leitete mit der Tri Met Mall [12] eine durchgreifende Reorganisation des zentralen Geschäftsviertels der Stadt ein. Das Büro in San Francisco erarbeitete eine Entwurfsstudie für die Firma Advanced Micro Devices [13], in der trapezförmige Gartenhöfe vorgeschlagen werden. Dem Southern California Operations Center der Wells Fargo Bank in El Monte [14] gab das Büro in San Francisco durch einen im Querschnitt dreieckigen Baukörper – der dem Bau-

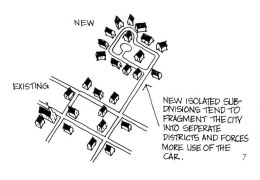

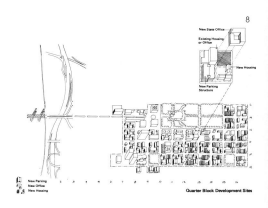

The West Coast

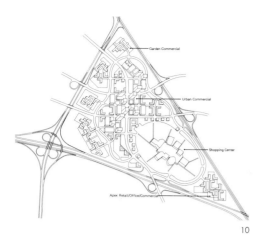

10

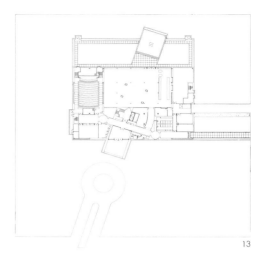

13

Is there a Western mind, some regional character in California's Bay Area or Washington's Puget Sound, that calls for distinctive architecture? Merely to raise that question sounded quaint as early as 1960. Much earlier, Western regionalism had excited architect Winsor Soule to imagine a Spanish style for Santa Barbara, and indigenous residential wooden forms still intrigued architects in the 1960's, even while the West Coast was losing its regional outlook and landscapes. Commercial, industrial and housing developments spread to valleys and mountainsides, and "Cry California!" was the plea that opened the West Coast's 1970's. It lamented problems that lie beyond the scope of regionalists' inquiry.

SOM/San Francisco led a forceful drive for planned regional growth. Encouraged by founding partner Nathaniel Owings, a leader in conserving Big Sur, SOM in 1971 prepared a California-wide model for conservation, the California Tomorrow Plan [2, 3]. Earlier, SOM had demonstrated a compact rural community in California's Carmel Valley Manor [4], and SOM's Mauna Kea Hotel [5] graces a beautiful shoreline in Hawaii.

SOM/San Francisco further developed its planning concepts in three seminal documents. For California's Napa Valley towns, whose vineyards were invaded by housing developments, SOM in 1974 showed how Saint Helena [6, 7] might improve its approaches, circulation, building lots and Main Street. In 1977, Sacramento [8, 9] received SOM's design for 75 acres of prime downtown land which had been cleared and turned into paved parking lots in the 1960's. For a triangular site created by three freeways at Irvine, SOM in 1981 planned a grid street plan and tall office buildings with plazas and gardens. Approached from elevated freeways, Irvine Center [10] promised to become an attractive land-saving, commercially successful alternative to strip highway sprawl.

In Oregon, partner David Pugh lead SOM/Portland, which earlier designed the Portland Center [11]. Later joined by James Christensen, SOM guided a reorganization of the downtown business district. The Tri-Met Mall [12] is often cited for its successful recapture of centralized shopping within a metropolitan region. SOM/San Francisco prepared a design for Advanced Micro Devices [13], which contains trapezoidal garden courtyards and an entrance past a polished green marble slab bearing AMD's logo. SOM/San Francisco dramatized the Southern California Operations Center of Wells Fargo Bank at El Monte [14]: a triangular prism connected to a block devoted to computer operations.

Ranging from regional plan to high-rise office buildings, SOM/San Francisco's work served an important clientele throughout the West Coast and, in the 1970's attracted commissions

10. Plan for Irvine Center, Irvine, California.
11. Portland Center, Portland, Oregon.
12. Tri-Met Mall, Portland, Oregon.
13. Office building for Advanced Micro Devices, Sunnyvale, California.
14. Wells Fargo Southern California Operations Center, El Monte, California.

11

12

14

15

17

16

block mit den Datenverarbeitungseinrichtungen vorgelagert ist – eine besondere Note.

Mit Projekten, die von Regionalplänen bis zu Bürohochhäusern reichen, hat das Büro in San Francisco nicht nur bedeutende Bauherren an der ganzen Westküste angesprochen, sondern in den siebziger Jahren auch Aufträge aus dem Osten der USA, aus Europa, dem Nahen Osten und Südostasien erhalten. Das im Jahr 1946 von dem SOM-Gründungspartner Nathaniel Owings eröffnete Büro gewann bald zwei seiner derzeitigen Partner für den Verwaltungsbereich hinzu: 1949 trat John Merrill und im Jahr darauf Walter Costa ein. Merrill, ein Sohn des verstorbenen SOM-Gründungspartners, schreibt das Verdienst für den von Anfang an bemerkenswerten Ideenreichtum des Büros Edward Bassett zu, der 1955 von Eero Saarinen zu SOM kam und für die meisten der unverwechselbaren Bauten des Büros in San Francisco verantwortlich ist. Sein Talent zog 1961 Marc Goldstein und 1968 Lawrence Doane als Entwurfsarchitekten ins Büro. 1982 haben diese drei Partner allein in San Francisco – wo SOM in Zusammenarbeit mit anderen Büros von 1969 bis 1971 die vielbeachtete Bank of America [15] baute – nahezu zwei Dutzend größere Bauwerke errichtet.

Bis zum Bau der Bank of America war San Francisco nicht unbedingt erpicht auf moderne Bauformen in seinen Banken- und Geschäftsvierteln. Die von Mies van der Rohe beeinflußten, als »östlich« bezeichneten Stilelemente in der von SOM entworfenen US Naval Station in Monterey sowie in den ebenfalls von SOM stammenden Gebäuden für Crown Zellerbach [16] und Alcoa [17] in San Francisco verringerten den Widerstand gegen die moderne Architektur nicht. Etwa 1957 griff dann Bassett beim John Hancock Building [18] auf klassische Formelemente zurück. Aber die Öffentlichkeit von San Francisco hielt sich mit ihrer Begeisterung zurück, bis die Hauptverwaltung der Bank of America [19] dem Neoklassizismus und Regionalismus eine neue Dimension hinzufügte und internationale Anerkennung fand.

In den nächsten Jahren, in denen es sich sein gegenwärtiges hohes Ansehen erwarb, realisierte das Büro in San Francisco vier herausragende Bauten: das Oakland-Alameda County Coliseum [20], den Campus des Laney College [21], die Wohnsiedlung Carmel Valley Manor [22] und die Hauptverwaltung der Weyerhaeuser Company in der Nähe von Tacoma [23]. Wie auch ein fünftes großes Werk des Büros – das Mauna Kea Hotel auf Hawaii [24] – zeichnen sich alle diese Bauten durch spannungsvolle Massengliederung, harmonische Einpassung in ihre Umgebung, Formenreichtum und lebendige Raumfolgen aus. Der Erfolg des Weyerhaeuser-Gebäudes brachte dem SOM-Büro in San Francisco in den siebziger Jahren einen weiteren Auftrag des Holzkonzerns ein, das auf demselben Gelände erbaute Forschungszentrum der Firma.

Los Angeles war immer schon aufgeschlossen

19

18

15. Bank of America, San Francisco, California.
16. Crown Zellerbach Building, San Francisco, California.
17. Alcoa Building, San Francisco, California.
18. John Hancock Building, San Francisco, California.
19. Bank of America, San Francisco, California.

20

in eastern states and in Europe, the Middle East and Southeast Asia. Opened in 1946 by founding partner Nathaniel Owings, the office soon gained two of its current administrative partners, John O. Merrill in 1949 and Walter Costa the following year. Merrill, who is the son of SOM's late founding partner, attributes the office's initial brilliance to Edward C. Bassett, who, joining SOM from Eero Saarinen's office in 1955, has created most of SOM/San Francisco's distinctive buildings. Fully founded in his craft but also inventive and whimsical, Bassett early sensed the formal, classical tone of San Francisco's financial leaders, and his architectural talent attracted designers Marc Goldstein in 1961 and Lawrence Doane in 1968. By 1982, those three design partners could count almost two dozen major buildings in San Francisco alone, where SOM, with associated firms, designed the celebrated Bank of America, built in 1969–71.

Until the Bank of America Headquarters [15], San Francisco was not avid about modern form in its downtown financial and commercial districts. Following its 1906 earthquake, San Francisco had been rebuilt predominantly with classical buildings: The Italianate Pacific Union Club and Fairmont Hotel, the Roman downtown banks, Bernard Maybeck's Fine Arts Palace, and Arthur Brown, Jr.'s Opera House and City Hall. An ardent and skillful practitioner, Timothy Pfleuger, at 450 Sutter made Aztec and Mayan ornament enhance an otherwise classical composition. Willis Polk's glazed and metallic Hallidie Building and Frank Lloyd Wright's later Morris Store were considered to be aberrations from classical success, as was the previously cited Bay Regional style. The Miesian or "Eastern" aspect of SOM's early U.S. Naval Station at Monterey and SOM's Crown Zellerbach [16] and Alcoa Buildings [17] in San Francisco did not lessen resistance to modern architecture. Then, about 1957, Bassett drew upon classical references for the John Hancock Building [18]. Still San Franciscans withheld enthusiasm. At that point the Bank of America Headquarters [19] added a new dimension to lingering classicism and regionalism, winning international respect.

While earning its current eminence, SOM/San Francisco completed four outstanding projects: the Oakland-Alameda stadium and arena [20]; the Laney College campus [21], the Carmel Valley Manor [22], and the Weyerhaeuser Company Headquarters outside Tacoma [23]. Like another superb example, SOM's Mauna Kea Hotel in Hawaii [24], all are admirable for their strong massing, harmonious fit to site, rich elaboration of form, and sculptured spatial sequences. The success with Weyerhaeuser led to SOM/San Francisco's being recalled in the 1970's to design Weyerhaeuser's new research center at Tacoma.

In Los Angeles, long hospitable to modern architecture, SOM developed a strong presence in the 1970's with both SOM/Los Angeles,

22

23

24

21

20. Oakland-Alameda County Coliseum, Oakland, California.
21. Laney College, Oakland, California.
22. Carmel Valley Manor, Carmel Valley, California.
23. Weyerhaeuser Headquarters, Tacoma, Washington.
24. Mauna Kea Beach Hotel, Kamuela, Hawaii.

25

28

26

gegenüber der modernen Architektur gewesen. SOM war dort in den siebziger Jahren sehr aktiv sowohl mit einem eigenen, von dem Partner Richard Ciceri geleiteten Büro als auch mit Arbeiten des Büros in San Francisco. Auf einem abfallenden Grundstück zwischen zwei Schnellstraßen gruppierte Marc Goldstein vom Büro in San Francisco die Bürogebäude der 70/90 Universal City Plaza [25] für die Music Corporation of America in einer niedrigen, terrassierten Anlage. Maris Peika, Partner im Büro in Los Angeles, brachte auf einem heruntergekommenen Grundstück in Santa Monica die First Federal Savings and Loan Association in einem gestaffelten, zwölfgeschossigen Gebäude unter, dessen Fassaden aus dunkelgrauen Fensterbändern und tief kannelierten Betonelementen einen schönen Platz rahmen [26]. Die Stadt Los Angeles regte große Banken, Hotelkonzerne und andere bedeutende Unternehmen zum Bau von Hochhäusern im Bunker-Hill-Viertel an. Angrenzend an sich in mehreren Ebenen überschneidenden Schnellstraßen erhebt sich dort mit zwei rechtwinklig zueinander angeordneten, im Grundriß trapezförmigen Türmen das Crocker Center von SOM [27]. Die beiden von Goldstein entworfenen, mit poliertem Granit und bronzefarbenem Glas verkleideten Hochhäuser beherrschen das Zentrum mit ihren großen abgewinkelten Flächen und messerscharfen Kanten.

Immer noch ist es aber das Gebiet um die Bay von San Francisco, wo SOM seine bedeutendsten Bauten errichtet hat. Wichtige städtische Projekte sind dem Büro dort anvertraut worden. Als das Schnellbahnsystem Bay Area Rapid Transit von Oakland-Berkeley aus über die Bay nach San Francisco ausgedehnt wurde, entwarf SOM die BART-Stationen Powell Street und Montgomery Street [28], die 1972 fertiggestellt wurden. Der von SOM entworfene Transbay Terminal [29, 30] soll ein weitgehend verglaster Busbahnhof mit mehreren Ebenen werden. Am Angelpunkt zwischen dem Einkaufs- und dem Bankenviertel von San Francisco stellt das Crocker Center von SOM [31] mit seiner dreigeschossigen, überdachten Einkaufsarkade ein wichtiges Verbindungselement dar; eine ähnliche Funktion haben auch die offenen Ladenstraßen des Five Fremont Center von SOM [32]. Der Ergänzungsbau für die Bechtel Corporation, 45 Fremont Street, erhebt sich mit seinem eleganten Stahlskelett von etwa neun auf zwölf Metern Spannweite über einer weiten Terrasse. Wenn das 1981 fertiggestellte, mit silberfarben anodisierten Aluminiumtafeln verkleidete Hochhaus 444 Market Street [33] auch vornehmlich wegen der Dachsilhouette seiner Terrassen in Erinnerung bleiben wird, so liegt doch in der sägezahnförmigen Abstaffelung des Grundrisses und der dadurch erzielten Ausweitung des Fußgängerbereichs die größere Bedeutung dieses Bauwerks.

Zu dem regen Interesse, das SOM für die städtebaulichen Belange von San Francisco zeigt,

25. 70/90 Universal City Plaza, Universal City, California.
26. First Federal Square, Santa Monica, California.
27. Crocker Center, Los Angeles, California.
28. BART station at Montgomery Street, San Francisco, California.
29, 30. Transbay Terminal, San Francisco, California.
31. Crocker Center and Galleria, San Francisco, California.
32. Five Fremont Center, San Francisco, California.
33. 444 Market Street, San Francisco, California.
34. Paramount Theater, Oakland, California.

27

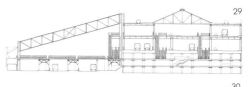

29

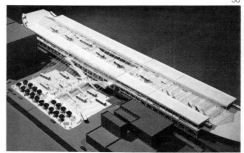

30

31

33

led by partner Richard Ciceri, and SOM/San Francisco working there. For a sloped site between two highways, SOM/San Francisco's Goldstein modeled low, terraced office buildings for the Music Corporation of America at 70/90 Universal City Plaza [25], and, on a previously disarrayed site in Santa Monica, SOM/Los Angeles partner Maris Peika installed Santa Monica's First Federal Savings and Loan Association in a terraced twelve-story building whose dark gray glass ribbons and deeply channelled concrete walls shape a fine plaza [26]. Investing heavily to concentrate financial and commercial activity, Los Angeles encouraged banking headquarters, convention-sized hotels and national companies to build tall buildings around Bunker Hill. There, abutting multilevel, interlaced freeways, SOM's Crocker Center [27] rises in two towers, each trapezoidal in plan, set perpendicular to each other. Polished granite and bronze-glazed, the towers designed by Goldstein dominate the core with tall angled planes and knife-edge corners. As the Crocker Center opened with prestigious tenants in 1982, hopes were stirred for filling the emptiness in downtown Los Angeles.

Still, the Bay Area is where SOM has made its greatest mark on the West Coast. Important urban space has been entrusted to SOM. When the Bay Area Rapid Transit was extended across the Bay from Oakland-Berkeley to San Francisco, SOM prepared BART's underground stations for Powell and Montgomery Streets [28], finished in 1972. The proposed Transbay Terminal [29, 30] is intended to be a glazed, multilevel interchange for passengers transferring between buses. At the hinge joining San Francisco's retail and financial districts, SOM's Crocker Center [31] contributes a three-story enclosed shopping arcade, and SOM's Five Fremont Center [32] rises from a retail courtyard. At 45 Fremont Street, SOM's newest Bechtel Building springs its 30- and 40-foot steel frame bays from a broad terrace, and, while 444 Market Street [33], completed in 1981, will be remembered for its silver-anodized aluminum skyline terraces, its groundline serrations and sidewalk setbacks make a greater urban gift.

Added to SOM's concern for San Francisco's urban spaces is great care for its architectural heritage. Urged by Edgar Kaiser and Stephen Bechtel, SOM restored Oakland's Paramount Theater [34], a 1931 cinema, to its splendor of colored velvets, exuberant lighting and stylized lily, tulip and scimitar ornament. At the Crocker Center in San Francisco, SOM plans to remove the banal existing tower but preserve its fine banking hall, which will support an outdoor roof garden, adjacent to the new Crocker tower. For the Civic Center, designed in the 1920's by the talented classicist, Arthur Brown, Jr., SOM succeeded in making new buildings relate successfully to their important neighbors. The addition to the Opera House [35] repeats

32

34

35

37

36

kommt die Sorgfalt im Umgang mit dem architektonischen Erbe der Stadt. Aufgefordert von Edgar Kaiser und Stephen Bechtel, ließ SOM das Paramount Theater in Oakland [34], ein 1931 entstandenes Kino mit farbigen Samtbezügen, üppiger Beleuchtung und stilisierten Art-Déco-Ornamenten in seinem alten Glanz wiedererstehen. Beim Crocker Center in San Francisco gab SOM zwar das architektonisch unbedeutende alte Bankhochhaus zum Abriß frei, sorgte jedoch für die Erhaltung der Bankhalle. Im Bereich des Civic Center – das in den zwanziger Jahren von dem Neoklassizisten Arthur Brown jr. gestaltet worden war – gelang SOM mit seinen Neubauten eine einfühlsame Anpassung an die bestehende Architektur. Im Anbau des Opernhauses [35] wiederholen sich neoklassizistische Formelemente, und der Entwurf für das State Office Building [36] übernimmt kompositorische Motive der umliegenden Bauten und richtet den Innenhof des Neubaus in einer Diagonale zum Rathaus aus. Auf denselben zentralen Punkt ist auch die Louise M. Davies Symphony Hall [37] hin orientiert. Der auf einem sehr engen Grundstück untergebrachte Bau mit einem akustisch brillanten Konzertsaal für 3000 Zuhörer erwies dem neoklassizistischen Rathaus zugleich mit seinen stilistischen Anspielungen seine Reverenz.

Die Fähigkeit, moderne Bauten mit ihrer älteren Umgebung zu einem harmonischen Zusammenspiel zu bringen, zeigt sich auch bei der 1977 fertiggestellten California First Bank und dem 1983 fertiggestellten Federal Reserve Building in San Francisco [38]. In der unverkennbaren Handschrift des Partners Edward Bassett ist bei der California First Bank [39] der Kern mit den Vertikalelementen in einen eigenen Bauteil ausgegliedert, während sich die verglaste Bankhalle durch weit auseinandergerückte Stützen zur Kolonnade der 1908 erbauten Bank of California hin öffnet. Bei der Planung der Federal Reserve Bank, dem jüngsten der von ihm in San Francisco errichteten Bauten, lehnte es Bassett ab, sich einfach einem nüchternen Bauprogramm zu unterwerfen. Statt dessen terrassierte er das breite, acht Geschosse hohe Bauwerk in Stufen von jeweils zwei Geschossen über einer viergeschossigen Sockelzone ab. Mit der vorgelagerten Loggia gelang eine überzeugende Aufwertung einer Baustruktur zu einem Symbol.

Mit seinen zahlreichen und vielgestaltigen Arbeiten im amerikanischen Westen gelang es SOM zweifellos, Modelle für Verwaltungs- und Wohnstätten, integrierte Bürohochhäuser, Orte der Kultur und Regierungsbauten sowie nicht zuletzt für Landschaftsschutz und Denkmalpflege zu entwickeln, die alle bemerkenswerte Antworten auf die mannigfaltigen Probleme an der Westküste geben.

35. Addition to the San Francisco Opera House, San Francisco, California.
36. State Office Building, San Francisco, California.
37. Louise M. Davies Symphony Hall, San Francisco, California.
38. The Federal Reserve Bank of San Francisco, California.
39. The California First Bank, San Francisco, California.

39

its classical forms, and the proposed State Office Building [36] bears compositional themes in neighboring buildings and aligns its interior court on a diagonal to City Hall. That focus also set the orientation for the Louise M. Davies Symphony Hall [37], which, on a tight site, develops an acoustically vibrant 3,000-seat auditorium within a building that offers grace notes to the Civic Center's classicism.

The rare imagination that creates modern images which harmonize with classical settings appears again in San Francisco's California First Bank, completed in 1977, and the Federal Reserve Building [38] completed in early 1983. Unmistakably the artful work of SOM's Bassett, California First Bank [39] offsets its service core and stretches long spans between columns to open a glazed banking lobby to vistas towards the colonnade of the 1908 Bank of California. Smooth and textured precast concrete (probably the best any architect has summoned) carries to the roofline where the twelve columns' tips reappear in an echo of function and articulated joinery. In the Federal Reserve, his most recent building in San Francisco, Bassett refused to succumb to a prosaic program and stepped a broad eight-story building in two-story increments over a four-story base. Recessed from Market Street, the facade marries themes in neighboring classical buildings, and the loggia is a deft triumph of structure serving as symbol.

Thus, in its extensive, multiple Western presence, SOM demonstrated models of conservation, preservation, office and residential development, integrated transportation systems, high-rise office buildings, places for cultural assembly, and symbols of government – all admirable responses to the cries for rescuing the splendid but endangered West Coast.

38

The California First Bank,
San Francisco, California

The site of this 23-story office tower, completed in 1977, is a 19,000-square-foot corner in the city's financial district. The client required a headquarters building that could provide adequate space for its own needs, including a major banking hall, as well as prestige office space for tenants.
While the tower is free-standing on three sides, the fourth side is joined to an adjacent party wall by means of a recessed link element. This is an offset core which contains seven passenger elevators arranged in two banks, as well as a service elevator and utility spaces on the tower floor levels. The tower lobby entrance is at the podium level of the core with a ramp down at the rear for truck delivery, executive parking and service areas. Offsetting the core achieved unencumbered office floors for maximum flexibility and efficiency, and more important, enabled the podium level of the tower to be devoted entirely to the banking hall.
The steel frame structure is clad with precast concrete units composed of a matrix of white cement and Sierra white granite aggregate, the most common granite in use throughout San Francisco. Contrasting horizontal bands of smoothly cast and of heavily sandblasted surfaces make up the spandrel panels. The plinth, entry porch and steps are of the same stone. On the tower facades, a frameless glazing system of 3/8-inch-thick solar grey glass is set flush between spandrel panels and the round tower columns. On the uppermost executive floor level, glazing is recessed behind the columns and the spandrel line in order to achieve a strong shadow at the top of the building.

The California First Bank,
San Francisco, Kalifornien

Für den 1977 fertiggestellten, 23geschossigen Büroturm stand ein etwa 1.770 m² großes Eckgrundstück im Bankenviertel der Stadt zur Verfügung. Der Bauherr wünschte ein Hauptverwaltungsgebäude, das neben ausreichendem Raum für die eigenen Bedürfnisse einschließlich einer großen Bankhalle auch vermietbare Büroflächen mit gehobener Ausstattung bietet.
Auf drei Seiten steht der Bau frei, während er auf der vierten Seite mit einem eingezogenen Verbindungselement an die Nachbarbebauung anschließt. Hier liegt die Kernzone mit sieben Personenaufzügen und einem Lastenaufzug in zwei Blocks sowie Sanitärräumen in den Obergeschossen und einer Aufzugshalle im Erdgeschoß. Hinter der Aufzugshalle ist die Einfahrtsrampe zum Untergeschoß angeordnet, in dem Anlieferung, Parkplätze für leitende Mitarbeiter und Technikräume untergebracht sind. Die Anordnung der Kernzone am Rand kam sowohl den Büroflächen, die, von keinerlei Einbauten gestört, ein Höchstmaß an Flexibilität bieten, als auch der das ganze Erdgeschoß einnehmenden Bankhalle zugute.
Die Fassadenverkleidung des Stahlskelettbaus besteht aus vorgefertigten Sichtbetonelementen. Als Zuschlagstoffe kamen weißer Zement und Splitter aus weißem Sierra-Granit zur Verwendung, einem vielverwendeten Baustoff in San Francisco. Glatt geschalte und stark gesandstrahlte Oberflächen wechseln sich in horizontalen Bändern auf den Elementen ab. Die Sockelzone mit Vorplatz, Stufen und Eingangsbereich wurde mit Platten verkleidet, die ebenfalls aus weißem Sierra-Granit bestehen. Die rahmenlos verglasten Fensterflächen aus etwa 9 mm dickem, grau getöntem Sonnenschutzglas liegen im Bereich der Normalgeschosse bündig zwischen den Brüstungselementen, während die halbrunden Stützen hier stark plastisch vor die Fassade treten. Im obersten Bürogeschoß, in dem sich die Räume der Firmenleitung befinden, wurde die Verglasung vollständig hinter die Außenstützen und Brüstungen zurückgesetzt, so daß sich diese Ebene durch eine stärkere Schattenlinie abzeichnet und den Gebäudeabschluß unterstreicht.

1. The 23-story office tower occupies a prominent corner site in downtown San Francisco.
2. Access from the street to the high banking hall (to the left) is from a podium level. The tower lobby is located in a recessed link between the tower and an existing party wall.

1. Das 23geschossige Bürohochhaus erhebt sich auf einem prominenten Eckgrundstück in der Innenstadt von San Francisco.
2. Die hohe Bankhalle (links im Bild) ist von einer Podiumsebene aus zugänglich. Die Eingangshalle mit den Aufzügen zu den Bürogeschossen liegt in einem zurückgesetzten Bauteil zwischen dem Hochhaus und einer bestehenden Brandwand.

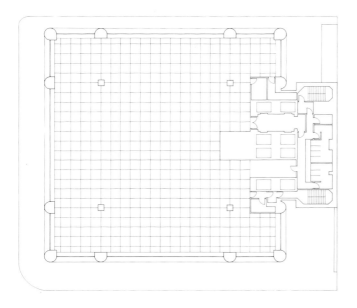

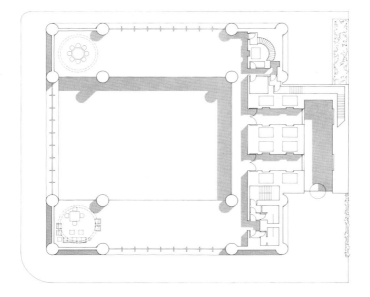

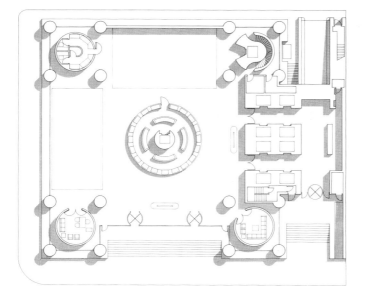

3. Plans (street level, mezzanine level, typical floor).
4. The tower seen from the west. An expression of classical building elements was achieved within a contemporary architectural vocabulary.

3. Grundrisse (Straßenebene, Zwischengeschoß, Normalgeschoß).
4. Ansicht des Hochhauses von Westen. Mit den Ausdrucksmitteln der modernen Architektur wurde eine klassische Gebäudegliederung erreicht.

30'

444 Market Street,
San Francisco, California

The site of this 36-story office tower, completed in 1980, abuts the strong diagonal of Market Street, San Francisco's major avenue. To the north, a party wall is shared with an adjacent structure, and the two remaining sides are aligned with the normal city grid. Working within the economic restrictions of normal rental office patterns and the geometry of the site, the elevation along Market Street has a sawtooth shape, while core elements such as elevators and other vertical services are grouped along the party wall to the north. This results in five desirable corner offices along the tower's most important side and provides floors of about 19,000 square feet for flexible subdivision. At the top of the tower on the east side, the building steps back at the 33rd, 34th and 35th floors, permitting office spaces to open out on extensively planted terraces protected by windscreens.
Between the tower and an adjacent building to the west, a two-story wing defines a small plaza, an extension of the adjacent Mechanics' Monument Plaza. The principle entrance to the tower lobby is from this space. The lobby is treated as an arcade leading to the street to the east. The lobbies of three elevator banks, including 16 passenger elevators and one freight elevator, open into it, as do the adjacent rental areas.
The tower has a welded steel moment frame with lightweight concrete fill on metal deck floors. The curtain wall is an aluminum stick system with insulated spandrel panels in anodized silver used in conjunction with ⅜-inch tinted grey glazing. The air conditioned building is fully sprinklered for fire protection. Individual floor control capability with fan rooms on every third floor was provided to save energy through close adaption to user needs.

444 Market Street,
San Francisco, Kalifornien

Die Market Street, eine der Hauptstraßen San Franciscos, schneidet das Grundstück, auf dem das 1980 fertiggestellte, 36geschossige Bürogebäude errichtet wurde, schräg an. Im Norden mußte an die Brandwand eines alten Nachbarhauses angebaut werden. Aus diesen besonderen Bedingungen entwickelten die Architekten im Rahmen der bei Mietbürohäusern gegebenen Einschränkungen und Erfordernisse eine eigenwillige Grundrißform. Nach Südosten, zur Market Street hin, ist die Fassade sägezahnartig abgestaffelt, die Aufzüge und Nebenräume sind entlang der Brandwand im Norden angeordnet. Dadurch ergaben sich je Geschoß fünf der begehrten Eckbüros auf der wichtigsten Gebäudeseite, und es entstanden zusammenhängende, flexibel unterteilbare Geschoßflächen von je etwa 1.770 m². Auf der Ostseite treppt sich der Bau im 33., 34. und 35. Geschoß terrassenartig ab, und die Büros öffnen sich hier auf bepflanzte und durch Glaswände gegen Wind geschützte Dachgärten. Zu den Brandwänden der nach Westen anschließenden Bebauung hin wurde der baumbestandene Platz vor dem Neubau durch einen zweigeschossigen, dreieckigen Anbau mit Dachgarten abgeschlossen. Der Platz selbst, der eine optische Erweiterung der Mechanics' Monument Plaza bildet, dient als Hauptzugang zu der Eingangshalle des Gebäudes. Die Halle wurde als Fußgängerpassage ausgebildet, die von dem kleinen Platz zu der Straße im Osten führt. Zu ihr öffnen sich neben den angrenzenden Verkaufsflächen die Warteräume der drei Aufzugsblocks mit sechzehn Personen- und einem Lastenaufzug.
Das Tragwerk des Hochhauses ist ein geschweißtes, biegesteifes Stahlskelett. Die Stahlzellendecken haben eine Leichtbetonauflage. Für die vorgehängte Fassade wurden Rahmenprofile und Brüstungstafeln aus silberfarbenem Aluminium sowie etwa 12 mm dickes, grau getöntes Glas gewählt. Zum Brandschutz wurde der vollklimatisierte Bau durchgehend mit Sprinkleranlagen ausgestattet. Geschoßweise Einzelsteuerung der Klimaanlagen – bei Zusammenfassung der Ventilatorenräume für jeweils drei Geschosse – führt zu Energieeinsparungen durch Anpassung an den jeweiligen Bedarf.

1. Section.
2. The tower rises from a tree-lined open space which is a visual enlargement of Mechanics' Monument Plaza on Market Street.

1. Schnitt.
2. Das Hochhaus steht auf einem mit Bäumen bepflanzten Platz, der eine optische Erweiterung der Mechanics' Monument Plaza an der Market Street bildet.

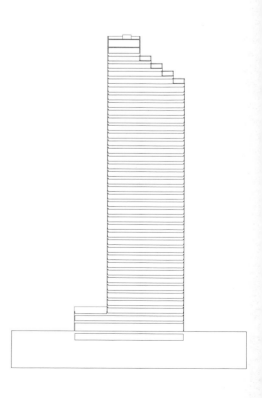

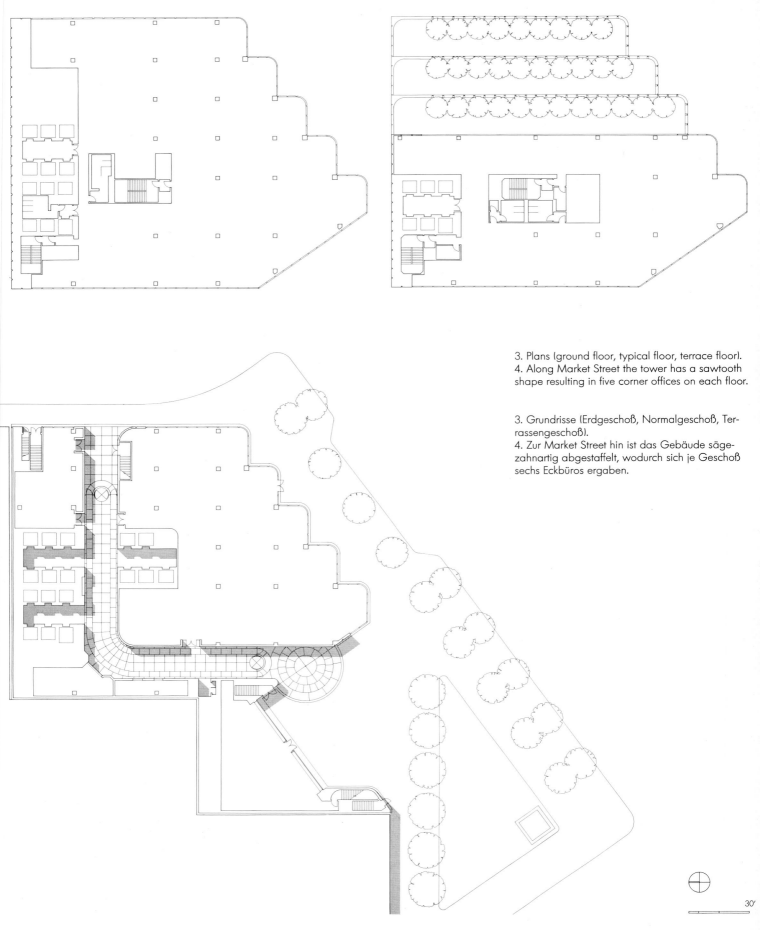

3. Plans (ground floor, typical floor, terrace floor).
4. Along Market Street the tower has a sawtooth shape resulting in five corner offices on each floor.

3. Grundrisse (Erdgeschoß, Normalgeschoß, Terrassengeschoß).
4. Zur Market Street hin ist das Gebäude sägezahnartig abgestaffelt, wodurch sich je Geschoß sechs Eckbüros ergaben.

30'

45 Fremont Street (Bechtel Building),
San Francisco, California

The Bechtel Corporation headquarters building, constructed in San Francisco in 1967 for this engineering and building enterprise, had become too small to provide the space needed in the early seventies. Overflow departments had to be located in a new structure located on an adjacent site. The small size of the site required a highly economical building shape and a flush exterior skin.

The dimensions of the tower, 150 feet by 120 feet, were the maximum allowed by the San Francisco Planning Code. The building has an area of 780,000 gross square feet. A small planted plaza is shared by both the original building and the new structure. They also share the provision of access to rapid transit on the site.

The steel moment frame structure rests on pile foundations and has five bays of 30 feet in the long direction as well as three bays of 40 feet on the short side. An oblong, centrally placed interior core, containing elevators, staircases and restrooms allows the interior planning to use flexible partitioning. Connections to the original building are made below grade and by a glazed sky-bridge.

The elevation design clearly reflects the long spans of the structural system. Aluminum spandrel members of up to 40 feet in length were prefabricated and installed in one piece. The building was one of the first projects with such an aluminum skin to receive a matt paint finish which is light beige in color. Windows are formed by 10-foot sections of monolithic bronze-tinted glass and are set into the aluminum skin with but a minimal difference between closed and glazed surfaces. The street level entrance is finished in a travertine clad core and exterior brick paving.

45 Fremont Street (Bechtel Building),
San Francisco, Kalifornien

Die 1967 vollendete Zentrale der Bechtel Corporation war schon in den frühen siebziger Jahren voll belegt, und viele Abteilungen mußten ausgelagert werden. Einem umfangreichen Raumprogramm für den 1978 fertiggestellten Neubau stand allerdings ein nur relativ kleines Grundstück im Anschluß an den Bau aus dem Jahr 1967 gegenüber. Die Architekten mußten daher auf jede gestalterische Differenzierung des Baukörpers verzichten, um die höchstmögliche Geschoßfläche zu erzielen. Die Grundrißdimensionen von etwa 46 × 37 m waren das Maximum dessen, was der San Francisco Planning Code erlaubt. Das Gelände konnte mit einer Bruttogeschoßfläche von etwa 72.500 m² überbaut werden, wobei auf Grund der Anlage eines parkartig bepflanzten Platzes zwischen Alt- und Neubau sowie eines Zugangs zur U-Bahn auf dem Grundstück Zuschläge zur zulässigen Geschoßflächenzahl in Anspruch genommen wurden.

Der auf Pfählen gegründete, biegesteife Stahlskelettbau hat in der Länge fünf Stützenfelder mit etwa 9 m Spannweite und in der Tiefe drei Felder mit etwa 12 m Spannweite. Der Aufzüge, Treppen und Sanitärräume enthaltende Kern liegt langgestreckt im Zentrum des Gebäudes, wodurch sich an den Längsseiten tiefe, flexibel unterteilbare Arbeitsflächen ergaben. Auf Untergeschoßniveau und über eine verglaste Fußgängerbrücke wurden Verbindungen zwischen dem Altbau und dem Neubau hergestellt.

In der Fassadengestaltung sind die großen Spannweiten des Tragwerks klar ablesbar. Bis zu etwa 12 m lange Aluminiumbrüstungstafeln wurden in einem Stück hergestellt und montiert. Als eines der ersten Gebäude mit einer Aluminiumaußenhaut erhielt der Bau einen Anstrich, hier in einem matten Hellbeige. Die Verglasung besteht aus etwa 3 m breiten Scheiben in Bronzetönung, die nahezu bündig in die Aluminiumfassaden eingesetzt sind. Die geschlossenen Flächen des zurückgesetzten Eingangsgeschosses sind mit Travertin verkleidet; der Bodenbelag der Eingangsebene besteht aus Ziegelsteinen.

1. Plan (typical floor).
2. The facade clearly reflects the long spans of the steel structural system.

1. Grundriß (Normalgeschoß).
2. In der Fassadengestaltung sind die großen Spannweiten des Stahltragwerks klar ablesbar.

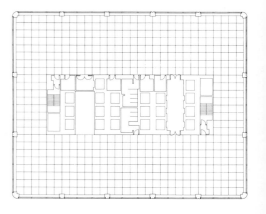

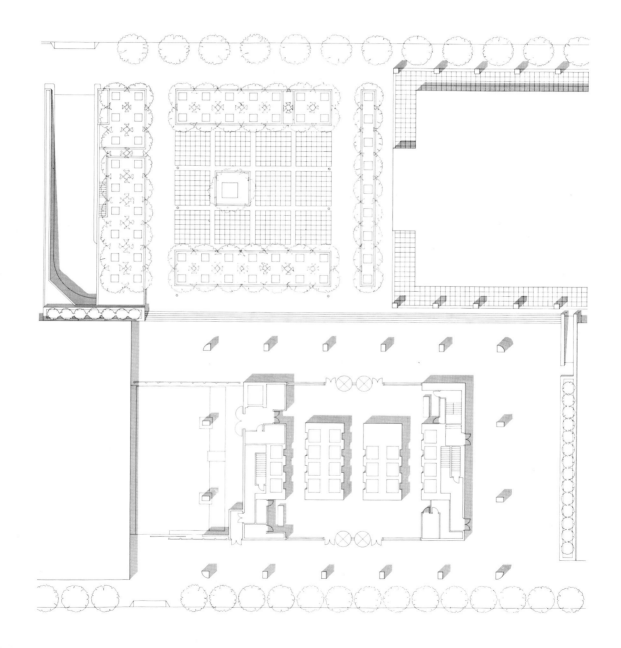

30'

3. Plan (ground level).
4, 5. View of the pedestrian plaza between the 1967 headquarters building and the new tower.

3. Grundriß (Erdgeschoßebene).
4, 5. Blick auf den Fußgängerplatz, der zwischen dem Hauptverwaltungsgebäude aus dem Jahr 1967 und dem neuen Hochhaus liegt.

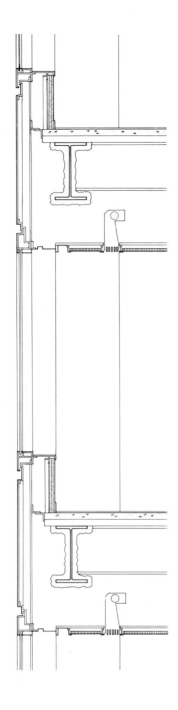

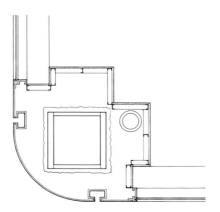

6. Facade detail. Windows are formed by 10-foot sections of monolithic bronze-tinted glass, which are set into the aluminum skin with minimal difference between closed and glazed surfaces.
7. The travertine-clad core and the brick-paved landscaped plaza contribute towards a pleasant pedestrian environment.

6. Fassadendetail. Die Verglasung besteht aus etwa 3 m breiten Scheiben in Bronzetönung, die nahezu bündig in die Aluminiumfassaden eingesetzt sind.
7. Aus dem Zusammenwirken der mit Travertin verkleideten Kernelemente und der gärtnerisch gestalteten Platzanlage ergibt sich ein anziehender Fußgängerbereich.

Five Fremont Center,
San Francisco, California

The site is situated at the edge of the financial district south of Market Street, San Francisco's main business artery, facing the Transbay Regional Bus Terminal. This central location, convenient to all traffic systems, led to the creation of two new pedestrian paths across the site. These paths are formed by the residual spaces between two low retail structures and the 43-story tower. The entire complex is woven together at street level by a consistently patterned series of facades, colonnades and arcades.

The tower rises 600 feet, given identity by sawtooth corner setbacks of increasing depth, set within continuous seams of vertical bay windows. Employing these rather minor variations in shape, a convincing design is created with strong vertical emphasis. In addition, a large number of desirable corner offices are provided, especially at the top of the tower.

The steel structure of the tower portion is developed as a tube system with perimeter columns at 15 feet on center, deep column-free office areas and a classic central structural core. The exterior walls are clad with travertine panels and silver-colored reflective glass.

Five Fremont Center,
San Francisco, Kalifornien

Das Five Fremont Center liegt am Rande des Bankenviertels südlich der Market Street, der Hauptgeschäftsstraße von San Francisco, und gegenüber dem Transbay Regional Bus Terminal. Diese zentrale und verkehrsgünstige Situation führte zur Planung von zwei Fußwegverbindungen über das Grundstück. Diese Wege nehmen den verbleibenden Raum zwischen zwei niedrigen Ladenzeilen und dem 43geschossigen Hochhaus ein. Der ganze Komplex wird auf der Straßenebene durch eine gleichartig gestaltete Folge von Fassaden, Kolonnaden und Arkaden zusammengebunden.

Das rechteckige, gedrungene Hochhaus erreicht eine Höhe von etwa 180 m. Durch zunehmend tiefer werdende Ausklinkungen mit einer vertikal durchlaufenden erkerartigen Verglasung erhielt es eine unverwechselbare Gestalt. Die verhältnismäßig geringfügige Variation der Grundform führte nicht nur zu einer überzeugenden vertikal betonten Gliederung, sondern ließ besonders im oberen Bereich des Turmes auch eine größere Anzahl der begehrten Eckbüros entstehen.

Das Stahltragwerk des Hochhauses ist als Rohrkonstruktion mit einem Achsabstand der außen umlaufenden Stützen von etwa 4,60 m, tiefen stützenfreien Nutzflächen und einem tragenden Kern im Gebäudezentrum ausgebildet. Die äußere Verkleidung besteht aus Travertinplatten mit Fensterflächen aus silberfarben reflektierendem Glas.

1. Plan (typical floor).
2, 3. The tower was given identity by minor variations of its basically rectangular plan.

1. Grundriß (Normalgeschoß).
2, 3. Durch geringfügige Veränderungen der rektangulären Grundform gewann das Hochhaus einen eigenen Ausdruck.

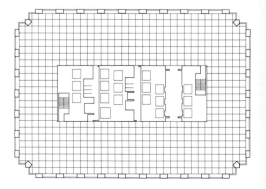

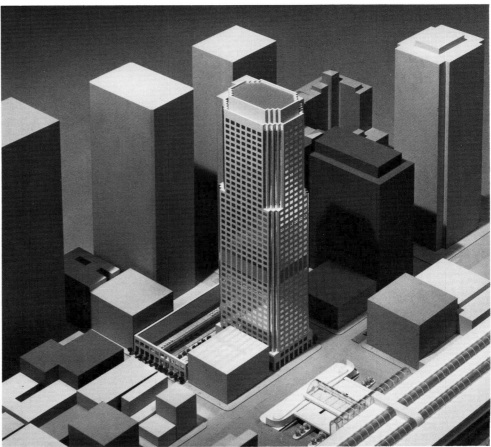

4. Plan (ground level).
5. Tower elevation and section of the two-story retail arcade.

4. Grundriß (Erdgeschoßebene).
5. Aufriß des Hochhauses und Schnitt durch den zweigeschossigen Ladenkomplex.

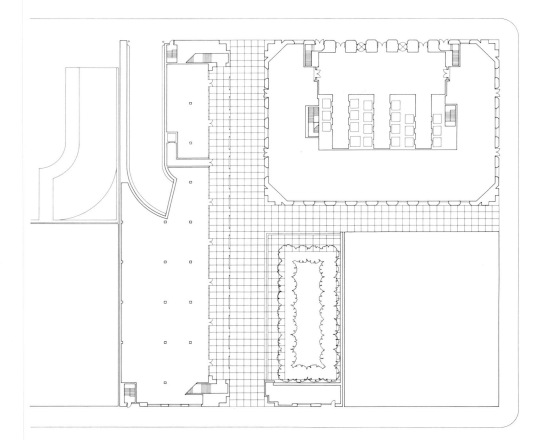

60'

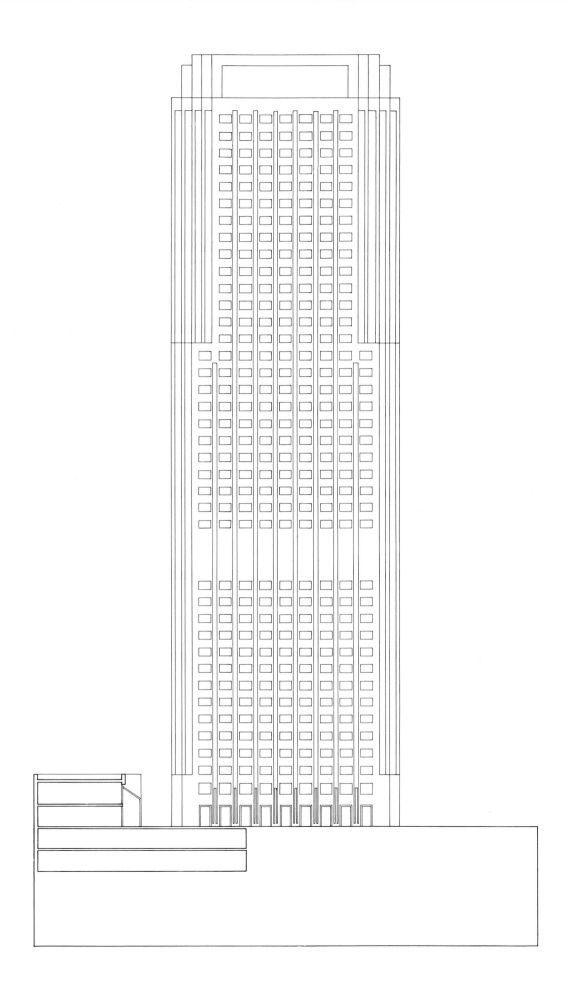

The Federal Reserve Bank of San Francisco,
San Francisco, California

The site of The Federal Reserve Bank is nearly an entire city block on the south side of Market Street, at its eastern end near the waterfront, and at that point where California Street (San Francisco's second most important street) intersects Market. It is flanked by two handsome, older commercial structures: The Southern Pacific Building to the east and the Pacific Gas and Electric (PG&E) Building to the west.

The program of some two-thirds of a million square feet is complex, including traditional office building functions and services, public exhibit and educational facilities, and highly technical accommodations for the movement, storage and recording of large amounts of currency.

The design solution is a building which extends the full length of the block to a height of eight stories, striking a balance between its lower neighbor to the east and the higher one to the west. The facade steps back slightly in two-story increments permitting the handsome upper story and cornice treatments of the neighbors to be seen effectively. The wall treatment is restrained, employing granite in two finishes, applied horizontally in concert with the strip windows. The stone color harmonizes with the brick of one neighbor and the enamelled window frames, setback railings and other metal parts are colored to match the accents of the other.

The building is set back from Market Street in order to permit the introduction of a pedestrian loggia, or porch, for the full block as an open colonnade. It is a separate structure, treated differently in detail and material, related purposely in scale and rhythms to the base of its neighbors and to the details and materials of newly reconstructed Market Street.

The loggia is designed to receive intensive and large-scale planting for its full length, including a variety of full size trees and large shrubs. The intent is to create a memorable architectural and landscape incident at an important place in the city.

The Federal Reserve Bank of San Francisco,
San Francisco, Kalifornien

Die Federal Reserve Bank of San Francisco nimmt nahezu einen ganzen Straßenblock auf der Südseite der Market Street ein, und zwar an deren östlichem Ende in der Nähe der Bay, wo die California Street (San Franciscos zweitwichtigste Straße) in die Market Street mündet. Der Komplex wird flankiert von zwei qualitätsvollen älteren Geschäftsbauten: dem Southern Pacific Building auf der östlichen und dem Pacific Gas and Electric (PG & E) Building auf der westlichen Seite.

Das komplexe, etwa 60.000 m² umfassende Raumprogramm forderte neben üblichen Büroräumen auch Platz für öffentliche Ausstellungen und Schulungseinrichtungen sowie technisch aufwendige Anlagen für Transport, Lagerung und Registrierung von Geld.

Der Baukörper gliedert sich in eine viergeschossige Sockelzone mit sehr tiefen Geschossen und größeren Stockwerkshöhen und eine Zeile mit acht Bürogeschossen normaler Höhe an der Market Street. Dort fügt sich das Projekt harmonisch zwischen die Altbauten ein, deren differenzierte Gebäudeecken durch ein Zurücktreppen des Neubaus in jedem zweiten Geschoß frei gestellt und betont werden. Die in zwei Ausführungen verwendeten Granitplatten der Außenwände haben in Übereinstimmung mit den Streifenfenstern eine horizontale Gliederung. Der Farbton des Steines harmoniert mit der Ziegelsteinfassade des einen Nachbargebäudes, während die Fensterrahmen, Geländer und anderen Metallteile in ihrer Farbe auf entsprechende Akzente des anderen Nachbargebäudes abgestimmt sind.

Die Gebäudefront ist von der Market Street abgerückt, so daß Platz für eine offene Loggia gewonnen wurde, die sich über die gesamte Straßenfront erstreckt. Sie stellt ein eigenes Bauteil dar, das in Detail und Material vom übrigen Komplex abgesetzt ist; im Maßstab und Rhythmus bezieht sie sich auf die Basisgeschosse der Nachbargebäude, in den Details und Materialien auf Elemente der kürzlich sanierten Market Street.

Die Loggia soll auf der vollen Länge eine dichte Bepflanzung aufnehmen, darunter auch große Bäume und Büsche. Man will auf diese Weise an einem wichtigen Punkt der Stadt einen erinnerungswürdigen architektonischen Ort schaffen.

1. The freestanding pedestrian loggia fronting Market Street.
2. View of the complex across Market Street.

1. Ansicht der frei stehenden Fußgängerloggia an der Market Street.
2. Blick über die Market Street hinweg auf den Komplex.

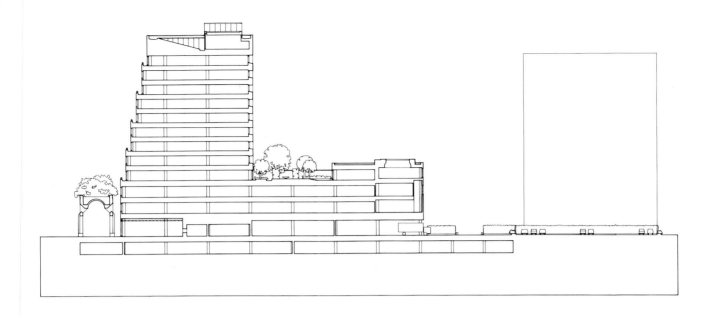

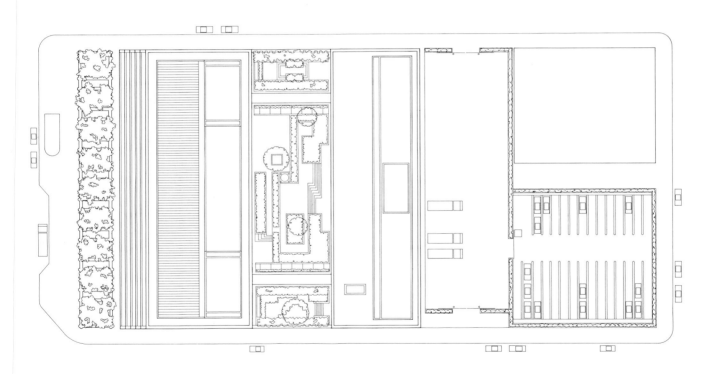

60'

3. Site plan and section.
4. The facade of the office block is substantially
set back from Market Street, permitting the rich or-
namentation of its two handsome neighbors to be
seen effectively.

3. Lageplan und Schnitt.
4. Die Gebäudefront ist von der Market Street
weit zurückgesetzt, so daß die reichhaltige Orna-
mentierung der beiden stattlichen Nachbarbauten
ungehindert zur Geltung kommt.

5, 6. Along Market Street the loggia creates pedestrian scale and establishes an important element of continuity.

5, 6. Die Fußgängerloggia gibt der Straßenfront an der Market Street Maßstäblichkeit und stellt so ein wichtiges Element der Kontinuität dar.

Crocker Center and Galleria,
San Francisco, California

The client is a major West Coast bank, on an important site located at the juncture of the retail and financial districts. A portion of the site has been occupied by the institution for many years. The master plan called for construction of a new office tower and a block-long retail galleria, followed by the removal of the bank's present offices above its banking hall, and finally the restoration of the hall and installation of a garden upon its roof.

The focus of the complex is the open ended, three-level retail galleria, covered by a large glazed vault. The galleria joins two important retail streets and also connects the new 38-story office tower with the existing banking hall, providing a variety of new pedestrian movements at a significant point in the city. The property slopes strongly down from west to east, permitting the tower lobby to coincide with the mid-level of the galleria, and the lower level of the galleria to the banking hall. The tower lobby is pushed to the rear, permitting shops to occupy the street edge at the bottom of the tower.

Renovation of the banking hall will improve pedestrian flow, but will otherwise be limited to careful enhancement and restoration of the existing traditional interior. After demolition of the tower above, elevators will carry the public to the new garden on the roof.

Above the specialized shopfront treatment at street level, the tower walls are a skin of stone and reflective glass. The stone is a warm colored granite from Texas in a pattern of polished and thermal finishes, reflecting the structural frame behind, with the glass set flush in a minimum frame. Window washing equipment will be engaged by a pattern of stainless steel studs that project from the wall.

The tower is framed as a steel tube with a 12-foot module at the exterior wall. The office floors are 20,180 square feet in area and are column free. The floors are fully electrified steel deck with concrete fill. The building is completely air conditioned and incorporates the latest life safety techniques.

Crocker Center and Galleria,
San Francisco, Kalifornien

Der Bauherr dieses 1982 fertiggestellten Komplexes ist eine der großen Banken an der Westküste; das Grundstück liegt an der Nahtstelle zwischen dem Einkaufs- und dem Bankenviertel der Stadt. Gefordert waren der Neubau eines Bürohochhauses und einer den ganzen Block durchquerenden Galleria mit Läden sowie der nachfolgende Abriß des bestehenden Bürogebäudes der Bank über deren Bankhalle und schließlich die Renovierung der Bankhalle, verbunden mit der Einrichtung eines Gartens auf deren Dach.

Kernstück der Anlage ist die dreigeschossige Einkaufsgalleria mit einer verglasten Tonne als Überdachung. Diese Galleria verbindet nicht nur den 38geschossigen Büroturm mit der Bankhalle, sondern auch zwei wichtige Einkaufsstraßen; sie schafft somit eine wesentliche neue Fußgängerverbindung an einem bedeutsamen Punkt der Stadt. Das Gelände fällt von Westen nach Osten stark ab, so daß die Eingangshalle des Hochhauses auf der mittleren und die alte Bankhalle auf der unteren Ebene der Galleria liegen. Die Eingangshalle des Hochhauses ist in den Hintergrund gerückt, wodurch es möglich war, auch an den Straßenseiten des Turmes im Erdgeschoß Läden vorzusehen.

Von der Südostecke des Komplexes führt eine zusätzliche Fußgängerverbindung schräg durch die Bankhalle auf die Eingangshalle des Büroturmes zu, wobei die Galleria gekreuzt wird. Das historische Interieur der alten Bankhalle wird im übrigen sorgfältig renoviert. Nach dem Abriß des alten Turmes über der Halle werden die Aufzüge die Besucher auf den neuen Dachgarten führen.

Über der andersartig behandelten Schaufensterfront auf der Straßenebene sind die Außenwände des Turmes eine Haut aus Stein und reflektierendem Glas. Der Stein ist Granit aus Texas, verlegt in einem sich auf das dahinter liegende Tragwerk beziehenden Muster mit abwechselnd polierten und thermisch behandelten Oberflächen; die Glasscheiben sitzen fast bündig mit den Granitplatten und sind in sehr schmalen Rahmen gefaßt.

Das Stahltragwerk des Büroturms ist als Rohrkonstruktion mit einem Achsabstand der außen umlaufenden Stützen von etwa 3,65 m ausgebildet. Zwischen Außenwänden und Kern sind die etwa 1.880 m² großen Geschoßflächen stützenfrei.

1. Plan (typical floor).
2. Plan (ground level).

1. Grundriß (Normalgeschoß).
2. Grundriß (Erdgeschoßebene).

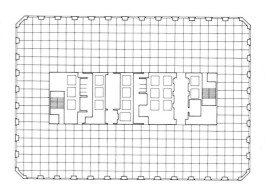

58

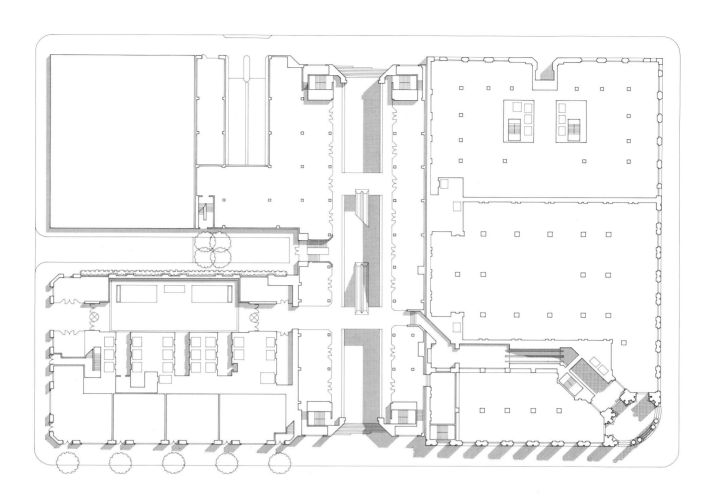

3. Section through the galleria. Where the various parts and functions of the complex meet, the three-story glass-vaulted retail galleria creates a significant pedestrian axis.
4. The galleria seen from the south with the new tower rising behind it.

3. Schnitt durch die Galleria. Am Schnittpunkt der verschiedenen Bauteile und Nutzungszonen ist durch die dreigeschossige, mit einem Glasdach überwölbte Einkaufsgalleria ein wichtiger Fußgängerbereich entstanden.
4. Ansicht der Galleria von Süden mit dem Bürohochhaus im Hintergrund.

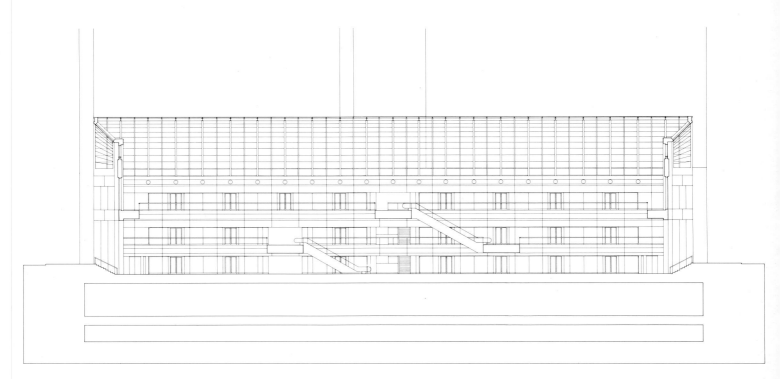

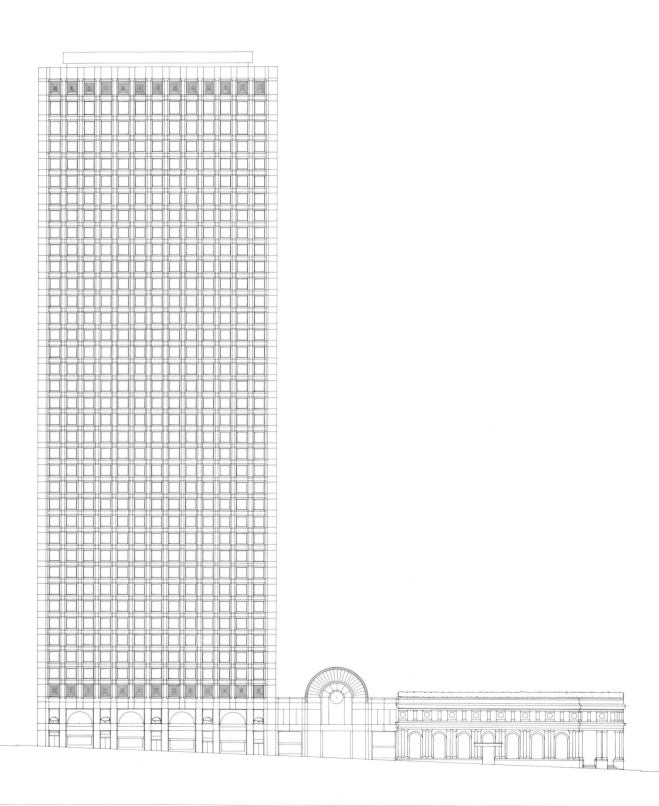

San Francisco Civic Center,
San Francisco, California

Grouped around a large, landscaped plaza, the San Francisco Civic Center includes city, state and federal government agencies' offices and courts, as well as cultural and recreational facilities.

At a pivotal point west of the plaza stands the City Hall, designed by architects Bakewell and Brown in a French Renaissance style. The building was completed in 1915 following the complete destruction of the original City Hall by the fire and earthquake of 1906. The Civic Center consists of two "subcenters", divided by the nature of their activities, which share certain facilities and combine to form a unified whole. Public buildings predominantly occupy the district north and east of the Civic Center Plaza. Cultural and recreational buildings, including the Museum, the Opera House, and an exposition building are situated to the south and west.

Located on a site southwest of City Hall ist the SOM-designed Louise M. Davies Symphony Hall. Another project completed by SOM is the addition of backstage facilities to the San Francisco Opera House.

San Francisco Civic Center,
San Francisco, Kalifornien

Im Civic Center von San Francisco sind um einen großen begrünten Platz eine Reihe von öffentlichen Gebäuden gruppiert.

Nach der Zerstörung des alten Rathauses durch Erdbeben und Feuer im Jahr 1906 wurde 1915 von den Architekten Bakewell und Brown das heutige Rathaus, die City Hall, in französischem Renaissancestil am Westrand des Platzes errichtet. Weitere Gebäude für die kalifornische und die bundesstaatliche Verwaltung folgten. Neben öffentlichen Bauten, die sich vorwiegend östlich und nördlich des Platzes ansiedelten, entstanden auf der Süd- und Westseite auch Kultur- und Freizeiteinrichtungen wie ein Museum, ein Opernhaus und ein Ausstellungsgebäude.

Um den Niedergang der Innenstadt an dieser Stelle aufzuhalten, wurde 1953 vom Bürgermeister ein Komitee ernannt, das 1956 den Entwicklungsplan für das Civic Center, den Civic Center Development Plan, vorlegte. Dieser Plan war von den Architekturbüros Wurster, Bernardi and Emmons und SOM sowie dem Ingenieurbüro De Leuw-Cather ausgearbeitet worden. Der wichtigste Vorschlag war der, die bestehenden Bauten zu renovieren und mit neuen Bauteilen unter Bewahrung der Ensemblewirkung in der Höhenentwicklung und den Proportionen zu ergänzen.

SOM baute auf einem Grundstück südwestlich der City Hall die Louise M. Davies Symphony Hall; außerdem stammt die Erweiterung des Opernhauses durch eine Hinterbühne von SOM.

1. Site plan. To the west are, showing from north to south, the proposed State Office Building, the Veterans Building, the Opera House and the Louise M. Davies Symphony Hall. To the east is the City Hall.

1. Lageplan. Im westlichen Teil des Areals liegen, von Norden nach Süden, das geplante State Office Building, das Veterans Building, das Opernhaus und die Louise M. Davies Symphony Hall. Im östlichen Teil befindet sich die City Hall.

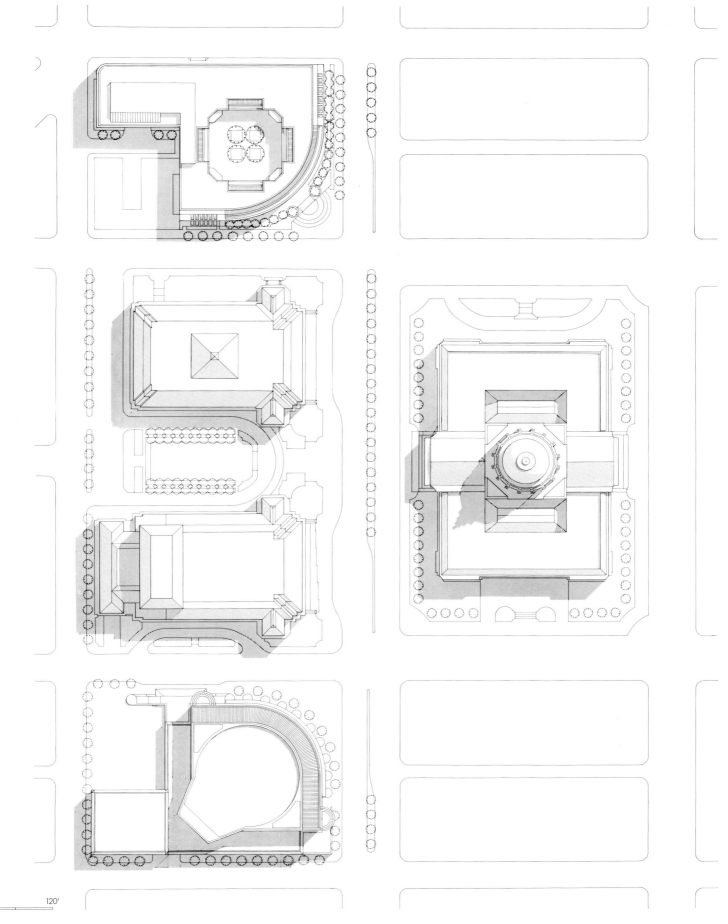

Louise M. Davies Symphony Hall,
San Francisco, California

The Louise M. Davies Symphony Hall, completed in 1980, is the newest addition to the San Francisco Civic Center.

The program required a hall of approximately 1 million cubic feet to seat an audience of 3,000, along with public related foyers, lobbies and lounges, and administrative offices, rehearsal spaces, television and recording facilities, storage and other back-of-the-house requirements.

The site is a part of, but not directly in the formal geometry of the Civic Center. It is therefore slightly relegated, dictating that the building's curved facade fall on a diagonal axis with the City Hall, and suggesting that the lobbies at each level act as glazed promenades so that the audience itself is on display and the building presents an animated and festive facade to the city streets. The design intent was to find an architectural idiom thoroughly contemporary in its expression, but consciously related in its scale and parts to the neighboring buildings, matching cornices, roof forms, colors and textures wherever possible.

The hall proper is a moderate fan shape, distributing the audience between a main orchestra level and two balcony levels. The lower balcony continues around the orchestra. Wall and ceiling surfaces are shaped for best acoustic response and consist of either painted concrete or plaster except for the wood orchestra surround at stage level. Acrylic reflector discs are suspended above the stage as required. The wall above and behind the stage is to receive a concert organ in 1983.

The structure is a composite of structural steel and reinforced concrete, depending upon the nature of the structural or acoustical need. The building is completely air conditioned. The ventilation system is designed to current best practice for sound control.

Louise M. Davies Symphony Hall,
San Francisco, Kalifornien

Schräg gegenüber der City Hall und neben dem Opernhaus im Herzen der Stadt gelegen, ist die 1981 fertiggestellte Louise M. Davies Symphony Hall das jüngste Bauwerk des San Francisco Civic Center.

Das etwa 28.000 m² umfassende Raumprogramm forderte neben einer Konzerthalle mit 3.000 Plätzen Räume für die Verwaltung des Orchesters und die üblichen Bühneneinrichtungen wie Probenräume und Lager sowie Aufnahme- und Fernsehstudios.

Die neue Konzerthalle verleugnet nicht die Zeit, in der sie entstand. Sie vermeidet sowohl modisches Formenspiel als auch falschen Historizismus. In der Baukörpergliederung, den Baustoffen mit ihren Oberflächen und Farben sowie den Details wurde ein bewußtes und ausgewogenes Zusammenspiel mit den übrigen Bauten des Civic Center angestrebt. Dabei wurde besonderes Gewicht auf die Beziehung zur City Hall gelegt, der sich das halbrunde Foyer und der Baukörper des Saales diagonal zuwenden. Der Konzertsaal ist allseitig von einer Stahlbetonwand umschlossen, deren Funktion zugleich akustische Abschirmung und statische Aussteifung ist. In seinen übrigen Teilen besteht der Bau aus einer Skelettkonstruktion mit Stahlbetonscherwänden zur Aufnahme sowohl der Windlasten als auch der in San Francisco einzukalkulierenden seismischen Lasten. Als Tragwerk der Balkone und der Verkleidung aus Fertigbetontafeln im Saal dienen biegesteife Stahlrahmen; die Decken und Balkone sind aus Ortbeton. In den Bauteilen außerhalb des Saales fanden genietete Stahlrahmen und Profilstahldecken mit Leichtbetonauflage Verwendung. Das Dach und die abgehängte Decke werden von etwa 4,25 m hohen Stahlfachwerkbindern getragen.

Die Klimaanlagen des Gebäudes umfassen sowohl Niedergeschwindigkeitssysteme mit konstantem Luftwechsel als auch variabel steuerbare Mittelgeschwindigkeitsanlagen. Alle Motoren und das Leitungsnetz mußten auf die hohen akustischen Anforderungen ausgelegt werden.

1. Plans (street level, orchestra level, loge level, first balcony level, second balcony level).

1. Grundrisse (Straßenebene, Orchesterebene, Logenebene, erster Rang, zweiter Rang).

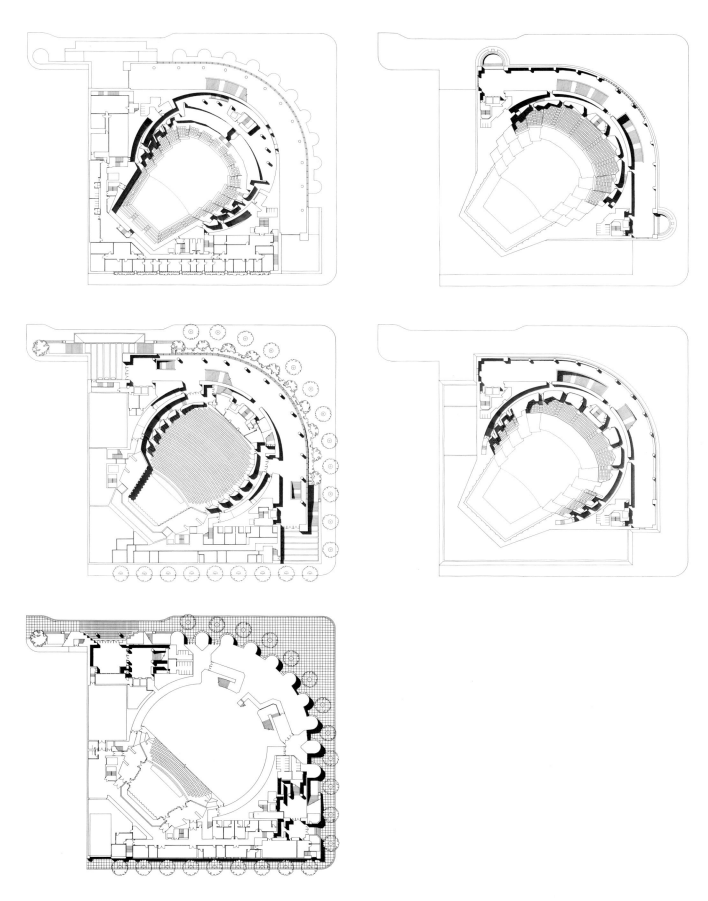

60'

2. Section. The roof and ceiling over the hall are supported by 14-foot-deep steel trusses.
3. A flight of exterior stairs lead to the upper foyer level at the northwest corner of the building.

2. Schnitt. Das Dach und die Decke über dem Saal werden von etwa 4,25 m hohen Stahlfachwerkbindern getragen.
3. Über eine Flucht von Außentreppen an der Nordwestecke des Gebäudes erreicht man die obere Ebene des Foyers.

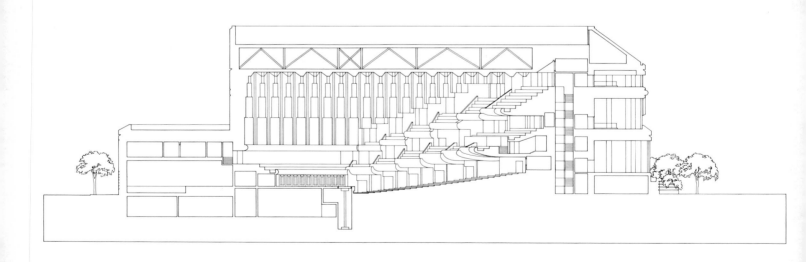

4, 5. Exterior and interior view of the glazed semi-circle of the foyer, which is oriented diagonally towards the Civic Center.
6, 7. Interior views of the hall. Wall and ceiling surfaces are shaped for best acoustic response, consisting of either painted concrete or plaster except for the wood orchestra surround at stage level. Acrylic reflector discs are adjusted above the stage as required.

4, 5. Außen- und Innenansicht des verglasten Foyerhalbrunds, das diagonal auf das schräg gegenüberliegende Civic Center hin orientiert ist.
6, 7. Innenansichten des Konzertsaals. Die Wand- und Deckenverkleidungen wurden nach akustischen Gesichtspunkten ausgebildet. Sie bestehen – mit Ausnahme der hölzernen Umkleidung des Orchesterbereichs – aus gestrichenem Beton oder Putz. Die Reflektoren aus Acrylglas über dem Bühnenraum können nach Bedarf verstellt werden.

Addition to the
San Francisco Opera House,
San Francisco, California

The Opera House addition was built in 1979 to rectify an important and crippling lack of backstage facilities, caused when the original construction was curtailed for lack of funds.
The new addition extends back from the stagehouse for its full length and to a height of four stories plus basement. In addition to the primary need for stage set storage, the program included offices, performers' lounges and dressing rooms, practice and rehearsal facilities for musicians, and ballet, wig and costume studios, and other miscellaneous spaces.
The structure is a fireproofed steel frame with slab floors. The exterior is clad with precast units, carefully adjusted to the color and texture of the terra-cotta on the original building. All masonry details, carvings, metal roof and other parts were carefully reproduced and continued in the spirit of the original in order that the addition be scarcely discernible.

Anbau an das
San Francisco Opera House,
San Francisco, Kalifornien

Als das Opernhaus von San Francisco in den frühen dreißiger Jahren gebaut wurde, fielen die Hinterbühnenbereiche Sparmaßnahmen zum Opfer. Dieser Mangel sollte mit einem Anbau im rückwärtigen Bereich hinter dem Bühnenhaus behoben werden.
Der 1979 errichtete Anbau erstreckt sich über die volle Länge des Altbaus und hat eine durchgehende Verbindung zum Bühnenraum. An beiden Seiten des viergeschossigen, unterkellerten Bauwerks befinden sich Zufahrten für Lastwagen. Gegenüber drei Kulissensätzen vor Errichtung des Anbaus können nun sieben gleichzeitig auf Lager genommen werden. Neben dem eigentlichen Hinterbühnenbereich fanden in dem Anbau Verwaltungsräume, Ruheräume für Schauspieler, Probenräume für Musiker und Ballettkünstler, Perücken- und Kostümwerkstätten sowie eine Reihe verschiedener anderer Räume Platz.
Das Stahlskelett des Anbaus wurde mit vorgefertigten Betonelementen verkleidet, die in Form, Farbe und allen Details exakt dem Baubestand nachgebildet worden sind. Auf diese Weise wurde der Anbau zu einem kaum unterscheidbaren Teil des Ganzen.

1. Side view with the new addition on the left which is set off from the existing building through a slight recess.
2. Rear view of the Opera House with the backstage addition. The concrete panels of the addition were carefully adjusted to the facade elements of the original building.

1. Seitenansicht mit dem neuen Anbau (links), der vom bestehenden Gebäude durch einen leichten Rücksprung abgesetzt ist.
2. Rückansicht des Opernhauses mit dem neuen Hinterbühnenbereich. Die Betonverkleidung des Neubauteils wurde den Fassadenelementen des Altbaus sorgfältig nachgebildet.

Wells Fargo Southern California Operations Center, El Monte, California

The Wells Fargo Data Center is located in a suburban zone east of Los Angeles. The property, some 4.5 acres, was large enough to comfortably hold both the existing and new buildings. The new facility houses the check-handling, data processing and account services for Wells Fargo Bank's southern California operations as well as a cafeteria and parking for the entire complex.

By collecting the parking into a four-level structure, enough site area was saved to create a significant park, internal to the site, which is immediately accessible to occupants of both buildings. Oriented towards the park in front of the five-story data center is an entry structure with the cafeteria, serving as a central space for the people who inhabit the buildings of the complex. The sloping front facade of this element is not only a pleasant "frontispiece" for the mass of the data center but also a desired back-drop for the park. The sloping wall is sheathed in clear anodized aluminum with flush glazed vertical slots to admit light to the cafeteria. All entries to the work areas of the data center are through the generous space beneath the sloping facade which, with its lush interior landscaping, becomes an extension of the park on which it faces, and serves as a convenient meeting place for employees. Directly behind the entry structure – but for security reasons separated from it – the mechanical heart of the complex is compacted in a core stretching the entire length of the buildings. This core is stacked vertically through all five working levels and contains sophisticated mechanical and electrical equipment, allowing for the operation of the data center during normal conditions as well as during power failures.

The data center and cafeteria building is a steel moment frame structure, sheathed – with the exception of the sloping cafeteria wall – with aluminum windows and glass fibre-reinforced concrete. The window sash is extruded sheet aluminum and the entire building surface is painted in values ranging from off-white to dark brown. With relatively little glass area on any one elevation, the darker value serves to "enlarge" the windows and provide a balanced relationship of open to opaque wall area. The parking structure, constructed in a combination of precast and poured-in-place concrete, is detailed and painted to harmonize with the data center.

Wells Fargo Southern California Operations Center, El Monte, Kalifornien

Die Betriebszentrale für den Geschäftsbereich Südkalifornien der Wells Fargo Bank wurde in einem östlichen Vorort von Los Angeles errichtet. Mit etwa 1,8 ha war das Gelände groß genug, um darauf neben einem älteren Gebäude bequem die neuen Einrichtungen unterzubringen. Zu diesen gehören neben der Betriebszentrale selbst mit den Abteilungen Scheckbearbeitung, Datenverarbeitung und Kontoführung eine Kantine und Parkraum für die gesamte Anlage.

Der Block der Betriebszentrale wurde so angeordnet, daß zwischen ihm und dem Altbau ein von den Straßen abgeschirmter Grünraum entstand, auf den beide Bauten bezogen sind. Diese Lösung war möglich, weil alle Parkstände in einer viergeschossigen Hochgarage auf der dritten Seite des Freiraums zusammengefaßt wurden. Mit Orientierung auf diesen Grünraum ist der fünfgeschossigen Betriebszentrale ein Eingangsbau mit der Kantine vorgelagert, der als Mittelpunkt der Gesamtanlage allen Beschäftigten dient. Mit seiner geneigten Fassade bildet dieser Bauteil sowohl einen guten Abschluß für die Baumasse der Betriebszentrale als auch eine Kulisse für den Park. Die schräge Außenwand ist mit naturfarbenen Aluminiumtafeln verkleidet, die sich mit bündig verglasten Vertikalschlitzen zur Belichtung der Kantine abwechseln.

Der einzige Zugang zu den Arbeitsplätzen in der Betriebszentrale führt durch den großzügigen Raum unter der geneigten Fassade, der durch seine intensive Bepflanzung den Park davor optisch erweitert und einen idealen Treffpunkt für die Mitarbeiter bildet. Unmittelbar hinter dem Eingangstrakt – von diesem jedoch aus Sicherheitsgründen abgeschlossen – wurde in einer Kernzone, die ebenso lang wie der Baukörper ist, das technische Herz der Anlage untergebracht. Dieser Teil hat – wie die Arbeitsbereiche – fünf Geschosse und enthält die komplizierten mechanischen und elektronischen Einrichtungen für das Funktionieren der Betriebszentrale sowohl unter Normalbedingungen als auch bei Netzausfall.

Das Tragwerk des Blockes der Betriebszentrale besteht aus einem biegesteifen Stahlskelett, das – mit Ausnahme der schrägen Wand des Kantinentrakts – mit Aluminiumfensterbändern und glasfaserarmiertem Beton verkleidet wurde. Die Außenwände des aus Stahlbetonfertigteilen und Ortbeton konstruierten Parkhauses wurden in ihrer Durchbildung auf den Block der Betriebszentrale abgestimmt und auch in derselben Farbskala gestrichen.

1. Site plan. The two new buildings are located in the western portion of the site.
2, 3. The sloping front facade of the cafeteria structure is sheathed in clear anodized aluminum with flush glazed vertical window slots.

1. Lageplan. Die Neubauten wurden auf dem westlichen Grundstücksteil errichtet.
2, 3. Die geneigte Längsfassade des Kantinentrakts ist mit Tafeln aus naturfarben anodisiertem Aluminium verkleidet, die sich mit bündig eingesetzten Fensterschlitzen abwechseln.

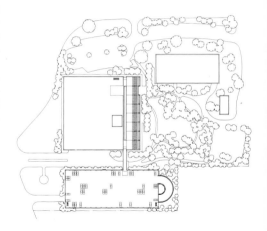

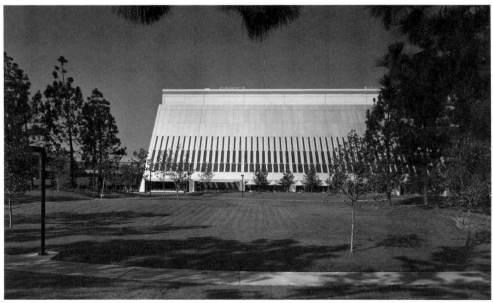

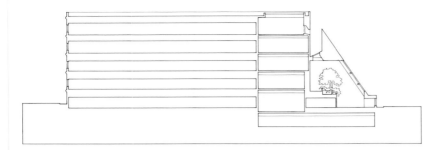

4. Plans (ground level, mezzanine level) and section.
5. Interior view of the cafeteria which serves as a central meeting place for the employees of the entire complex.

4. Grundrisse (Erdgeschoßebene, Zwischengeschoß) und Schnitt.
5. Innenansicht der Kantine, die als zentraler Treffpunkt für die Mitarbeiter der ganzen Anlage dient.

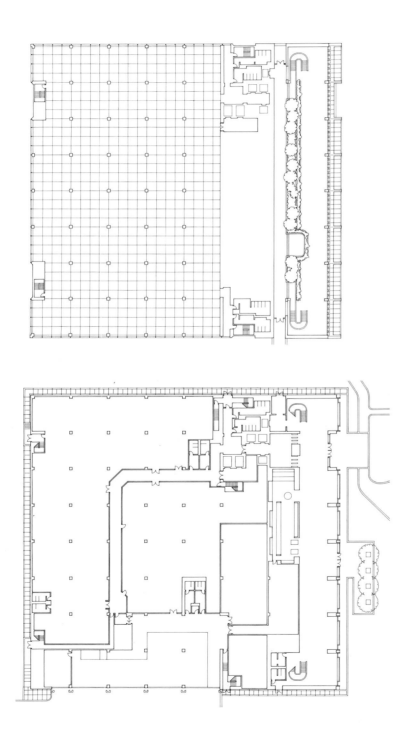

60'

70/90 Universal City Plaza,
Universal City, California

Originally the site, which is part of a 420-acre development known as Universal City, was occupied by parking as well as by a group of cottages containing office space for film and television producers. The facilities for the producers, as well as the parking, were to be replaced and expanded. Additional office space was to be provided for rental purposes. Finally, commercial space at grade level fronting on Lankershim Boulevard was required. As an inviting alternative to a highrise office structure, SOM proposed a lowrise garden-terrace environment.
In total the complex includes 280,000 square feet of office and commercial space with parking for 800 cars. Along the boulevard, the first-floor area is occupied by commercial uses, whereas office spaces occupy the upper floors. Three depressed parking levels are contained under a planted roof behind the commercial frontage. Multiple entries and elevator locations were dispersed over the length of the structure allowing for flexible use of space and rentals to a variety of tenants.
A sequence of lively spaces – terraces and courtyards, overlooked by balconies – is created by the stepped plans and sections of the structure which follows the course of the boulevard. The result is an environment of work spaces suitable to the mild southern California climate. Lush landscaping reinforces these indoor-outdoor space relationships and complements the rectangular forms of the buildings which are sheathed in pale Italian travertine and grey heat-absorbing glass.

70/90 Universal City Plaza,
Universal City, Kalifornien

Ursprünglich befanden sich auf dem Gelände, das Teil der etwa 170 ha großen Universal City ist, neben zahlreichen Parkplätzen eine Reihe von Behelfsbauten mit Büros von Film- und Fernsehproduzenten. Dem Programm des Bauherrn zufolge sollten sowohl die Einrichtungen für die Produzenten als auch die Parkplätze erneuert und vergrößert werden. Außerdem sollten weitere Büros zur Vermietung und, in der Erdgeschoßzone am Lankershim Boulevard, Läden entstehen. Als Alternative zu den üblichen Bürohochhäusern schlug SOM hier eine niedrige Terrassenanlage mit starker Begrünung vor.
Insgesamt umfaßt der Komplex etwa 26.000 m² Büro- und Ladenflächen sowie 800 Parkplätze. Entlang dem Boulevard entstanden im Erdgeschoß des im wesentlichen viergeschossigen Baukörpers großzügige Läden, die darüber liegenden drei Geschosse nehmen Büroflächen ein. Dahinter wurden im Inneren des Komplexes drei niedrigere Parkebenen mit begrüntem Dach angeordnet. Eingänge und Aufzugsanlagen verteilen sich so auf das Gebäude, daß flexible Unterteilungen und Vermietungen an eine Vielzahl von Benutzern möglich sind.
Die starke Grundrißgliederung des Baukörpers, der dem schrägen Straßenverlauf folgt, sowie Vor- und Rücksprünge auch im Querschnitt, führten zu abwechslungsreichen Raumfolgen mit Balkons, Terrassen und Höfen, die alle begrünt und von den Büros aus zugänglich sind. Damit entstand eine ruhige Arbeitsatmosphäre in Verbindung mit Erholungsmöglichkeiten, wie sie dem milden Klima Südkaliforniens angemessen ist. Eine intensive gärtnerische Gestaltung unterstreicht diese Beziehung zwischen Innen- und Außenräumen und kontrastiert zu den rechteckig-kubischen Architekturformen aus hellem italienischen Travertin und grau getöntem Wärmeschutzglas.

1. Plan (third floor) and section.

1. Grundriß (3. Geschoß) und Schnitt.

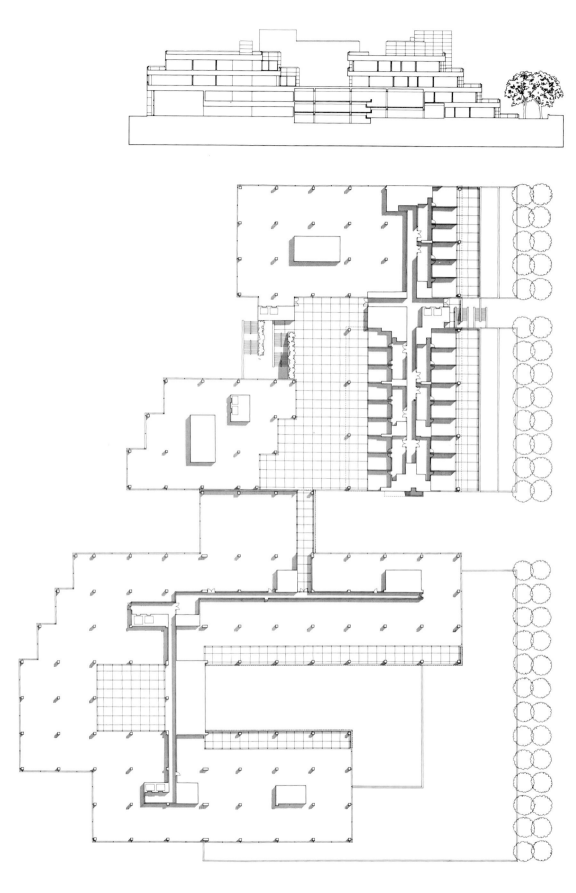

60'

2–6. As an inviting alternative to conventional, sealed high-rise office structures, a low-rise garden terrace environment suitable to the mild Southern California climate was created.

2–6. Als einladende Alternative zu den üblichen vollklimatisierten Hochhausbüroanlagen wurde hier eine niedrige Terrassenlösung mit bepflanzten Balkons geschaffen, die dem milden Klima Südkaliforniens entspricht.

First Federal Square,
Santa Monica, California

The corporate headquarters for First Federal Savings and Loan Association of Santa Monica was completed in June 1982. The 12-story steel framed structure rises in alternating bands of dark gray glass framed by burgundy colored sills and heads and white precast concrete above four levels of underground parking.

The need to maintain an existing outdated building on the site while the new building was constructed resulted in an opportunity to set the building back from the main street, creating an open plaza after the old structure was removed.

The building facade angles away from Wilshire Boulevard to allow for an entry plaza which is framed by a landscaped arbor along the side street. A chevron pattern of burgundy and white terrazzo is developed on the plaza paving in response to the angled building facade, the arbor and the planter-benches. The lower three floors step out from the tower with landscaped roofs to provide larger floors for the administrative offices and the main branch on the ground floor.

The building consists of 220,000 gross square feet of office space with four levels of below grade parking.

First Federal Square,
Santa Monica, Kalifornien

Der Hauptsitz der First Federal Savings and Loan Association of Santa Monica wurde 1982 fertiggestellt. Der zwölfgeschossige Stahlskelettbau, der sich über einer viergeschossigen Tiefgarage erhebt, ist in seiner äußeren Erscheinung gekennzeichnet durch die horizontale Schichtung von Bändern aus weißen Fertigbetonelementen sowie aus dunkelgrauem, oben und unten in burgunderroten Rahmen gefaßtem Glas.

Die Notwendigkeit, während der Bauzeit ein auf dem Grundstück vorhandenes veraltetes Gebäude zu erhalten, gab die Möglichkeit, den Neubau von der Hauptstraße, dem Wilshire Boulevard, zurückzusetzen und ihm nach dem Abbruch des Altbaus eine Plaza vorzulagern.

Das Gebäude springt entlang dem Wilshire Boulevard so zurück, daß man von dort auf die Eingänge an der Seitenstraße, an der die Plaza durch eine Pergola gefaßt ist, hingelenkt wird. Das keilförmige Muster aus burgunderroten und weißen Terrazzoplatten spiegelt in der Bodenfläche der Plaza die abgewinkelte Form des Gebäudes, der Pergola und der Pflanzbecken. Die unteren drei Geschosse springen gegenüber dem Turm mit bepflanzten Dächern vor und bieten auf diese Weise größere Geschoßflächen für die Verwaltung und die Kundenräume im Erdgeschoß.

Das Gebäude bietet eine Bruttogeschoßfläche von etwa 20.500 m², zu der noch die Autoabstellflächen in den Untergeschossen hinzukommen.

1. Site plan.
2. View of the building from the south.

1. Lageplan.
2. Südansicht des Gebäudes.

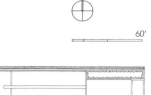

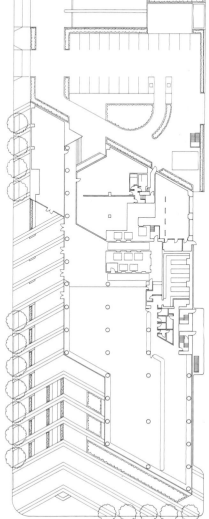

60'

Master plan for
Irvine Center,
Irvine, California

The problem presented by the Irvine site and program is a classic one. A large tract of land with few natural boundaries has been made valuable for commercial development because of the convergence of three major freeways. In fast growing areas of the country where shopping centers prevail and regional development has spread endlessly along high speed roadways, the master plan for the Irvine Center site represents a radical departure.

The intent of the master plan is to create a multi-purpose retail office district that will serve as a "downtown" for the various village clusters that have been developed or planned for the surrounding region, a total population of approximately 500,000.

The main concept of the urban design plan for Irvine Center is to cluster a core of taller buildings within a traditional grid of streets in order to create a compact pedestrian environment. These buildings are located in a checkerboard pattern to maximize tenant views and to create a distinctive skyline. The surrounding garden zone is developed with informal clusters of lowrise commercial office space. The contrast between the informal garden commercial district and the more formal urban commercial district becomes a device which sharply defines the Center's image and creates a clearly perceived place in the region. In addition, the ground floor uses are planned to promote pedestrian connections between buildings. The plan creates a lively and comfortable pedestrian environment through landscaping and other amenities such as sidewalk shelters and rest areas.

The program for Irvine Center includes approximately 2.2 million square feet of retail space, 3.8 million square feet of office space and 1 million square feet of hotel space. In addition, there are approximately 3.1 million square feet of structured parking and 0.1 million square feet of civic space. One of the most important concepts of the plan is the creation of a 360-foot square block which establishes a pattern of equal, 180-foot square parcels. These parcels allow a development framework that is flexible to the inevitable program changes that will occur over time.

Entwicklungsplan für das
Irvine Center,
Irvine, Kalifornien

Auf der dreieckigen Schnittfläche zwischen drei großen Schnellstraßen war mit der Anlage eines großen regionalen Einkaufszentrums der Anfang einer Bebauung gemacht worden. Die drei Schnellstraßen haben das Aussehen des Gebietes erheblich verändert, weil das ursprünglich für die Landwirtschaft bewässerte Land nun mit der zunehmenden Verstädterung Südkaliforniens anderen Nutzungen zugeführt wird. Der Strukturplan, den SOM für das Zentrum entwickelt hat, stellt für eine Region, deren Bild von endlosen, ungeordneten Korridorsiedlungen entlang den Autobahnen geprägt wird, eine radikale Neuerung dar.

Auf den Flächen um das Einkaufszentrum soll nun ein Geschäfts- und Bürogebiet mit Mehrfachnutzungen entstehen, womit die etwa 500.000 Bewohner der in der Umgebung aus dem Boden geschossenen Wohnsiedlungen so etwas wie ein »Stadtzentrum« erhalten.

Entlang einer Haupterschließungsstraße, dem Irvine Center Drive, soll ein Kern von Hochhausgruppen mit Arbeitsplätzen und Geschäften in verdichteter Form angelegt werden. Diese Kernzone wird das Aussehen eines größeren Stadtzentrums mit übersichtlichem Verkehrsnetz und einer Reihe von städtischen Grünflächen haben. Darum herum legt sich eine parkartige Grünzone mit lockeren Gruppen niedriger Bürobauten. Im Kontrast zwischen dem strenger gegliederten Innenbereich und diesem Ring drückt sich ein wesentliches Element des planerischen Ordnungsprinzips der Architekten für das Irvine Center aus. Im Gegensatz zu der bisherigen Lehrmeinung, die eine strikte Trennung von Fuß- und Fahrwegen forderte, wird es hier im Interesse einer dichten städtischen Atmosphäre wieder wie früher Straßen mit beidseitigen Gehsteigen geben.

Das Programm für das Irvine Center sieht etwa 205.000 m² für Verkaufsflächen, etwa 355.000 m² für Büroflächen und etwa 93.000 m² für Hotelflächen vor. Zusätzlich sind etwa 290.000 m² für Parkierungsflächen und etwa 9.300 m² für öffentliche Flächen vorgesehen.

Die Realisierung des Planes wird sich über mehrere Jahre erstrecken. Durch die Unterteilung in etwa 55 × 55 m große, stufenweise realisierbare Zonen soll ein Rahmen geschaffen werden, der gegenüber unausweichlichen Programmänderungen in der Zukunft ein Höchstmaß an Flexibilität bietet.

1. Building prototypes.
2. Parcelization plan. A regular grid of 180 by 180 feet is overimposed over the site except for an oval shaped area at the southeastern end of the site for which a shopping center has been planned.
3. Infill and phasing plan. Phasing starts at the center of the site, where tall buildings are located to form an urban center.

1. Prototypen der verschiedenen Gebäude.
2. Parzellierungsplan. Auf einem oval zugeschnittenen Geländeteil im südöstlichen Grundstücksbereich soll ein großes Einkaufszentrum errichtet werden; über das restliche Grundstück wurde ein gleichmäßiges Raster aus Quadraten mit einer Seitenlänge von etwa 55 m gelegt.
3. Bauabfolgeplan. Mit der Bebauung soll in der Mitte des Geländes begonnen werden, wo hohe Baukörper ein städtisches Zentrum bilden sollen.

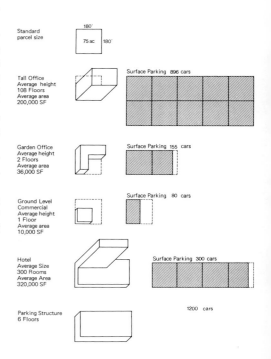

Standard parcel size 180' / 75 ac / 180'

Tall Office
Average height 108 Floors
Average area 200,000 SF
Surface Parking 896 cars

Garden Office
Average height 2 Floors
Average area 36,000 SF
Surface Parking 155 cars

Ground Level Commercial
Average height 1 Floor
Average area 10,000 SF
Surface Parking 80 cars

Hotel
Average Size 300 Rooms
Average Area 320,000 SF
Surface Parking 300 cars

Parking Structure 6 Floors
1200 cars

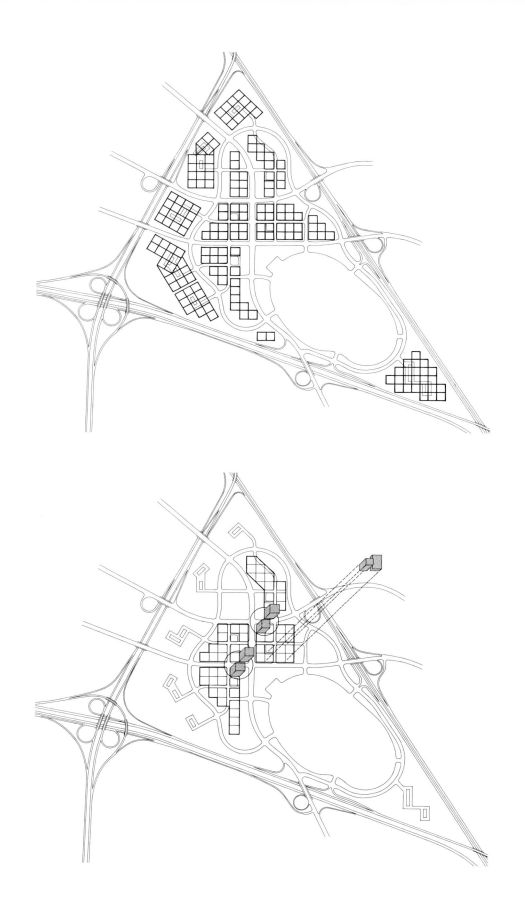

1200'

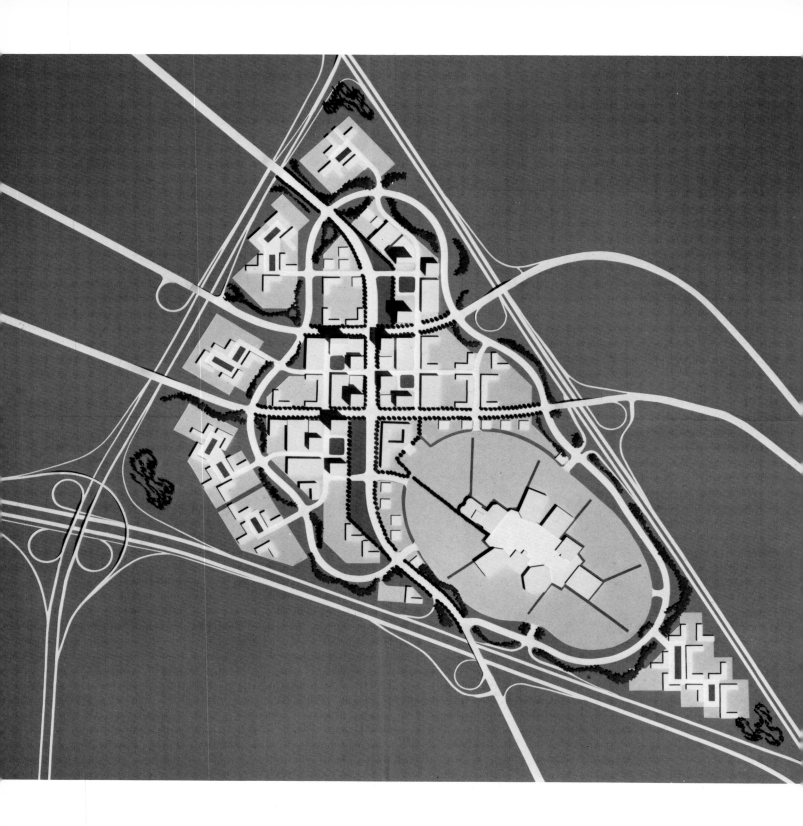

4, 5. General views (model and axonometric drawing).

4, 5. Gesamtansichten (Modell und Axonometrie).

Crocker Center,
Los Angeles, California

The site for the Crocker Center project is situated on the highest elevation on Bunker Hill, the business and financial hub of downtown Los Angeles. Given its high visibility at a pivotal point in this part of the city, it was intended to provide a rich variety of options for people to eat, shop and be entertained.

Two office towers of 54 and 44 stories in height sit in balanced juxtaposition to one another on the east portion of the large rectangular site, while to the west a glazed pavilion is embedded in a terraced commercial structure descending the hill.

The pavilion will be enclosed in a 40-foot-high structure supporting a clear glass roof – allowing visitors views of the towers above. Constantly changing patterns of light and shadows are cast on the atrium floor. An extensive palette of cool greens, rose, copper and bronze for interior plaster surfaces, mullions, trellises, light standards and planters, as well as exterior aluminum wall panels was chosen.

Both towers are sheathed in polished red granite fitted with windows of copper-bronze insulating glass.

Crocker Center,
Los Angeles, Kalifornien

Das Grundstück des Crocker Center liegt auf dem höchsten Punkt des Bunker Hill, des Geschäfts- und Finanzzentrums von Los Angeles. Wegen seiner exponierten Lage war eine sorgfältige Einpassung in die städtebauliche Situation von ausschlaggebender Bedeutung. Zugleich sollte ein reichhaltiges Angebot an Geschäften und Unterhaltungsstätten geschaffen werden.

Zwei gleichartige Bürotürme mit 54 und 44 Geschossen stehen sich auf der Ostseite des großen rechteckigen Grundstücks in spannungsreicher Beziehung gegenüber, während im Westen ein dreigeschossiges Ladenzentrum als Zeilenbau mit einer terrassierten Fassade den Straßenraum begrenzt. Zwischen diesen Baukörpern liegt als Mittelpunkt der Anlage ein lichtdurchflutetes Atrium.

Um Ausblicke auf die Bürotürme und die bepflanzten Terrassen der niedrigen Bauteile zu ermöglichen, wird das etwa 12 m hohe Atrium nach oben mit einem verglasten Raumfachwerk geschlossen. Der wechselnde Sonneneinfall wirft auf den Boden wandernde Schattenbilder. Mitarbeiter, die in den Bürotürmen des Crocker Center tätig sind, wie auch Besucher, finden hier inmitten des Geschäftszentrums von Los Angeles einen einmaligen Treffpunkt für Restaurant- und Ladenbesuche vor, der die früher üblichen, unwirtlichen und kaum nutzbaren Pflasterplätze vor Bürohochhäusern ersetzt. Für die verputzten Flächen, Metallrahmen, Jalousien, Beleuchtungskörper und Pflanzkästen im Inneren sowie für die Aluminiumelemente an den Fassaden entwickelten die Architekten eine reiche Farbskala aus kühlen Grün-, Rosa-, Kupfer- und Bronzetönen.

Die beiden Bürotürme wurden mit poliertem roten Granit verkleidet und erhielten Fenster aus kupferbronzefarben getöntem Wärmeschutzglas.

1. General view from the southeast (model).
2. Plans (ground floor, typical floor) and section.

1. Gesamtansicht von Südosten (Modell).
2. Grundrisse (Erdgeschoß, Normalgeschoß) und Schnitt.

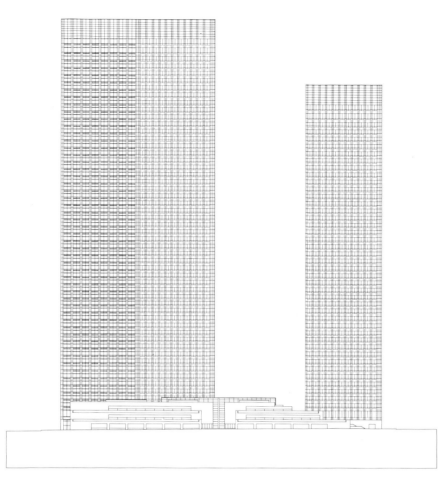

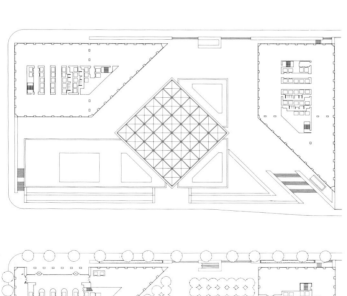

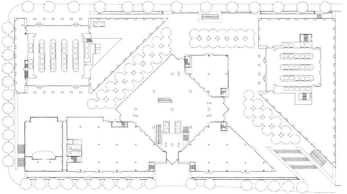

120'

**Weyerhaeuser Technology Center,
Tacoma, Washington**

In 1971 the corporate headquarters of the Weyerhaeuser Company, one of the world's largest manufacturers of wood products, was built on a 480-acre site in suburban Tacoma. At the same time a system of roadways and paths was planned for a number of future structures on the site.

In 1974 the new building was planned to provide a close mixing of office, laboratory and development as well as support spaces in a configuration that would promote as much visual and physical contact between researchers working in different disciplines or projects as possible. Laboratories and all other work spaces were to be undedicated and anonymous, allowing for maximum functional and personnel flexibility.

The final design has three distinct but connected parts. First, a two-story glazed pavilion, the second story of which is free of exterior walls. This contains laboratory and office space. Second, a parallel link on two levels containing entry lobbies, cafeteria, meeting rooms and library. Third, a two-story space containing large-scale development equipment which is totally without exterior glazing.

The entire property was originally heavily wooded. This was partially cleared to provide a site for the corporate headquarters. The Technology Center is sited in the portion that remains wooded in a manner that as few trees as possible were cleared for the building or exterior parking. The glazing of the pavilion is clear rather than tinted or reflective glass with the result of not changing the perception of being next to a green wall. The fact that the offices are entirely planned to be in the open makes these exterior views possible throughout the building. In addition to the open office plan, all light fixtures for general illumination are contained within the furniture pieces and no lighting is contained in the ceiling.

The structural system for the office, laboratory pavilion is a system of heavy timber girders and columns. Foundations and suspended floor slabs are of reinforced concrete. Concrete masonry shear walls brace this support structure and anchor the 220,000-square-foot plywood diaphragm roof. The development area has masonry walls which are clad with modular cedar panels.

**Weyerhaeuser Technology Center,
Tacoma, Washington**

1971 entstand auf einem etwa 195 ha großen, dicht bewaldeten Gelände im Vorortbereich von Tacoma die Hauptverwaltung der Weyerhaeuser Company, die eine der größten Gesellschaften für Holzprodukte der Welt ist. Zugleich wurde damals ein Netz von Straßen und Wegen gebaut, das schon auf eine weitere Bebauung hin ausgelegt war.

1974 wurde dann mit der Planung eines zentralen Neubaus für die Forschungs-, Entwicklungs- und Konstruktionsabteilung des Unternehmens begonnen. Man strebte dabei einen kompakten Bau mit vielen optischen und physischen Kontaktmöglichkeiten zwischen den in unterschiedlichen Bereichen – oder an verschiedenen Projekten – arbeitenden Forschungsingenieuren an. Die Arbeitsräume und Labors sollten außerdem nicht personalbezogen, sondern möglichst flexibel ausgelegt werden, um ein Maximum an Nutzungsneutralität zu erreichen.

Die Entwurfslösung besteht aus drei eng miteinander verbundenen Bauteilen verschiedener Art. Ein verglaster Pavillonbau mit zwei Geschossen enthält Großraumbüros und innenliegende Laborräume. Parallel an eine der Längsseiten des Pavillons lehnt sich ein ebenfalls zweigeschossiger Verbindungsbau mit Eingangshalle, Kantine, Besprechungsräumen und einer Bibliothek an. Der dritte Bauteil ist ein zweigeschossiges Gebäude ohne Fenster, in dem neue Herstellungs- und Verfahrenstechniken erprobt werden.

Beim Bau der Hauptverwaltung wurde die ursprünglich dichte Bewaldung des Grundstücks teilweise gelichtet. Für das Technology Center und die anschließenden Parkplätze wurden dann allerdings so wenig Bäume wie möglich gefällt. Die Scheiben der Verglasung des Pavillons sind weder getönt noch beschichtet, sondern klar, so daß der Ausblick auf den Wald nicht geschmälert wird. Da es sich bei den Büros, wie bereits erwähnt, um Großräume handelt, ist der Ausblick von überall möglich. Die Beleuchtung in den Büros ist gänzlich in die Möblierung integriert; es gibt hier also keine Lampen in den Decken.

Das konstruktive System des Komplexes besteht aus verleimten Holzbindern und Stützen mit Ausfachungen aus Glas und Mauerwerk sowie Fundamenten und Zwischendecken aus Stahlbeton. Der Aussteifung des Tragskeletts und des etwa 20.500 m² großen Daches, das aus einer Sperrholzmembran besteht, dienen Wände aus Betonsteinmauerwerk. Die geschlossenen Mauerwerkswände des Versuchsgebäudes sind mit Elementen aus Zedernholz verkleidet.

1. The building seen from the south.
2. Site plan. The Technology Center is located north of the corporate headquarters.

1. Südansicht des Gebäudes.
2. Lageplan. Das Technology Center liegt nördlich der Hauptverwaltung.

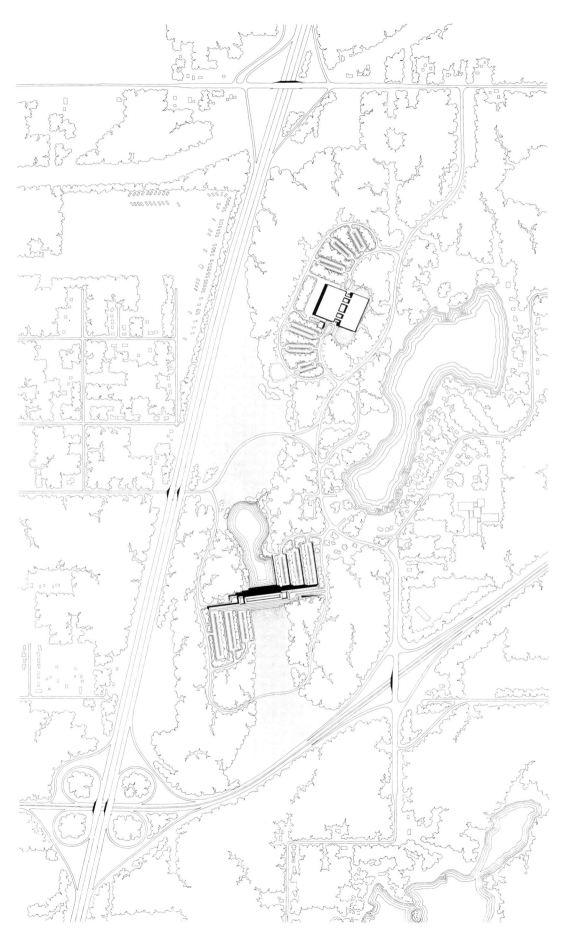

1200'

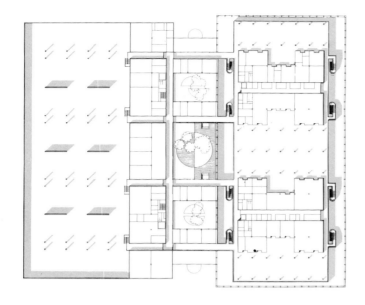

3. Plans (ground floor, second floor).
4. The Technology Center is sited in a heavily wooded portion of the site, where as few trees as possible were cleared.

3. Grundrisse (Erdgeschoß, 2. Geschoß).
4. Das Technology Center liegt in einem stark bewaldeten Bereich des Grundstücks, wo so wenige Bäume wie möglich gefällt wurden.

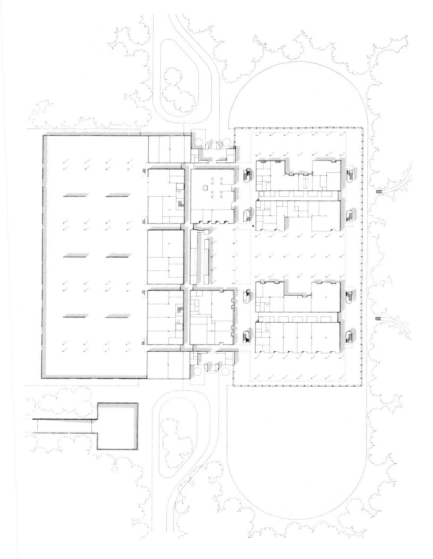

120'

5. View of the main entrance.
6. The glazing of the office pavilion is clear glass with the result of not changing the perception of being next to a green wall.

5. Ansicht des Haupteingangs.
6. Der Bauteil mit den Büros hat Fenster aus ungetöntem Glas, damit der Ausblick auf die grüne Wand des umliegenden Waldes nicht geschmälert wird.

The Portland Transit Mall,
Portland, Oregon

The Portland Transit Mall extends eleven blocks along two parallel streets in the heart of downtown Portland. Completed in 1978 as the hub of a regional transit system, the mall harmoniously combines circulation systems for buses, private vehicles and pedestrians. The transit mall provides convenient transfers between bus routes and serves as a link between suburban transit stations and future light rail lines. Coordinated signals, street lights, bollards, widened sidewalks and reduced street widths establish an exclusive one-way circulation corridor which enables buses to make five stops in each direction in less than half the time previously required.

The design of the transit mall creates a lively streetscape tailored to Oregon's rainy climate. Red brick paving banded by light gray granite curbs orders the system of bus shelters, information kiosks, vendors' booths, fountains and sculptures that enrich the pedestrian experience. The broad sidewalks are landscaped with over 300 London Plane and Red Maple trees. Flowers and shrubs placed in 100 planter tubs provide additional texture and color. Refurbished light fixtures dating from the 1920's and historic cast bronze drinking fountains add a link with Portland's past.

The transit mall has 31 bronze-clad, walk-through bus shelters. At both ends of the lozenge-shaped shelter, large glass walls allow commuters to watch for buses while protected from inclement weather. The transparent overhanging roof provides additional shelter for up to 60 commuters. There are seats inside the shelter for elderly and handicapped persons. A closed-circuit television system in each bus shelter displays bus arrival and departure times. Used for the first time in the United States, the system includes back-lit maps and instructions which help the passengers use the regional transit system. Each shelter is coded by a color and a symbol keyed to seven geographic service areas. Eight trip planning kiosks feature the closed-circuit screen, a keyboard to inquire about route numbers and bus schedules, and a free telephone linked to an information line.

SOM planned and designed the transit mall in association with Lawrence Halprin and Associates.

The Portland Transit Mall,
Portland, Oregon

Die 1978 fertiggestellte Portland Transit Mall erstreckt sich über elf Blocks im Herzen der Stadt und umfaßt zwei parallele Straßen. Als Angelpunkt eines neuen Verkehrsprogramms ermöglicht sie ein harmonisches Nebeneinander von Bussen, Privatautos und Fußgängern. Durch aufeinander abgestimmte Lichtsignale, Boller und verringerte Fahrbahnbreiten benötigen die Busse in den nur noch in einer Richtung befahrbaren Straßen für jeweils fünf Halts weniger als die Hälfte der früher dafür aufgewendeten Zeit. Der Individualverkehr zu Parkgaragen und Hoteleingängen ist auf eine gesonderte Fahrspur verwiesen worden, die jeweils nur über die Länge von drei Straßenblocks durchgeführt wurde, um den Durchgangsverkehr fernzuhalten.

Das Straßenpflaster besteht jetzt aus Ziegeln, die im Fischgrätmuster verlegt sind und von Randsteinen aus grauem Granit gesäumt werden. Kreuzungen, an denen sich die Verkehrswege von Fußgängern, Autos und Bussen überschneiden, wurden durch große Kreise aus Granitpflaster mit Rändern aus Ziegeln besonders markiert. An den beiden Straßen wurden über 300 Platanen und Ahornbäume gepflanzt; Blumen und Büsche in Pflanzbehältern sorgen für eine weitere Textur- und Farbbereicherung. Instand gesetzte Straßenlampen aus den zwanziger Jahren und alte Trinkbrunnen aus Bronze stellen eine Verbindung zur Vergangenheit von Portland her. Glasüberdachte, bronzeverkleidete Wartehäuschen bieten Busfahrgästen Schutz vor der Witterung. Erstmalig in den Vereinigten Staaten unterrichtet ein Kabelfernsehsystem die Fahrgäste über Ankunfts- und Abfahrtszeiten an jeder Haltestelle. Übersichtspläne und Hinweistafeln ergänzen dieses Informationssystem. Die Wartehäuschen sind durch verschiedene Farben und Symbole gekennzeichnet, die bestimmten Verkehrszonen entsprechen. In acht Informationspavillons können über Bildschirme und Streckenpläne Auskünfte über einzelne Routen und Fahrpläne eingeholt werden; darüber hinaus stehen Telefone mit Anschluß an eine zentrale Informationsstelle zur Verfügung.

SOM plante und entwarf die Portland Transit Mall in Zusammenarbeit mit Lawrence Halprin and Associates.

1. Location plan of Portland. Key: 1 The Portland Transit Mall.
2. View of a walk-through bus shelter.

1. Situationsplan von Portland. Legende: 1 Portland Transit Mall.
2. Ansicht eines offenen Wartehäuschens für Busfahrgäste.

Pages 98/99:
3–15. The Transit Mall is a lively colorful pedestrian environment.

Seiten 98/99:
3–15. Die Transit Mall ist ein lebendiger und farbiger Fußgängerraum.

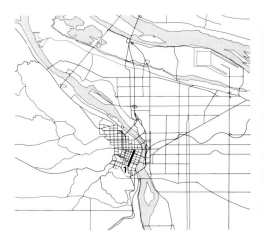

Der Mittlere Westen

Nur wenige Architekten konnten mit ihrem Werk Zeichen setzen, die bestimmend für Maßstab und Charakter einer ganzen Stadt wurden. Zu solchen Zeichen gehören zweifellos das John Hancock Center (»Big John« genannt) und der Sears Tower, beide Werke des SOM-Büros in Chicago, die allgemein bewundert werden, weil sie den Maßstab Chicagos erweitert haben und mit ihrer Silhouette die Lebendigkeit, ja Kühnheit der Stadt unterstreichen. Auch sonst stößt man in Chicago überall auf Plätze und Bauwerke, die SOM entworfen hat: so in der Innenstadt Inland Steel [2], Harris Trust, Brunswick [3], Hartford Fire Insurance und Three First National Plaza, am südwestlichen Rand der Innenstadt der Chicago Circle Campus [4] der University of Illinois und am östlichen Rand die Erweiterungsbauten für das Art Institute of Chicago.

Die Stärke des Chicagoer SOM-Büros beruht auf der Verbundenheit mit der baulichen Tradition dieser Stadt. Immer noch die vorherrschende Ausdrucksform in der zeitgenössischen Architektur, kündigte sich der besondere Stil Chicagos um 1895 mit dem Reliance Building von John Welborn Root und dem Kaufhaus Carson, Pirie, Scott (ehemals Schlesinger & Mayer) von Louis Sullivan an.

Chicago selbst begann erst vor kurzem sein architektonisches Erbe zu schätzen. Während Sullivan in Buffalo das Prudential Building, in St. Louis das Wainwright Building und in Owatonna die National Bank bauen konnte, wurden ihm in Chicago keine größeren Aufträge anvertraut. Auch sein berühmtester Schüler, der höchst kreative Frank Lloyd Wright, sollte die wichtigen Gebäude dieser Stadt nicht entwerfen. Chicago favorisierte statt dessen oft neoromanische und neogotische Entwerfer. Die Vorstellung, daß sich Architektur aus Raumprogramm, Technik und kulturellem Umfeld entwickeln müsse – wie Sullivan nachdrücklich betont hatte –, blieb ein Traum, der – wenn man einmal von Wright absieht – mit Sullivans Tod im Jahr 1924 nahezu unterging.

Ist es daher nicht sonderbar, die Halle von Sullivans großartiger Stock Exchange im Komplex der Erweiterungsbauten von SOM für das Chicago Art Institute [5] wiederzufinden? Der Raum fand hier, im Zentrum des Kunstlebens von Chicago, eine neue Bleibe und wurde mit Hilfe von SOM liebevoll restauriert, während der Eingangsbogen der Börse als frei stehende Skulptur nunmehr in der von SOM geplanten Gartenanlage steht.

Durch einen Glücksfall – er hatte es ein Jahr zuvor abgelehnt, an die Harvard University zu gehen – wurde Ludwig Mies van der Rohe für Chicago gewonnen. Bereits weithin bekannt durch seinen Deutschen Pavillon auf der Weltausstellung in Barcelona und das Haus Tugendhat in Brünn, gelang es Mies nach und nach, Aufträge an sich zu ziehen. Zugleich schuf er sich durch seine intellektuelle Disziplin,

3

1. Skyline of Chicago, Illinois.
2. Inland Steel Building, Chicago, Illinois.
3. Brunswick Building, Chicago, Illinois.
4. University of Illinois, Chicago Circle Campus, Chicago, Illinois.
5. Art Institute of Chicago, Chicago, Illinois.
6. Oak Ridge, Tennessee.
7. Lake Meadows Housing, Chicago, Illinois.

2

4

6

The Midwest

Few architects have created landmarks that set the scale and tone of an entire city. Yet SOM/Chicago's John Hancock Center ("Big John") and Sears Tower are popularly admired for lofting Chicago's scale and skylining Chicago's vitality, even its audacity. At groundline, Chicago is punctuated with SOM's plazas and buildings: Inland Steel [2], Harris Trust, Brunswick [3], Hartford Fire Insurance, and Three First National Plaza, all in Chicago's Loop. Southwest, SOM's University of Illinois Chicago Circle Campus [4] is a crossroads of intellectual and social vitality, and eastward, towards Lake Michigan, SOM's Chicago Art Institute additions form an edge to the lakeside park. Those buildings reveal three decades of SOM's achievement, developed in powerful symbols for the Midwest's financial and cultural capital.

SOM/Chicago's strength rests upon adherence to Chicago's architectural tradition. Still the dominant expression within the modern movement, Chicago's special architecture was intimated about 1895 by John Welborn Root in his Reliance Building and Louis Sullivan in his Carson, Pirie, Scott (Schlesinger & Mayer) store. They featured slender structure, large voids, glazed transparencies, metallic arises and moulded finishes, all unified by central axes, symmetry, and tripartite facades, as in Sullivan's Prudential (Guaranty) Building in Buffalo. The Prudential, Sullivan wrote in 1896, is a tall, rational expression of the technology that carries buildings high. That ideal suffered from Root's early death and Sullivan's eclipse, but when in 1981 he stated SOM/Chicago's goal, the late SOM/Chicago partner Fazlur Khan reaffirmed that ideal: "the visible expression of technology in architecture."

Chicago itself has only recently cherished its heritage. Although Buffalo gained Sullivan's Prudential, St. Louis his Wainwright and Owatonna his National Bank, Chicago ignored Sullivan for major commissions. Even his most celebrated disciple, the incomparably fecund Frank Lloyd Wright, did not design Chicago's important commercial or civic buildings. Instead, Chicago often sought Roman and Gothic designers, and their Wrigley and Chicago Tribune Buildings of about 1925 resemble the Gothic scenery the philanthropist, John D. Rockefeller, gave to the University of Chicago, despite Thorstein Veblen's championship of a functional alternative. That architecture might spring from program, technology and native culture, as Sullivan urged, was a dream which, save Wright, nearly died with Sullivan in 1924.

How ironic therefore to find Sullivan's great Stock Exchange Hall preserved inside SOM's new buildings for the Chicago Art Institute [5]! There, at Chicago's center of the arts, Sullivan's Trading Room has been moved and lovingly conserved with SOM's help, and the Ex-

5

7

8

die ihren Ausdruck fand in Zusammenschau, Objektivierung und symbolhafter Darstellung, eine Anhängerschaft. Bruce Graham trat 1949, unmittelbar nach Abschluß seines Studiums an der University of Pennsylvania, in das Büro von SOM in Chicago ein und fand – wie so viele junge Entwurfsarchitekten – in Mies einen Meister, den er bewunderte.

Als Graham nach Chicago kam, hatte sich SOM bereits mit den militärischen Ausbildungseinrichtungen am Hafen von Chicago und den Laborbauten in Oak Ridge [6] Anerkennung erworben. In den fünfziger Jahren stellte SOM die Wohnanlage Lake Meadows [7] fertig, begann mit dem Bau der Air Force Academy, nahm bedeutende Projekte für die Staatsuniversitäten von Iowa und Illinois in Angriff, errichtete die Bürohäuser für Harris Trust und Inland Steel und vollendete das außergewöhnliche Kitt Peak National Observatory in Arizona. Der Entwurf für diese Sternwarte stammt von Myron Goldsmith, dessen Vorliebe für präzise, von der Konstruktion geprägte Bauformen auch bei der von ihm in den sechziger Jahren in Columbus, Indiana erbauten Druckerei für die Zeitung »The Republic« sichtbar wird. Offensichtlich ganz andersartig war die eindrucksvolle Formensprache, die Netsch bei seinen Projekten für die UICC und die Air Force Academy benutzte. Und wiederum anders waren die Arbeiten des jungen Graham, der 1960 nach der Fertigstellung der Gebäude für Inland Steel und Harris Trust zum Partner gewählt wurde.

Die zwischen 1954 und 1957 geplante und von 1956 bis 1962 erbaute Air Force Academy in Colorado Springs bewies das formale Talent, die technische Meisterschaft und das organisatorische Können der Firma. In den fünfziger und sechziger Jahren wäre kein anderes Architekturbüro in der Lage gewesen, ein so umfassendes Bauvorhaben mit einer derartigen konzeptionellen Reife, Qualität und Perfektion sowie in so kurzer Zeit fertigzustellen. Es ist nahezu dreißig Jahre her, seit 1957 das Inland Steel Building der Stadt Chicago die Möglichkeiten einer neuen urbanen Architektur offenbarte; wenig später wurde das Harris Trust Building [8] mit seinem doppelgeschossig zurückspringenden und hier das Stahlskelett offen zeigenden Installationsgeschoß unmittelbar neben einen herkömmlichen Mauerwerksbau gestellt. Darauf folgte das Hartford Fire Insurance Building [9], wo die Suche nach einem konstruktiven Realismus sich verjüngende Stützen, dünne Pilzdecken und Versteifungsecken zwischen Decken und Stützen zur Folge hatte. Beim John Hancock Building [10] wurde mit größter konstruktiver Logik ein atemberaubend hohes Bauwerk entwickelt, bei dem offen gezeigte Diagonalstreben in das Stahlskelett integriert sind. Höhepunkt dieser Entwicklung war schließlich der Sears Tower [11] mit etwa 450 Metern Höhe und der gewaltigen Bruttogeschoßfläche von etwa 410000 Quadratmetern, eingeschlossen in einem Bündel von außentragenden Rohrele-

8. Harris Trust and Savings Bank, Chicago, Illinois.
9. Hartford Fire Insurance Building, Chicago, Illinois.
10. John Hancock Center, Chicago, Illinois.
11. Sears Tower, Chicago, Illinois.
12. Headquarters of Baxter Travenol, Deerfield, Illinois.
13. American Republic Insurance Headquarters, Des Moines, Iowa.

9

10

12

change's arched entrance is now a free-standing sculpture in SOM's gardens. In the years between the classical Art Institute and SOM's new additions lies a story of Chicago's growing pride, which was encouraged by a succession of SOM partners, including Hartmann, Graham and Netsch who won the confidence of Chicago's civic leaders.

What Chicago's leaders wanted was strong imagery announcing corporate and cultural presence in urban settings. Fortunately, (and the fortune lay in his declining to go to Harvard a year earlier), Ludwig Mies van der Rohe was attracted to Chicago. Heralded by his elegant German Pavilion at Barcelona and Tugendhat House at Brno, Czechoslovakia, Mies slowly won commissions. Meanwhile, his intellectual discipline in synopsis, generalization and symbol compelled a following. Arriving in Chicago fresh from study at the University of Pennsylvania, Bruce Graham joined SOM's office in 1949, and, like many designers, found in Mies a master to admire.

When Graham joined its Chicago office, SOM already enjoyed respect for its wartime training centers on Chicago's piers and Oak Ridge Laboratories [6] where SOM designers Walter Netsch and Myron Goldsmith had won their partnerships. In the 1950's, SOM completed the Lake Meadows Housing [7], started the Air Force Academy, began major projects for the State Universities of Iowa and Illinois, erected the office buildings for Harris Trust and Inland Steel, and finished the extraordinary Kitt Peak National Observatory in Arizona. The observatory was designed by Goldsmith whose fidelity to refined structural shapes is visible in his printing plant for "The Republic" in Columbus, Indiana, built in the 1960's. Visibly different were the arresting forms Netsch composed for UICC and the Air Force Academy. And still different was the work of the rising designer, Graham, who was elected partner in 1960, after completing Inland Steel and Harris Trust. The diversity among SOM/Chicago's designers was greater than any differences among their geometries or structural expressions. Each artistically creative and intellectually avid, the three enjoyed different types of client and perceptions of architecture. Graham led the colossal office building projects for John Hancock and Sears, while Netsch made award-winning university buildings and sought to relate SOM to liberal causes. Goldsmith was fascinated by esoteric technical problems, like the Kitt Peak Observatory, where technical precision was paramount.

The Air Force Academy at Colorado Springs (designed 1954–1957; built 1956–1962) proved SOM's aesthetic talent, technical skill and project organization. In the 1950's and 1960's, no other architectural firm could have carried so vast a project to such depth of concept, quality, and refinement or speed in completion. Nearly thirty years ago (1957), the Inland Steel Building showed Chicago the promise of

11

13

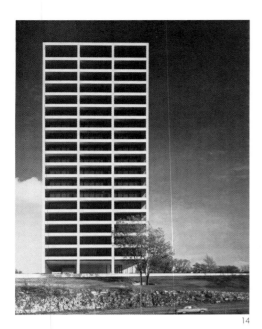

menten, die, wie es Graham und Khan als die Entwerfer des Gebäudes beabsichtigten, bestimmend sind für die architektonische Form. SOM-Bauten, die die Konstruktion sinnbildhaft zum Ausdruck bringen, findet man an vielen Orten des Mittleren Westens. Manche drükken ihr statisches Prinzip unmittelbar aus, wie das Zentralgebäude der Hauptverwaltung von Baxter Travenol [12] mit seinem abgehängten Dach. Die vier Paare von Gelenkträgern der Hauptverwaltung der American Republic Insurance Company in Des Moines, Iowa [13] sind dramatisch hervorgehoben. Im Gegensatz zu diesen Beispielen ist der Ausdruck der Konstruktion in anderen Fällen abstrakt, so bei der Hauptverwaltung der Business Men's Assurance Co. of America in Kansas City, Missouri [14]. Während der siebziger Jahre trat der Ausdruck der Baustruktur bei den Bauten des Chicagoer Büros dann – ähnlich wie bei denen des Büros in San Francisco – oft zurück. Formale Absichten verschleierten gelegentlich das Konstruktionssystem, das sich – wie bei der Industrial Trust & Savings Bank in Muncie, Indiana [15] und der Fourth Financial Bank in Wichita, Kansas [16] – nur bei nächtlicher Beleuchtung abzeichnet. Beim Centennial Center in Schaumburg, Illinois war für SOM der Ausdruck der Konstruktion oder der Funktion weniger wichtig als die Gestaltung der formalen Hülle. Zwei lange, mit Ziegelmauerwerk verkleidete Kragarme am Eingang des vom Büro in San Francisco entworfenen Rathauses von Columbus, Indiana [17] ordnen die Konstruktion formalen Überlegungen unter. Im Ganzen gesehen blieb der gestalterische Ausdruck bei den Arbeiten von SOM im Mittleren Westen jedoch von der Technik bestimmt. Die spannungsvolle Massengliederung des Gebäudes One Magnificent Mile in Chicago [18] und die artikulierte Fassade des dortigen Olympia Centre [19] haben ihren Ursprung in der vielseitigen Ausformbarkeit tragender Rohrsysteme. Durch die kompakte Bauform wurden beim 28geschossigen Bürogebäude 33 West Monroe Street in Chicago [20] die Außenfassaden und vertikalen Versorgungselemente in ihrer Größe reduziert, und die Büros sind auf drei mehrgeschossige Atrien hin orientiert. Die Knotenpunkte und Raumfolgen des Caterpillar Tractor Training Center [21] stellen den Bezug zur artikulierten Formensprache bei Netschs Kapelle der Air Force Academy und den UICC-Gebäuden für Verhaltensforschung [22] und Architektur vom Beginn der sechziger Jahre her. Als graphische Darstellungen von Computern seine dreidimensionalen Untersuchungen erleichterten, konnte Netsch eine plastische Auswahl treffen; das Lindquist Center der University of Iowa [23] und das Kunstmuseum der Miami University in Oxford, Ohio sind bemerkenswerte Beispiele dieser Studien.
In den siebziger Jahren wurde in den Arbeiten von SOM im Mittleren Westen zunehmend ein Bewußtsein für die Beziehung des Gebäudes zu seiner Umwelt sichtbar. James DeStefano,

14

14. Business Men's Assurance Headquarters, Kansas City, Missouri.
15. Industrial Trust & Savings Bank, Muncie, Indiana.
16. Fourth Financial Center, Wichita, Kansas.
17. Columbus City Hall, Columbus, Indiana.

16

15

17

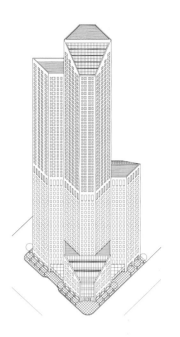

18. One Magnificent Mile, Chicago, Illinois.
19. Olympia Centre, Chicago, Illinois.
20. 33 West Monroe Street, Chicago, Illinois.
21. Caterpillar Training Center, Peoria, Illinois.
22. Behavioral Sciences Building, University of Illinois, Chicago Circle Campus, Chicago, Illinois.

modern urban form. Shortly, Harris Trust [8] juxtaposed its two-story plenum and open steel frame against its classical masonry neighbor. Then came the Hartford Fire Insurance Building [9], where structural realism demanded the tapered columns, thin floor slabs and inflected connections. For the John Hancock Building [10], structural logic was carried to a breathtakingly tall structure rising from only a fraction of its site, and the exposed diagonals were tied into the steel exoskeleton at strategic intersections. The epitome was the Sears Tower [11], 1,470 feet tall, enclosing a gigantic 4.4 million square feet, all carried by perimetal tubes, which determined architectural form, as designers Graham and Khan intended.

SOM's structurally based emblems appear often throughout the Midwest. Some are literal, like the cables and suspended roof of Baxter Travenol [12]. In Des Moines, Iowa, a view of the American Republic Insurance Headquarters [13] dramatizes four pairs of steel hinges. In contrast to literalism, structural expression is sometimes abstract, as beside the freeway in Kansas City, Missouri, where the Business Men's Assurance Headquarters [14] brings welded steel piers and spandrels to one vertical surface without differentiation throughout the 19-story tower. In the 1970's, SOM/Chicago, like SOM/San Francisco, often subordinated structural expression. The allusive form sometimes hid structure until revealed by interior illumination, as in the Industrial Trust Building in Muncie, Indiana [15], and the Fourth Financial Bank in Wichita, Kansas [16]. Neither structural nor functional expression was so compelling as the formal envelope for SOM/Chicago's Centennial Center at Schaumburg, Illinois. At the City Hall in Columbus, Indiana [17], designed by SOM/San Francisco, two long cantilevers, clad in brick masonry, subordinate structure to emblematic intent. Still, the dominant expression in SOM's midwestern work remained technological. The vibrant massing of Chicago's One Magnificent Mile [18] and the articulated fenestration in Chicago's Olympia Centre [19] originate in the versatility of tube structural systems. Chicago's 33 West Monroe Street [20], a compact 28-story building, reduces exposed surfaces and mechanical core, clads its compact mass with deep spandrels and thermal glass, and wraps its offices around three multistory atria.

SOM/Chicago has never been monolithic. The transitional nodes and sequential spaces in the Caterpillar Tractor Training Center model [21] reflect earlier articulated form in Netsch's Air Force Academy Chapel and UICC buildings for Behavioral Sciences [22] and Architecture of the early 1960's. Intent upon defining spaces by angled walls and roofs, Netsch aimed at solving three problems simultaneously: identity of structural points, integration of mechanical equipment, and creation of spaces formed by integrating wall, roof and floor. Basing his initial planning on

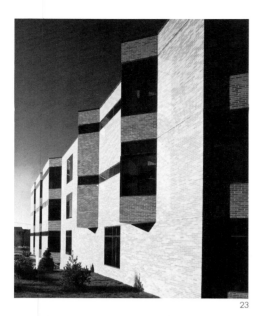

23. Lindquist Center, University of Iowa, Iowa City, Iowa.
24. The Menninger Foundation, Topeka, Kansas.
25. St. Paul Town Square, St. Paul, Minnesota.
26. First Wisconsin Plaza, Madison, Wisconsin.
27. Lutheran Brotherhood Building, Minneapolis, Minnesota.

Partner im Chicagoer Büro, fand bei dem Komplex der Menninger Foundation in Topeka, Kansas [24] einen Maßstab, der mit dem der bestehenden Bauten harmoniert. Sowohl das Pillsbury Center in Minneapolis als auch der Komplex Town Square in Saint Paul [25] beziehen öffentliche Verkehrsanlagen sowie Zonen für Fußgänger mit ein und bieten bedeutsame Sichtbeziehungen. Die Industrial Trust & Savings Bank in Muncie respektiert die bestehenden Traufhöhen, und das Rathaus in Columbus wendet sich mit seinem Platz und Vorhof der historischen Hauptstraße der Stadt und dem County Courthouse zu. Der Rücksichtnahme auf den städtebaulichen Kontext entsprangen auch die gebrochenen Silhouetten der First Wisconsin Bank in Madison [26], des Lutheran Brotherhood Building in Minneapolis [27] sowie der Gebäude One Magnificent Mile und Three First National Plaza [28] in Chicago. Zu diesen gestalterischen Bezügen zur umliegenden Bebauung kamen die Vorteile, die witterungsgeschützte Plätze, Atrien und Hallen für das städtische Umfeld bieten. So ist die Eingangshalle des Gebäudes Three First National Plaza ein mehrgeschossiger Verkehrsknoten, und in dem acht Geschosse hohen Atrium des Pillsbury Center – das von einer Fußgängerbrücke in der Ebene des ersten Obergeschosses durchschnitten wird – liegen Läden und Restaurants. Die große Halle im Komplex Town Square in Saint Paul bietet auf drei Ebenen neben Läden und Restaurants Brunnen, Wasserbecken und Wasserfälle; außerdem steht sie mit einem großen Kaufhaus in Verbindung. Wohnungen wurden nicht nur bei dem Gebäude One Magnificent Mile mit Geschäfts- und Bürogeschossen kombiniert sondern auch beim Olympia Centre, wo ein Kaufhaus um ein von oben belichtetes Atrium herum angeordnet wurde.

1971 begann das Chicagoer Büro mit der städtebaulichen Untersuchung eines etwa 2800 Hektar großen Areals im Zentrum von Chicago. Das Ergebnis war der unter Leitung des Partners Roger Seitz erarbeitete Chicago 21 Plan [29]. In der 1977 begonnenen, etwa 16 Hektar großen Wohnanlage Dearborn Park [30] werden in parkartiger Umgebung dreitausend Wohnungen geschaffen. Der Chicago 21 Plan ist ein deutlicher Beweis für das Vertrauen, das dem Chicagoer SOM-Büro von den Vertretern der Öffentlichkeit und des kulturellen Lebens der Stadt entgegengebracht wird. Ein weiterer Beweis für dieses Vertrauen ist die 1982 dem Büro anvertraute Planung der für 1992 in Chicago vorgesehenen Weltausstellung [31]. Hier bietet sich eine großartige Gelegenheit, bleibende städtebauliche Einrichtungen und Symbole für Chicago und den gesamten Mittleren Westen zu entwickeln.

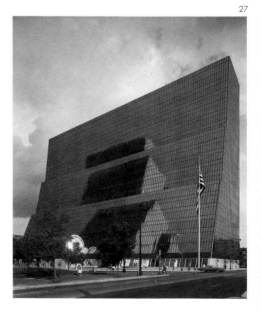

28

28. Three First National Plaza, Chicago, Illinois.
29. Chicago 21 Plan.
30. Dearborn Park, Chicago, Illinois.
31. Chicago World's Fair 1992.

30

29

superimposed rotated squares, Netsch selected mass or void from the diagonals, points and hexagons within a lattice or field. After computer graphics assisted his three-dimensional study, Netsch's selection was a plastic choice, and his Lindquist Center at the University of Iowa [23] and Art Museum for Miami University at Oxford, Ohio, justify his hard-won study.

An increasing concern for building's context is evident in SOM's Midwestern work in the 1970's. For the Menninger Foundation in Topeka, Kansas [24], SOM/Chicago partner James DeStefano, starting with clustered bedrooms, cottages and courtyards, achieved a scale compatible with existing buildings. Both the Pillsbury Center and St. Paul Town Square towers [25] accommodate transitways, enclose pedestrian circulation, and sustain significant vistas. Muncie's Industrial Trust & Savings Bank respects existing cornice lines, and Columbus' City Hall directs its plaza and forecourt towards historic Main Street and the County Courthouse. A similar care for context explains the faceted profile of the First Wisconsin Bank in Madison [26], Minneapolis' Lutheran Brotherhood [27], One Magnificent Mile in Chicago, and Three First National Plaza [28], also in Chicago. Massing its tallest tower on Chicago Avenue, the Olympia Centre presents only its lower elements to Michigan Avenue. Added to those formal contextual responses were the urban amenities gained by having enclosed plazas, atria and lobbies. The lobby at Three First National Plaza is a multilevel interchange, and the eight-story atrium at Pillsbury Center, which traverses a second level skyway, contains shops and restaurants, while the concourse at Town Square in St. Paul offers fountains, pools, and waterfalls among restaurants and stores disposed on three levels, all related to a major department store. Residential, retail and office space are combined in One Magnificent Mile and also in the Olympia Centre, where a department store surrounds a skylighted atrium.

In 1971, SOM/Chicago conducted a two-year study of 7,000 acres in the center of Chicago. Guided by SOM/Chicago partner Roger Seitz, the Chicago 21 Plan [29] evolved a New Town, proposed to be a total environment south of the central business district, recreational parks on the Lake front, apartments on the Chicago River shoreline, and a transitway along a State Street shopping corridor. Started in 1977, 40-acre Dearborn Park [30] will offer 3,000 housing units in parklike settings. The Chicago 21 Plan reflects the talent that has won SOM/Chicago the confidence of Chicago's civic and cultural leaders, who in 1982 awarded SOM/Chicago responsibility for planning the Chicago World's Fair [31] scheduled for 1992 – a great opportunity to evolve enduring urban functions and symbols for Chicago and the Midwest.

31

33 West Monroe Street,
Chicago, Illinois

The primary goal in designing the 33 West Monroe building was to create an energy efficient, investment office building for a developer's budget at the time of an unpredictable leasing period in Chicago. The solution was to optimize all building systems, including the substructure, superstructure, HVAC, exterior and vertical transportation. The savings thus achieved permitted the designers to add tenant amenities that would create a marketable, institutional quality building.
During the conceptual design phase, two building configurations were developed. The first was a traditional 1,000,000-square-foot, slender 45-story building with small floors. This design was compared with the atrium building design which was a 28-story building occupying the entire site and containing a total of 1,000,000 square feet with office floors ranging from 30,050 square feet to 37,400 square feet. The atrium design optimized all the necessary building systems, making both the construction cost and operating costs more economical than the first design.
The final solution for 33 West Monroe was to vertically stack three atria formed by overhanging office floors rising 7 to 12 stories. The atria serve as lobbies for the floors that rise above. Glass-enclosed office floors overlook each atrium, illuminated by natural light from the exterior window wall. The atrium concept provides greater perimeter glass for each floor, a stronger leasing concept and a tremendous mechanical advantage. An energy efficient exterior envelope using dual glazed, semi-reflective glass reduces heat gain, minimizes heat loss and affords a comfortable work environment.
The building's relationship to surrounding buildings is reinforced by the choice of exterior paint color which harmonizes with the stainless steel Inland Steel Building directly across the street to the north. The 28-story 33 West Monroe Building further respects the neighboring 19-story Inland Steel Building in its massing which begins to step back from the street at the 19th floor. Its orientation along the edge of the side visually anchors the building to the corner, reinforcing the open space of the First National Bank Plaza across the street.
Designed in the tradition of the Chicago School, the building is a pure expression of the simple structural frame.

33 West Monroe Street,
Chicago, Illinois

Das Hauptziel beim Entwurf dieses Mietbürogebäudes war die Verbindung außerordentlicher Wirtschaftlichkeit mit einem räumlichen Angebot, das die Vermietung auch in geschäftlich schwierigen Zeiten sicherstellt. Man optimierte daher alle baulichen Systeme, von der Gründung über das Tragwerk und die Außenhaut bis hin zur Energieversorgung, und verwendete die auf diese Weise eingesparten Mittel für die Schaffung einer großzügigen Raumatmosphäre.
Entgegen dem naheliegenden Schema eines schlanken Hochhauses von etwa 45 Geschossen mit Plaza wurde ein kompakter Baukörper von 28 Geschossen gewählt, der das gesamte Baugrundstück ausfüllt. In diesem Baukörper wurden dann drei nach Norden orientierte, voneinander durch überhängende Geschoßebenen getrennte Atrien übereinander angeordnet, zu denen sich die Nutzflächen U-förmig in der Tiefe gestaffelt orientieren. Die Atrien haben unmittelbare Sichtbeziehung zum Straßenraum. Die vermietbaren Nutzflächen der Geschosse variieren von etwa 2.800 m² bis etwa 3.500 m² und sind damit außerordentlich groß. Insgesamt hat das Gebäude eine Bruttogeschoßfläche von etwa 93.000 m².
Der Bau ist sorgfältig in den städtebaulichen Kontext eingefügt. So harmonisiert der Außenanstrich mit den Fassaden aus rostfreiem Stahl an dem direkt nördlich gegenüber liegenden Inland Steel Building. Ab der Oberkante dieses Gebäudes, das 19 Geschosse hoch ist, beginnt auch die Abtreppung des 28geschossigen Neubaus nach Süden. Für die schräg gegenüber liegende Plaza der First National Bank bildet der Bau einen kräftigen baulichen Abschluß nach Südosten.
In seiner strengen Fassadengestaltung, die ein unmittelbares Diagramm der einfachen Tragstruktur ist, steht der Bau in der besten Tradition der Chicago School. Die Außenwände des Gebäudes bestehen aus Aluminiumelementen und reflektierendem Zweischeibenglas. In den Atrien ist die feuerbeständig ummantelte einfache Stahlkonstruktion aus Stützen und Trägern – die nur in den Außenwandebenen zur Aufnahme der Windlasten biegesteif verbunden zu werden brauchten – ohne Unterbrechung durchgeführt.

1. Section.
2. View of the building from First National Bank Plaza. The 28-story building respects the neighboring 19-story Inland Steel Building in its massing which begins to step back at the 19th floor.

1. Schnitt.
2. Ansicht des Gebäudes von der First National Bank Plaza. In seiner Baukörpergliederung nimmt der 28geschossige Bau Bezug auf das gegenüberliegende 19geschossige Inland Steel Building, indem es ab dem 19. Geschoß zurückspringt.

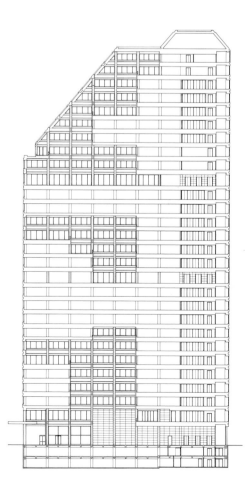

3. Plans (ground floor, typical donut floor, typical U floor, typical full floor).

3. Grundrisse (Erdgeschoß, Normalgeschoß mit mittigem Ausschnitt, Normalgeschoß mit U-förmiger Nutzfläche, Normalgeschoß mit voller Nutzfläche).

30'

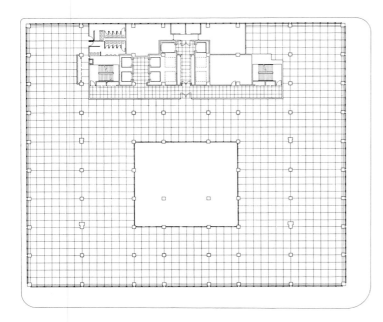

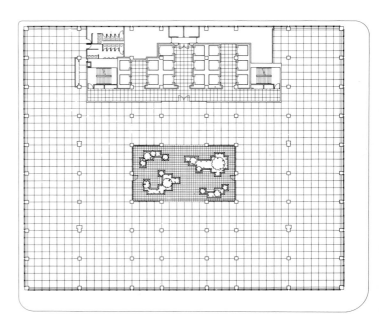

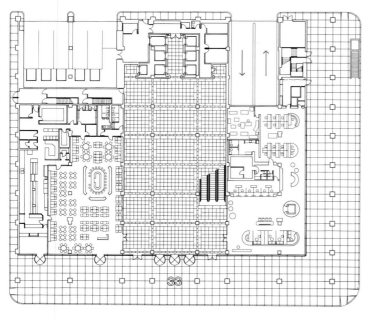

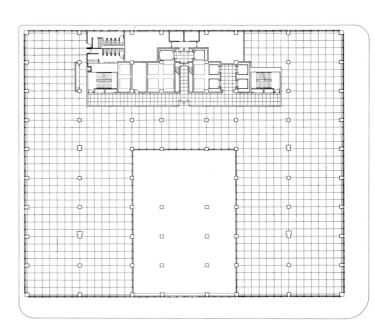

4, 5. The building is a pure expression of the simple structural frame.

4, 5. Das Gebäude ist ein unmittelbares Diagramm der einfachen Tragstruktur.

Three First National Plaza,
Chicago, Illinois

Completed early in 1982, the Three First National Plaza complex occupies a prime partial-block location near the financial center and downtown commercial district of Chicago's Loop. The project comprises a 57-story tower, an 11-story element which engages an existing private club, and a central nine-story glazed public lobby.

The configuration of the new tower was designed to retain a degree of openness along busy Madison Avenue and to minimize the disruption of views from the neighboring 60-story First National Bank Building. The sawtooth geometry, which provides multiple corner offices, makes a transition on the top six levels to stepped greenhouse offices with views over the city toward Lake Michigan. Just as the massing of Three First National Plaza is designed to relate to its neighbor tower, the carnelian granite cladding reinforces their complementary relationship. A second level walkway further links the two structures.

Bay windows, a traditional element of Chicago turn-of-the-century architecture, are a central feature of the tower, designed to provide light and views for prestige tenants. Projecting from the structural tube, the bays emphasize the tower's vertical expression. Cantilevered from the concrete and steel structural system, the bronze reflective glass bays are framed in warm gray aluminum spandrels which act as louvers for the decentralized mechanical system.

On three sides, office areas and mezzanine balconies look onto the central nine-story public space. A stepped steel truss structure, repeating the sawtooth geometry on a horizontal plane, supports the clear glass enclosure. Connected below grade both to Chicago's rapid transit system and underground commercial arcade network, the lobby is designed as an indoor plaza in the Chicago tradition of open public spaces. A Henry Moore sculpture will enhance the plaza which is designed to add street-level animation with its granite paving, bronze detailing, landscaping and specialty shopping area.

Three First National Plaza,
Chicago, Illinois

Das 1982 fertiggestellte, 57geschossige Bürohochhaus Three First National liegt unmittelbar gegenüber dem um drei Geschosse höheren, etwa 15 Jahre alten Bau der First National Bank im Zentrum der Stadt. Auf dem östlichen Teil des einen halben Straßenblock einnehmenden Grundstücks entstand zusätzlich ein elfgeschossiges winkelförmiges Gebäude, das Bezug nimmt auf den älteren Bau eines Privatklubs, und eine neun Geschosse hohe verglaste Eingangshalle. Um zwischen der First National Bank im Süden – zu der eine Brücke im 1. Obergeschoß über die Straße führt – und dem Neubau keine Straßenschlucht entstehen zu lassen, ist dieser nach Norden sägezahnförmig abgestaffelt. Diese Abstaffelung wird in den obersten sechs Geschossen des Hochhauses durch begrünte Wintergärten mit Ausblick über die Stadt hinweg auf den Lake Michigan hin fortgesetzt.

Wesentliches Gestaltungselement des zur Aufnahme der Windlasten als Stahlbetonrohrkonstruktion mit einem Minimum an Innenstützen konzipierten Hochhauses sind die vorspringenden Erkerfenster, die die Tradition des berühmten »Bay-window« der Chicago School zu Ende des vorigen Jahrhunderts in abgewandelter Form wieder aufgreifen. Die vor die Öffnungen der Rohrfassade in einer leichten Konstruktion aus bronzefarben reflektierendem Glas und grauen Aluminiumelementen vorspringenden Erker betonen die Vertikalität des Turmes. Sie sind als in der Höhe durchlaufende Elemente klar von dem mit rötlichem Granit verkleideten Tragwerk des Turmes abgesetzt. Im Inneren erhöhen die Vor- und Rücksprünge der Außenwand den Lichteinfall und die Möglichkeiten des Ausblicks nach verschiedenen Richtungen.

Die Rundstahlkonstruktion der Eingangshalle nimmt mit abgeknickten Fachwerkbindern die Abtreppungen der flankierenden Bauteile auf und steigt von drei Geschossen im Eingangsbereich an der Straße nach Norden zu bis auf neun Geschosse an. In dieser außen vollständig mit Klarglas verkleideten Halle, zu der sich die dreiseitig angrenzenden Gebäudebereiche mit Balkons öffnen, wird eine Skulptur von Henry Moore als Blickpunkt aufgestellt. Unterirdische Fußgängerstraßen stellen Verbindungen zu den umliegenden Gebäuden und zur Untergrundbahn her.

1. The sawtooth geometry of the building provides multiple corner offices.
2. In its stairstepped shape the steel truss structure of the atrium repeats the sawtooth configuration of the enclosing building walls.

1. Die sägezahnförmige Abstaffelung des Baukörpers hat eine große Zahl von Eckbüros zur Folge.
2. Die abgeknickten Stahlträger des Atriums nehmen den sägezahnförmigen Umriß der flankierenden Gebäudewände auf.

114

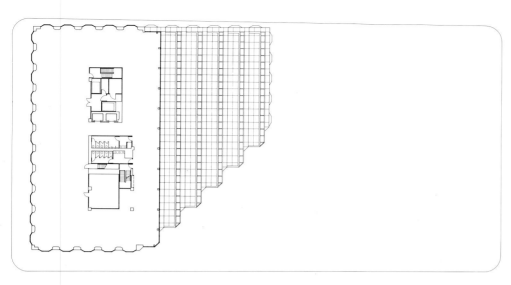

3. Plans (ground plan, typical floor, upper floor).
4. Axonometric view of the upper portion of the tower.

3. Grundrisse (Erdgeschoß, Normalgeschoß, Geschoß im oberen Turmbereich).
4. Axonometrie des oberen Turmbereichs.

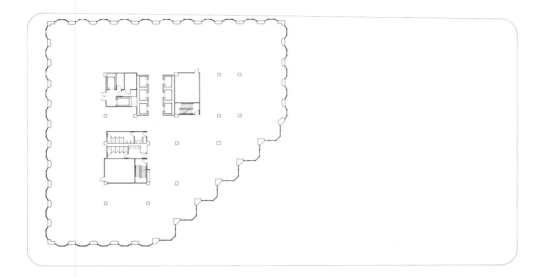

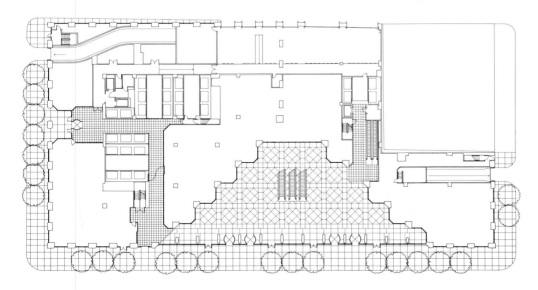

30'

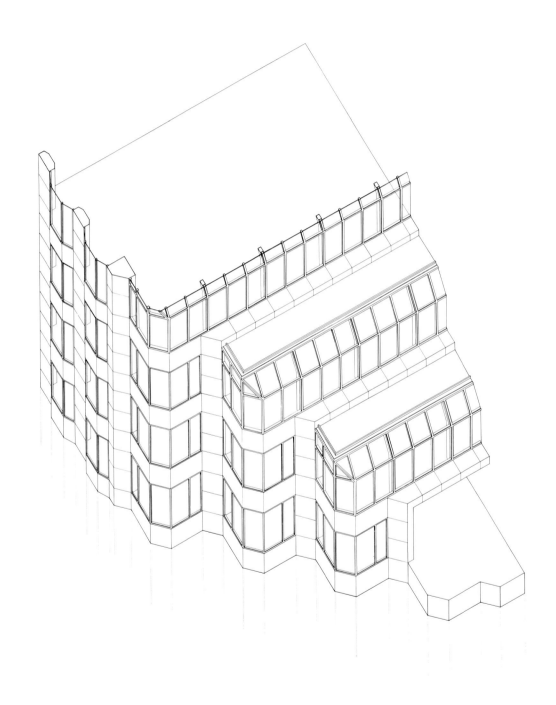

One Magnificent Mile,
Chicago, Illinois

One Magnificent Mile, to be completed in 1983, is situated at the northern end of one of the most elegant and prestigious shopping avenues in the nation. The multi-use tower will contain commercial space on the first three levels, office space on floors four to 19, and 181 luxury condominiums at the top of the building.

The building floor plans and profile were developed as an expression of both the problems and opportunities of the small, angular lot at the corner of Oak Street and Michigan Avenue, and of the logic and structural possibilities of the bundled-tube system. Three hexagonal concrete tubes with punched window openings, rise 57, 49 and 21 stories and are joined together to resist wind loads as a bundled tube. The top of the 21-story element bears a two-story mechanical floor, which, as it is carried across the entire tower floor area, sharply divides the office levels from the residential floors by a broad horizontal line. Following interior functions, the fenestration is treated in different manners below and above this visual division.

The tubes' geometric shapes and varying heights result from extensive studies of desirable views from the high-rise condominiums and of the potential shadow cast over the nearby Oak Street park and beach. Computer simulation determined the optimum height at which no shadow would blight these recreation areas. In addition, the faceted shape skillfully avoids the impression that the new building turns its back on any of its significant neighbors, relating well to adjacent structures, to Lake Shore Drive and to the high-rise buildings on Michigan Avenue.

The 57-story tower element in the middle of the bundle is topped by a glazed roof, sloping towards the northeast, with a view of the beach and the lake, and covering greenhouses and recreation facilities for tenants' use. Reflecting this scheme, a five-story hexagonal entrance pavilion in front of this high tower element also has a glazed roof sloping northeast towards the corner of Michigan Avenue and Oak Street.

The tower will be clad in granite with clear windows at the commercial level, grey reflective glass for the offices and grey tinted glass for the condominiums.

One Magnificent Mile,
Chicago, Illinois

Der 1983 fertiggestellte Komplex liegt am nördlichen Ende der Michigan Avenue, der vornehmsten Einkaufsstraße Chicagos. Zwei Drittel der Gesamtfläche werden von 181 Luxuseigentumswohnungen eingenommen, die oberhalb der drei Ladengeschosse und der 16 Bürogeschosse liegen.

Die Grundriß- und Gebäudeform ist in logischer Konsequenz einerseits aus dem winkelförmigen Eckgrundstück an der Einmündung der Oak Street in die Michigan Avenue, andererseits aus den Gesetzmäßigkeiten und Möglichkeiten der Rohrkonstruktion entwickelt worden. Drei sechseckige Stahlbetontürme verschiedener Höhe sind über jeweils eine Gebäudekante miteinander so verbunden, daß die als eingespannte Rohre mit ausgeschnittenen Fensteröffnungen fungierenden Elemente als einheitliches Gesamtsystem, als gebündelte Rohre, zusammenwirken. Auf der Höhe des oberen Endpunkts des niedrigsten, 21geschossigen Bauteils ist ein zweigeschossiges Installationsgeschoß angeordnet, das die gesamte Geschoßfläche einnimmt und so die in Abhängigkeit von ihrer Funktion verschiedenartig befensterten Büro- und Wohngeschosse voneinander optisch durch eine breite horizontale Linie trennt.

Die unterschiedliche Höhenstaffelung der Turmelemente ergab sich aus intensiven Studien über die besten Ausblicke aus den Wohnungen in den oberen Geschossen und über den Schattenwurf des Gebäudes. Mit Hilfe eines Computers wurden die Höhen ermittelt, bei denen eine Beschattung des nahe gelegenen Parks an der Oak Street und des Erholungsgebietes am Seeufer noch ausgeschlossen ist. Die vielfach gebrochene Form des Gebäudes ergab zudem nach keiner Richtung hin eine weniger befriedigende Rückseite; es werden vielmehr zum gesamten Nachbarbereich harmonische Beziehungen hergestellt.

Das mittlere, mit 57 Geschossen höchste Turmelement ist oben nach Nordosten hin abgeschrägt. Unter dem abfallenden Dach wurden mit Blick auf den See Freizeiteinrichtungen für die Bewohner untergebracht. In gleicher Orientierung ist diesem Bauteil ein fünf Geschosse hoher, sechseckiger Eingangsbau vorgelagert, dessen Glasdach im gleichen Winkel wie das auf dem Turm zur Ecke zwischen Michigan Avenue und Oak Street hin abfällt.

Die äußere Verkleidung des Gebäudes besteht aus Granitplatten mit Fensterflächen aus Klarglas in den Ladengeschossen, grau reflektierendem Glas in den Bürogeschossen und grau getöntem Glas in den Wohngeschossen.

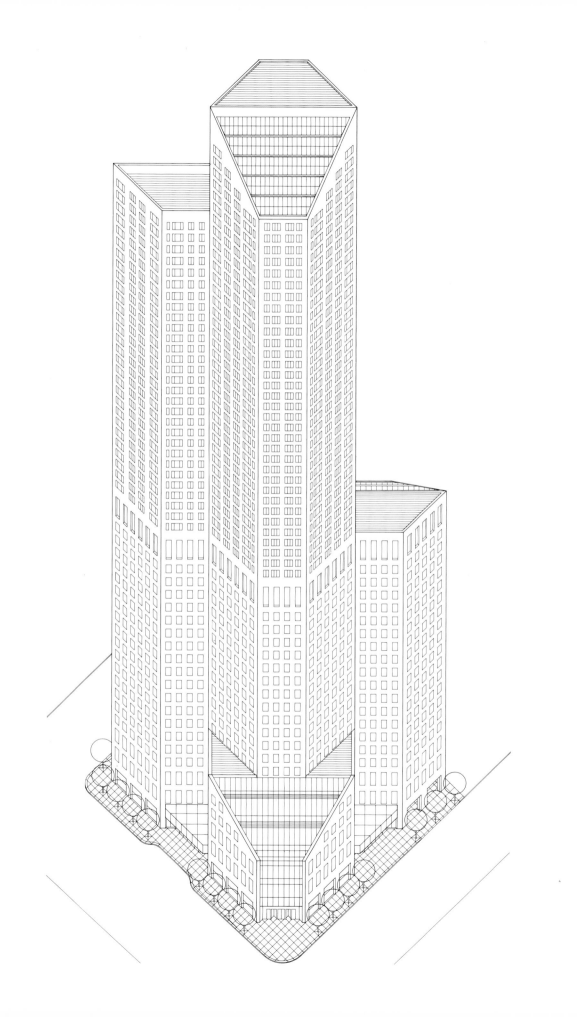

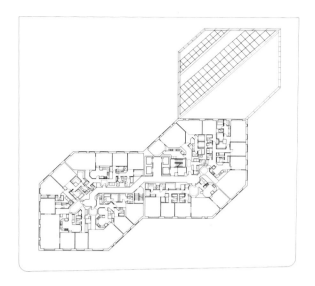

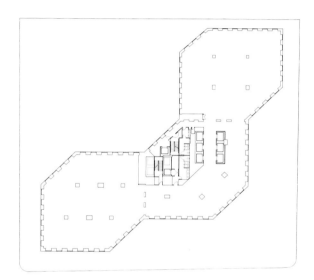

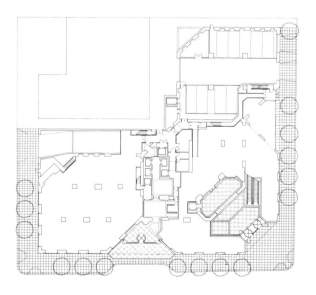

2. Plans (ground level, typical office floor, typical condominium floor).
3. View across Michigan Avenue from Oak Street Beach (model).
4. View of the five-story hexagonal entrance pavilion with the glazed roof sloping northeast towards the corner of Michigan Avenue and Oak Street (model).

2. Grundrisse (Erdgeschoßebene, Normalgeschoß im Bürobereich, Normalgeschoß im Bereich der Eigentumswohnungen).
3. Blick von der Oak Street Beach über die Michigan Avenue hinweg auf das Gebäude (Modell).
4. Ansicht des fünf Geschosse hohen, sechseckigen Eingangsbaus mit verglastem Dach, das nach Nordosten zur Ecke zwischen Michigan Avenue und Oak Street abfällt.

30'

Reorganization and Expansion of the
Art Institute of Chicago,
Chicago, Illinois

In 1970, the Art Institute of Chicago commissioned SOM to develop a comprehensive master plan for the reorganization and physical expansion of the museum and its art school. The plan comprised a long-range plan for new space to the east at Columbus Drive and on air rights over the railroad tracks to the north and south, and a specific phased construction program.

New construction in the first phase provided a circulation spine toward the ultimate East Entrance and additional gallery areas by adding as second level above the galleries around McKinlock Court. To reduce the apparent scale of the addition yet accommodate large 20th century works, a sloping roof was designed. Window openings respect the rhythm and character of the original court designed by Coolidge and Hodgson in 1924.

Major elements of the 1977 Columbus Drive additions are the School of Art, an auditorium, the Chicago Architecture Gallery, a members' lounge overlooking Lake Michigan and two public restaurants.

The 110,000-square-foot School of Art addition was designed to accommodate 1,000 full-time students as well as student enrichment programs and adult education. A school gallery integrates the addition into the museum while providing independent access and security. The simple form and detailing of the addition result from the physical and visual context of the lakefront Grant Park and are an extension of the materials of the original buildings.

The low, central element at Columbus Drive houses the Chicago Architecture Gallery. On axis with the three-story main building, the reverse pediment of the East Additions allows the original museum to be seen from Grant Park and Lake Shore Drive. Limestone cladding, slim mirror glass windows and sloped metal roofs were designed to complement the earlier structures and make the additions a restrained contemporary foreground to the 1892 main building.

The Chicago Architecture Gallery now incorporates the restored Adler and Sullivan Stock Exchange Trading Room. Working with Vinci & Kenny, architects for the reconstruction, SOM designed the building shell with skylights to illuminate the original clerestories of the 1893 Trading Room.

Reorganisation und Erweiterung des
Art Institute of Chicago,
Chicago, Illinois

Die Museumsleitung erteilte im Jahr 1970 den Architekten den Auftrag für eine umfassende Reorganisation und Erweiterung der Museumseinrichtungen mit gleichzeitiger Integration einer zugehörigen Kunstschule. Der Gesamtplan schlug eine Überbauung der unmittelbar hinter dem Altbau verlaufenden Eisenbahntrasse sowie einen Neubaukomplex entlang dem Columbus Drive jenseits dieser Schneise vor.

In der ersten Phase der Realisierung dieses Planes wurde eine Verbindungsschiene zu einem neuen Osteingang und eine Aufstockung der Galerieräume um den McKinlock Court durchgeführt. Diese Aufstockung erhielt ein schräges Dach, das die notwendige große Raumhöhe für Kunstwerke des 20. Jahrhunderts ergab, ohne die neue Baumasse allzu stark zu betonen. Die Fensteröffnungen des zusätzlichen Stockwerks passen sich dem Rhythmus und Charakter des im Jahr 1924 von Coolidge und Hodgson erbauten Hofes an.

Die Hauptelemente der im Jahr 1977 fertiggestellten Erweiterungen am Columbus Drive sind die Kunstschule, ein Auditorium, die Chicago Architecture Gallery, eine Lounge für die Mitglieder des Museums mit Blick auf den See und zwei öffentliche Restaurants.

In der etwa 10.200 m² großen Kunstschule können 1.000 Studenten ausgebildet und darüber hinaus Erwachsenenbildungsprogramme durchgeführt werden. Ein Schulausstellungsbereich liegt am Übergang zu den übrigen Museumseinrichtungen und ist wechselseitig nutzbar.

An die Baugestaltung des neuen Ostflügels wurden hohe Anforderungen gestellt, zumal jenseits des Columbus Drive einer der großen Seeuferparks Chicagos, der Grant Park, liegt. Die Architekten haben versucht, den Geist des alten Hauptgebäudes von 1892 in einer zeitgemäßen Gestaltung weiterzuführen. Daraus entstand eine sehr differenzierte, im Grundriß von diagonalen Einschnitten unterbrochene, in der Höhenentwicklung und den Dachformen jedoch ruhige und großzügige Bebauung. Der Altbau bleibt dabei vom Grant Park und dem Lake Shore Drive aus noch als Hintergrund der Neubauten sichtbar.

Die 1972 beim Abbruch der 1893 von Louis Sullivan und Dankmar Adler erbauten Old Stock Exchange gerettete Holzvertäfelung und Ausstattung des Börsensaals wurde in Zusammenarbeit mit den Architekten Vinci & Kenny in der Chicago Architecture Gallery wieder aufgebaut.

1. General view of the Art Institute with the new additions in the foreground.

1. Gesamtansicht des Art Institute mit den neuen Bauteilen im Vordergrund.

123

2. The entrance to the new wing is oriented on a diagonal and overlooks Columbus Gardens.
3. Overall plan and elevation.

2. Der Eingang zu dem neuen Flügel ist diagonal ausgerichtet und auf die Columbus Gardens orientiert.
3. Gesamtplan und Aufriß.

120'

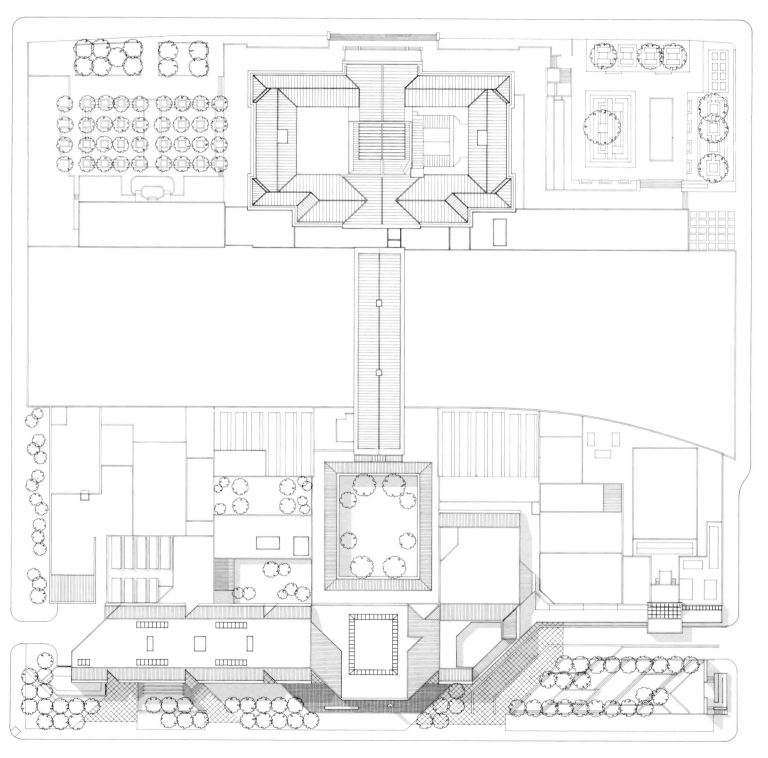

4. The Sullivan arch, saved from the demolished Stock Exchange Building forms the gateway to the eastern portion of the museum.
5, 6. A glazed facade acts as a backdrop for Isamu Noguchi's sculpture "Celebration of the 200th Anniversary of the Founding of the Republic" which is enhanced by an ornamental reflecting pool.

4. Der Sullivanbogen, der beim Abbruch des Stock Exchange Building sichergestellt wurde, bildet das Tor zum östlichen Teil des Museums.
5, 6. Eine verglaste Fassade bildet den Hintergrund für Isamu Noguchis Skulptur "Celebration of the 200th Anniversary of the Founding of the Republic", deren Wirkung von einem dekorativen Spiegelteich unterstrichen wird.

919 North Michigan Avenue,
Chicago, Illinois

1. Plan (ground floor).
2. View of the main building entrance.

1. Grundriß (Erdgeschoß).
2. Ansicht des Haupteingangs zum Gebäude.

The cast iron and nickel bronze storefronts of the 1929 Palmolive Building by Holabird & Root were replaced by a black aluminum and dark glass facade during the early 1970s. The present owners of the building wanted to revitalize the basement, ground and second floors with new commercial tenancy on the prime corner location and believed it necessary to replace the existing character with a conservative, sophisticated facade more in keeping with the building itself. The basic design goal was to complement the original architectural vocabulary within a budget that would not permit full restoration.

The new facade is composed of large lites of glass suspended in a steel structural framework applied to the building shell. Bays of clear glass and steel mullions, varying from 8 to 10 feet, are framed by ribbed lintels and fluted columns of extruded aluminum which replicate the remaining second-level cast iron columns and lanterns. Detailing allows the eventual addition of pediments and medallions similar to the original Art Déco ornaments.

The commercial arcade ot the original Palmolive Building, designed to accommodate multiple small shops, clearly demarcated the first and second levels with painted sign band spandrel panels. As the new commercial tenants occupy larger, often two-story spaces, a continuous two-story expression was chosen for the projecting bays. Soffits are set back and the bay is a single open volume where the same tenant occupies both floors. New backlit sign panels are positioned directly above the two symmetrical commercial entries on Michigan Avenue.

The office lobby was refurbished with back-painted glass, patterned terrazzo and Tennessee pink marble. The original elevator cabs, carved wooden elevator doors and a nickel bronze mail box cover were preserved.

919 North Michigan Avenue,
Chicago, Illinois

Anfang der siebziger Jahre waren die ursprünglich aus Gußeisen und Nickelbronze gefertigten Ladenfronten des 1929 von Holabird & Root erbauten Palmolive Building durch eine Front aus schwarzem Aluminium und dunklem Glas ersetzt worden. Nach einem Besitzerwechsel beschlossen die neuen Eigentümer, Untergeschoß, Erdgeschoß und 1. Obergeschoß dieses Gebäudes in bevorzugter Ecklage zu renovieren und neu zu vermieten. Dabei sollte die vorhandene Ladenfront durch eine konservative, differenziert gestaltete Fassade im Charakter des Altbaus ersetzt werden. Während die zur Verfügung stehenden Mittel eine vollständige Restaurierung nicht zuließen, wollte man hierdurch immerhin eine Angleichung an das Architekturvokabular der alten Bausubstanz erreichen.

In den neuen Fassaden fachen große Scheiben aus Klarglas ein am Gebäudeskelett befestigtes, selbsttragendes Stahlrahmenwerk aus. Die in der Breite zwischen etwa 2,40 und 3,00 m variierenden Felder werden durch profilierte Stürze und gekehlte Stützen aus gezogenem Aluminium eingefaßt, die Nachbildungen der noch vorhandenen Gußeisenstützen und Laternen im 1. Obergeschoß des Gebäudes sind. Die Durchbildung der neuen Bauteile erlaubt die spätere Anbringung von Ziergiebeln und Medaillons in der Art der Art-Déco-Ornamente des Originals.

Im ursprünglichen Zustand mit einer Vielzahl kleiner Läden entlang der Straße bildete ein durchlaufendes Brüstungsband aus gemalten Firmenschildern eine deutliche Zäsur zwischen Erdgeschoß und 1. Obergeschoß. Die neuen Ladenmieter benötigten jedoch größere Verkaufsflächen, die sich oftmals auch über beide Geschosse erstrecken; deshalb fassen die vorspringenden Glasfelder in ihrer Erscheinung beide Geschoßebenen zusammen. Die Laibungen sind zurückgesetzt, und bei Läden, die beide Ebenen einnehmen, wurden die Felder als einheitliches, doppelgeschossiges Element ohne Zwischenglieder gestaltet. Unmittelbar über den beiden symmetrisch angeordneten Ladeneingängen an der Michigan Avenue wurden neue, von rückwärts beleuchtete Firmenschilder angebracht.

Die Eingangshalle mit den Aufzügen zu den Bürogeschossen erhielt eine neue Ausstattung mit schwarzen Glasflächen, gemustertem Terrazzoboden und Verkleidungen aus rosafarbenem Marmor aus Tennessee. Von der ursprünglichen Ausstattung blieben die Aufzugskabinen mit ihren geschnitzten Holztüren und ein Briefkasten aus Nickelbronze erhalten.

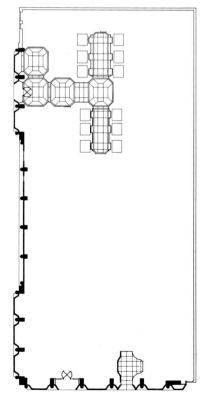

30'

Headquarters of Baxter Travenol, Inc., Deerfield, Illinois

Completed in 1975 on a rolling, 179-acre site northwest of Chicago, the corporate headquarters for Baxter Travenol, Inc. was designed to accommodate the pharmaceutical company's continuous reorganization and expansion. The master plan concept consists of a flexible cluster of modular office pavilions expanding north and south from a central facilities building and parking garages. Linked by an underground pedestrian network and by corner second-level bridges, the long-span steel structures function as autonomous modules or larger shared spaces. Future expansion can be achieved by additional modules followed by a new, similarly flexible cluster.

Within the campus plan, two double-helix garages are centrally located to minimize walking distances and eliminate open-air car parks. All four stories of the stepped steel structures are bordered with planter boxes concealing automobiles from view.

The central facilities building, which houses an auditorium and training center on the bermed lower level, features a 1,000-seat cafeteria on the 24-foot-high main level. A stayed-cable suspended roof is supported by two steel pylons rising 35 feet above its metal deck. Visible from an adjacent expressway, the twin masts give an easily recognized identity to the complex.

Four office pavilions and a low executive building complete the original campus. These two- and three-story modules each have a dominant interior color scheme for easy orientation. Closed offices are placed along the short elevations so that open-plan work stations benefit from the maximum light and views over the site. In the executive pavilion, perimeter suites surround central conference and board rooms.

The crisp exterior cladding of off-white painted metal and infill panels of full-height, semi-reflective dual glazing in stainless steel mullions reflect the client's precise, clean image.

Landscaping, more formal near the buildings and roadways, recreates natural Midwest prairie conditions over most of the site. Man-made ponds provide drainage, stormwater retention and flood control.

Hauptverwaltung der Baxter Travenol, Inc., Deerfield, Illinois

Als Grundstück für den 1975 fertiggestellten Komplex stand ein etwa 72,5 ha großes Gelände an einer Autobahn nordwestlich von Chicago zur Verfügung. Die Gebäudegruppe dient als Zentrale eines Konzerns, der mit der Herstellung pharmazeutischer Produkte erhebliche Zuwachsraten erzielt und deshalb eine Lösung forderte, die spätere Erweiterungen begünstigt.

Um die als offene Doppelrampe ausgeführte viergeschossige Garagenanlage im Mittelpunkt der Anlage gruppieren sich im Norden drei Büroeinheiten, im Süden eine weitere und der Bauteil der Direktionsbüros sowie im Osten der Zentralbau.

Insgesamt nehmen die sowohl durch verglaste Brücken im 1. Obergeschoß als auch durch unterirdische Gänge miteinander verbundenen Baukörper nur einen sehr kleinen Teil der leicht welligen Prärielandschaft ein. Durch die Unterbringung der Autos in Garagen konnte die Anlage großer Flächenparkplätze entfallen, und die Entfernung vom Parkplatz zum Arbeitsplatz wurde erheblich verkürzt.

Im unteren, auf Zufahrtsebene liegenden Geschoß des Zentralgebäudes befinden sich die Empfangshalle, ein Auditorium sowie die Ausbildungsabteilung. Diese Ebene ist allseitig angeböscht, so daß die darüber liegende, etwa 7,30 m hohe Halle mit einer Kantine für 1.000 Mitarbeiter erdgeschossig erscheint. Das Stahlprofildach dieser allseits verglasten Halle ist von zwei in der Mitte angeordneten Rundstützen aus Stahl, die sich etwa 10,50 m über das Dach erheben, abgehängt. Starke Farbkontraste mit Tönungen in Chinesisch-Rot, rötlichem Braun und besonders abgestimmten Gelbschattierungen schaffen in dem lichtdurchfluteten Saal, der durch Bäume in voller Größe und Pflanzentröge einen gartenartigen Eindruck macht, eine warme, einladende Atmosphäre.

In den vier Büropavillons sind die nach Norden und Süden orientierten Längsseiten frei von Einbauten, damit von den Großraumbüros, die durch eine entsprechende Farbgebung voneinander unterschieden sind, ein ungehinderter Blick in die umgebende Landschaft möglich ist. Einzelbüros befinden sich nur an den Schmalseiten. Im Flachbau der Firmenleitung gruppieren sich die Büroräume um eine Innenzone mit Konferenzräumen, Sitzungssaal und Nebeneinrichtungen.

Die landschaftsgärtnerische Gestaltung des Geländes stellte durch die Verwendung heimischer Gräser und Pflanzen den Charakter der mittelwestlichen Prärie soweit wie möglich wieder her. Im Osten zur Autobahn hin und im Norden wurden Seen mit stark modulierten Uferkonturen angelegt, die zugleich als Stauraum bei den in dieser Gegend jährlich wiederkehrenden Überflutungen dienen.

1. Section of the central facilities building.
2. Site plan.

1. Schnitt durch das Zentralgebäude.
2. Lageplan.

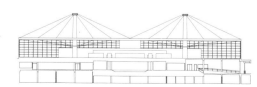

240'

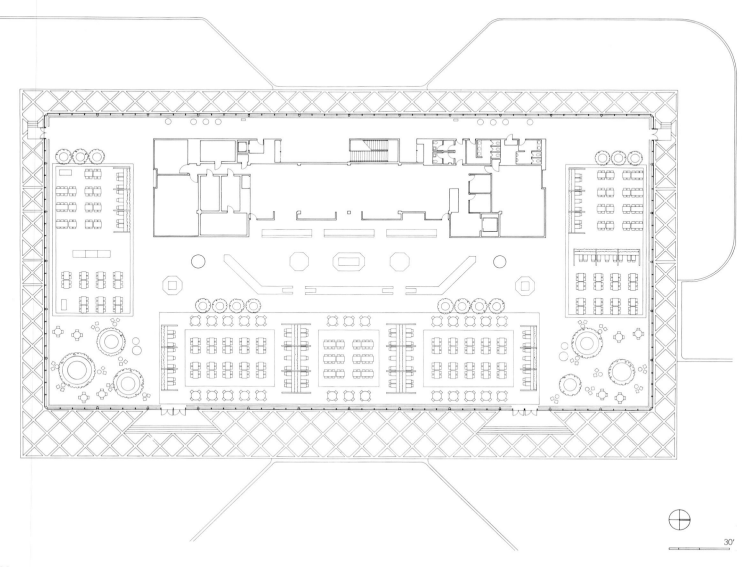

30'

3. Plan of the central facilities building (main level).
4. The 1000-seat cafeteria accommodating the entire staff at one sitting offers a variety of seating possibilities along the glass-walled perimeter.

3. Grundriß des Zentralgebäudes (Hauptgeschoß).
4. Die Kantine mit 1.000 Sitzplätzen, in der die gesamte Belegschaft gleichzeitig Platz findet, bietet entlang der verglasten Außenwände eine Vielzahl von Sitzmöglichkeiten.

Pages 134/135:
5. The dramatic cable-suspended roof structure of the central facilities building gives an easily recognizable identity to the complex.

Seiten 134/135:
5. Die spektakuläre, mit Stahlseilen verspannte Hängedachkonstruktion des Zentralgebäudes verleiht der Anlage eine einprägsame Gestalt.

First Wisconsin Center,
Milwaukee, Wisconsin

The corporate headquarters for the largest bank in Wisconsin was completed in downtown Milwaukee in 1974 on a six-acre site composed of three city blocks. There is a substantial slope from north to south and the southern portion of the site is bisected by a major roadway. The character of the development was significantly influenced by these site conditions as well as the owner's previously announced plans to build a 40-story tower.

The solution for the design problem of creating two distinctive images for the banking facility and announced office tower was to set a 40-story tower toward the center of the site above a double level glass-enclosed podium. This low-rise structure respects the scale of existing buildings while softening the transition between the horizontal street and vertical tower. On the first level of the banking facility are the main banking hall, safe-deposit area and a landscaped garden. This feeling of openness within a weather protected park-like space is continued on the second level by a skylit galleria which contains the commercial lending divisions, shops, restaurants and clubs.

The galleria bridges the street to a separate 850-car garage on the southern segment of the site. The truss bridge provides a sheltered pedestrian path through the superblock and is the first element in a potential expansion of an elevated covered walkway system.

The white-coated aluminum tower provides smaller floor areas for the corporate and rental offices. Although a 40-foot structural grid was established for the site, the efficiency of the tower structure required a reduced perimeter column spacing of 20 feet. The transfer of this structure back to the larger podium grid is achieved through V-shaped transfer beams expressed as a distinctive exterior design element. The structural system for the steel tower is based on the framed tube concept combined with belt trusses.

First Wisconsin Center,
Milwaukee, Wisconsin

Die 1974 fertiggestellte Hauptverwaltung der größten Bank von Wisconsin liegt auf einem in Längsrichtung von Norden nach Süden um nahezu eine Geschoßhöhe abfallenden, etwa 2,4 ha großen Grundstück, das drei Stadtblocks im Zentrum von Milwaukee umfaßt. Die Beschaffenheit der im südlichen Drittel von einer Hauptstraße geteilten Baufläche und die vom Bauherrn getroffene Entscheidung, ein 40geschossiges Hochhaus zu bauen, bestimmten den Charakter des Komplexes in wesentlicher Weise.

Ein zweigeschossiger, vollverglaster Unterbau nimmt nahezu die gesamte Fläche des Baugrunds ein. Dieses Podium verbindet die durch die Verkehrsschneise getrennten Grundstücksteile und leitet von der Straßenebene maßstäblich zur Baumasse des 40geschossigen Hochhauses über. Im Erdgeschoß des Flachbaus liegt in einem mit großen Bäumen landschaftsgärtnerisch gestalteten, zum Teil durch beide Geschosse durchlaufenden Atrium die Bankhalle mit anschließendem Tresor. Das Obergeschoß ist eine von oben belichtete Galerie, die im Norden die Kreditabteilung der Bank und südlich des Kernbereichs des Turmes Läden, Restaurants und Klubs aufnimmt. Die Galerie stellt über die Straße hinweg die Verbindung zu der auf dem südlichen Grundstücksteil gelegenen Garage für 850 Wagen her. Als witterungsgeschützter Fußgängerbereich kann sie den Ausgangspunkt für ein umschlossenes innerstädtisches Fußwegenetz bilden.

Der zur Erzielung eines leichten Erscheinungsbildes mit weißen Aluminiumelementen verkleidete Turm nimmt sowohl bankeigene als auch vermietete Büros auf. Das Grundraster von etwa 12 × 12 m ist aus konstruktiven Gründen an den Außenwänden auf die Hälfte reduziert. Den Übergang zwischen dem engeren Fassadenraster des Hochhauses und dem weiteren Raster des Podiums bilden V-Stützen, die die äußere Erscheinung des Komplexes wesentlich bestimmen. Das Stahltragwerk des Hochhauses ist als eine mit Gürtelträgern kombinierte Rohrkonstruktion ausgebildet.

1. Plan (typical office floor).
2. General view of the complex.

1. Grundriß (Normalgeschoß des Bürohochhauses).
2. Gesamtansicht der Anlage.

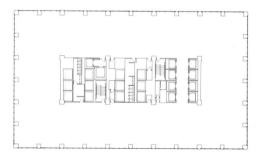

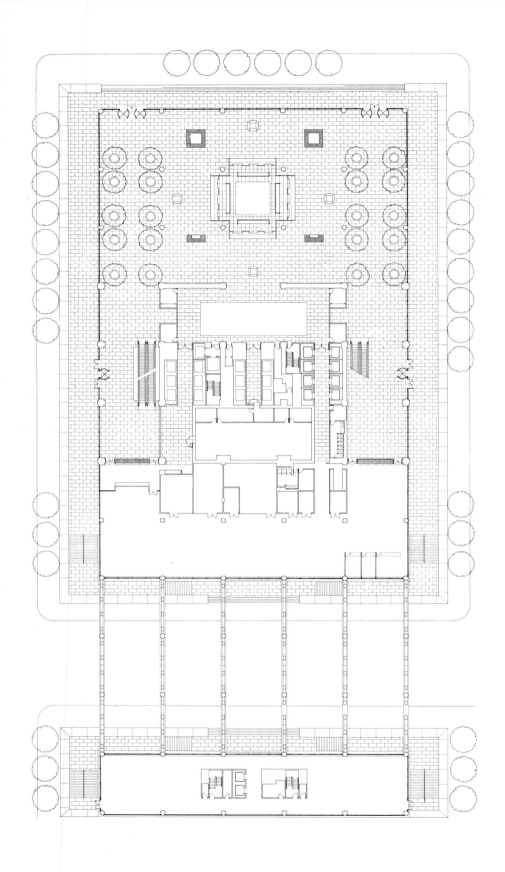

30'

3. Plan (ground level).
4. View of the banking hall situated on the ground level.
5. View of the two-story skylit atrium. Mezzanine floors along the side bays form a visual enclosure for the parklike interior.

3. Grundriß (Erdgeschoßebene).
4. Ansicht der Bankhalle im Erdgeschoß.
5. Blick in das zweigeschossige, von oben belichtete Atrium. Zwischengeschosse in den seitlichen Stützenfeldern geben dem parkartig gestalteten Innenraum einen optischen Abschluß.

Pages 140/141:
6. The structural system for the steel tower is based on the framed tube concept combined with belt trusses.

Seiten 140/141:
6. Das Stahltragwerk des Hochhauses ist als eine mit Gürtelträgern kombinierte Rohrkonstruktion ausgebildet.

First Wisconsin Plaza,
Madison, Wisconsin

1. Southwest elevation.
2. Plan (ground floor) and section.

1. Aufriß der Südwestseite.
2. Grundriß (Erdgeschoß) und Schnitt.

This nine-story bank and office building was completed in 1974 on a site in downtown Madison. In an area designated for redevelopment, the building directly faces the State Capitol across Capitol Square, a parkland mall. The 500,000-square-foot building includes 140,000 square feet of banking space, 175,000 square feet of tenant offices, a commercial mall, a restaurant and health club, and 130,000 square feet of parking space.

The northeastern exposure of the building faces the street with a straight nine-story wall of glass, while the exposure facing Capitol Square is staggered down with sloping glass roofs to first floor height. Offices on the upper floors wrap around a fourth floor roof garden on three sides, gaining an attractive view of the Capitol Square in the southwest. This treatment of the building adds scale and compatibility with the picturesque architecture of the 19th century Capitol.

Rather than an open plaza, the Wisconsin climate dictated an open airy internal environment sheathed in glass. The Bauhaus-style curtain wall eliminated typical spandrel panels while providing an economical solution for the building's skin of white painted aluminum mullions and double glazed glass in 3-foot by 5-foot panels. The mechanical system is expressed as a design element of the curtain wall. A series of air risers and induction units painted blue and water risers painted yellow is exposed and set behind an outer grid of white mullions. On the main banking floor, five murals designed by the artist Valerio Adami integrate the open spaces with the bright color scheme of the rest of the interiors. Three-story greenhouses expand from the structural bays creating internal garden spaces.

This was one of the first adaptations in an office building of the atrium concept which has since gained considerable importance in the United States. The energy efficient design allows the curtain wall to capture sunlight, yet the heating load and ratio of glass to square footage are very efficient in spite of full glazing.

First Wisconsin Plaza,
Madison, Wisconsin

Der 1974 fertiggestellte, neungeschossige Komplex, der unmittelbar an die Grünanlage des Kapitols des Bundesstaates Wisconsin grenzt, enthält auf einer Gesamtfläche von etwa 46.500 m² die Räume des Bauherrn, der First Wisconsin Bank, Mietbüros, eine Ladenstraße, ein Restaurant, einen Gesundheitsklub und eine Garage.

Während das Gebäude – von dem zuerst lediglich der zwei Drittel des etwa 5.300 m² großen Baugrunds umfassende nordwestliche Teil ausgeführt wurde – nach Nordosten zu eine ungebrochene neungeschossige Fassade hat, ist es auf der Platzseite in drei Stufen bis zum Erdgeschoß abgestaffelt. Die oberen Bürogeschosse umgeben dreiseitig eine auf dem 3. Obergeschoß liegende Gartenterrasse, die als Blickpunkt dient und sich auf der Südwestseite zum Platz hin öffnet. Diese Gliederung gibt dem großen Bau Maßstäblichkeit und den notwendigen Bezug zu der Architektur des aus dem 19. Jahrhundert stammenden Kapitols.

Wegen des häufig trüben Wetters in Madison entschloß man sich zu einer Vollverglasung aller Außenwände mit etwa 0,90 × 1,50 m großen Doppelscheiben in weiß gestrichenen Aluminiumrahmen. Das Gebäude hat ein Ortbetonskelett mit Rundstützen im Abstand von etwa 9 m und Kassettendecken mit etwa 90 cm Rippenabstand. Nach Südwesten zu sind diesem Skelettsystem über drei Geschosse reichende Gewächshäuser mit schrägen Dächern vorgelagert. Die offen hinter den weißen Sprossen der Vorhangwand geführten Installationskanäle bilden ein wesentliches Gestaltungselement des Gebäudes. Zuluftkanäle und Induktionsgeräte sind blau, Wasserleitungen gelb gestrichen. In der Bankhalle leiten fünf Wandbilder von Valerio Adami zu der lebhaften Farbskala der Innenräume über.

Es handelt sich hier um eines der ersten Bürogebäude, bei denen das »Atrium«-Prinzip zur Verwendung kam, das heute in den USA eine große Bedeutung gewonnen hat. Das Verhältnis der Fassadenflächen zur Gebäudemasse ist so günstig, daß für den klimatisierten Bau durch die Vollverglasung keine zusätzlichen Heizkosten entstehen, und wegen der relativ geringen Sonnenscheindauer in Madison sind auch die Kühllasten nicht besonders hoch. Man ist im Gegenteil oft über die Sonneneinstrahlung als zusätzliche Wärmequelle froh.

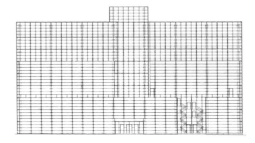

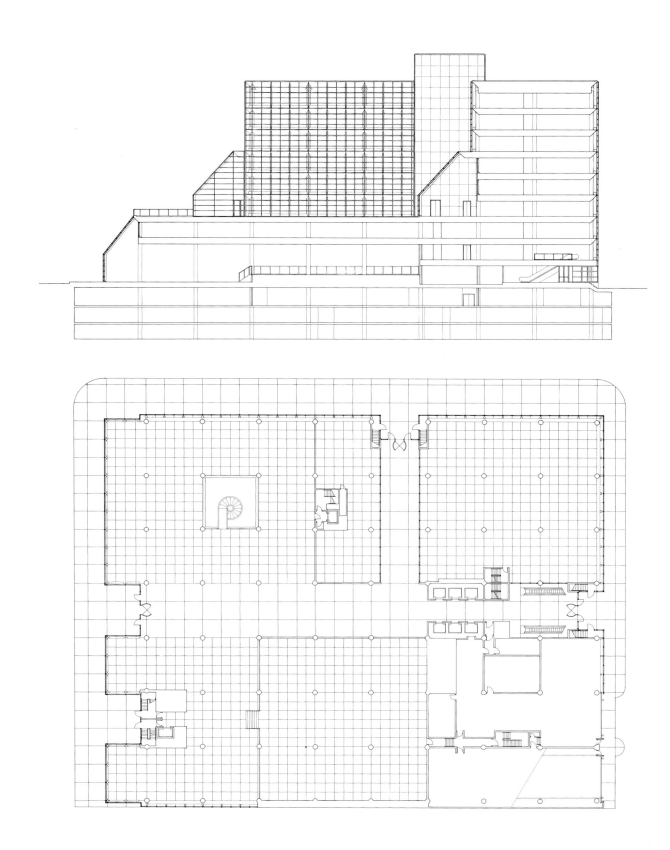

30'

143

3, 4. Three-story greenhouses expand from the structural bays creating internal garden spaces.

3, 4. Den Stützenfeldern sind drei Geschosse hohe Gewächshäuser vorgelagert, die als innenliegende Gartenzonen fungieren.

Pages 145–147:
5, 6. An open, airy environment sheathed in glass was chosen in response to Wisconsin's harsh climate.

Seiten 145–147:
5, 6. Als Antwort auf das strenge Klima in Wisconsin schuf man eine offene, luftige Glashülle.

Pillsbury Center,
Minneapolis, Minnesota

The design of the Pillsbury Center 1,900,000-square-foot investment office complex on a full block in the city center had to integrate the requirements of two primary tenants, a highly structured urban site and one of the most stringent energy codes in the United States.

Two identically shaped towers of 40 and 22 stories, stepping down in two-floor increments at the eight lower levels, were designed to give distinct identities and discrete, flexible facilities to the Pillsbury Company and the First National Bank of Minneapolis. The towers were sited on a strong diagonal axis, allowing separate landscaped plazas which further distinguish the dual occupancies. Both height and massing were also a direct response to the urban context. Along the diagonal axis, views of the historic city hall are preserved at the pedestrian level and from the neighboring 51-story IDS Center to the southwest.

A key design intent was to establish the complex as a major focal node in the city's extensive skyway system. Linking the two towers, a stepped eight-story atrium lobby with multi-faceted triangular panels of clear glazing accommodates second-level pedestrian bridges to surrounding buildings to the north and west and also allows an additional link to the east. Inserted along the narrow diagonal axis, the atrium is carved into the towers' stepped elements to form opposing geometries beneath column transfer trusses. With shops and restaurants on two levels, the atrium is designed to become a spacious indoor plaza and year-round activity center for the city. Paved in dark carnelian granite and accented by stainless steel finishes, the bright, column-free space is highlighted by a suspended Loren Madsen gravity sculpture.

Light travertine and grey-tinted glass, set off above dark carnelian plinth and plazas, were chosen to complement and illuminate the physical forms within the context of the surrounding urban environment. Heavy insulation applied to the concrete structural frames and dual glazing attenuate heat loss and solar gain while extensive use of outside air for cooling reduces energy consumption. The city's first major office complex to be designed in compliance with the Minnesota Energy Code, Pillsbury Center employs a heat pump system and central supply from the city's underground steam distribution network.

Pillsbury Center,
Minneapolis, Minnesota

Der 1982 fertiggestellte Komplex, der einen vollen Straßenblock in der Innenstadt von Minneapolis einnimmt, ist ein Gemeinschaftsprojekt der Pillsbury Company und der First National Bank of Minneapolis.

Die Bauherren verlangten die Unterbringung der eigenen Büros und zusätzlicher Mietbüros mit insgesamt etwa 177.000 m² Fläche in zwei getrennten Gebäuden, um auch nach außen hin ihre Identität zu wahren. Aus städtebaulichen Gründen wurden die beiden Bürotürme, ein 40geschossiges Gebäude für die Pillsbury Company und ein 22geschossiges Gebäude für die First National Bank, diagonal auf dem Grundstück angeordnet. Entscheidend für die Höhenentwicklung, Gebäudeform und Stellung der Neubauten war zugleich die Rücksichtnahme auf den städtebaulichen Kontext. So erlaubt die diagonale Anordnung einen Durchblick zwischen dem 51geschossigen IDS Center im Südwesten und dem historischen Rathaus im Nordosten.

Ein wesentliches Entwurfskriterium war die Einbeziehung des Komplexes in das ausgedehnte »Skyway«-System der Stadt, wozu zwischen den beiden Bürotürmen ein achtgeschossiges Atrium mit Läden und Restaurants angeordnet wurde. Vom 8. Geschoß nach unten sind die Hochbauten in Abschnitten von zwei Geschossen abgetreppt, so daß hier größere Geschoßflächen entstehen. Zwischen diesen Abtreppungen liegt das von oben belichtete Atrium als ansteigender, stützenfreier, von Stahlfachwerkträgern überspannter Raum. Fußgängerbrücken, die den Atriumraum durchqueren, verbinden das Pillsbury Center mit der First National Bank im Westen und dem Gebäude der Northwest Bell im Norden. Eine weitere Verbindung ist zu dem östlichen Nachbargebäude geplant.

Für die Gestaltung der Außenhaut der Hochhäuser waren sowohl städtebauliche Gesichtspunkte als auch die sehr strengen Vorschriften von Minnesota zur Energieeinsparung maßgebend. Das Stahlbetontragwerk wurde stark wärmegedämmt und erhielt eine Verkleidung aus hellen Travertinplatten mit Öffnungen aus grau getöntem Zweischeibenglas. Im Gegensatz dazu sind die Fußgängerbereiche und Sockelzonen sowie die Böden des Atriums mit rötlich getönten Granitplatten belegt. Für das Kühlsystem wird soweit wie möglich Außenluft herangezogen; weitere Maßnahmen zur Energieeinsparung waren die Installation eines Wärmepumpensystems und der Anschluß an das unterirdische Dampfverteilungsnetz der Stadt.

1. General view of the complex.
2. View of the atrium from the mezzanine level.

1. Gesamtansicht der Anlage.
2. Blick in das Atrium von der Mezzaninebene aus.

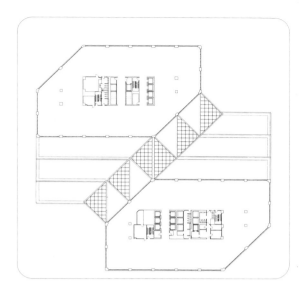

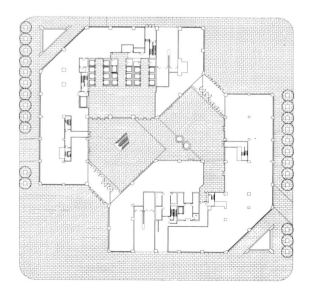

3. Plans (ground level, second floor, typical floor).
4. Elevation of the 40-story tower with section through the atrium.

3. Grundrisse (Erdgeschoßebene, 2. Geschoß, Normalgeschoß).
4. Aufriß des 40geschossigen Büroturms und Schnitt durch das Atrium.

60'

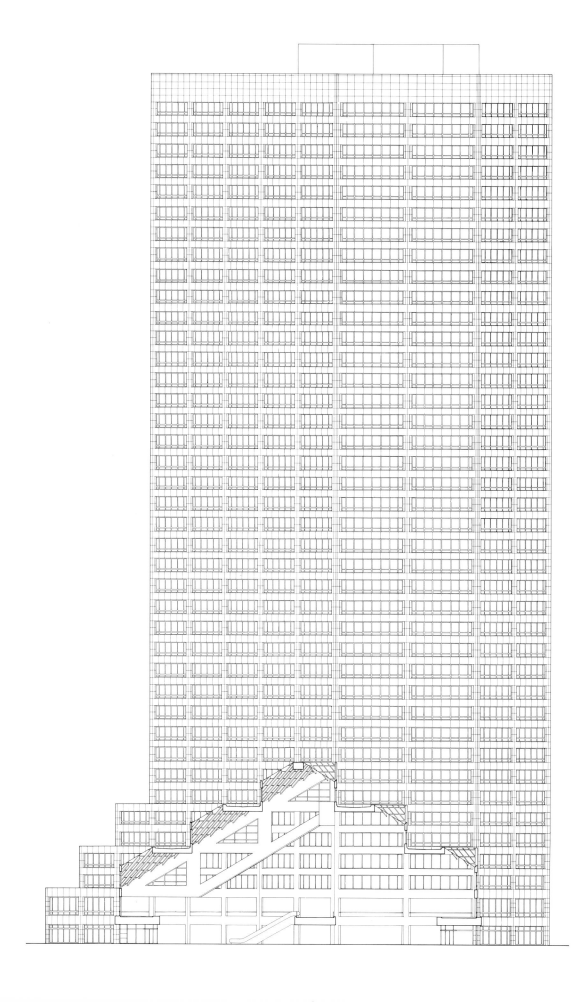

St. Paul Town Square,
St. Paul, Minnesota

Town Square, completed in 1980, is a prime example of an economically viable combination of office, retail, and commercial spaces integrated with recreational and civic-oriented uses to draw people to the city's core. It includes a large, two-block retail podium containing retail shops and restaurants and a major department store; office towers of 25 and 27 stories; a 16-story, 250-room hotel; underground parking for 500 vehicles; and an enclosed city-owned park.
Town Square is the focal point of three urban transitways in St. Paul: pedestrian circulation along 7th Street; the extensive downtown skyway system; and a planned people mover system connecting the large populations of the capitol area and near suburbs with the downtown core. Siting of the various elements of the project respond directly to these factors. The juxtaposed towers are chiseled in plan allowing the people mover system to pass between them, while circulation and structure are likewise designed to accommodate the future station at the podium's roof level.
The podium is kept at two levels to relate to the scale of neighboring buildings. A strong theme of rounded columns and curved spandrels is used on the exterior and interior shopping areas. These rounded forms, extended to the cladding of the office towers, provide sculptured facades that continually change with the movement of the sun.
A 2.5-acre public park under the glazed atrium further emphasizes Town Square's role as a focal point of the downtown core. Over 300 species of plants can be found throughout the greenhouse area. The protected oasis includes an amphitheater, a children's play area, lecture and display areas, and is also suitable for concerts, parties and cultural events.
Visual unity and spaciousness for all levels is provided by abundant greenery, extensive skylights, large openings between levels, and a fountain which visually flows from the park level down to the concourse level.
Well water from St. Paul's aquifer, with a constant temperature of 55 degrees, is used in heat pumps to heat and cool the complex, lowering energy consumption to approximately half that used by conventional high-rise buildings.

St. Paul Town Square,
St. Paul, Minnesota

Die Schwesterstädte Minneapolis und St. Paul begannen bereits vor etwa 20 Jahren damit, ihre Innenstadtbereiche wiederzubeleben und auszubauen. Die Planungen wurden ein voller Erfolg, und heute gehört die Doppelstadt zu den vitalsten Zentren im Norden der USA. SOM hat dort eine Reihe von größeren Bauten realisiert, darunter den im Jahr 1980 fertiggestellten, zwei Straßenblocks im Zentrum von St. Paul einnehmenden St. Paul Town Square. Der Komplex besteht aus einem die gesamte Grundstücksfläche einnehmenden Sockelbereich mit Läden, Restaurants und einem großen Warenhaus, zwei Bürotürmen mit 25 und 27 Geschossen, einem 16geschossigen Hotel mit 250 Gastzimmern, einer Tiefgarage für 500 Fahrzeuge sowie einem umschlossenen, stadteigenen Park.
Die sich über den Sockelbereich erhebenden Bürotürme fügen sich in ihrer Anordnung und Höhenentwicklung der umgebenden Bebauung ein und dominieren nicht die von dem Kapitol von Minnesota und der Kathedrale bestimmte Stadtsilhouette. Außerdem entsprechen sie den Wünschen der beiden Bauherren, die jeweils einen eigenen Büroturm zu ihrer Identifikation für notwendig hielten. Der diagonale Durchlaß zwischen den beiden Türmen ist auf das von der Stadt geplante öffentliche Personenbeförderungssystem abgestellt, dessen eine Linie dort hindurch zum Kapitol führen soll.
Minnesota hat extrem kaltes Winterwetter. Der in die Anlage einbezogene Town Square wurde deshalb nicht als offener Platz, sondern als verglastes Atrium ausgeführt. Dieser zentrale Bereich liegt über der Straße zwischen den beiden Grundstücksteilen, die hier überbaut wurde, und setzt als über 1 ha großer, witterungsgeschützter Park die Tradition von St. Paul als einer Stadt der Parks und Gartenanlagen fort. Über Rolltreppen erreicht man von der 7th Avenue aus den durchgehenden Hallenbereich über der Durchfahrt. Auch die Bürogeschosse werden nicht direkt von der Straße, sondern über die Hallenzonen erschlossen. Unter dem Gewächshausdach sind über 300 Pflanzenarten sowie eine Voliere und ein Aquarium zu finden. Außerdem gibt es hier ein Amphitheater, einen Kinderspielplatz, Konferenzräume und Ausstellungsflächen.
Für die Heizung und Kühlung des Komplexes wurden Wärmepumpen installiert, für deren Betrieb Brunnenwasser mit einer konstanten Temperatur von etwa 13 °C verwendet wird. Der Energiebedarf der Anlage beträgt nur etwa die Hälfte des für Hochhäuser üblichen Verbrauchs.

1. General view of the complex (modell).
2. On top of a large retail podium featuring an enclosed town square environment two office towers and a hotel are located.

1. Gesamtansicht der Anlage (Modell).
2. Zwei Bürotürme und ein Hotel erheben sich auf einem großen Sockelbau, der einen witterungsgeschützten Stadtplatz mit Läden umschließt.

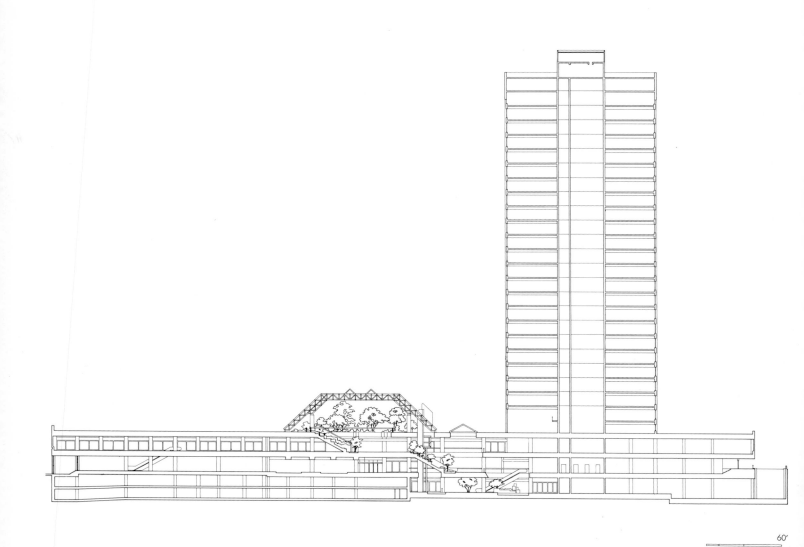

60'

3. Section through one of the office towers and the atrium.

3. Schnitt durch einen der Bürotürme und das Atrium.

4. View into the public park under the glazed atrium.

4. Blick in den öffentlichen Park unter dem Glasdach des Atriums.

Lutheran Brotherhood Building,
Minneapolis, Minnesota

The shape of the Lutheran Brotherhood Building is the result of urban context and owner's requirements. The site, which is flat and uneventful, is centrally placed and has a number of important neighbors, especially the monumental Hennepin County Government Center immediately across the street. Studies indicated that the best relationship to the Government Center was obtained when the mass of the new building became horizontal rather than vertical, and that the small park across the street was framed most successfully when the building's length extended the full block. Two programmatic factors strongly influenced the building's form. The first was the large variation in the size and nature of the spaces required – ranging from typical floors of individual offices to those of open landscape, data processing and computers. In addition, the client's important place in the cultural as well as business life of the community demanded more public space than customary, including areas for assembly and exhibition, a library, appropriate customer and building services, and a large and flexible dining facility.
The design responds through a long 17-story rectangle whose main facade steps up in a series of three tilted and stepped planes. The lowest typical office floor is considerably less than the public floors at the street and skyway levels, but more than twice the area of the uppermost floor. The building's vertical services are distributed along the vertical plane of the northeast facade to assure the flexibility of the office floors and to leave the public spaces below unencumbered.
The major part of the dining facility is expressed as a glazed, barrel-vaulted room extending out from the building mass and overlooking the park. The building's exterior wall is a flush skin of brightly reflective and energy-efficient copper tinted glass, set in dark red enamelled aluminum frames. The street level is a rusticated pink granite from Texas.

Lutheran Brotherhood Building,
Minneapolis, Minnesota

Die überraschende Form des Gebäudes der Versicherungsgesellschaft Lutheran Brotherhood ergab sich aus der Lage des Grundstücks und den Forderungen des Bauherrn, die die Architekten gern aufgriffen, um darin den Schlüssel und die Chance für eine eigenständige Lösung zu finden. Das Grundstück befindet sich in der Innenstadt und ist mehreren wichtigen Bauten benachbart – insbesondere dem monumentalen Hennepin County Government Center aus den sechziger Jahren. Die Architekten kamen bald zu der Überzeugung, daß der Neubau nicht aus einer Turmlösung wie dem Verwaltungszentrum bestehen sollte, sondern daß für dieses ein betont horizontaler Charakter angemessen sei. Um der Grünfläche auf der anderen Straßenseite einen Abschluß zu geben und um den Straßenraum zu fassen, wurde der Neubau auf die ganze Länge des Baugrundstücks ausgedehnt und an die Straße herangerückt.
Ein wichtiger Gesichtspunkt für die Bauform war der Wunsch des Bauherrn nach Geschoßflächen sehr unterschiedlicher Größe. Die Architekten ließen daher die Stockwerke in drei Höhenzonen von Westen nach Osten kontinuierlich zurückspringen, so daß die untersten Stockwerke mehr als doppelt so groß sind wie die obersten. Aufzüge, Treppen und Vertikalschächte liegen an der Ostfassade, die über die gesamte Bauhöhe ungebrochen aufsteigt. Die drei unterschiedlich geneigten Fassadenebenen auf der Straßenseite sind durch kleine, die Horizontalität unterstreichende Terrassen getrennt. Eine Vorhangwand aus reflektierendem Isolierglas verleiht dem 1982 fertiggestellten Gebäude eine glänzende, prismatische Form, die sich von der schweren Steinfassade des gegenüber liegenden Gebäudes abhebt. Vor dem oft grau verhangenen Himmel von Minneapolis setzt die warme Kupfertönung der Verglasung einen willkommenen Akzent.
Das Gebäude ist im 1. Obergeschoß mit einem vor der Ostfassade verlaufenden Gang an das »Skyway«-System von Minneapolis angeschlossen. Eine teilweise über beide Eingangsgeschosse reichende Halle verbindet die beidseitigen Zugänge im Erdgeschoß mit jenem auf der Fußgängerebene. In diesen beiden Geschossen – und einem kleinen, mit einem Tonnendach gedeckten Anbau vor der Westfassade – liegen Ausstellungs- und Galerieräume, eine Halle für musikalische Veranstaltungen, Seminare, Filmvorführungen oder den Ostergottesdienst und eine Bibliothek mit Lesebereich. Als zusätzliche Einrichtungen sind auf beiden Geschoßebenen Läden sowie eine Cafeteria untergebracht.

1. Section.
2. The main facade rises in a series of three tilted and stepped planes.

1. Schnitt.
2. Die Hauptfassade besteht aus drei verschiedenartig geneigten, durch Abtreppungen getrennten Ebenen.

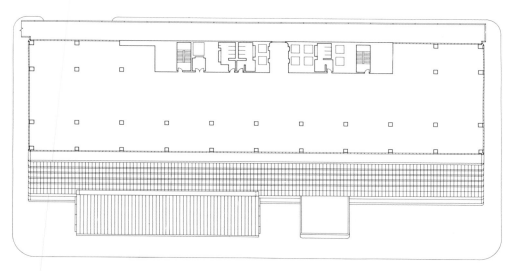

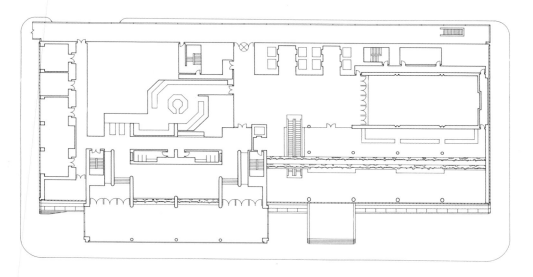

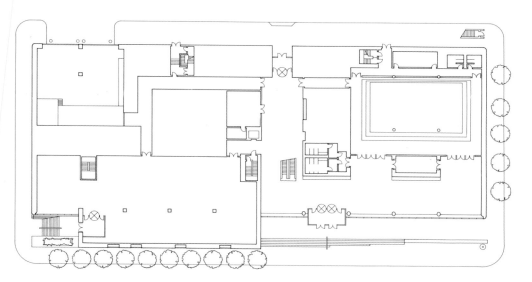

3. Plans (ground floor, second floor, midrise office floor).
4. View of the main entrance from the southwest. The glazed barrel-vaulted extension is part of the dining facility.

3. Grundrisse (Erdgeschoß, 2. Geschoß, Bürogeschoß auf mittlerer Höhe).
4. Ansicht des Haupteingangs von Südwesten. Der tonnenförmige, gläserne Vorbau ist Teil des Speisesaals.

60'

The Menninger Foundation,
Topeka, Kansas

1. Site plan.

1. Lageplan.

The Menninger Foundation, a center for treatment, research and education in psychiatry, is dedicated to the treatment of the whole person in mind and body, within a caring and accepting environment. The physical facility needed to be a manifestation of that philosophy in its organization, architecture and environment. The development of a new 332-acre campus, completed in 1982, included master planning and space programming, architectural and interior design of 20 new buildings, rehabilitation of two existing facilities, and extensive landscaping.
The new complex retains the easily recognized orthogonal grid of Midwestern American towns and cities. Undulating walkways reflect the natural rise and fall of the site as they approach buildings on the diagonal, varying perspectives of form and mass. As the master plan bars automobiles from the campus, the existing tree-lined drive became a main walkway connecting patient activity centers. Covered brick walkways connect sheltered courtyards, residential quarters and related patient therapy and professional offices. Great care was taken to retain the natural beauty of the original estate. Less than five percent of the large stand of mature evergreens and shade trees were lost.
New buildings include professional offices, commons/dining, a conference center, arts and education studios, living units, and a gymnasium. The low, white-painted brick buildings incorporate a wide range of structural shapes: pitched and flat roofs, one- and two-stories, arcades, porches, atria, terraces, and garden walls. A series of courtyards binds together the new elements and red-brick older buildings. The existing tower building, a near replica of Philadelphia's Independence Hall, has become a museum and visitor center and is the focal point of the community.
The philosophy of treating patients in a community setting is reflected in the 166-bed adult psychiatric hospital spread across the brow of a hill. Early programming studies indicated the need for both integrated activities and opportunities for more private exchanges. Eight independent, one- to three-story living units grouping single and double rooms allow patients to live and interact in small groups yet be part of the larger community. Corridor window-seat alcoves offer quiet places to visit and talk. In the patient rooms, built-in furniture, natural wood ceilings and a soft-toned palette of fabrics create an inviting, comfortable atmosphere.

The Menninger Foundation,
Topeka, Kansas

Das von der Menninger Foundation auf einem etwa 135 ha großen Parkgelände unterhaltene psychiatrische Zentrum dient sowohl der Vorbeugung und Behandlung als auch der Forschung und Ausbildung. Die Stiftung hat sich die ganzheitliche Behandlung ihrer Patienten in einer liebevollen Atmosphäre der Zuwendung zum Ziel gesetzt. Umgebung, Architektur und Organisation sollen diesem Ziel dienen und es zum Ausdruck bringen.
Neben der Instandsetzung der vorhandenen Gebäude mit etwa 11.700 m² Nutzfläche waren Neubauten mit einer Fläche von etwa 23.700 m² zur Aufnahme von Praxen, Speisesälen, Krankenzimmern, Gemeinschaftsräumen, Kunst- und Unterrichtssälen sowie eines Konferenzzentrums und einer Turnhalle zu errichten. Der Komplex konnte 1982 übergeben werden. Mittelpunkt des Altbestands ist die Nachbildung der Independence Hall in Philadelphia. Dieses Gebäude wurde zu einem Besucherzentrum mit Museum umgebaut.
Die Behandlungsphilosophie der Stiftung drückt sich in der lockeren Planung des neuen psychiatrischen Krankenhauses für Erwachsene mit 166 Betten aus, das auf der Kuppe eines Hügelzugs südöstlich des alten Zentralbaus errichtet wurde. Acht selbständige Wohneinheiten mit Einzel- und Doppelzimmern gruppieren sich als ein- bis dreigeschossige, weiß gestrichene Ziegelbauten mit braunen Schindeldächern um großzügige Grünhöfe. Die Patienten leben hier in überschaubaren Gruppen, wobei sie sich gleichzeitig als Teil einer größeren Gemeinschaft fühlen können. Zwischen den Zimmergruppen liegen ruhige, nach außen orientierte Besuchs- und Gesprächsecken. Die Zimmer sind mit Einbaumöbeln, Naturholzdecken und Textilien in zurückhaltenden Farbtönen wohnlich gestaltet.
Die langgestreckten, niedrigen Neubauten wurden mit dem Altbestand zu einem einheitlichen Ganzen verbunden. In Windungen verlaufende Fußwege passen sich dem natürlichen Geländeverlauf an und eröffnen vielseitige Blickbeziehungen zu den Bauten. Wesentlicher Bestandteil der Planungsaufgabe war die Erhaltung und Weiterentwicklung der natürlichen Schönheit des hügeligen Parkgeländes. Es gelang, die Bauten so anzulegen, daß weniger als 5% der vorhandenen Bäume den Neubauten weichen mußten.
Da der Kraftfahrzeugverkehr aus dem Gelände herausgenommen wurde, konnte die breite Allee, die früher als Zufahrt diente, in eine Fußgängerzone umgewandelt werden.

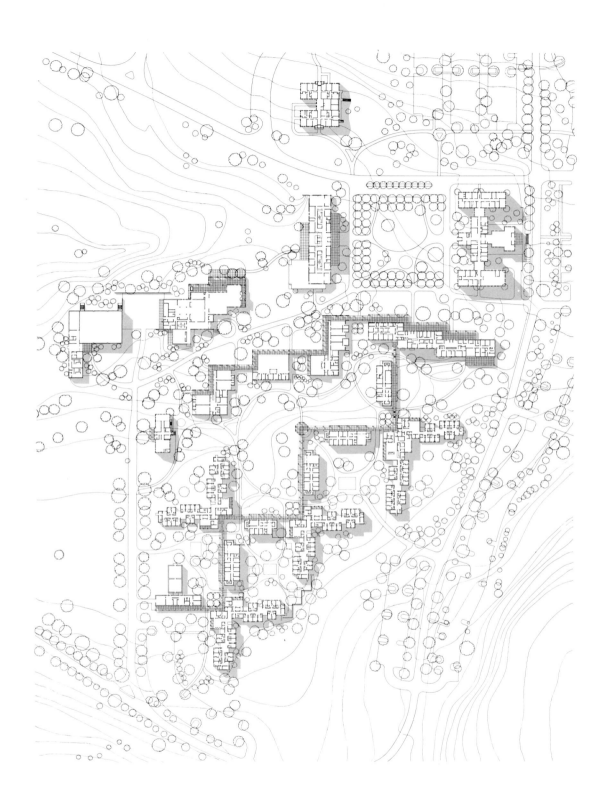

120'

2. Partial view of the complex.
3. Elevation with the remodeled tower building at left.
4. Plan of a hospital unit.

2. Teilansicht der Anlage.
3. Aufriß mit dem renovierten Turmgebäude auf der linken Seite.
4. Grundriß einer Betteneinheit.

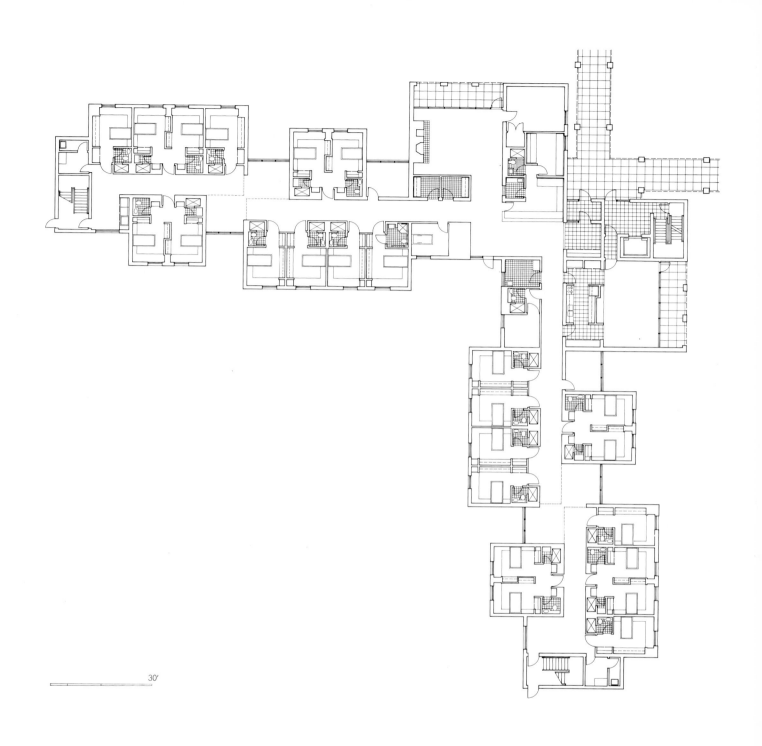

5. A parklike setting retains the natural beauty of the original estate.

5. Durch die sorgfältige Einbindung der Bauten in das Parkgelände blieb dessen ursprüngliche Schönheit erhalten.

6. Covered brick walkways connect courtyards, residential quarters and the other facilities.

6. Gedeckte und mit Ziegeln befestigte Fußwege verbinden Höfe und Wohnbereiche mit den anderen Einrichtungen.

Fourth Financial Center,
Wichita, Kansas

The nine-story headquarters building of the Fourth Financial Bank and Trust Company was completed in 1974 on the edge of a deteriorating shopping area in downtown Wichita. The client perceived this project as a catalyst to the future development of the community and wanted this first element in the planned renewal of the city's Central Business District not to be a conventional office tower but rather a unique structure generating public activity.

In addition to the bank's own facilities, the building contains rental offices on the upper floors and commercial space, a restaurant and a 200-seat meeting room on two underground levels. A glazed pedestrian bridge on the second level links the building to the downtown walkway system of the city and to a parking garage across the street. The focus of the building is a nine-story, glass-enclosed and landscaped atrium. This large atrium is oriented towards the street corner and glazed all the way up to the full building height. An Alexander Calder mobile suspended in this space underlines its vitality. The steel roof structure of the atrium is topped by a pyramidal skylight system bringing light into the center of the hall.

On the upper levels, floor areas of 33,400 square feet flank the square court in two tiers of equal length. The L-shape, with a service core at the intersection of the legs, results in excellent possibilities to subdivide the floors for use by larger or smaller tenants. Towards the south and west, offices on these floors face the atrium with window walls being at the same time protected from direct sun.

The relatively low profile of the nine-story structure is scaled to the surrounding neighborhood. As an additional advantage, the low atrium building provides smaller exterior wall surfaces, fewer elevators and a less expensive structural system than a conventional office tower. Mechanical costs and energy consumption were reduced as the interior courtyard has an insulating effect in conserving energy. While the atrium curtain wall reduces heat loss in winter, the tinted glass reduces solar heat gain in the summer, yet allows the use of natural illumination at all times during bright days.

Fourth Financial Center,
Wichita, Kansas

Die 1974 fertiggestellte, neungeschossige Hauptverwaltung der Fourth Financial Bank and Trust Company liegt am Rand des Einkaufsgebietes im Zentrum der Stadt. Der Bauherr wollte einen Katalysator für eine Reaktivierung des etwas heruntergekommenen Viertels schaffen und gab deshalb diesem aus dem Rahmen fallenden Gebäude den Vorzug gegenüber einem konventionellen Büroturm.

In dem Gebäude sind neben den Räumen der Bank Mietbüros und in den beiden Untergeschossen Läden und ein Restaurant sowie ein Versammlungsraum mit 200 Plätzen untergebracht. Im 1. Obergeschoß verbindet eine verglaste Fußgängerbrücke den Neubau mit der zugehörigen Hochgarage und mit einem innerstädtischen Fußwegenetz. Zentraler Anziehungspunkt des Baus ist ein zur Straßenecke hin orientiertes, über die gesamte Bauhöhe reichendes, verglastes Atrium. Es bezieht zugleich die Stadt in den Bau ein und bietet Schutz vor dem unwirtlichen Wetter in Kansas. Trotz reicher Bepflanzung hat das Atrium nicht den Charakter eines ruhigen Gartens, sondern vielmehr den eines innerstädtischen Platzes der Aktivität und Begegnung. Ein großes Mobile von Alexander Calder unterstreicht diese Funktion. Das Hallendach ist in pyramidenförmige Oberlichter aufgelöst, so daß die Ausleuchtung auch im inneren Bereich außerordentlich gut ist.

In den Obergeschossen legen sich jeweils etwa 3.100 m² große Nutzflächen mit Büros in gleichen Schenkeln L-förmig um die quadratische Halle. Diese Grundrißform mit einem Aufzugs- und Sanitärkern an der Innenseite der L-Form ergibt gute Unterteilungsmöglichkeiten für die Vermietung größerer und kleinerer Teilflächen.

Diagonal gestellte Ortbetonhohlstützen mit vertikaler Sichtbetonstruktur im Achsabstand von etwa 24 m bilden in Verbindung mit etwa 1 m hohen, feuerbeständig ummantelten Stahlträgern das außerordentlich weit gespannte Tragwerk des Gebäudes. In den Hohlstützen sind Treppen und Installationsschächte untergebracht.

Mit der niedrigen Bauhöhe von neun Geschossen fügt sich das Gebäude gut in die Nachbarschaft ein. Zugleich hat diese geringe Höhe den Vorteil, daß sich dadurch kleinere Fassadenflächen, weniger Aufzüge und geringere Kosten für die Rohbaukonstruktion gegenüber einem Büroturm üblicher Art ergeben, so daß die zusätzlichen Kosten der etwa 48 × 48 m großen, neun Geschosse hohen, öffentlichen Halle durch diese Einsparung gedeckt werden konnten. Auch bei den Installations- und Betriebskosten waren Einsparungen von 25% zu erzielen.

1. Section.
2. The focus of the building is a nine-story, glass-enclosed and landscaped atrium.

1. Schnitt.
2. Zentraler Anziehungspunkt des Gebäudes ist ein neun Geschosse hohes, vollverglastes und bepflanztes Atrium.

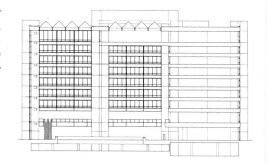

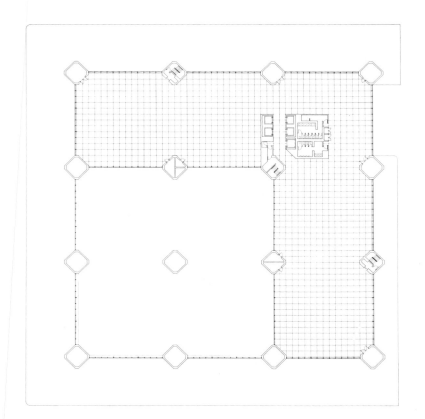

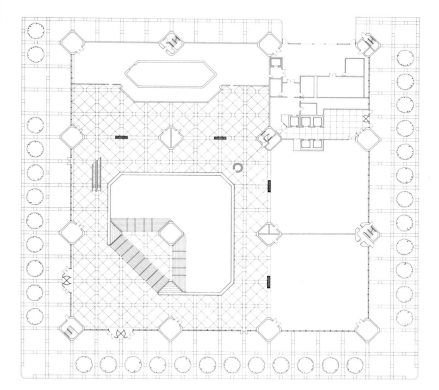

3. Plans (ground floor, typical floor).
4. View of the atrium.

3. Grundrisse (Erdgeschoß, Normalgeschoß).
4. Ansicht des Atriums.

60'

Caterpillar Training Center,
Peoria, Illinois

Traditionally based in this farmbelt town, The Caterpillar Tractor Co. selected for its training center a downtown site which offered accessibility and convenient accommodations for dealers and visitors and which reaffirmed the company's commitment to Peoria's urban revitalization. Caterpillar's goal for this prominent 22-acre site near the new Civic Center was a sophisticated design which would represent the company's high-technology image yet relate well to the surrounding residential area and mixed-use core.

The training center's interior organization evolved from the program requirements for centralized general offices, classroom areas and factory-scale laboratory components able to accommodate a constantly changing array of mammoth equipment. Along an interior street nearly three blocks in length, tiered and stacked classrooms and offices are located opposite related two-story laboratories in repetitive modules. Four skylit circulation nodes, each 60 feet square, which give a sense of scale and place to the long central spine, are used for displays and special events. Second-level gallery walkways from three core areas skirt the open nodes to establish an orthogonal secondary circulation pattern.

Within the five-acre floor plan, all the modules, access points and interior circulation corridors are oriented to respond to the orthogonal grid of nearby residential areas, or rotated 45 degrees to follow the strong diagonal central spine parallel to an adjacent city thoroughfare. Rectangular laboratory modules, related loading docks and service yard are located on the slopes of the descending site and enclosed by a landscaped buffer. Further expansion of the facility is foreseen by adjoining additional repetitive modules and circulation nodes.

Each element is distinctly articulated to give a more appropriate scale to the 312,350-square-foot facility. Similarly, exterior stairs set off from the notched diagonal facade break the long horizontal line of the more visible southeastern face. Crisp, white Alaskan brick in keeping with Caterpillar's high-technology image, was chosen to accentuate the apparent mass of the steel-frame structure. The horizontal planes are broken only by two bands of grey-tinted thermopane windows or a single high band of laboratory clerestories.

Caterpillar Training Center,
Peoria, Illinois

Die Caterpillar Tractor Company ist traditionell eng mit der Stadt Peoria inmitten des agrarischen Mittelwestens der USA verbunden. Sie entschied sich deshalb, ihr neues Ausbildungs- und Schulungszentrum, das 1984 fertiggestellt werden soll, im Zentrum der Stadt zu errichten. Von dem Neubau in der Stadtmitte profitiert sowohl die Stadt – die Unterstützung für ihre innerstädtischen Sanierungspläne erhält – als auch die Gesellschaft selbst durch die hervorragende Lage unmittelbar am Civic Center. Der Bauherr wünschte eine dem Standort gemäße anspruchsvolle Gestaltung, die zugleich etwas von dem technologischen Image der Firma vermittelt.

Das etwa 8,9 ha große dreieckige Grundstück ist allseitig von Straßen umgeben. Im Norden liegt das Civic Center, im Westen soll ein lockeres Einfamilienhausgebiet entstehen, und im Süden und Osten schließt sich ein Mischgebiet mit älterer Bebauung an. Parallel zur Jefferson Street ist eine breite, von oben belichtete Verkehrszone angeordnet, die vom Eingangsplatz im Nordosten – gegenüber dem Civic Center – ausgehend alle Funktionen übersichtlich erschließt und dem zweigeschossigen Flachbau ein optisches Rückgrat verleiht. In einem im Winkel von 45° entsprechend der Richtung der Fisher Street im Westen gedrehten Grundrißsystem sind im Südosten Büros und Kursräume sowie im Nordwesten Ausbildungs- und Entwicklungslabors angeschlossen. Platzartige Ausweitungen der Verkehrszone an Kreuzungspunkten des Erschließungssystems dienen Ausstellungszwecken und Veranstaltungen. Die zweigeschossige Lösung entspricht sowohl dem starken Publikumsverkehr als auch dem Streben nach geringem Energieverbrauch. Das Tragwerk des Gebäudes ist ein Stahlskelett, als Außenhaut wurde Sichtmauerwerk aus weißen Ziegelsteinen mit Öffnungen aus grau getöntem Zweischeibenglas gewählt.

Der Gerätehof wurde in die Böschung des nach Nordwesten ansteigenden Grundstücks eingeschnitten, so daß er gegenüber den Ausbildungseinrichtungen zurücktritt; zu dem benachbarten Wohngebiet und einer Kirche ist er durch einen dicht bepflanzten Grüngürtel abgeschlossen. Insgesamt soll die Hälfte des Baugrundstücks von Grünanlagen und begrünten Parkplätzen eingenommen werden. Nach Südwesten hin sind auf dem Grundstück Erweiterungsmöglichkeiten für alle Bereiche gegeben.

1. General view of the complex (model).
2. Site plan.

1. Gesamtansicht der Anlage (Modell).
2. Lageplan.

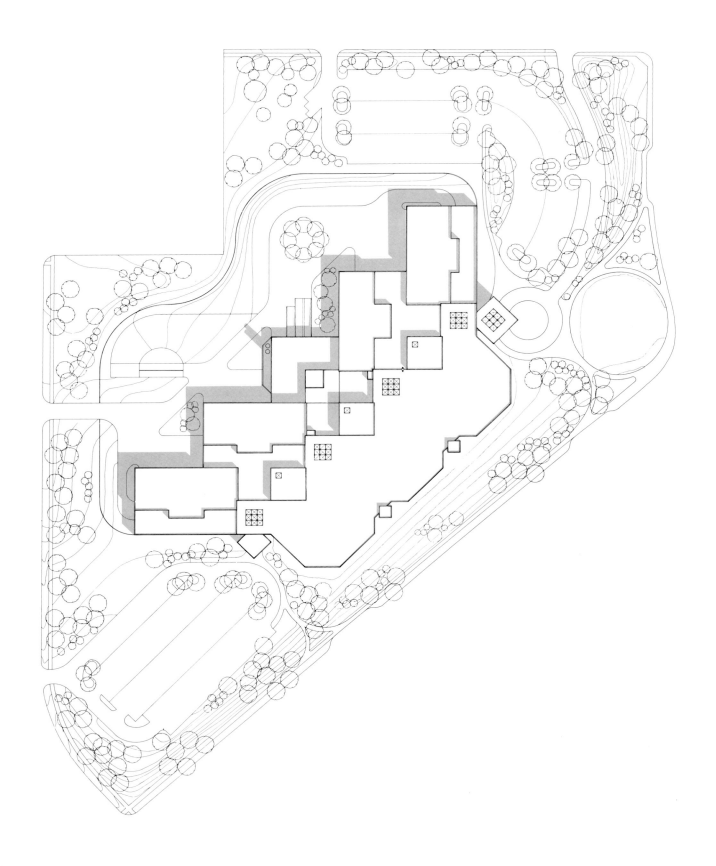

120'

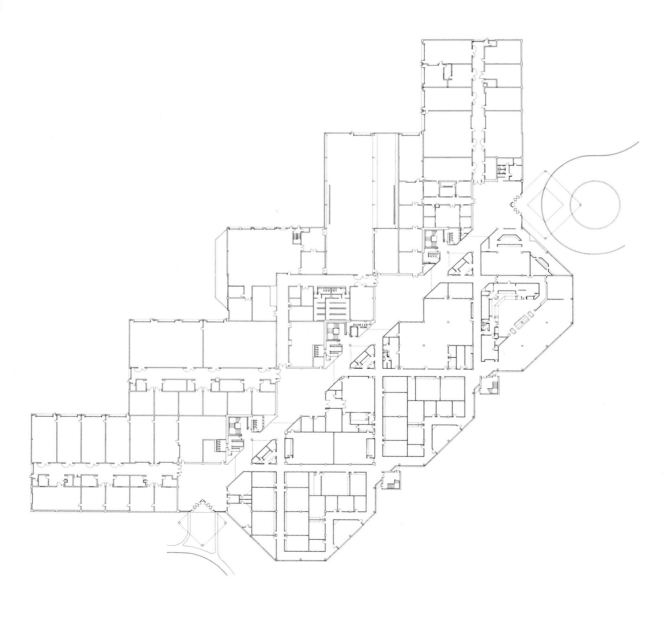

60'

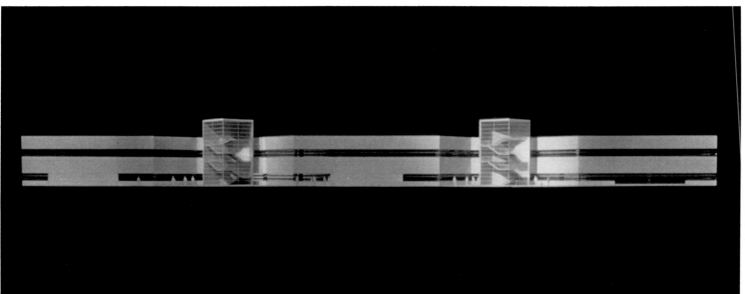

Miami University Art Museum,
Oxford, Ohio

The Miami University Art Museum, completed in 1979, rises from the crest of its four to five acre site like a sculpturesque sequence of changing architectural forms. The proportion and scale of the building elements are geometrically organized both horizontally and vertically and are highlighted by constantly changing light and shadow throughout the day.

The 24,000-square-foot museum was conceived as an active center for art and artifacts. It needed to be flexible enough to display many genres of art, and the surrounding woodlands had to be an integral part of the design. These objectives were met in a single-story barrier-free structure containing both intimate exhibit areas and large skylit spaces, as well as a 115-seat auditorium which accommodates a variety of media presentations. A reflecting pool and three exterior areas can accommodate outdoor sculpture. Through large windows and clerestories, the surroundings are visible from galleries bathed in natural light.

A small gallery, housing drawings, prints and photographs, begins a sequence of galleries adjacent to the entry lobby. Two spacious galleries reserved for larger work are followed by two intimate spaces for decorative arts and primitive works. The visitor is guided through the succession of expanding galleries by a high wall separating exhibit areas from the art storage and research areas which share natural light from the clerestories. Recesses along the wall contain media alcoves. Rearprojection screens supplement exhibits and present work which cannot be installed within traditional small museums. Pocketed sliding display panels within each alcove contain additional prints and materials for study and research.

Northern clerestories in the three larger galleries rise from a flat roof, providing a wash of natural light without exposing artwork to direct sunlight. The sloped clerestory roofs are supported by exposed white-painted wooden trusses which support supplemental, moveable indoor lighting.

The entry plaza focuses on a reflecting pool and the glass-enclosed media center with moveable seats which provide flexible space for receptions and lectures. The entry vestibule allows independent access to the media center which is available at all times for academic and community use.

Miami University Art Museum,
Oxford, Ohio

Das 1979 fertiggestellte Museum der Miami University liegt auf dem höchsten Punkt des leicht abfallenden Universitätsgeländes. Das Gebäude stellt sich dem Besucher als eine Abfolge von in Proportion und Maßstab verschiedenen geometrischen Formen dar, die im Verlauf des Tages mit dem wechselnden Spiel von Licht und Schatten ihr Aussehen ständig ändern.

Der Bauherr wünschte auf einer Nutzfläche von etwa 2.200 m² ein Ausstellungszentrum für Kunst und Kunstgewerbe von großer Lebendigkeit und Flexibilität in der Nutzung. Die bewaldete Umgebung sollte in das Entwurfskonzept einbezogen werden. Diesem Anliegen kamen die Architekten mit einem eingeschossigen Bau nach, der unterschiedlich große Ausstellungsräume bietet und durch große Öffnungen Ausblicke in die Landschaft ermöglicht.

Neben dem Eingang liegt ein dreieckiges, weitgehend verglastes Auditorium mit 115 Sitzplätzen. Über ein Wasserbecken hinweg, in dem auch Plastiken aufgestellt werden, geht der Blick von hier auf die bewaldete Landschaft. Der in vielfacher Weise nutzbare Saal steht der Universität und der Öffentlichkeit gleichermaßen zur Verfügung. Er ist deshalb von der Eingangshalle aus getrennt erschlossen.

Die Galerieräume mit Oberlicht sind nordöstlich einer Trennwand, hinter der Lagerräume und Studios sowie Sanitärräume untergebracht sind, aneinandergereiht. Nächst dem Eingang liegt der kleinste Raum, in dem Zeichnungen, Drucke und Photographien ausgestellt werden. Darauf folgen ein Raum mittlerer Größe und schließlich ein noch größerer. Am Ende dieser drei von oben belichteten Räume schließen zwei intime Ausstellungsräume ohne Oberlicht, in denen Kunstgewerbe und primitive Kunst zu sehen sind, die langgestreckte Anlage ab. Nischen in der Trennwand nehmen Einrichtungen für zusätzliche Informationen auf. Hier werden über Rückprojektionstafeln auch Kunstwerke dargestellt, die in den üblichen kleinen Universitätsmuseen nicht gezeigt werden können. Verschiebbare Ausstellungstafeln enthalten darüber hinaus zusätzliche Drucke und Materialien für vertiefende Studien.

Die Wände bestehen aus Kalksandsteinmauerwerk, das in nach oben hin breiter werdenden Bändern gegliedert wurde. Sie tragen eine Flachdachkonstruktion aus Holz. Durch die von weiß gestrichenen Holzfachwerkbindern mit Stahlzugseilen gebildeten Shedoberlichter wird die Landschaft in die lichtdurchfluteten Innenräume einbezogen, ohne daß die Sonne direkt einfallen kann.

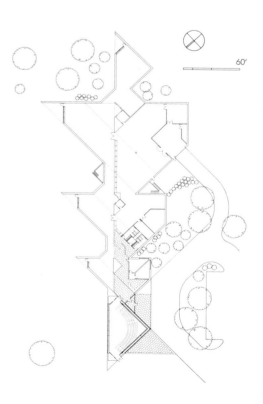

60'

1. Plan.
2. In the three larger galleries northern clerestories provide a wash of natural light without exposing artwork to direct sunlight.

1. Grundriß.
2. Die drei größeren Galerieräume werden durch Nordoberlichter mit Tageslicht durchflutet, ohne daß die Kunstwerke direktem Sonnenlicht ausgesetzt sind.

Pages 176/177:
3. The museum is situated on the crest of a gently sloping site. To the visitor the structure reveals a sequence of geometrically organized forms, highlighted by the movement of light and shadow.

Seiten 176/177:
3. Das Museum liegt auf dem höchsten Punkt des leicht abfallenden Grundstücks. Dem Besucher bietet sich die Anlage als eine Abfolge geometrischer Formen dar, deren Wirkung durch die Bewegung von Licht und Schatten unterstrichen wird.

Louisville Galleria,
Louisville, Kentucky

The Louisville Galleria, completed in 1982, is the largest mixed-use project ever undertaken in Kentucky. Totaling approximately 1,500,000 square feet, the project covers a full block in the heart of downtown Louisville. It serves as the focal point for the major business, government and entertainment centers of the city, and is the hub of the popular pedestrian skyway system. The complex is comprised of two 26-story office towers, the renovated Kaufman-Straus Building within a glass-enclosed, seven-story galleria, retail space, and a garage. The central circulation spine for the complex, an extension of the River City Mall, runs through the galleria and is anchored at either end by the 415,000-square-foot towers. The galleria, with its lush plantings, brightly colored seasonal banners, and interior piazza, provides a lively enclosed urban space which promotes year-round activity.

The space frame of the galleria slopes from the top of the historic Kaufman-Straus Building across the mall to the second retail level. The steel truss system glazed with a reflective insulating glass roof and clear glass walls is designed to highlight and preserve the historic structure. The ornate facade of the 75-year old building was restored to its original character with the interior adapted for office and retail space. The exterior walls of the first two levels were rebuilt in a complementary buff colored brick. The third level accommodates a food court which provides shoppers with a space to eat and relax overlooking the park-like setting below.

The towers are sheathed with an insulating reflective glass curtain wall. The glass minimizes the impact of the towers on the skyline and harmonizes with the glazed galleria, while the light-beige painted aluminum mullions match the brick facade of the Kaufman-Strauss Building and local buildings of Indiana limestone and brick. The rounded columns throughout the project soften the angularity of the galleria and its flanking towers. The structural system for the towers consists of an exterior gravity-loaded steel frame and an interior concrete core which resists lateral loads. The floors are composite lightweight concrete decks supported by steel beams.

Louisville Galleria,
Louisville, Kentucky

Die 1982 fertiggestellte Louisville Galleria ist der größte Komplex mit Mehrfachnutzung in Kentucky. Mit einer Gesamtfläche von ungefähr 140.000 m² umfaßt die Anlage ein ganzes Straßengeviert und bildet den Kristallisationspunkt für die Geschäfts-, Verwaltungs- und Unterhaltungsaktivitäten der Stadt und zugleich den Kernpunkt des beliebten Fußwegesystems, das auf der Ebene des 1. Obergeschosses das Stadtzentrum durchzieht. Der neue Komplex besteht aus zwei 26geschossigen Bürotürmen, dem renovierten Kaufman-Straus Building – das in eine vollverglaste, sieben Geschosse hohe Galleria mit Läden eingebunden ist – und einer Hochgarage. Die zentrale Verkehrsachse der Anlage ist als Verlängerung der River City Mall durch die Galleria geführt und wird an ihren beiden Endpunkten von den jeweils etwa 38.600 m² Fläche bietenden Bürotürmen gefaßt. Mit reichhaltiger Bepflanzung, wechselnden buntfarbigen Bannern und einem innenliegenden Platz wurde ein witterungsgeschützter Stadtraum geschaffen, der zu jeder Jahreszeit von Leben erfüllt ist.

Ein Raumfachwerk bildet Dach und Außenwände der Galleria. Das Dach fällt vom Traufgesims des Kaufman-Straus Building über die große Halle zur 2. Einkaufsebene ab und ist mit reflektierendem Isolierglas ausgefacht, während die Stahlträgerkonstruktion an den Außenwänden mit Klarglas geschlossen wurde. Diese Lösung soll die Qualität des vor 75 Jahren errichteten Altbaus zur Geltung bringen, dessen reichdekorierte Fassade originalgetreu wiederhergestellt wurde, während man das Innere den neu eingerichteten Büros und Läden anpaßte. Die ersten beiden Geschosse erhielten Außenwände aus Sichtziegelmauerwerk in einem zum Bestand passenden Beigeton. Die Bürotürme sind mit einer Vorhangwand aus beschichtetem Isolierglas verkleidet, die ihre Masse in der Stadtsilhouette kleiner erscheinen läßt und sich der Galleriaverglasung anpaßt. Zugleich versuchten die Architekten durch einen Anstrich der Aluminiumsprossen in einem hellen Beige eine Abstimmung auf die Ziegelfassade des Kaufman-Straus Building und andere benachbarte Bauten mit Verkleidung aus Indiana-Kalkstein und Sichtmauerwerk zu erreichen. Runde Stützenverkleidungen mildern die Rechtwinkligkeit des Komplexes. Das Tragwerk der Türme besteht aus einem äußeren Stahlskelettsystem, das lediglich Vertikallasten aufnimmt, und einem biegesteif ausgebildeten Stahlbetonkern.

1. Site plan.
2. View of the central circulation spine towards the galleria entrance.
3. Interior view of the galleria with the Kaufman-Straus Building on the right.

1. Lageplan.
2. Blick über die zentrale Fußgängerachse auf den Eingang zur Galleria.
3. Innenansicht der Galleria mit dem renovierten Kaufman-Straus Building auf der rechten Seite.

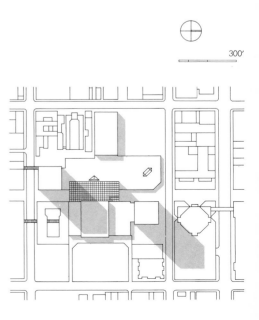

300'

Industrial Trust & Savings Bank, Muncie, Indiana

The primary consideration in designing this bank completed in 1980, was scaling it to fit into the context of the surrounding small-scale downtown area. To respect the existing cornice heights in the area, the 52,000-square-foot building rises only three stories.

The building has a dual focus. One side faces a mall with a strong pedestrian environment. The opposite orientation, from which the majority of customers arrive, is a landscaped parking area which is separated from the building by three drive-through teller stations. The geometry of the building, with its strong vertical and horizontal module, is a simple nine-part square with the center deleted to create a three-story atrium. Establishing the three floors at the same height creates the desired intimate scale at ground level. To complement both the pedestrian and parking areas, deep shadowed entries are recessed into the facade wrapping the building in a tight glass skin.

The glass panels are interposed according to interior space uses and solar orientation. The reflective glass becomes a filter system, diminishing solar loading. The tinted glass is in the vision areas and the back-painted spandrel glass is at opaque surface areas. Each face of the building is tempered to respond to the climatic conditions of its orientation.

The massing and volume systems once defined, the interior organization was established. The original intent for the interior was to maintain the feeling of accessibility that existed in the bank's previous building. The three-story atrium space allows for this. It is open to column-free offices on three sides with the service core on the fourth side.

In order to make the atrium a functional space and not just a lobby, the teller area was chosen to be the atrium's central focus. In contrast to the building exterior, which is subdued to integrate into the surrounding quiet community, the atrium space is defined by bands of bright colors. Orange is used in public areas along the atrium's edge, blue indicates non-public areas and red covers the walls of the core. Offices are divided by low partition system with glass clerestories in the upper modules. This allows for privacy yet maintains a visual awareness of the exterior surface system.

Industrial Trust & Savings Bank, Muncie, Indiana

Der 1980 fertiggestellte Neubau der Bank wurde sorgfältig in seine kleinstädtische Umgebung eingefügt. Mit Rücksicht auf den Maßstab der Nachbarbauten beschränkte man sich bei der eine Bruttogeschoßfläche von etwa 4.800 m² umfassenden Bank auf nur drei Geschosse. Es ist eine Orientierung nach zwei Richtungen gegeben: Auf der einen Seite liegt ein Einkaufszentrum mit Fußgängerzone, auf der entgegengesetzten Seite – durch drei Autoschalter von der Bank getrennt – ein dicht bepflanzter Parkplatz, von dem aus die meisten Kunden kommen. In seiner Grundrißorganisation besteht der Bau aus neun Quadraten, von denen das mittlere sich als Atrium zu einem Oberlicht öffnet. Alle drei Geschosse haben die gleiche Höhe; auch im Erdgeschoß ergab sich daher ein intimer Maßstab. Sich gegenüber liegende Eingänge, die auf die Fußgängerzone und den Parkplatz ausgerichtet sind, bilden tiefe Einschnitte in der Fassade, die als straffe Glanzglashaut das Gebäude ummantelt.

Die Glaspaneele gibt es entsprechend dem inneren Aufbau und der Orientierung zur Sonne in drei verschiedenen Ausführungen: aus reflektierendem oder getöntem Glas im Sichtbereich sowie aus Glas mit rückseitiger opaker Schicht vor Decken und Brüstungen.

Die innere Gliederung ergab sich aus der Baukörperform und der Grundrißorganisation. Ausgehend von dem Gebäude, in dem die Bank früher untergebracht war, sollte auch hier eine Atmosphäre der Offenheit und unmittelbaren Zugänglichkeit herrschen. Dieses Ziel wurde durch das dreigeschossige Atrium erreicht, an dem an drei Seiten stützenfreie Büroflächen und an der vierten Seite der Kernbereich liegen.

Die Architekten wollten das Atrium in der Gebäudemitte nicht einfach zu einer Lobby machen, sondern an dieser Stelle einen funktional sinnvollen Raum schaffen, weshalb sie in dessen Zentrum den Bankschalter setzten. Während die Fassaden mit Rücksicht auf die ruhige Umgebung sehr zurückhaltend gestaltet sind, wird das Atrium von starken Farbkontrasten bestimmt. Die öffentlichen Bereiche um das Atrium herum sind in Orange und die nichtöffentlichen Zonen in Marineblau gehalten; die Wände des Gebäudekerns sind rot. Die Bürozonen wurden durch niedrige Trennwände mit Glaselementen in den oberen Feldern unterteilt. Dadurch ergab sich die notwendige Abgeschlossenheit, gleichzeitig blieb aber der Durchblick zu den Außenwänden erhalten.

1. Section.
2. Deep shadowed entries are recessed into the facade, wrapping the building in a tight glass skin.

1. Schnitt.
2. Die Eingänge bilden tiefe Einschnitte in der Fassade, die als straffe Ganzglashaut das Gebäude ummantelt.

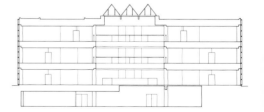

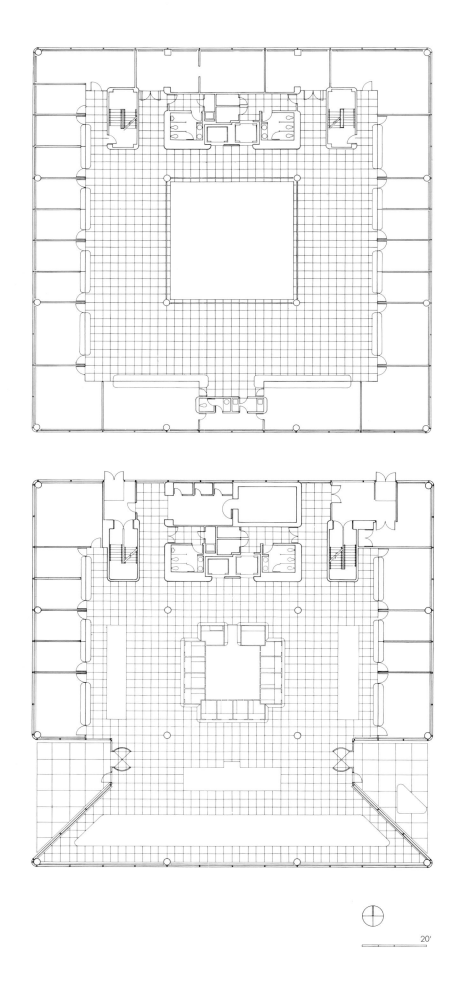

20'

3. Plans (ground floor, second floor).
4. Offices are divided by low partions with glass clerestories in the upper modules. This allows for privacy, yet a visual awareness of the exterior is maintained from all points.

3. Grundrisse (Erdgeschoß, 2. Geschoß).
4. Die Bürozonen wurden durch niedrige Trennwände mit Glaselementen in den oberen Feldern unterteilt. Dadurch ergab sich die notwendige Abgeschlossenheit, gleichzeitig blieb aber der Durchblick zu den Außenwänden erhalten.

Columbus City Hall,
Columbus, Indiana

In 1972 SOM executed an inner city redevelopment scheme for Columbus, a county seat south of Indianapolis, Indiana. Phased implementation of this plan has greatly enhanced the city's core area. Extending from north to south, the historic main street of this city of 38,000, Washington Street, is dominated at its southern end by the Bartholomew County Courthouse. Diagonally across from this landmark – and across from the low, glazed rectangle which SOM built for the city's daily newspaper in 1972 – is the new City Hall completed in 1981.

Columbus City Hall is a three-story building, triangular in plan with the hypotenuse forming a strong diagonal facing directly towards the Courthouse. The front presents a two-story high, essentially opaque and monumental facade above a large lawn, which rises with a wide approach walk and steps to a glazed semi-circular entrance courtyard. Behind the glass is a circulation gallery rising full height to the second floor balcony, also a circulation gallery, and reached by stairs at each end. These two floors contain the various service departments of the city government in addition to several conference rooms, the Council Chamber on the upper floor, and an Assembly Hall at court level. The first floor is given over almost entirely to the Police Department.

It is treated as a plinth, cased in limestone and emerging out of the lawn at the front, but a full story in height on the two flanking elevations, with pierced openings onto the planted parking areas. The upper two stories, except for the entrance court, are veneered in a softly-colored sand struck brick with a tinted, wide mortar joint. The window openings are carefully proportioned with tinted glass set flush in narrow dark frames and revealed from the brick. The limestone is detailed to recall earlier attitudes towards monumental masonry. The building's structure is a composite of poured-in-place concrete (the plinth) and a light steel upper frame with steel decking and block infill behind the brick. The building is fully air-conditioned. In conclusion, the materials and most details are consistent with an adequate but austere budget. There is an ongoing civic-sponsored art program for the building.

Columbus City Hall,
Columbus, Indiana

Für den zentralen Bereich der südlich von Indianapolis gelegenen Bezirksstadt Columbus hatte SOM bereits 1972 einen Sanierungsplan ausgearbeitet, auf Grund dessen eine spürbare Aufwertung der Innenstadt erreicht werden konnte. Hauptstraße der etwa 38.000 Einwohner zählenden Stadt ist die von Norden nach Süden verlaufende Washington Street, an deren südlichem Ende dominierend das Bartholomew County Courthouse liegt. Diagonal gegenüber diesem Baudenkmal – und direkt gegenüber dem 1972 von SOM erbauten Flachbau der örtlichen Tageszeitung – liegt das neue Rathaus, das 1981 fertiggestellt wurde.

Der dreigeschossige Bau, in dem auch die städtische Polizeiverwaltung Platz fand, erhielt eine seiner Bedeutung entsprechende unverwechselbare Form. Bestimmend ist die Diagonalbeziehung zu dem Courthouse und dem Stadtzentrum. Auf dieser Seite ist dem Neubau eine Rasenfläche nach Art traditioneller Vorplätze vorgelagert. In der Achse der Diagonale erreicht man über eine Folge breiter Stufen das erhöhte, zweigeschossige Längsseite des rechtwinkligen Gebäudedreiecks und betritt einen halbkreisförmigen Innenhof. Dieser ist auf der Ebene des Obergeschosses durch zwei etwa 10,50 m auskragende, mit Ziegelmauerwerk verkleidete Stahlbinder gegenüber der Stadt optisch abgesetzt. Hinter der sprossenlosen, von durchgehenden Tafeln aus grün getöntem Dickglas gebildeten Hoffassade liegt auf zwei Ebenen im Halbrund eine große Halle als Zugangsbereich zu den Büros der Stadtverwaltung und den Sitzungssälen.

Die Galerie auf der oberen Ebene wird durch zwei dem Radius der Fassade folgende Treppen erschlossen. Zugang, Eingangshof und öffentliche Bereiche ergeben eine überaus eindrucksvolle Atmosphäre, die Offenheit, Übersichtlichkeit und Bürgernähe ausstrahlt. Der große Sitzungssaal auf der Eingangsebene ist für 200 Personen ausgelegt; der Ratssaal im Obergeschoß hat 50 Plätze.

Die dicht mit Bäumen bepflanzten Parkplätze sind winkelförmig den beiden parallel zu den Ortsstraßen verlaufenden kurzen Seiten des Gebäudes vorgelagert und erstrecken sich über den gesamten verbleibenden Teil des Grundstücks. Sie liegen tiefer und sind deshalb vom Haupteingang nicht einsehbar. Nach diesen Seiten hin drücken dreigeschossige Lochfassaden in starkem Gegensatz zur Eingangssituation die Funktion der hierher orientierten Verwaltungsräume des Rathauses aus. Zugleich nehmen die flächigen Wände aus Ziegelmauerwerk mit Elementen aus Kalkstein eine Beziehung zur traditionellen Bauweise öffentlicher Gebäude im Zentrum von Columbus auf.

1. The new City Hall in its urban context (model).
2. View of the main entrance. The monumental facade is approached by a wide walk with steps, which lead across a traditional "front lawn".

1. Das neue Rathaus in seinem städtebaulichen Umfeld.
2. Ansicht der Haupteingangsseite. Man nähert sich der imposanten Eingangsfront auf einem breiten Stufenweg, der über eine Rasenfläche nach Art traditioneller Vorplätze führt.

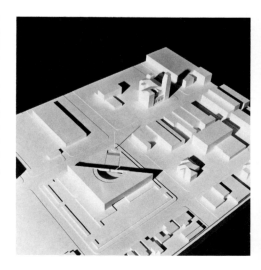

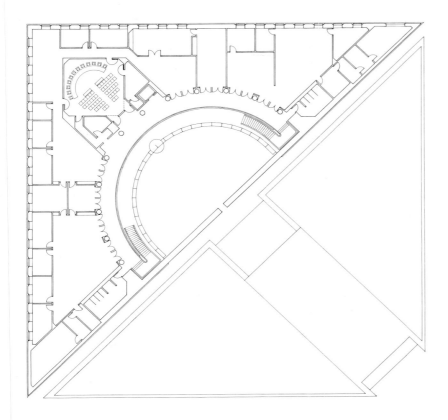

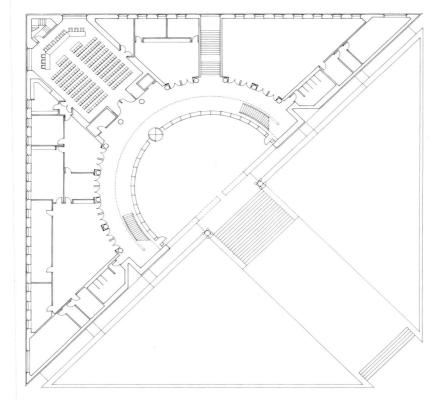

3. Plans (second floor, third floor).
4. Behind the tinted glazing of the curved courtyard wall is a large two-story gallery.

3. Grundrisse (Eingangsgeschoß, Obergeschoß).
4. Hinter der Fensterwand aus getöntem Glas, die den halbkreisförmigen Innenhof begrenzt, liegt eine große zweigeschossige Galerie.

30'

2

Der Südwesten

In den siebziger Jahren wurde der Südwesten der Vereinigten Staaten Teil einer nordsüdlichen Finanzachse. Ausgehend von Houston und New Orleans am Golf von Mexiko, erstreckt sich der »Energy Belt« nach Westen und Nordwesten über Denver bis nach Calgary in Kanada. Öl und Erze in diesen Gebieten zogen amerikanische und kanadische Prospektoren und Investoren an, und im Südwesten kam es zu einer außerordentlichen Belebung der Bautätigkeit.

Jedes der älteren SOM-Büros hat sich im Südwesten seit geraumer Zeit mit bemerkenswerten Arbeiten ausgezeichnet. Den Anfang machte Ende der fünfziger Jahre das New Yorker Büro mit dem Entwurf des Hochhauses der First City National Bank in Houston [2]; 1962 folgte dann das Büro in San Francisco mit dem Tenneco Building für die Tennessee Gas Corporation [3]. Dieses nunmehr zwanzig Jahre alte Hochhaus erntet immer noch Anerkennung für die differenzierte Behandlung der Bank- und Bürogeschosse sowie die ausdrucksvolle Aluminiumfassade mit den in die Randbalken integrierten Sonnenblenden. 1971 entwarf das Chicagoer Büro das 50geschossige, nach der Doppelrohrbauweise konstruierte Stahlbetongebäude One Shell Plaza in Houston [4]. Unter Leitung von Walter Netsch befaßte es sich 1955 bis 1962 beim Bau der U.S. Air Force Academy im Wüstengebiet unterhalb des majestätischen Ostabhangs der Rocky Mountains bei Colorado Springs [5] mit vielschichtigen Problemen des Maßstabs, der Verkehrserschließung und des Symbolcharakters. Myron Goldsmith vom Chicagoer Büro war verantwortlich für den Bau des Sonnenteleskops in Kitt Peak, Arizona [6], und kurz nach 1970 entwarf Gordon Bunshaft vom New Yorker Büro die Lyndon Baines Johnson Library in Austin, Texas [7].

Bei diesen von SOM in früheren Jahren entworfenen Bauten stand das Streben nach einer monumentalen und zeichenhaften Gestaltung im Vordergrund. So ist beispielsweise die Hauptverwaltung von Boise Cascade in Boise, Idaho [8] ein einzelner, frei stehender Baukörper mit zentralem Innenhof, der von Brückenverbindungen zwischen den außenliegenden Bürozonen durchschnitten wird. Die vom Bauherrn gewünschte großzügige – aber unrentable – Anordnung von Nutzflächen und Verkehrsbereichen entsprach natürlich nicht den Erwartungen der Bauträger, die in den siebziger Jahren im Energy Belt tätig wurden. Diese Bauherren forderten statt dessen eine möglichst rationale Nutzung der Gebäudeflächen und der Energie, wie sie sich etwa bei dem vom Chicagoer Büro entworfenen 28geschossigen Pan American Life Building in New Orleans zeigt. Zu den bemerkenswertesten Arbeiten des von Kenneth Soldan und Robert Holmes geleiteten SOM-Büros in Denver zählt der Bürokomplex der Gulf Mineral Resources

3

4

1. Skyline of Houston, Texas.
2. First City National Bank, Houston, Texas.
3. Tenneco Building, Houston, Texas.
4. One Shell Plaza, Houston, Texas.

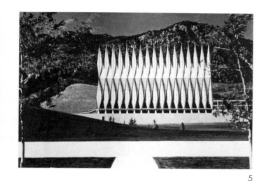

5

8

The Southwest

During the 1970's the southwestern United States, which had long enjoyed business alliances with Chicago, New York and San Francisco, developed a north-south financial axis. Starting with Houston and New Orleans along the Gulf, the Energy Belt stretched west-northwest through Denver to Calgary in Canada. Its oil and minerals attracted American and Canadian prospectors and investors, and the Southwest saw a spectacular spurt in building. Dallas, Fort Worth, and Denver amassed dense aggregations of towers containing rentable office space. Downtown Houston leapt from SOM's 33-story Tenneco Building of the early 1960's to the 71 stories of SOM's Allied Bank Tower nearing completion in 1983.

Each of SOM's older offices has had a long and distinguished presence in the Southwest. Starting in the late 1950's, SOM/New York designed Houston's First City National Bank [2], and, in 1962, SOM/San Francisco designed the Tenneco Headquarters for the Tennessee Gas Corporation [3]. A model solar screened tower, now 20 years old, its expression of banking and office floors in articulated aluminum louvers and spandrels still commands admiration. In 1971, SOM/Chicago designed a 50-story tube-within-tube reinforced concrete structure, Houston's One Shell Plaza [4]. Led by Walter Netsch in 1955–1962, SOM/Chicago addressed the awesome problems of scale, circulation and symbolism attendant upon building the U.S. Air Force Academy in the desert foothills beneath the majestic east face of the Rockies near Colorado Springs [5]. Raising its tetrahedron trusses high above the low buildings, the Chapel turns a brilliant horizontal order into a masterly expression of site. At Kitt Peak, Arizona, SOM/Chicago's Myron Goldsmith designed the National Observatory [6], and, at Austin, Texas, shortly after 1970, SOM/New York's Gordon Bunshaft designed the Lyndon Baines Johnson Library [7].

Central to those earlier SOM buildings was the intention to be monumental and emblematic. Thus SOM's Boise Cascade Headquarters in Boise, Idaho [8], is a freestanding, single mass, with a central courtyard crossed by bridges connecting peripheral offices. While wanted by the corporate client, comparable arrangements of generous but unrentable space and circulation would not be demanded by the developers who arrived in the Energy Belt in the 1970's. Rather, they sought efficient use of space and energy, as shown in SOM/Chicago's 28-story Pan American Life Building in New Orleans, which reduces office heights, compacts circulation, and stacks two tall atria to achieve a high ratio of floor to exterior wall. Among the remarkable designs now emanating from SOM/Denver, led by partners Kenneth Soldan and Robert Holmes, the Gulf Mineral Resources Company office buildings [9] arrange incremental units along enclosed

6

7

5. U.S. Air Force Academy, Colorado Springs, Colorado. Chapel.
6. Robert R. McMath Solar Telescope, Kitt Peak National Observatory, Kitt Peak, Arizona.
7. Lyndon Baines Johnson Library, University of Texas, Austin, Texas.
8. Boise Cascade Home Office, Boise, Idaho.

Company [9]. Hier sind auf Erweiterung ausgelegte Bauteile durch straßenartige Korridore miteinander verbunden. Außerdem wurden innenliegende, von oben belichtete Atrien und zweischalige Solarfassaden vorgesehen. Die vom Chicagoer Büro geplanten Bürohäuser River Center [10], 1515 Poydras [11] und One Shell Square [12] in New Orleans sind Ausdruck der Forderung ihrer Bauherren nach möglichst rationeller Raumausnutzung und wirtschaftlichem Betrieb.

SOM sah sich in den letzten Jahren anstelle eines einzigen Bauherrn, der für seine eigene Gesellschaft ein repräsentatives Gebäude errichten will, viel öfter einem Team von Finanzverwaltern gegenüber. Diese vertraten Anlegergruppen, die selbst – wenn überhaupt – nur einen kleinen Teil der Gebäude beziehen wollten und schnellen Mietertrag sowie volle Verzinsung ihres Kapitals verlangten. Ihr Ziel lag in der Verringerung nichtvermietbarer Flächenanteile, der Schaffung zusätzlicher Geschosse und der marktgerechten Kombination von Geschäfts- und Büroräumen. Wie das Gebäude Great Western Plaza in Denver zeigt, mußten sich auch die Entwurfsarchitekten des dortigen Büros – zunächst unter Leitung von Donald Smith aus dem New Yorker Büro – mit derartigen Forderungen herumschlagen. Das Büro erhielt dann aber die Aufträge für das Anaconda Building [13] und die Denver National Bank [14] und hatte bis 1982 wichtige Bauten in der von der 16th und der 17th Street gebildeten zentralen Achse geplant.

Gemessen an seinen Hochhäusern, ist Houston sicherlich interessanter als Denver. Wenn man von Westen über den Sam Houston Park blickt, stellt sich das Geschäftsviertel von Houston als großartiges Häusergebirge dar, das sich abrupt hinter offenem Land und niedrigen öffentlichen Gebäuden erhebt. Zu den von SOM entworfenen Bürotürmen InterFirst Plaza [15], Tenneco Building, One Shell Plaza und Allied Bank werden sich bald das Four Houston Center [16] und der Campeau Tower [17] gesellen. In der Nähe befinden sich Hochhäuser von Philip Johnson und John Burgee, von leoh Ming Pei und dem in Houston ansässigen Büro CRS.

Viele Arbeitgeber haben für ihre Mitarbeiter nicht nur im Arbeitsbereich, sondern auch für Erholungszwecke außergewöhnliche Einrichtungen geschaffen. Beispielhaft dafür ist Tennecos neues Employee Benefits Center [18], das von Richard Keating aus dem SOM-Büro in Houston geplant und 1982 fertiggestellt wurde. Die Bürotürme von Houston sind Ausdruck der Notwendigkeit des rationellen Umgangs mit der Zeit, wie sich an Garagenanlagen, Schnellaufzügen und Datenverarbeitungseinrichtungen zeigt, sowie Ausdruck der Notwendigkeit, sich als leistungsfähig und erfolgreich darzustellen, wie es das Streben nach angesehenen Adressen und der Mitgliedschaft in Klubs sowie die großzügigen Eingangshallen offenbaren. Mit ihren möglichst charakteristi-

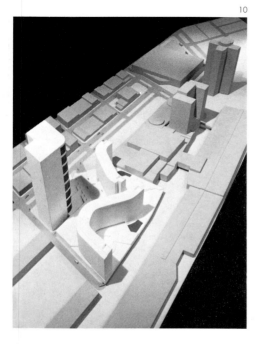

13

14

streets, with internal skylighted atria and solar envelopes. In New Orleans, SOM/Chicago's River Center [10], 1515 Poydras [11], and One Shell Square [12] reflect their owners' concern for efficient space and economical operation. Now, instead of a corporate personality seeking an emblematic building his company would occupy, SOM was more likely to meet a team of financial managers who represented groups of investors who would occupy only a small part of a building, if any, and expected quick rentals and full return on capital. Profit lay in reducing nonrentable space, gaining additional floors, and building a marketable mixture of commercial and office space. The requirements were impersonal: the number of net rentable square feet, the dollars to be expended, and the quality of finishes and furnishings. Having begun with such requirements, as evident in Denver's Great West Plaza, SOM/Denver's designers, initially led by SOM/New York's Donald Smith, steadily won commissions for the Anaconda Building [13] and Denver National Bank [14] and by 1982 had proposed important buildings for the vital spine created by 16th and 17th Streets where Denver needs a strong architectural expression.

Measured by its individual towers, Houston is more rewarding. Seen from the west across Sam Houston Park, Houston's financial district forms a grand massif rising sheer behind open land or low public buildings. SOM's InterFirst Plaza [15], Tenneco Building, One Shell Plaza, and Allied Bank are expected to be joined by Four Houston Center [16] and Campeau Tower [17]. Nearby are towers designed by Philip Johnson and John Burgee, Ieoh Ming Pei, and Houston's CRS. Some twenty blocks of densely packed towers soar fifty and seventy stories, making one crystalline mass that is striated vertically and breaks into cubistic and faceted summits at the skyline.

In Houston, modern architects meet a city whose plan has neither a mercantile nor cultural base. Downtown Houston is built for people who drive automobiles to offices where they work with messages. Their world has manifest dependencies on oil and electricity for its physical energy and on money and risk for its psychic energy. Companies have made extraordinary provisions for their employees, not only in work space, but in recreational space, notably Tenneco's new Employee Benefits Center [18], designed by SOM/Houston's Richard Keating in 1982. The office towers speak of the need to manage time efficiently, expressed in garages, fast elevators, computers, and push-button access, and the need to display competence and success, expressed in prestigious addresses, club memberships, art-filled conference rooms and generous lobbies. The tower then is given a distinctive summit, and the summits are emblems of identity and prestige.

That the architectural result can be elegant has been demonstrated repeatedly in towers spon-

15

9. Gulf Mineral Resources Headquarters, Denver, Colorado.
10. River Center, New Orleans, Louisiana.
11. 1515 Poydras, New Orleans, Louisiana.
12. One Shell Square, New Orleans, Louisiana.
13. Anaconda Building, Denver, Colorado.
14. Denver National Bank, Denver, Colorado.
15. InterFirst Plaza, Houston, Texas.

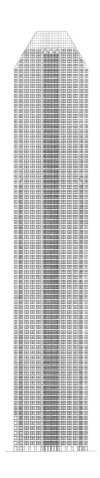

16

schen oberen Abschlüssen versucht man schließlich, die Hochhäuser zu Sinnbildern der Individualität und des Prestiges zu machen.

Daß sich dabei durchaus elegante architektonische Lösungen ergeben können, das hat sich wiederholt bei den Bürotürmen des tatkräftigen und aufgeschlossenen Bauträgers Gerald Hines gezeigt, der zunächst das Hochhaus One Shell Plaza und dann eine ganze Reihe weiterer Gebäude baute, die sowohl wirtschaftlichen als auch ästhetischen Ansprüchen vollauf gerecht werden. Zu den gelungensten der fünf von SOM in Houston errichteten Türme gehört das von Hines finanzierte sowie von Doane und Bassett vom Büro in San Francisco entworfene Gebäude InterFirst Plaza. Die spannungsvolle und heitere Anlage atmet überall Großzügigkeit – von der großen Plaza über die luftige Bankhalle mit den kaskadenartig auf diese ausgerichteten Büros bis hin zum strahlenden oberen Abschluß des Gebäudes. Das Vorbild von Hines und der Erfolg von InterFirst Plaza ermutigten auch andere Bauträger. Das Tenneco-Gebäude sowie die Hochhäuser InterFirst Plaza und One Shell Plaza vor Augen, beauftragte der Bauträger Kenneth Schnitzer SOM mit dem Entwurf des Neubaus der Allied Bank [19]. Dieses von Keating vom Büro in Houston in Zusammenarbeit mit Bassett aus San Francisco entworfene Hochhaus ist in seiner Erscheinung ebenso ungewöhnlich wie gelungen. In dem von zwei Viertelzylindern gebildeten schlanken, gläsernen Gebäudeschaft werden gekrümmte und gerade Flächen so einander gegenübergestellt, daß sich bis hinunter auf die Straßenebene ein abwechslungsreiches Spiel von Licht und Spiegelung bietet und die differenzierte Gliederung von InterFirst Plaza und One Shell Plaza in ungewöhnlicher Weise apostrophiert wird.

So gelungen aber jeder dieser Bürotürme auch sein mag – was den Städten im Energy Belt fehlt, sind innerstädtische Bereiche mit einem Angebot an die Bewohner, das über Büroflächen hinausgeht. In New Orleans gelingt es oft, Märkte mit Wohnungen, Arbeitsplätze und Erholungseinrichtungen sowie Ausbildungsstätten zu mischen. Den SOM-Büros in Houston und Denver wurden nur zögernd Aufträge erteilt, sich mit einigen der dortigen städtebaulichen Probleme zu befassen. Dabei könnten sich beide Städte gut auf die Studie über den San Antonio River Corridor [20] beziehen, die das Büro in San Francisco 1973 anfertigte. Ausgehend von der Notwendigkeit der Hochwasserregulierung, wurde in dieser Studie eine etwa zehn Kilometer lange Zone mit neuen Wohn- und Geschäftsvierteln inmitten von Erholungsparks vorgeschlagen – man sollte die Städte im Energy Belt ermutigen, dieser städtebaulichen Lösung nachzueifern!

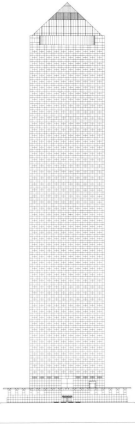

17

sored by the forceful, enlightened developer, Houston's Gerald Hines, who built Houston's One Shell Plaza and thereafter a succession of buildings that meet both financial and aesthetic measures. Among the five towers in Houston designed by SOM, Hines' InterFirst Plaza is clearly a masterpiece. Buoyant, generous and cheerful, its generosity starts with a large plaza, cascades interior offices in the airy banking lobby, and ends in an exuberant almost incandescent summit, the whole being the brilliant concept of San Francisco's Lawrence Doane and Edward C. Bassett. Hines' leadership and InterFirst Plaza's success encouraged other developers. Now, with Tenneco, InterFirst and One Shell Plaza in place, developer Kenneth Schnitzer asked SOM to propose a tower for Allied Bank [19]. Designed by Houston partner Keating in collaboration with San Francisco partner Bassett, the tower is as unexpected as it is successful: a 71-story turning point in Houston's western skyline. Formed by two quarter cylinders, the slender glazed shaft juxtaposes curves and straight planes that play with light and reflections even at street level, where, seen against the background of InterFirst or One Shell, the dark green shaft marks a sharp apostrophe to their complex forms.

Still, however fine each tower may be, the Energy Belt cities lack downtown urban districts that support residents' needs for more than office space. New Orleans often succeeds in mixing markets, residence, work, recreation, and education. By 1980, Denver seemed to be awakening, but there was less assurance that Houston had. SOM's Houston and Denver offices were only beginning to be asked to address some of those cities' urban problems. Both cities might well refer to the San Antonio River Corridor Study [20] SOM/San Francisco completed in 1973. Impelled by the need for flood control, that Study proposed a six-mile stretch of new residential and commercial districts in recreational parks, an urban ideal that Energy Belt cities should be encouraged to emulate.

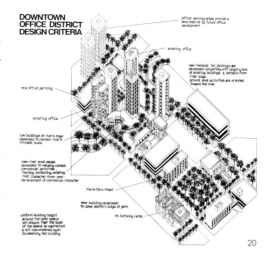

DOWNTOWN OFFICE DISTRICT DESIGN CRITERIA

20

InterFirst Plaza,
Houston, Texas

The 55-story office tower of the First International Corporation in Houston is clad in polished rose-colored granite combined with matching reflective glass. The building is 748 feet tall and contains a total gross area of 1.9 million square feet, of which 1.2 million is rentable office and commercial space. Each typical floor of the steel and concrete framed tube has a net usable area of approximately 22,000 square feet.

The building is adjacent to Tenneco, designed by SOM in 1963, Shell by SOM in 1971, and just several streets from the First National Bank of Houston by SOM in 1961.

Approach to the building entrance is on the northeast side by way of a plaza with a large Dubuffet polychromed sculpture.

The tower has climate controlled underground access across the street to the adjacent hotel with its restaurants and convention facilities as well as to a 1,500-car parking garage just to the west. These pedestrian walkways are part of an extensive tunnel system between almost every major building in downtown Houston, required by the adverse climatic conditions of the Southwest.

To the southeast, the banking hall is placed at an angle to the tower which is bevelled in various ways as it rises. On this side a sawtooth pattern is carried up the entire height resulting in a multitude of desirable corner offices. The tower wall configuration is repeated in the treatment of the hall's roof. The bevelled exterior wall which forms the envelope on this side of the tower extends down unchanged to flank the bank lobby. Supported by girders 15 feet in height, the roof of the hall steps down in a pyramid of levels from north to south where a maximum span of about 162 feet is reached. Linear skylights fill the horizontal intervals between the Z-shaped girders, and a large northern window wall faces the plaza.

The building is air-conditioned with the most advanced systems of controls and security, including the electronic dispatching for the tower's 27 passenger elevators.

InterFirst Plaza,
Houston, Texas

Das mit Platten aus poliertem, rosafarbenem Granit und dazu passend getöntem Glas verkleidete, 55geschossige Bürohochhaus der First International Corporation ist etwa 228 m hoch und hat eine Bruttogeschoßfläche von etwa 176.700 m², von denen knapp 112.000 m² als Büros und sonstige Geschäftsräume weitervermietet sind. Ein Normalgeschoß des als Rohrkonstruktion ausgeführten, kombinierten Stahl- und Stahlbetongebäudes hat etwa 2.050 m² Nutzfläche.

Trotz seiner Lage inmitten des Geschäftszentrums von Houston hat der Bau auf der Westseite eine unverbaubare Aussicht über niedrige Gebäude der Stadtverwaltung hinweg auf eine große Grünanlage, die hier die Innenstadt begrenzt.

Man betritt das Hochhaus von der Nordostseite her über einen gärtnerisch gestalteten Platz, auf dem eine große polychrome Skulptur von Jean Dubuffet steht. Klimatisierte, unterirdische Passagen führen zu dem gegenüber liegenden Hyatt-Regency-Hotel mit seinen Restaurants und Kongreßeinrichtungen sowie zu einer unmittelbar westlich gelegenen Hochgarage für 1.500 Wagen. Diese Verbindungen sind Teil eines ausgedehnten Passagensystems zwischen den Hochhäusern im Zentrum von Houston, das Schutz vor dem ungünstigen Klima im Südwesten der USA bietet.

Auf der Südostseite, im Winkel zu dem im Höhenverlauf wechselnd abgestuften Hochhaus, ist die Bankhalle angeordnet. Die auf dieser Seite durchgehend sägezahnartige Ausformung der Hochhausfassade – die eine große Zahl der begehrten Eckbüros ergab – wurde in der Form des Daches der Bankhalle wiederholt. Dadurch entstand eine spannungsreiche optische Verbindung der beiden Bauteile. Die abgestaffelten Fassadenstützen, die die Rohrkonstruktion der Außenwand an dieser Seite des Hochhauses bilden, laufen auch an der Begrenzung zur Bankhalle unverändert durch. Durch die pyramidenförmige Abtreppung des Hallendachs von Norden nach Süden ergaben sich etwa 4,50 m hohe Träger. Sie erreichen auf der Südseite der Halle eine Spannweite von über 49 m. Zwischen diesen Z-förmigen Deckenträgern liegen horizontale Lichtbänder, die der Halle im Zusammenwirken mit der Verglasung der hohen Nordwand einen einladenden, lichtdurchfluteten Charakter geben.

Das vollklimatisierte Hochhaus verfügt über 27 Personenaufzüge; ein elektronisches Steuerungssystem sorgt für geringstmögliche Wartezeiten.

1. Section through the banking hall and tower elevation.
2. In spite of its location in the heart of downtown Houston, the tower enjoys unobstructed views.

1. Schnitt durch die Bankhalle und Aufriß des Hochhauses.
2. Trotz seiner Lage inmitten des Stadtzentrums von Houston erfreut sich das Hochhaus unverbaubarer Ausblicke.

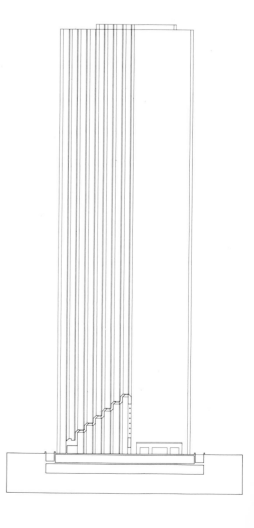

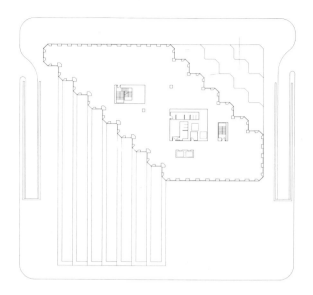

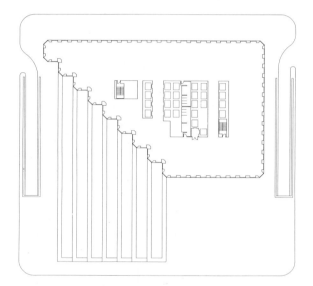

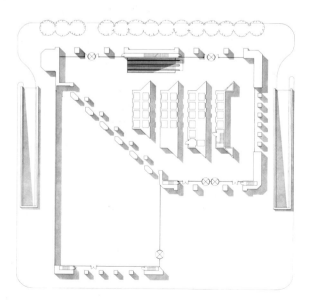

3. Plans (ground floor, typical floor, top floor).
4. The faceted angles of the tower's southeast wall reflect the intense southern sunlight in a very lively way.

3. Grundrisse (Erdgeschoß, Normalgeschoß, oberstes Geschoß).
4. Die kleinteilig abgewinkelten Flächen der Südostfassade des Hochhauses reflektieren in lebhafter Weise das intensive südliche Sonnenlicht.

60'

Tenneco Employee Center,
Houston, Texas

On a block across the street from the Tenneco Headquarters Building in downtown Houston, designed by SOM in 1963, is a seven-story parking garage. In 1980 and 1981 a two-story dining, recreational and training facility was added atop this garage structure.

For the exclusive use of Tenneco employees, the eighth and ninth floor addition contains a total of approximately 110,000 square feet. Facilities on the eighth floor incorporate a 500-seat employee cafeteria and a health facility including a 1/5 mile jogging track. Executive dining spaces and a training center are situated on the ninth floor. Dining areas open out onto a two-story park landscaped with full-height trees organized around a series of water fountains. There is also a smaller, more formal garden on the ninth floor, which similarly includes fountains and separates the main executive dining area from five private dining rooms. All garden areas have an inviting character created through the use of skylights. Designed to accommodate the client's request to provide a facility attractive to the employees, which would be in turn productive for the company, a great deal of attention was paid to the quality of the spaces: The dining facilities are competitive with, if not above the quality of nearby private clubs. The exercise facilities include Nautilus equipment, racquetball courts, aerobic studios, a jogging area, a sauna and whirlpools.

The exterior of the parking garage was remodeled and the metal cladding painted a color related to the Tenneco Building, resulting in visual compatibility as its backdrop. A steel-framed structure, enclosed by a small-scale window wall, was used for the additional floors. Surrounded by bronze anodized aluminum mullions, the reflective, insulated bronze glass contributes to energy conservation. Sunset red Texas granite was used as a paver, achieving further continuity with the Tenneco Building. This same granite, used throughout the interiors, serves as a basis for those color schemes.

Tenneco Employee Center,
Houston, Texas

Gegenüber dem 1963 von SOM in der Innenstadt von Houston errichteten Tenneco Building befindet sich auf einem quadratischen Grundstück mit etwa 75 m Seitenlänge eine siebengeschossige Hochgarage. In den Jahren 1980 und 1981 wurden auf dieses Garagengebäude zwei weitere Geschosse mit Einrichtungen für die Angestellten der Tenneco aufgesetzt.

Insgesamt wurde in den beiden neuen Obergeschossen eine Fläche von etwa 10.200 m² geschaffen. Im 8. Geschoß befinden sich eine Kantine mit 500 Plätzen und ein Fitneßzentrum mit einer außen umlaufenden Joggingbahn, während im 9. Geschoß Speiseräume für die Firmenleitung und ein Schulungszentrum entstanden. An der Nordwestseite öffnen sich die Speisesäle auf eine große doppelgeschossige Gartenhalle hin orientiert, die mit hohen Bäumen bepflanzt und durch Wasserbecken gegliedert ist. Im 9. Geschoß liegt zwischen dem Hauptspeiseraum der Firmenleitung und fünf kleineren Speiseräumen ein weiterer, kleinerer Gartenhof mit Wasserbecken. Oberlichtkonstruktionen geben den Gartenbereichen einen hellen, einladenden Charakter. Während im 8. Geschoß eine umlaufende doppelte Außenwandkonstruktion entstand (im Zwischenraum fand die Joggingbahn ihren Platz), liegt im 9. Geschoß ein Teil der Räume direkt an der Außenwand.

Die neuen Stockwerke wurden als Stahlkonstruktion mit kleinteiligen, weitgehend verglasten Fassaden ausgebildet. Im Rahmen der Bauarbeiten erhielten auch die Garagengeschosse eine geänderte, zum Verwaltungsgebäude der Tenneco passende Außenwandverkleidung aus Aluminiumelementen. Bronzefarben reflektierendes Isolierglas in bronzefarben anodisierten Aluminiumrahmen trägt zur Energieeinsparung bei. Im Erdgeschoß sowie in den Verkehrsbereichen und Eingangsräumen der neuen Obergeschosse wurde ein Bodenbelag aus dunkelrotem Granit gewählt; der Speisesaal der Firmenleitung erhielt einen Teppichboden.

1. Section.
2. The two-story garden on the eighth floor.

1. Schnitt.
2. Der zwei Geschosse hohe Garten auf dem 8. Geschoß.

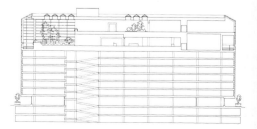

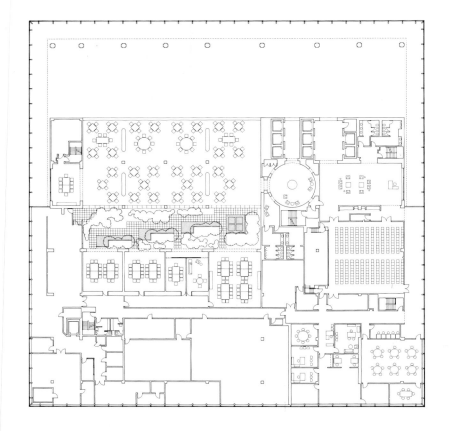

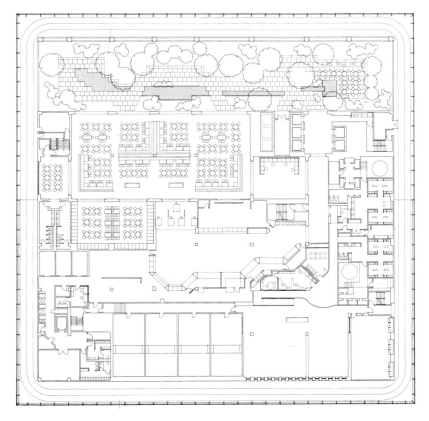

3. Plans (eighth floor, ninth floor).
4, 5. In order to provide a facility with exceptional attraction for the employees, a great deal of attention was paid to the quality of the spaces.

3. Grundrisse (8. Geschoß, 9. Geschoß).
4, 5. Um für die Mitarbeiter der Firma eine Erholungseinrichtung von besonderer Anziehungskraft zu schaffen, verwandten die Architekten große Aufmerksamkeit auf eine hohe Qualität der Innenraumgestaltung.

30'

Allied Bank Plaza,
Houston, Texas

The 71-story Allied Bank Plaza in downtown Houston, under construction since 1980, is directly adjacent to three other SOM buildings: the Tenneco Building to the east, One Shell Plaza to the north and First International Plaza to the south.

Allied Bank commands its own identity through its distinctive design, yet also complements and ties together its surroundings. By forcing the site west, SOM created a linear open space along Louisiana Street. East, across Smith Street, the scale of the downtown business district gives rise to Allied Bank – dramatizing its prominence.

The tower was conceived as a bundled tube, rising without setbacks, over a plan formed by two quarter-circles. A sequence of steel columns, set at 15-foot on center, follows the round and rectangular plan and is so effective structurally that no additional interior columns or bracing walls in the core section are required. The typical floor areas of 25,000 gross square feet allow flexible space planning.

Allied Bank is sheathed in a curtain wall of energy efficient, high insulating blue-green reflective glass. An overall grid of dark green vertical and horizontal mullions and vertical stainless steel window washing tracks at the column lines subtly express the structural system and give scale to the huge expanses of glass.

The main entrance to Allied Bank, on Louisiana Street, is connected to Houston's climate-controlled underground tunnel system at a large landscaped plaza area which features a fountain.

Allied Bank Plaza,
Houston, Texas

Die Innenstadt von Houston ist durch relativ kleine, quadratische Straßenblocks von nur etwa 75 m Seitenlänge gekennzeichnet. Auf einem dieser Blockgrundstücke im Mittelpunkt des Geschäftszentrums ist seit 1980 der 71geschossige Büroturm der Allied Bank im Bau. Das Straßengeviert ist auf den drei zur Innenstadt gelegenen Seiten von Hochhäusern umgeben, die ebenfalls von SOM geplant wurden: dem Tenneco Building im Osten, dem Gebäude One Shell Plaza im Norden und dem Gebäude First International Plaza im Süden.

SOM entwickelte ein Gebäude mit starker eigener Identität, das sich jedoch gleichzeitig in die städtebauliche Situation einfügt. Entlang der Louisiana Street nach Osten hin wurde ein fortlaufender Freiraum durch die Plätze vor den Hochhäusern geschaffen. An der gegenüberliegenden, westlichen Seite des Grundstücks, an der Smith Street, endet das Geschäftszentrum Houstons mit niedrigen öffentlichen Bauten, einer großen Grünfläche und Verkehrsanlagen, so daß der Ausblick nach dorthin nicht behindert ist.

Das Hochhaus ist eine stufenlos über die gesamte Höhe durchlaufende Konstruktion aus gebündelten Rohren, die im Grundriß aus zwei gegeneinander um eine Stützenachse versetzten Viertelkreisen besteht. Die Außenwände sind sowohl in ihren geraden als auch in ihren geschwungenen Teilen in einen Kranz von Stützen mit einem Achsabstand von etwa 4,60 aufgelöst. Das Konstruktionssystem ist so effektiv, daß auf zusätzliche Innenstützen in den Nutzflächenbereichen von jeweils etwa 2.300 m² Größe und auch auf Aussteifungswände im Kernbereich verzichtet werden konnte.

Das eindrucksvolle Tragwerk wird mit einer Vorhangwand aus dunklem, blaugrün reflektierendem Glas verkleidet. Ein Netz aus dunkelgrünen Glasrahmen sowie vor den Stützen verlaufende Fensterschienen aus rostfreiem Stahl deuten das dahinter liegende Konstruktionssystem an und gliedern die großen spiegelnden Glasflächen.

Ein Großteil der Besucher erreicht das Gebäude von dem klimatisierten unterirdischen Tunnelsystem aus, das in Houston im Aufbau begriffen ist und bereits 25 Blocks des Geschäftszentrums miteinander verbindet. Um die Eingangsplaza an der Louisiana Street mit dieser Ebene zu verflechten, wurde der Tunnelbereich hier nach oben hin geöffnet. Die Plaza soll gärtnerisch gestaltet und mit einem Brunnen ausgestattet werden.

1. View of the 71-story tower (model).
2. Plans (ground level, typical floor).

1. Ansicht des 71geschossigen Hochhauses (Modell).
2. Grundrisse (Erdgeschoßebene, Normalgeschoß).

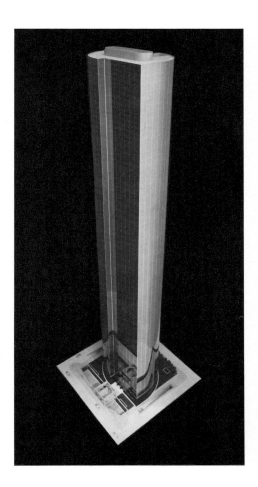

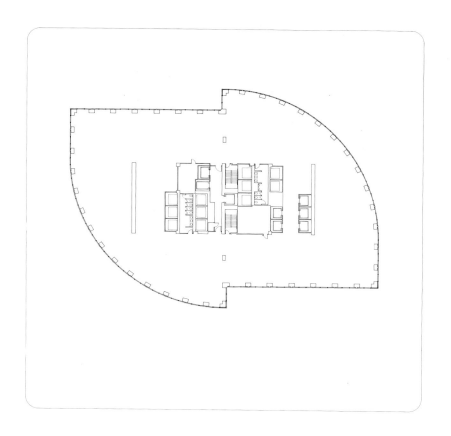

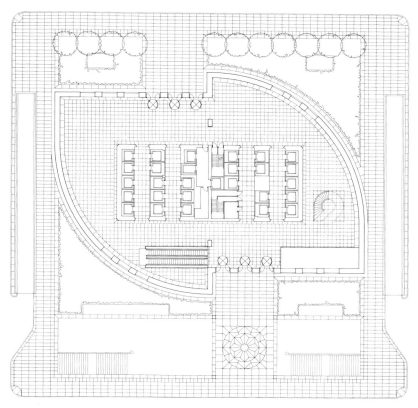

30'

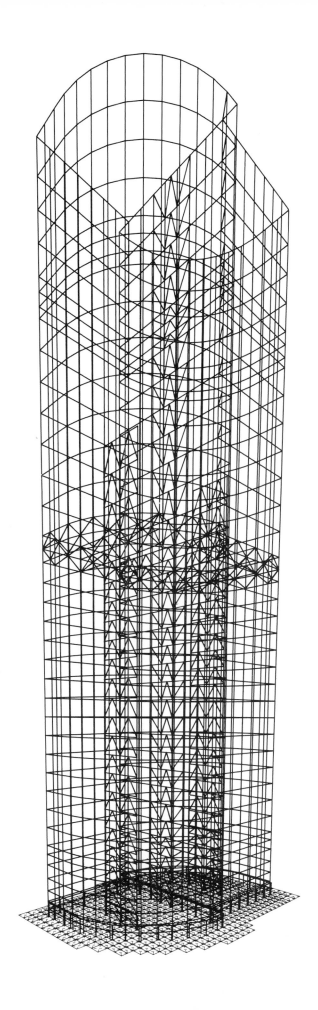

3. Computer drawing of the tower envelope.
4. Three SOM-designed towers on Houston's skyline: One Shell Plaza, Allied Bank Plaza and InterFirst Plaza (photomontage).

3. Computerzeichnung des Hochhausumrisses.
4. Drei von SOM entworfene Hochhäuser in der Stadtsilhouette von Houston: One Shell Plaza, Allied Bank Plaza und InterFirst Plaza (Photomontage).

Four Houston Center,
Houston, Texas

Four Houston Center will be located in downtown Houston, south of the city's present urban center. It is the fourth in a series of office towers which comprise the "Houston Center" project – an expanding mixed-use development of office buildings, hotels, retail and parking.

Four Houston Center is a 55-story tower reaching 860 feet in height. It is situated on a square site of approximately 62,500 square feet, bounded on four sides by streets. The tower is 155 feet square and rests symmetrically on a 250-foot square base. The base is one story in height and contains the tower entrance, retail space, executive parking, ramps to two basement parking levels, and building services at grade. The base is articulated by stepped granite planters and a pergola which encircles the tower and defines the edge of the terrace level. The main tower lobby is located at this terrace level – a condition which creates a strong visual and physical connection between both spaces. A mezzanine level will accommodate future bridge connections to adjacent properties.

The tower floor plan has a gross area of 24,025 square feet. An efficient 75-foot square core provides an open and flexible 40-foot lease span on all sides. 54 typical floors and one circular executive floor contain approximately 1,300,000 gross square feet.

The tower is a composite tube structure of steel and concrete ordered on a 15-foot module with a floor-to-floor dimension of 13 feet. The curtain wall consists of stainless steel and reflective glass. The wall clearly expresses the structural system in a taut graphic way, utilizing the reflective quality of the steel and glass to create a subtle and ever-changing image against the sky. A sloping stainless steel roof houses the mechanical equipment levels.

The conceptual development of Four Houston Center stemmed from the desire to establish a physical "point of order" in an otherwise undifferentiated context. The tripartite solution acknowledges the need for a strong base condition to respond to the activity of the street-level environment. The tower shaft accommodates the building's functional and programmatic requirements, and the development of the pyramidal roof satisfies the formal desire to resolve the tower form in a way which is consistent with the vocabulary of platonic geometries.

Four Houston Center,
Houston, Texas

Der 55geschossige, etwa 262 m hohe Büroturm wird auf einem etwa 5.800 m² großen, quadratischen Straßenblock am Rand des Geschäftszentrums von Houston in der Nachbarschaft einer Reihe isoliert stehender Hochhäuser errichtet.

Die Eingangshalle des Gebäudes liegt auf einer gegenüber dem Straßenniveau erhöhten Terrassenebene, die sich nahezu über das ganze Grundstück erstreckt und von einer über die Gehsteige auskragenden Pergola aus vorgefertigten Beton- und Holzelementen eingefaßt wird. Auf zwei Parkebenen unter dem Straßenniveau finden insgesamt 286 Wagen Platz. Die Straßenebene, die Terrassenebene und das als Mezzanin ausgebildete 1. Turmgeschoß nehmen eine Bankfiliale auf. Das Außenmaß des Turmes beträgt etwa 47 × 47 m. Da der ebenfalls quadratische Kern in der Mitte eine Seitenlänge von etwa 23 m hat, verbleibt eine umlaufende Nutztiefe von etwa 12 m, die stützenfrei und flexibel unterteilbar ist. Lediglich das oberste Geschoß unterhalb der Installationsanlagen, in dem die Direktion untergebracht wird, weicht von diesem Schema mit einem runden Grundriß ab. Die Bürogeschosse haben zusammen eine Bruttogeschoßfläche von etwa 121.000 m².

Die Vorhangwand aus reflektierendem Glas und rostfreiem Stahl ist in ihrer Gliederung ein klarer Ausdruck des Tragsystems, eine Rohrkonstruktion mit 1,50 m breiten Stützen, ebenso hohen Brüstungsträgern und etwa 3 m breiten Fensteröffnungen, die aus einem Stahlskelett mit Stahlbetonaussteifung besteht. Den oberen Abschluß des Turmes bildet ein pyramidenförmiges Dach aus rostfreiem Stahl.

Der Turm soll zu einem Orientierungspunkt unter weniger prominenten Nachbarn werden. Er zeichnet sich aus durch eine einfache, kristalline Form, die aus Funktion und Konstruktion gleichermaßen konsequent entwickelt wurde, und zugleich durch einen hohen Grad an Wirtschaftlichkeit.

1. Section.
2. View of the top of the tower (model). Mechanical equipment is contained under a pyramidal stainless steel roof.

1. Schnitt.
2. Ansicht der Spitze des Hochhauses (Modell). Die Technikräume sind unter einem pyramidenförmigen Dach mit einer Haut aus rostfreiem Stahl untergebracht.

3. Plans (ground level, fifth floor, typical floor, 55th floor).
4. Elevation.

3. Grundrisse (Erdgeschoßebene, 5. Geschoß, Normalgeschoß, 55. Geschoß).
4. Aufriß.

60'

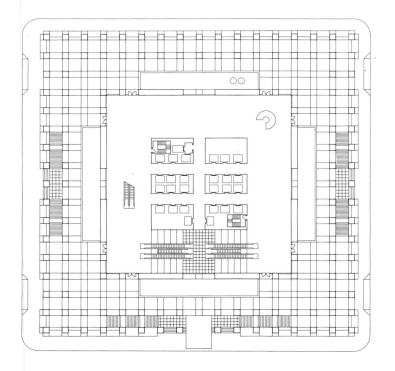

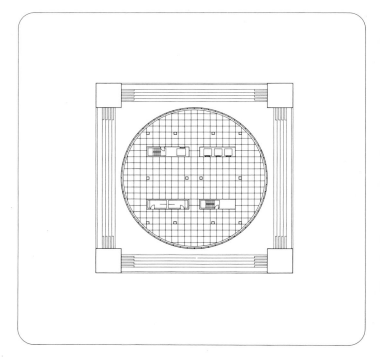

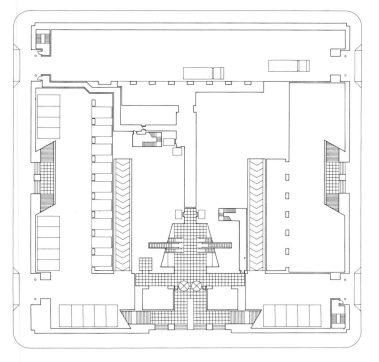

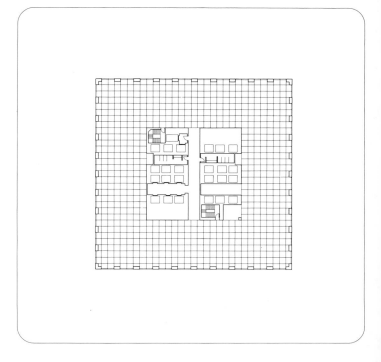

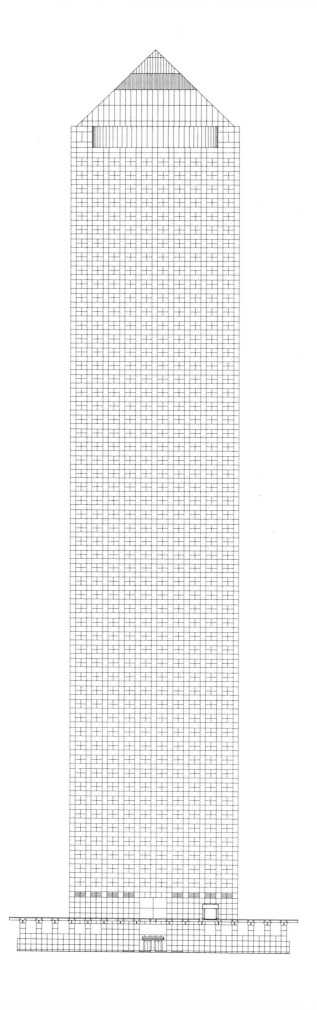

Campeau Tower,
Houston, Texas

The 80-story office tower for Campeau Corporation is located on the southern side of the central business district on a site affording it visual prominence in the Houston skyline. The tower is constructed in a composite system of rolled steel sections with a reinforced concrete cover. To accommodate high wind forces, a continuous tube at the perimeter of the building was selected as the most ideal structural concept.

The floor plan of the tower is developed essentially from a clear-span rectangular base. A series of open bays, which are an integral part of the structural system, project 45 degrees from the long sides in two different dimensions and rise to varying heights on the facade. The resulting plan accentuates the verticality of the design and provides a large number of desirable corner offices. Three different finishes of granite and reflective insulated glass in deep shades of rose combine with the different planes of the building, creating a constant interplay with sunlight on the exterior. The unique configuration at the top of the tower is formed by a sloped granite cap.

The main entrance on the west is accessible by way of a granite paved multi-level plaza with arcades of trees and a terraced water sculpture. The lobby will convey an individual spatial experience with its adjacent floor levels terraced off diagonally towards an eight-story atrium. This particular space is identified on the building exterior with a pattern of clear glass.

Below grade are two levels for parking and loading, as well as a lobby area which connects with Houston's pedestrian tunnel system. Retail lease space lines this concourse, which also links up to a 14-story parking garage serving the office tower. Retail space will occupy the tunnel and ground levels of this garage as well.

Two banks of six conventional elevators will provide access to the lower floors. Middle and upper level floors are served from the lobby and ground tunnel area by double-decker shuttles to two double skylobbies; one on the 39th and 40th floors and another on the 64th and 65th floors. From these skylobbies two banks of six each conventional local elevators provide service to the individual floors.

Campeau Tower,
Houston, Texas

Das 80geschossige Bürohochhaus der Campeau Corporation liegt an einer Stelle im südlichen Bereich des Geschäftszentrums von Houston, der in der Skyline dieser Stadt besondere Bedeutung zukommt; diesem Umstand wurde durch eine eigenständige, einprägsame Baugestalt Rechnung getragen. Als wirtschaftlichste Lösung für die Aufnahme der großen Windlasten des Turmes wurde eine Rohrkonstruktion aus Profilstahl mit Stahlbetonummantelung gewählt.

Der aus Aufteilungsgründen rechteckige Baukörper erhielt auf den Längsseiten Erker in zwei verschiedenen Größen, die unter einem Winkel von 45° aus der Fassade hervorspringen und auf verschiedenen Höhen enden. Zusätzlich sind in der Mitte der Schmalseiten drei Reihen von Erkern des kleineren Formates eingeschnitten. Die sich ergebende Grundrißfigur hat nicht nur den Vorteil einer Großzahl der begehrten Eckbüros mit Ausblick in mehrere Richtungen, sondern führte auch zu der beabsichtigten betont vertikalen Gebäudegliederung. Die vielfach gebrochenen Fassaden aus poliertem Granit in drei verschiedenen Oberflächen mit Öffnungen aus reflektierendem Isolierglas erzeugen ein ständig wechselndes Spiel des Lichtes auf dem Baukörper. Den oberen Abschluß des Gebäudes bildet eine pyramidenförmige Haube aus Granit.

Die Eingangshalle des Turmes erreicht man über eine mit Granitplatten belegte Plaza, die durch verschiedene Ebenen, Baumreihen und eine Wasserskulptur gegliedert ist. Auch die Eingangshalle erhielt als achtgeschossiges Atrium mit Diagonalabtreppung der anschließenden Geschoßebenen eine eigenwillige Form. Klarglas an den Fassaden setzt diesen Bereich vom übrigen Gebäude ab.

Unter dem Straßenniveau liegen zwei Geschosse für Anlieferung und Parken sowie eine Fußgängerzone, die Anschluß an Houstons unterirdisches Passagensystem hat. In dieser Zone sind Läden sowie der Zugang zu einer dem Büroturm angegliederten 14geschossigen Hochgarage untergebracht. Im Untergeschoß und Erdgeschoß des Garagenbaus befinden sich ebenfalls Läden.

Je sechs Normalaufzüge in zwei Blocks erschließen die unteren Geschosse des Turmes. Die mittleren und oberen Geschosse sind mit der Eingangshalle und der Tunnelebene durch doppelgeschossige Schnellaufzüge verbunden, die zu Umsteigehallen im 39. und 40. Geschoß sowie im 64. und 65. Geschoß führen. Von diesen Umsteigehallen aus geht es dann wiederum mit je sechs Normalaufzügen in zwei Blocks weiter.

1. Section.
2. One of the long sides of the building (model). The multi-faceted exterior, resulting from solar reflective glazing set flush into the cladding of polished granite in deep shades of rose, reflects Houston's intense sunlight.

1. Schnitt.
2. Eine der Längsseiten des Gebäudes (Modell). Die vielfach gebrochenen Fassaden aus poliertem Granit in dunklen Rosétönen mit bündig eingesetzten Scheiben aus reflektierendem Sonnenschutzglas reflektieren das intensive Sonnenlicht Houstons.

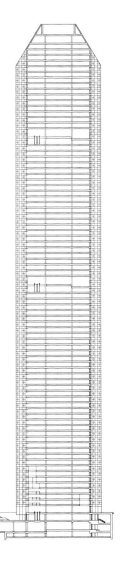

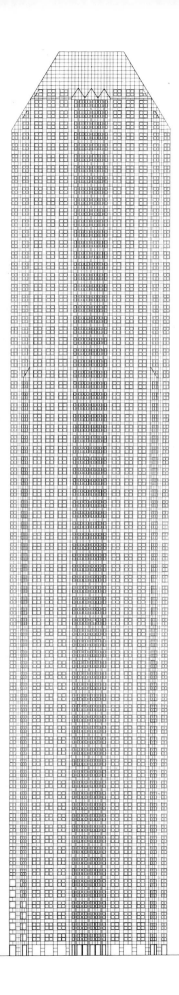

3. Elevation.
4. Plans (ground floor, typical floor).

3. Aufriß.
4. Grundrisse (Erdgeschoß, Normalgeschoß).

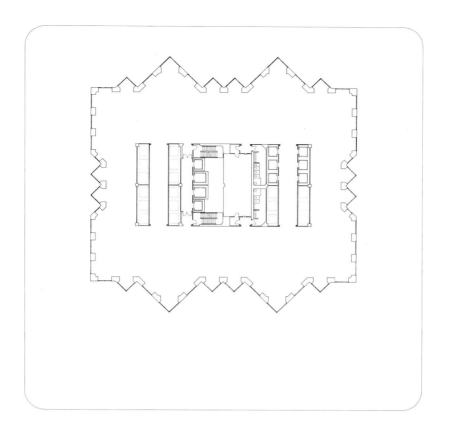

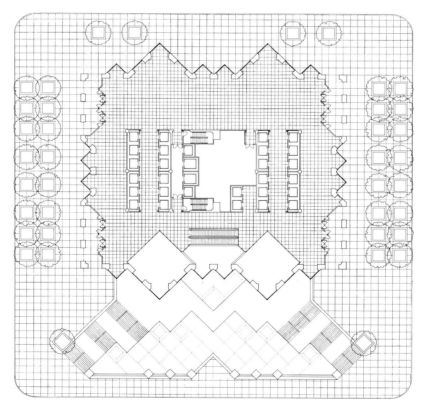

30'

Study on the
San Antonio River Corridor,
San Antonio, Texas

The San Antonio River is both the geographic and the spiritual heart of the 250-year old City of San Antonio, Texas. It flows through established residential neighborhoods as well as by historic buildings, including fragments of original Spanish settlements. 20 feet below street level, the river winds through a downtown which is the regional center for more than a million persons.

In 1972 and 1973 SOM, in joint venture with Marshall Kaplan Gans and Kahn, established a development program that used flood control improvements together with a variety of related public and private investments to make the river a catalyst for downtown revitalization. The total study area encompasses more than 3,000 acres surrounding a six-mile segment of the river. The plan develops specific policies and programs which treat the river as a unique and historic asset for residents and tourists, the downtown as a regional center with inner city neighborhoods, and an administrative body as a framework for both decision making and managing corridor revitalization.

At the regional scale, modifications to freeways and streets and other public transit recommendations make the central area more accessible. Because economic growth in the downtown is not unlimited, a principal recommendation at the project scale is to carefully locate new development so that it can maximize beneficial land uses and take advantage of the new river amenity and pedestrian environment.

Neighborhood revitalization is based on the introduction of new and rehabilitated housing in parallel with improvements in education and other inner-city community facilities. New high density sites and neighborhood centers are located in relation to inner landscape improvements. The newly landscaped river becomes an attraction for new residents and a gathering place for neighborhood services.

In order to insure that plan goals are implemented, a decision framework is developed which provides a recommended new agency, the Office of River Corridor Development, with a methodology for evaluating project proposals and accommodating citizen input. The greatest virtue of the plan is its ability to combine existing activities, historical assets and newly proposed open space and recreation areas.

Studie über den
San Antonio River Corridor,
San Antonio, Texas

Das geographische und städtebauliche Herz der 250 Jahre alten Stadt San Antonio in Texas ist der San Antonio River. An seinem Lauf liegen neben alten Wohnvierteln auch historisch bedeutende Bauten, darunter Reste von Siedlungen aus der spanischen Zeit. Schließlich durchquert der Fluß das innerstädtische Geschäftsviertel von San Antonio, das regionales Zentrum für mehr als eine Million Menschen ist.

In den Jahren 1972 und 1973 unternahm SOM in Zusammenarbeit mit Marshall Kaplan Gans and Kahn eine umfangreiche Untersuchung, in der Zielvorstellungen für die Umkehr der Verfallstendenzen im Bereich dieses Flußlaufs und des angrenzenden, etwa 1.200 ha großen innerstädtischen Gebietes entwickelt wurden. Ursprünglicher Anlaß für die Untersuchung war die Notwendigkeit, ein neues Hochwasserschutzsystem auf dem fast 10 km langen Flußabschnitt im Stadtgebiet zu bauen.

Neue Schnellstraßen sollen den starken Durchgangsverkehr – der zwei Drittel des Verkehrsaufkommens ausmacht – um das Stadtzentrum herumführen, während der Zielverkehr zu Parkplätzen an der Peripherie geleitet wird. Entlang dem Flußufer sollen anstelle von Parkplätzen neue Bürobauten entstehen. Der historische Stadtkern soll durch Fußwegverbindungen mit der Uferpromenade und durch Restaurierung historischer Gebäude aufgewertet werden.

In den Wohnvierteln am Flußkorridor leben heute vorwiegend Alte und Familien mit niedrigen Einkommen in überalterten Mietwohnungen. Die Untersuchung sieht sowohl eine Verbesserung der Wohnbedingungen für diesen Bevölkerungsteil als auch die Ansiedlung von wohlhabenderen Schichten vor. Läden und Kleingewerbe sowie Parks und Erholungseinrichtungen sollen das Umfeld der neuen Wohnbereiche bilden. An einigen Stellen ist auch an die Einrichtung von Nachbarschaftszentren mit Gesundheits- und Sozialdiensten gedacht.

Eine ganze Reihe von Organisationen und Behörden wird ihre Arbeit bei der Durchführung der in der Studie vorgeschlagenen Maßnahmen miteinander koordinieren müssen. Insbesondere geht es darum, Entscheidungsverfahren für die in der Studie vorgeschlagenen Alternativen zu entwickeln und Wege zu finden, die Bevölkerung an den Entscheidungen zu beteiligen. In ihrer Untersuchung haben die Architekten abschließend auch hierzu Anregungen gegeben.

1. Regional plan. Key: 1 San Antonio River Corridor study area.
2. The "dream" plan which summarizes the study's goals for rehabilitation of the river and 3,000 acres of land that surround it. Key: 1 flood control, 2 open space/recreation, 3 access, 4 CBD retail, 5 CBD office, 6 visitor services, 7 internal circulation, 8 housing.

1. Regionalplan. Legende: 1 Bereich der Studie über den San Antonio River Corridor.
2. Der »Idealplan«, in dem die Ziele der Untersuchung zur Wiederbelebung des Flusses und von etwa 1200 ha Fläche in seiner unmittelbaren Umgebung zusammengefaßt sind. Legende: 1 Hochwasserregulierung, 2 Freiräume und Erholungsbereiche, 3 Zufahrten, 4 innerstädtisches Einkaufsviertel, 5 innerstädtisches Büroviertel, 6 Einrichtungen für Besucher, 7 innere Erschließung, 8 Wohnanlagen.

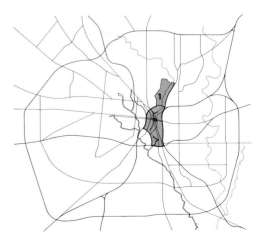

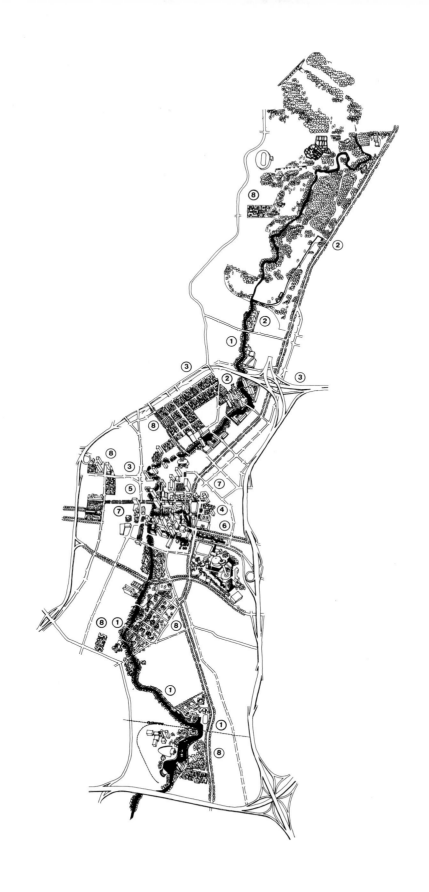

Lone Star Gardens

Roosevelt Park

bike path

promenade

ROOSEVELT LANDING

section 1

3. River sections. The natural potential and resources provided by the existing river will be put to use to transform the environment as a place of recreation and a site for attractive urban housing.
4. The plan of the environmental form which shows the impact of existing features on the plan.

3. Schnitte durch das Flußprofil. Das Potential und die Möglichkeiten, die der Fluß bietet, sollen zur Umwandlung des Gebietes in einen Ort der Erholung und des attraktiven städtischen Wohnens nutzbar gemacht werden.
4. Plan der Umweltbedingungen, aus dem der Einfluß der bestehenden Gegebenheiten auf den Entwurf hervorgeht.

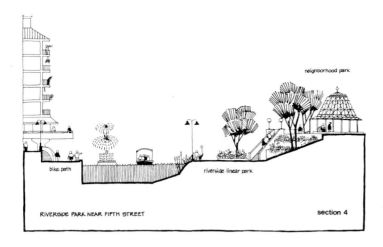

neighborhood park

bike path

riverside linear park

RIVERSIDE PARK NEAR FIFTH STREET

section 4

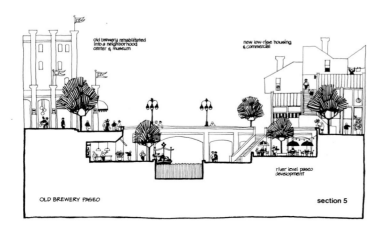

old brewery rehabilitated into a neighborhood center & museum

new low-rise housing & commercial

river level paseo development

OLD BREWERY PASEO

section 5

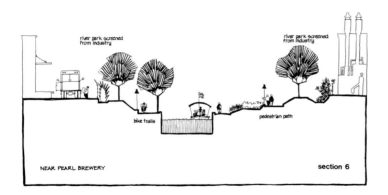

river park screened from industry

river park screened from industry

bike trails

pedestrian path

NEAR PEARL BREWERY

section 6

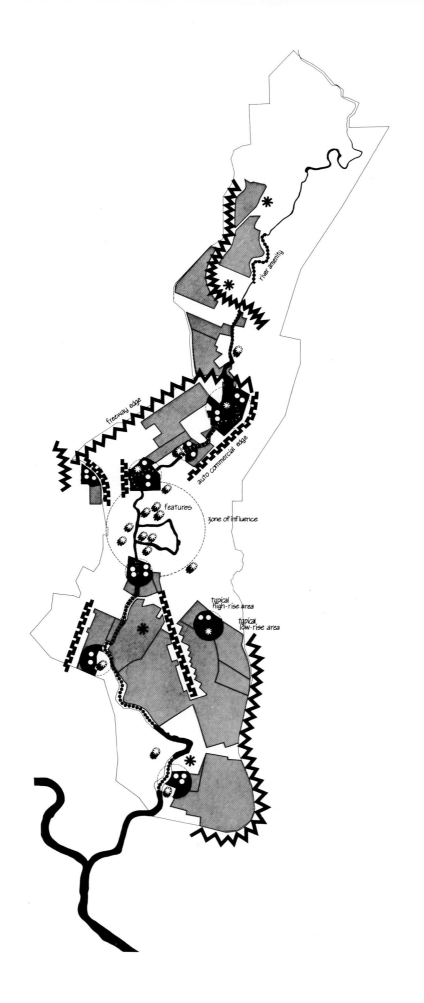

river amenity

freeway edge

auto commercial edge

features

zone of influence

typical
high-rise area

typical
low-rise area

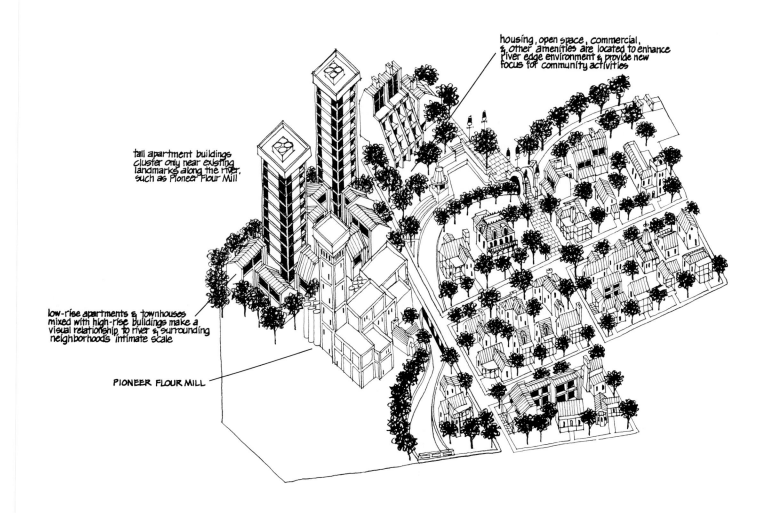

housing, open space, commercial, & other amenities are located to enhance river edge environment & provide new focus for community activities

tall apartment buildings cluster only near existing landmarks along the river, such as Pioneer Flour Mill

low-rise apartments & townhouses mixed with high-rise buildings make a visual relationship to river & surrounding neighborhoods intimate scale

PIONEER FLOUR MILL

5. Highrise housing design criteria.

5. Entwurfsrichtlinien für Wohnhochhäuser.

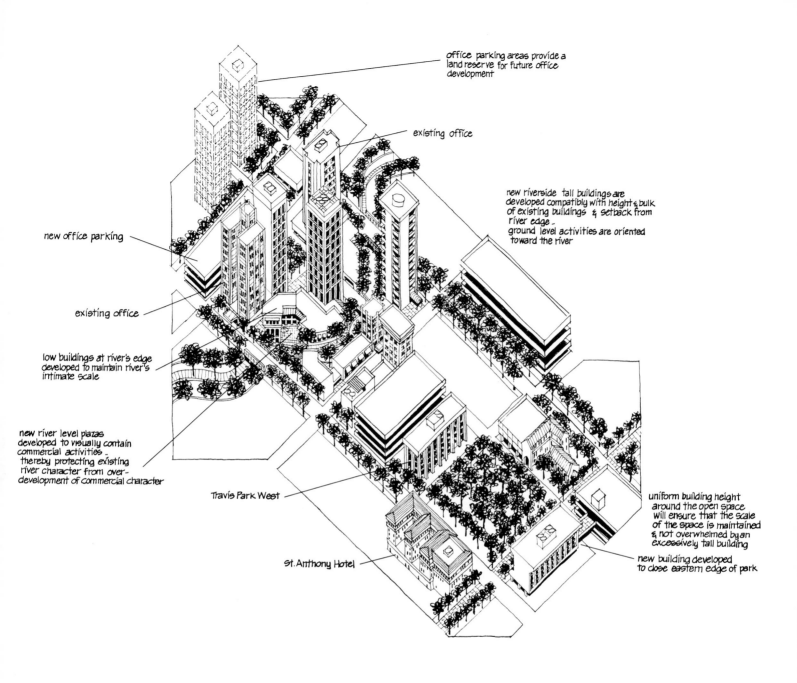

office parking areas provide a land reserve for future office development

existing office

new office parking

new riverside tall buildings are developed compatibly with height & bulk of existing buildings & setback from river edge. ground level activities are oriented toward the river

existing office

low buildings at river's edge developed to maintain river's intimate scale

new river level plazas developed to visually contain commercial activities _ thereby protecting existing river character from over-development of commercial character

Travis Park West

St. Anthony Hotel

uniform building height around the open space will ensure that the scale of the space is maintained & not overwhelmed by an excessively tall building

new building developed to close eastern edge of park

6. Downtown office district design criteria.

6. Entwurfsrichtlinien für das innerstädtische Büro-hausviertel.

Headquarters of the
Gulf Mineral Resources Company,
Denver, Colorado

The new corporate headquarters for the Gulf Mineral Resources Company (GMRC) is located on 26 acres in southeast Denver. Scheduled for completion in 1983, the first phase includes 230,000 square feet of space, with subsequent phases ultimately providing a total of 830,000 square feet. The site, located adjacent to a major vehicular corridor, slopes gently to the northwest, affording a clear view of Long's Peak, one of Colorado's tallest mountains.
In a modular building configuration, space is distributed among seven units which vary in height between two and three floors. This concept provides a sense of individual identity for each of GMRC's separate divisions, as well as flexibility for future organizational changes or expansion. Centrally located common areas include administrative, conference, and food service facilities. In contrast to an open office layout, the GMRC headquarters is planned primarily for private offices.
Precast concrete panels and clear glass are set between the building's precast structural frames. The northeast and southwest elevations are opaque, while the transparent, double skin envelopes on the southeast and northwest facades provide a prime element of energy conservation. In the winter, warm air is collected within the envelope space and circulated to the colder northwest facade through the insulated precast concrete tees which make up the structural system. In the summer, the envelope is ventilated to dissipate excess heat. Louvers between the skins are designed to alternately reflect or absorb heat.
Daylighting, the primary light source, is provided by either exterior windows or skylit interior atria, placing each work space within a maximum of 20 feet from a window wall. To further reduce the total energy consumption, a computerized system is used to sense natural light levels and adjust supplementary artificial lighting to operate only as needed.
A circular drive in the large central courtyard loads to the main public entrance of the complex. Visitors park beneath a canopy of trees along the drive's circumference and walk through the tree-planted courtyard to the entry. The reception area is glazed towards a planted terrace in a southeast courtyard.

Hauptsitz der
Gulf Mineral Resources Company,
Denver, Colorado

Die Hauptverwaltung der Gulf Mineral Resources Company wird zur Zeit auf einem etwa 10,5 ha großen, nach Nordwesten leicht abfallenden Grundstück im Südosten von Denver errichtet. Von dem Gelände bietet sich ein weiter Blick bis hin zum Long's Peak, einem der höchsten Berge Colorados. Die Fertigstellung des 1. Bauabschnitts mit etwa 21.400 m² Nutzfläche ist für 1983 vorgesehen; im Endausbau werden etwa 77.200 m² zur Verfügung stehen.
Auf der Grundlage einer streng geordneten Gliederung brachten die Architekten das Programm des 1. Bauabschnitts in sieben zwei- bis dreigeschossigen Einheiten unter. Diese Konzeption fördert die Identifikation der Mitarbeiter mit ihrer jeweiligen Abteilung und begünstigt zudem Erweiterungen sowie interne Veränderungen. In Querrichtung wird die im Gebäudeverlauf um zwei Geschosse nach Südosten zu entsprechend dem Geländeverlauf abgestaffelte Baugruppe von drei breiten Erschließungsschienen durchzogen, die nach Nordwesten zu erweitert werden können. In zentraler Lage sind die Verwaltung, Besprechungsräume und die Kantine angeordnet. In diesen Kontaktzonen liegen auch alle notwendigen Treppen, Aufzüge und Sanitärräume. Im Unterschied zu den meisten neueren amerikanischen Bürobauten wurden die Arbeitsplätze vorwiegend in Einzelbüros untergebracht.
Die Anlage hat ein Tragsystem aus vorgefertigten Stahlbetonelementen; die Außenwände bestehen aus ebenfalls vorgefertigten Sichtbetonplatten und ungetöntem Glas. Während die Nordost- und Südwestfassaden geschlossen sind, wurden die Südost- und Nordwestfassaden größtenteils verglast, wobei man zur Energieeinsparung zwei Scheiben hintereinander anordnete. Zwischen den beiden Scheiben sind verstellbare Jalousien angebracht, die je nach Bedarf die Sonnenstrahlen reflektieren oder absorbieren. Im Winter wird Warmluft aus den Zwischenräumen an den Südostfassaden durch Kanäle in der Stahlbetonkonstruktion an die kältere Nordwestseite geführt. Im Sommer wird der Zwischenraum entlüftet, so daß die überschüssige Wärme entweichen kann. Durch ein Computersystem wird die Beleuchtung der Helligkeit des Tageslichts entsprechend gesteuert und jeweils nur nach Bedarf zugeschaltet.
Der Haupteingang liegt an einem großen quadratischen Platz. Dessen Mitte wird von einem baumumstandenen Wendeplatz mit einigen Besucherparkplätzen eingenommen, von dem aus man unter den Bäumen hindurch zur Eingangshalle gelangt, die sich nach Südosten auf einen großen Innenhof hin öffnet.

1. Southeast view of one of the office modules (model).
2. Site plan.

1. Südostansicht einer der Büroeinheiten (Modell).
2. Lageplan.

120'

3. Plan (main floor).

3. Grundriß (Hauptgeschoß).

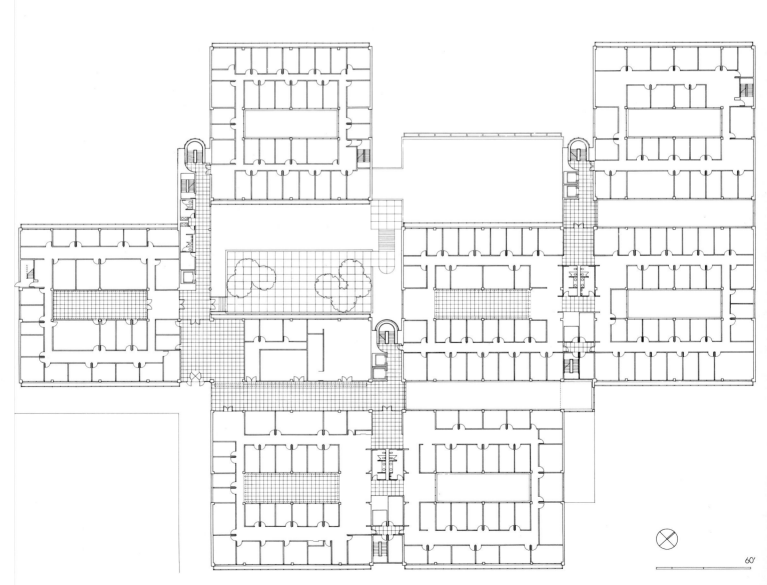

60'

224

4. General view from the east (model). The "seam" spaces between the building modules are marked by rounded stairtowers.

4. Gesamtansicht von Osten (Modell). Die »Naht«-Zonen zwischen den Büroeinheiten werden durch abgerundete Treppentürme betont.

2

4

Die Ostküste

Anfang 1982 gewann die Kreuzung der Park Avenue mit der 52nd und der 53rd Street beträchtlich an Weite und Licht. Das in Blockmitte gelegene Gebäude Park Avenue Plaza [2] setzte für die Park Avenue einen neuen Maßstab. Der als Spekulationsobjekt für die Fisher Brothers errichtete 44geschossige Büroturm konnte einige Geschosse höher werden als üblicherweise erlaubt, weil eine von Straße zu Straße reichende witterungsgeschützte Fußgängerplaza eingerichtet wurde. Dank der starken Nachfrage nach Büroraum im Zentrum von Manhattan war das Gebäude rasch vermietet. Bemerkenswerterweise ist der Bau aber auch in seiner formalen Gestaltung ein Erfolg. Die Sockelzone reicht so hoch wie das Gesims des Gebäudes des Racquet and Tennis Club; die Abschrägung im Osten ist zum Seagram Building hin orientiert; in der reflektierenden Fassade spiegelt sich das Lever House. Über diese Reverenzen vor bedeutenden Nachbarbauten hinaus hat der Entwurfsarchitekt von Park Avenue Plaza, Raul de Armas vom SOM-Büro in New York, einen neuen Blickpunkt etwas abseits der Park Avenue geschaffen, durch den der Straßenraum optisch erweitert wird.

Das gelungene Zusammenspiel zwischen dem Hochhaus Park Avenue Plaza und dem Gebäude des New York Racquet and Tennis Club lenkt die Aufmerksamkeit in dramatischer Weise auf nahezu ein Jahrhundert Architekturgeschichte in Manhattan, in dem sich die Entwicklung von der Bildwelt der Renaissance bei McKim, Mead & White hin zu den modernen Formen des Lever House von SOM [3] vollzog. Zu diesem Wandlungsprozeß trugen viele Architekten bei, aber der kreativste und klarste Verfechter einer modernen städtischen Firmenarchitektur war Gordon Bunshaft vom New Yorker SOM-Büro, der Entwurfsarchitekt des Lever House. Es ist offensichtlich, daß Bunshaft, der sich 1979 zur Ruhe setzte, mit seinem Sinn für großangelegten Maßstab und verfeinerte Details einen großen Einfluß auf die jungen New Yorker Partner Gordon Wildermuth, Donald Smith, Raul de Armas und Michael McCarthy ausübte. McCarthy entwarf für die Regierung des Kuwait die hervorragende Gesandtschaft in Washington, D.C., wo sich Präzision, formales Können und Eleganz in der besten Tradition von SOM vereinen.

Während der drei Jahrzehnte, die zwischen dem Lever House und dem Gebäude Park Avenue Plaza liegen, war es keineswegs sicher, daß die Städte im Nordosten der USA ihre Vitalität wiedergewinnen würden. SOM's Hochhaus One Liberty Plaza für die U.S. Steel wurde zwar in der Nähe der Wall Street erbaut, aber viele landesweit tätige Industriefirmen verließen gleichzeitig New York. Zu einer Zeit, als bedeutende Banken ins mittlere Manhattan zogen, stellte es eine außergewöhnliche Entscheidung dar, daß die Chase Manhattan

3

5

The East Coast

In early Spring 1982, the intersection of Park Avenue with 52nd and 53rd Streets gained new expanse and light. The midblock Park Avenue Plaza [2] set 45-degree angles to Manhattan's orthogonal grid and gave Park Avenue a different scale. A speculative investment by Fisher Brothers, the 44-story tower gained a few extra stories by providing a block-wide enclosed plaza and was quickly leased in a strong market for midtown office space close to Grand Central Station and corporate headquarters. Remarkably, the Plaza is also a successful aesthetic form. Its base strikes the Racquet Club's cornice; its eastern chamfer squares with the Seagram Tower; notches in its four-bay half chamfers resolve dualities; and its reflectivities receive Lever House. Beyond those acknowledgments to important neighbors, the Plaza's designer, SOM/New York's Raul de Armas, created a new lateral focus, broadening Park Avenue's corridor. Handsomely faceted, the Plaza's deformations denote a perimetal tubular frame and central columnar core. Neither structural nor mechanical expression mars its glistening, bevelled surfaces which end at the skyline without cornice or transition save the jagged silhouette of the crystal itself.

The happy congruence of Park Avenue Plaza and the New York Racquet and Tennis Club dramatizes nearly a century of Manhattan's architectural history, which turned from McKim, Mead & White's Renaissance imagery to the modern forms of SOM's Lever House [3]. The transformation was owed to many architects, but the seminal and purest advocate of modern urban corporate architecture was SOM/New York's Gordon Bunshaft, designer of Lever House. His 1954 Manufacturers Hanover Trust Building on Fifth Avenue at 43rd Street and his 1960 PepsiCola Building at 500 Park Avenue, corner of 59th Street, are glazed pavilions notable for fine proportions and refined detail. His Beinecke Library at Yale University is much more than an exhibition of translucent marble held in a precast concrete frame: its siting and cubic, angular silhouette wed it to the Gothic Revival and Beaux Arts buildings bordering its plaza. Retired in 1979, Bunshaft instilled his sense of dramatic scale and refined detail on younger partners Gordon Wildermuth, Donald Smith, Raul de Armas and Michael McCarthy. For the government of Kuwait, McCarthy drew the exquisite Kuwait Chancery in Washington, D.C., where precision, formality and elegance stand in SOM's best tradition.

During the three decades between Lever House and Park Avenue Plaza, it was not certain that America's northeastern cities would regain vitality. SOM's One Liberty Plaza for U.S. Steel was built near Wall Street, but many national manufacturing companies fled New York City. The Chase Manhattan Bank's decision to build SOM's building [4] downtown

229

10

Bank sich ihre Hauptverwaltung [4] von SOM im unteren Teil von Manhattan bauen ließ. Als 1982 der Manufacturers Hanover Trust das von der Union Carbide aufgegebene Gebäude an der Park Avenue [5] kaufte, kam man für den Umbau des Ende der fünfziger Jahre von Bunshaft entworfenen Gebäudes auf SOM zurück.

Im Verlauf der siebziger Jahre beschleunigte sich die Verlagerung in die Vororte und auf das Land; dahinter stand die Vorliebe älterer Manager für Hauptverwaltungen inmitten von Wiesen und Wäldern sowie in der Nähe von Schnellstraßen und kleinen Flughäfen. Derartige Firmenhauptverwaltungen auf dem Land hatte SOM in den sechziger Jahren für Emhart Manufacturing [6], Armstrong Cork, Reynolds Metal und American Can [7] gebaut. In den siebziger Jahren plante SOM für General Electric eine Gruppe von zwei Bürogebäuden auf einem steil abfallenden Grundstück am Merritt Parkway in Fairfield, Connecticut [8]. Außerdem erhielt Westinghouse einen Neubau als Aushängeschild für die bestehende Fabrikanlage, und Texaco kam zu einer Hauptverwaltung [9], die wegen ihrer sonnigen Lage und ihrer Baumgärten einmalig ist.

Bevor es den Städten im Osten der USA gelang, die Stadtflucht aufzuhalten, galt es eine Reihe von innerstädtischen Problemen zu lösen – insbesondere die des Verkehrs. In einem Gutachten des SOM-Büros in Boston wurde dem Gouverneur von Massachusetts empfohlen, Pläne für eine achtspurige Autobahn unter dem Hafen von Boston aufzugeben und statt dessen nur einen zweispurigen Straßentunnel für Busse und Mietwagen als Verbindung zwischen Boston und dem Logan Airport sowie den wachsenden Siedlungen im Norden zu bauen. Unter der Leitung des Partners Peter Hopkinson plante das Bostoner SOM-Büro den Trailways Bus Terminal in Boston [10] sowie den Umbau der U-Bahn-Station am Harvard Square in Cambridge [11]. Gleichzeitig befaßte sich das Büro in Washington mit dem Eisenbahnnetz des Verkehrskorridors im Nordosten der USA [12]. Der von der Bundesregierung erteilte umfangreiche Untersuchungsauftrag wurde unter Leitung des Partners David Childs bearbeitet. An der South Station in Boston kam es zu einer Verlegung der Gleisanlagen, die nun an der neuen Empfangshalle in dem restaurierten und wiederhergestellten alten Kopfbahnhof [13] enden. Die Stadt Providence erhielt nach Begradigung einer zu Verzögerungen führenden Gleiskurve ein neues Bahnhofsgebäude [14], dessen Kuppel mit dem nahe gelegenen Staatskapitol von Charles F. McKim korrespondiert. Die Bahnhöfe in New London, New Haven und Newark wurden renoviert, und der alte Bahnhof in Wilmington [15] – den Frank Furness entworfen hatte – erhielt einen neuen Innenraum und einen Vorplatz.

Während sich in den USA der Erfolg, den kanadische Städte mit der Anregung geschäftlicher Investitionen im Umkreis von innerstädtischen Eisenbahnstationen hatten, bisher nicht

12

11

10. Trailways Bus Terminal, Boston, Massachusetts.
11. Harvard Square Station, Cambridge, Massachusetts.
12. Northeast Corridor with Boston – Washington railway line.
13. Boston South Station, Boston, Massachusetts.
14. Providence Station, Providence, Rhode Island.
15. Wilmington Station, Wilmington, Delaware.
16. Vista International Hotel, New York, New York.

13

15

14

was exceptional at a time when major banks were moving midtown. In 1982, Manufacturers Hanover Trust bought the Park Avenue headquarters Union Carbide [5] vacated, and SOM was recalled to remodel the building it had designed in the late 1950's.

Accelerating throughout the 1970's, the drive to suburban and rural locations was led by senior officers' preference for having their headquarters on meadow and forested land near highways and small airports. In the 1960's, SOM had designed rural headquarters for Emhart Manufacturing [6], Armstrong Cork, Reynolds Metal, and American Can [7]. Now, in the 1970's, SOM gave General Electric a pair of buildings on a steep site bordering the Merritt Parkway in Fairfield, Connecticut [8]. Westinghouse received a frontispiece for its existing factories, and Texaco gained a headquarters [9] that is exemplary for its insolation and arboreal gardens.

Before eastern cities could reverse the exodus, several urban problems had to be overcome, beginning with transportation. Guided by SOM/Boston, Massachusetts' Governor was advised to abandon plans for an eight-lane road beneath Boston's Harbor and, instead, to tunnel only a two-lane road to connect buses and limousines from Boston to Logan Airport and the growing northern communities. The study also urged that money intended for an eight-mile road completing circumferential 495 should be diverted to Boston's subway and surface transit. Led by Boston partner Peter Hopkinson, SOM/Boston designed Boston's Trailways Bus Terminal [10] and redesigned the congested BMTA station at Cambridge's Harvard Square [11].

Meanwhile SOM/Washington studied the rail lines in the Northeast Corridor [12]. Still wary of waterways, Americans kept an unrequited faith in railroads, and the Federal Government now sponsored an extensive study led by SOM/Washington partner David Childs. Boston's South Station [13] would see its tracks redirected to arrive at a new concourse embraced by the restored and reconstructed old headhouse. Providence, with its delaying curve straightened, would gain a new station [14] with a low dome echoing Charles F. McKim's nearby State capitol. The stations at New London, New Haven and Newark were to be remodelled, and Wilmington's old station [15], which the fanciful Frank Furness had designed, would be given a new interior and plaza. Each step was encumbered, but the improvements encouraged hope for greater rail use.

While American downtown railroad stations did not yet confirm Canadian cities' success in generating commercial investment, American cities' major subway interchanges did attract such development. Near New York's World Trade Center, the first modern hotel in New York's financial district, the Vista Hotel [16] by SOM/New York partners Donald Smith and Leon Moed, opened in 1982 at the Cen-

16

17

18

19

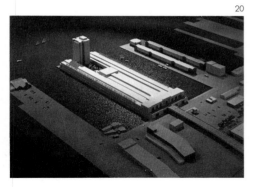

20

21

22

wiederholte, entwickelten sich hier die größeren U-Bahn-Umsteigestationen zu Anziehungspunkten für geschäftliche Aktivitäten. An der südwestlichen Ecke des New Yorker World Trade Center wurde 1982 das erste moderne Hotel im Bankenviertel der Stadt, das von dem Partner Donald Smith aus dem New Yorker SOM-Büro entworfene Vista Hotel [16], eröffnet. An der Kreuzung der G Street mit der 12th und der 13th Street im Geschäftsviertel von Washington profitierte das Metro Center [17] von einer sofort einsetzenden – und auch schon vorhergesagten – Nachfrage nach Mietflächen.

Ein hervorstechendes Merkmal des Metro Center ist die gekonnte Gegenüberstellung von alt und neu. In ähnlicher Weise gestaltete das Büro in Washington ein Bürogebäude mit terrassenartigen Abtreppungen über den Fassaden von Wohnhäusern beim Projekt 1777 F Street [18]. Beim Metropolitan Square [19] wurden zwei Gebäude im Beaux-Arts-Stil, das Keith Albee Theater und die National Metropolitan Bank, mit einem neuen Baukomplex verbunden und mit dem bestehenden Garfinkle's Department Store zu einer Anlage von der Größe eines Straßengevierts, das von einem zentralen, mit Glas überdachten Atrium durchdrungen wird, zusammengefaßt. Die Planung des Büros in Boston für den Commonwealth Pier V sieht auf der einen Hälfte dieser Landungsbrücke die Wiederherstellung der bestehenden Gebäude vor, während die andere Hälfte für ein neues Bürogebäude und ein Hotel freigemacht werden soll [20]. Bei dem ebenfalls in Boston, auf einem unregelmäßig geschnittenen Areal in der Nähe der Faneuil Hall und des Old State House gelegenen Hochhaus Sixty State Street [21] des Chicagoer SOM-Büros blieben 60 Prozent des Grundstücks einer öffentlichen Plaza vorbehalten. Außerdem wurden die verstellten Ausblicke auf die Faneuil Hall und das Old State House wiederhergestellt.

Solche historischen und räumlichen Bezüge sind heute häufig, aber Miami bildet hier eine Ausnahme. Mit dem an der Brickell Avenue vom New Yorker Büro errichteten Interterra Building [22] wurde – ähnlich wie auch bei dem vom Büro in San Francisco geplanten Southeast Financial Center [23] – versucht, eine neue Form zu schaffen. Das von dem Partner Donald Smith entworfene Gebäude vereinigt an einem baumbestandenen Boulevard Büros mit Läden, Wohnungen und Gartenanlagen. Das von Edward Bassett entworfene Southeast Financial Center besteht aus zwei Bauteilen, die durch eine freitragende, verglaste Dachkonstruktion miteinander verbunden sind. Auf Grund der kaskadenartig vorspringenden Fensterfelder des Hochhauses entstehen Eckbüros mit Orientierung nach Südosten zum Bay Front Park und nach Key Biscayne hin.

Oftmals bestimmte eine Vielzahl von Einflüssen die Gebäudeform. Beschränkungen in der Grundflächenzahl und der Geschoßflächenzahl führten in Manhattan dazu, daß das 1973

23

25

24

ter's southwest corner. At the juncture of G Street with 12th and 13th Streets in Washington's retail district, Metro Center [17] started an immediate and predicted demand for rental space. Seeing that opportunity, developer Oliver T. Carr, Jr. retained SOM/Washington to plan three blocks along G Street. Reminiscent of Washington's classical buildings, Childs' proposal envisages sympathetic bays and inflections and achieves remarkable urban open space.

One of several exceptional features in Metro Center is its skillful juxtaposition of the new with the old and preserved. Similarly, SOM/Washington terraced an office building over the one-bay deep facades of houses at 1777 F Street [18]. In Metropolitan Square [19], two Beaux Arts buildings, the Keith Albee Theater and the National Metropolitan Bank, were engaged into a new building and joined with the existing Garfinkle's Department Store, the resulting complex filling a city block punctuated by SOM's central glass-covered atrium. In Boston, SOM/Boston's plan for Commonwealth Pier V [20] restores buildings on half the pier, while the other half is to be cleared for an office building and hotel. Again in Boston, SOM/Chicago's tall Sixty State Street [21] on the irregular site near Faneuil Hall and the Old State House reserves sixty percent of its site for a plaza and restores the previously closed vistas to Faneuil Hall and the Old State House.

Such historic and spatial references were seldom absent. Miami was exceptional. On Brickell Avenue, SOM/New York's Interterra Building [22], like SOM/San Francisco's Southeast Financial Center [23], attempts to establish a new form. Designed by New York partner Donald Smith, the Interterra Building introduces landscape, shops and apartments in an office building on a tree-lined boulevard that has been rapidly disfigured by disparate buildings and empty plazas. Southeast Financial Center, designed by SOM/San Francisco partner Bassett, is meant to be seen in the round, two buildings connected by a glazed canopy; the tower's cascade of bays creates southeastern corner offices facing Bay Front Park and Key Biscayne.

More often, a medley of influences affected buildings' form. In Manhattan, limitations on land coverage and floor area ratios suggested that 9 West 57th Street [24], completed in 1973, take shape as a swoop-curved slab, devote 30 percent of its midblock site to a plaza, and cover only 40 percent of its site from its nineteenth floor upwards, expressed in a thin slab with exposed steel windbracing. A variant is the 50-story 780 Third Avenue [25], between 48th and 49th Streets, expected to be completed in 1983. Its concrete tube rises from only 40 percent of its site, resulting in a tall slender tower whose diagonal windbracing is expressed in granite wall patterns. In Atlanta, the Georgia-Pacific Center [26], completed in 1982, acknowledges Margaret Mitchell

17. Metro Center, Washington, D.C.
18. 1777 F Street, Washington, D.C.
19. Metropolitan Square, Washington, D.C.
20. Plan for Commonwealth Pier V, Boston, Massachusetts.
21. Sixty State Street, Boston, Massachusetts.
22. Interterra Building, Miami, Florida.
23. Southeast Financial Center, Miami, Florida.
24. 9 West 57th Street, New York, New York.
25. 780 Third Avenue, New York, New York.

26

fertiggestellte Gebäude 9 West 57th Street [24] eine sich nach oben verjüngende Form erhielt und daß 30 Prozent des in Blockmitte gelegenen Grundstücks als öffentliche Plaza gestaltet wurden. Eine Variante dieser Bauform ist das 50geschossige Gebäude 780 Third Avenue [25], das zwischen der 48th und der 49th Street liegt. Die schlanke, hohe Stahlbetonrohrkonstruktion erhebt sich auf einer Fläche, die nur 40 Prozent des Baugrunds einnimmt, so daß sich ein ungemein gestreckter Turm ergab, dessen diagonale Windversteifungen in den mit Granit verkleideten Fassaden ablesbar sind. Die Baumasse des 1982 in Atlanta fertiggestellten Georgia-Pacific Center [26] nimmt Rücksicht auf den Margaret Mitchell Square und betont die Bedeutung der Kreuzung der Peachtree Street mit der Houston Street. Zu den besonders geglückten Beispielen der Verdichtung derartiger formaler Determinanten zu einem zwingend erscheinenden Entwurf gehört das im unteren Manhattan, nördlich des World Trade Center gelegene Irving Trust Operations Center [27] des New Yorker Büros. Auf einem trapezförmigen Grundstück, das sich über zwei Straßenblocks erstreckt, verwandelte der Partner Raul de Armas die früher in der Mitte gelegene Straße in ein gebäudehohes, zwei Bauteile verbindendes Atrium. Die ganze Anlage faßte de Armas in einer niedrigen Baumasse zusammen, die sich durch Kompaktheit, sparsamen Energieverbrauch und natürliche Belichtung auszeichnet.

Die Arbeiten von SOM im Osten der Vereinigten Staaten offenbaren ein außergewöhnliches Geschick bei dem Bemühen, Charakter und Lebensfähigkeit heruntergekommener innerstädtischer Viertel zu stärken. An zwei besonderen Beispielen in Washington wird deutlich, mit welchem Können, welcher Einfachheit und Zurückhaltung David Childs und Walter Arensberg, beide Partner im Büro in Washington, vorgehen. Das Büro stellte für die Zweihundertjahrfeiern der USA 1976 die Achse der Mall – der zentralen Grünanlage am Kapitol – wieder her [28]; es verbannte dabei den Kraftfahrzeugverkehr vom Washington Drive und vom Adams Drive, schuf einen Baldachin aus Ulmen, richtete Fußwege ein und säumte diese mit einer passenden Straßenmöblierung. Anschließend plante das Büro auf einer Fläche von etwa 21 Hektar zwischen dem Spiegelteich und der Constitution Avenue die Constitution Gardens [29]. Sanft abfallende Rasenflächen, schattenspendende Bäume, ein etwa 2,5 Hektar großer See und gewundene Fußwege wurden so angeordnet, daß die Blickbeziehungen zum Lincoln Memorial und zum Washington Monument unterstrichen werden. So betont diese Parkanlage – die mit sicherer Hand in der klassischen Tradition des Landschaftsgartens geschaffen wurde – die Würde und Bedeutung dieser großen Denkmäler der amerikanischen Geschichte.

26. Georgia-Pacific Center, Atlanta, Georgia.
27. Irving Trust Operations Center,
New York, New York.
28. The Mall, Washington, D.C.
29. Constitution Gardens, Washington, D.C.

27

28

29

Square and accents the intersection of Peach-tree and Houston Streets. When such formal determinants converge in a design that seems inevitable, architects exult in their confluence. Such is the happy air surrounding SOM/New York's Irving Trust Operations Center [27], located in lower Manhattan north of the World Trade Center. The trapezoidal site, combining of two city blocks, conversion of the intervening street into an atrium, and joining of two separate buildings, one for Irving Trust's operations, the other for rental offices, were resolved by SOM/New York partner Raul de Armas within a low cube that boasts compactness, energy efficiency, natural light, and a dramatic conclusion to urban vistas.

SOM's work in the eastern United States displays exceptional talent in strengthening the character and performance of worn urban areas. Two special examples in Washington reveal the skill, simplicity and restraint exercised by SOM/Washington partners David Childs and Walter Arensberg. For the Bicentennial, SOM/Washington restored the Mall's central axis [28], removed automobiles from Washington and Adams Drives, planted elm canopies, made pedestrian paths, and bordered them with appropriate furnishings. Thereafter, SOM/Washington created Constitution Gardens [29] on the 52 acres between the Reflecting Pool and Constitution Avenue. Gently sloped meadows, shade trees, and a six-acre lake, all connected by meandering paths, are arranged to accent views towards the Lincoln Memorial and Washington Monument. Those great monuments of American history are dignified and dramatized by the Gardens, which were modestly and surely developed in the classical tradition of natural landscape.

Park Avenue Plaza,
New York, New York

Park Avenue Plaza, situated behind the New York Racquet and Tennis Club in the heart of the city, was completed in 1981. Forty-one office floors totaling approximately 25,000 square feet each surmount a 30-foot-high interior plaza with a retail area and mezzanine lobby.

Because of the building's 1,000,000-square-foot volume, it was designed to respond sensitively to its urban setting, specifically the adjacent McKim, Mead & White Racquet Club and the nearby Lever House and Mies van der Rohe's Seagram Building. This was accomplished in a number of ways: an angled geometric shape with chamfered corners and notched sides minimizes the building's bulk and recedes from the Racquet Club; tinted green glass sheathing with silvery mullions reflects the sky, relates to neighboring Park Avenue facades, and relieves the weight of the tower; the traditional street wall is maintained in a base which is flush with adjacent buildings; and the base of the tower continues the cornice line of the Racquet Club. An initial scheme distributed the volume at three levels to correspond with the heights of surrounding buildings. However, modifications in the client's program called for maximum floor area to be built for each story.

Soaring glass walls frame the indoor plaza, creating a feeling of light, air and spaciousness. Beyond the revolving glass doors, three-story high columns clad in stainless steel, and green polished marble walls define an enormous skylighted through-block public space enhanced by a 50-foot-wide waterfall, greenery, tables and chairs, and a pair of green painted glass kitchen kiosks serving restaurant patrons. This through-block arcade provides more amenities than the zoning resolution requires. The smaller shopping arcade recalls the intimacy of a variety of shops along narrow European streets. A sense of natural light is created overhead while the merchandise is spotlighted at eye level in the rounded bay windows. The shops relate to the public space through the continuous use of similar materials and details, such as clear and very dark tinted green glass, stainless steel and polished bronze. Escalators transport tenants and visitors from the street level to the lobby mezzanine where they board tower elevators. This area has been carefully planned to assure both unity of design and maximum security.

Park Avenue Plaza,
New York, New York

Der 1981 fertiggestellte Komplex liegt auf einem etwa 0,36 ha großen Grundstück hinter dem 1918 von McKim, Mead & White errichteten fünfgeschossigen New York Racquet and Tennis Club im Zentrum der Stadt. Er umfaßt einen Turm mit 41 Bürogeschossen und eine etwa 9 m hohe überdachte Plaza mit Läden, die einen ganzen Straßenblock einnimmt.

Trotz einer Gesamtgeschoßfläche von über 90.000 m² gelang den Architekten eine gute Anpassung des Komplexes an die Nachbarbauten, unter denen neben dem Racquet and Tennis Club das Lever House und Mies van der Rohes Seagram Building die prominentesten sind.

An den seitlichen Straßen wurde die anschließende Randbebauung in Höhe des Clubgebäudes bündig durchgezogen. Die Form des sich darüber erhebenden Büroturms, in dem etwa 4.000 Arbeitsplätze untergebracht sind, ist so gestaltet, daß die insgesamt etwa 175 m hohe Baumasse sehr schlank und leicht erscheint und von der Park Avenue aus hinter das Clubgebäude zurücktritt. Einkerbungen, die über die ganze Bauhöhe durchlaufen, kennzeichnen die beiden Straßeneingänge zur Plaza. Die Grundrißform ergab in jedem der etwa 2.300 m² großen Turmgeschosse zwölf der begehrten Eckbüros mit Ausblick nach mehreren Seiten über das Stadtpanorama von New York. Zur bestmöglichen Raumnutzung wurden die Stützen auf den Kernbereich und die Außenwände konzentriert, so daß flexibel aufteilbare Flächen von etwa 14 m Tiefe entstanden. Die Fassaden aus grün getöntem Sonnenschutzglas und einem gleichmäßigen Netz schlanker, silberfarbener Sprossen nehmen Bezug auf die Hochhausfassaden an der Park Avenue und geben dem Bau einen eleganten und leichten Ausdruck.

Die mit Bäumen bepflanzte Plaza hat eine Höhe von drei Bürogeschossen und erhält im Bereich der Brandwand zum alten Clubgebäude Tageslicht von oben. Durch vollflächige Klarglasfronten zu den beiden Seitenstraßen hin ergibt sich ein großzügiger, heller Eindruck. Über Rolltreppen erreicht man auf einem Halbgeschoß in der Halle die Aufzüge zu den Bürogeschossen. In Materialwahl und Raumgliederung wurde Einheitlichkeit mit der für eine öffentliche Halle erforderlichen Übersichtlichkeit und Zweckmäßigkeit verbunden. Unter dem Oberlicht wurde ein etwa 15 m breiter Wasserfall angelegt, um den sich Pflanzenkübel, Tische und Stühle sowie Imbißkiosks gruppieren.

1. Elevation.
2. View of the office tower across Park Avenue. The new building sensitively respects its urban context with an angled geometry and a reflecting curtain wall minimizing the building's bulk.

1. Aufriß.
2. Ansicht des Büroturms über die Park Avenue hinweg. Der neue Bau fügt sich mit seiner abgewinkelten Grundrißform und seiner reflektierenden Vorhangwand, die die Baumasse kleiner erscheinen läßt, rücksichtsvoll in den vorgegebenen städtebaulichen Rahmen ein.

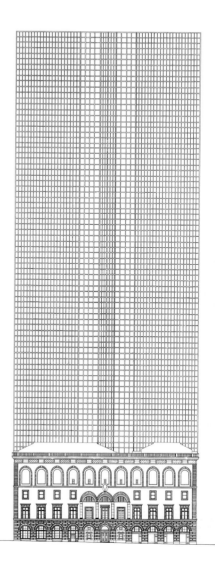

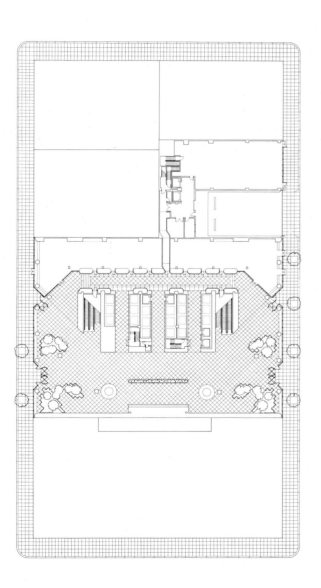

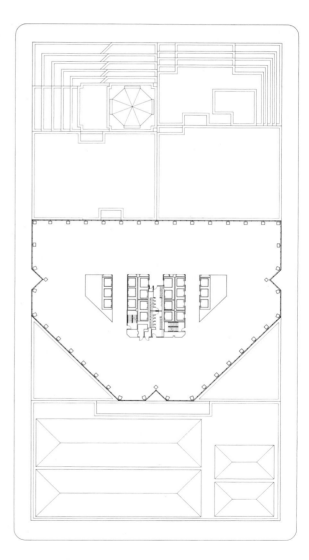

3. Plans (ground floor, typical floor).

3. Grundrisse (Erdgeschoß, Normalgeschoß).

30'

4. View of the indoor plaza.

4. Ansicht der überdachten Plaza.

Irving Trust Operations Center,
New York, New York

The design of the Irving Trust Company's operations center in New York City evolved from a response to the site, special Washington Street Urban Renewal District requirements, and programmatic needs of the bank. The two-acre site is located two blocks from the World Trade Center in lower Manhattan's densely built and populated financial district. A portion of Washington Street was closed, combining two city blocks into a trapezoidal plot.

The closed street became the footprint for a 60-foot-wide atrium which divides the structure into 23- and 16-story sections. Floors 17 through 23 in the 1,156,000-square-foot building will be leased until Irving Trust requires the additional floors for expansion. The steel frame structure, to be completed in 1983, is enclosed entirely with 6-foot by 4-foot glass panels. A polychromatic, ribboned effect is created by the use of three different types of glass. Partially reflective and clear vision glass bands wrap the building between white opaque glass spandrel panels. The partially reflective glass permits light to enter without glare, and therefore is positioned above the transparent, or vision, glass, set at eye level. Secondary light enters the atrium and penetrates interior glazed walls, so that an employee is never more than 45 feet from natural light and a view. The atrium also conserves energy, as one-third of the perimeter of the floor space is not subjected to the sun's direct heat, thereby reducing the air-conditioning load on adjacent office space.

Due to the technical nature of an operations center, virtually every desk can be equipped with a cathode-ray terminal. Because employees will spend a large portion of their day working on machines, the management felt it was necessary to provide space for employee interaction and relaxation. A landscaped cafeteria and lounge area will overlook the atrium from the top floor of the 16-story section beneath long span sloping steel trusses with clerestory windows.

Irving Trust Operations Center,
New York, New York

Die 1983 fertiggestellte Betriebszentrale der Irving Trust Company liegt am nördlichen Ende des Finanzviertels von Lower Manhattan, zwei Straßenblocks vom World Trade Center entfernt. Auf der Südwestecke des Grundstücks, das zum Sanierungsgebiet der Washington Street gehört, fanden die Architekten einen Altbau vor, der erhalten werden mußte. Um das verbleibende Grundstück sinnvoll mit einem kompakten Gebäude auf einem dem Quadrat angenäherten Grundriß nutzen zu können, wurde die von Norden nach Süden verlaufende Washington Street in diesem Bereich aufgehoben.

Ein etwa 18 m breites, durchgehendes Atrium in der Achse der Washington Street teilt die Anlage, die eine Bruttogeschoßfläche von etwa 107.500 m² umfaßt, in einen 23geschossigen und einen 16-geschossigen Block. Vom 17. Geschoß an aufwärts wurden Mietbüros vorgesehen, die bei Bedarf später vom Bauherrn übernommen werden können.

Ein frei stehender, monolithischer Turm im nördlichen Bereich des Atriums, der mit den Bürogeschossen durch Brücken verbunden ist, nimmt Aufzugsblocks und Vertikalschächte auf. Westlich und östlich dieses Turmes sind in den Bürogeschossen daher nur kleinere Kernelemente notwendig, so daß große, zusammenhängende Nutzflächenzonen zur Verfügung stehen.

Das Dach, das die beiden Bauteile verbindet, ist in Geschoßsprüngen nach Osten zu abgetreppt und verglast. Es überdeckt oberhalb des 16geschossigen Blocks eine große begrünte Halle mit Kantine, in der die geneigte Stahlfachwerkdachkonstruktion sichtbar gelassen wurde. Diese Halle öffnet sich auf ihrer vier Geschosse hohen Innenseite zu dem Atrium, das als witterungsgeschützter Innenraum sowohl zur Energieeinsparung beiträgt – indem die Klimaanlagen entlastet werden – als auch zusätzliche natürliche Belichtung für die angrenzenden Raumbereiche schafft. Da die Innenwände des Atriums verglast wurden, ist kein Büroarbeitsplatz weiter als 14 m von einem Fenster mit Ausblick entfernt.

Die aus etwa 1,80 × 1,20 m großen Glastafeln bestehende Vorhangwand teilt die Fassade geschoßweise in vier umlaufende Höhenbänder. Die Bänder, die im Bereich der Brüstungen und der Deckenkonstruktion liegen, sind mit undurchsichtigem weißen Glas geschlossen. Auf Sichthöhe wurde Klarglas verwendet, darüber reflektierendes Glas. Die Fassadenseiten des Atriums sind – bis auf undurchsichtige Streifen in Höhe der Bürogeschoßdecken – durchgehend mit transparenten Scheiben derselben Größe wie in den Büroblöcken verglast. Dadurch werden die beiden Bauteile optisch zu einer einheitlichen Baumasse zusammengefaßt.

1. General view from the southeast (model).
2. Section.

1. Gesamtansicht von Südosten (Modell).
2. Schnitt.

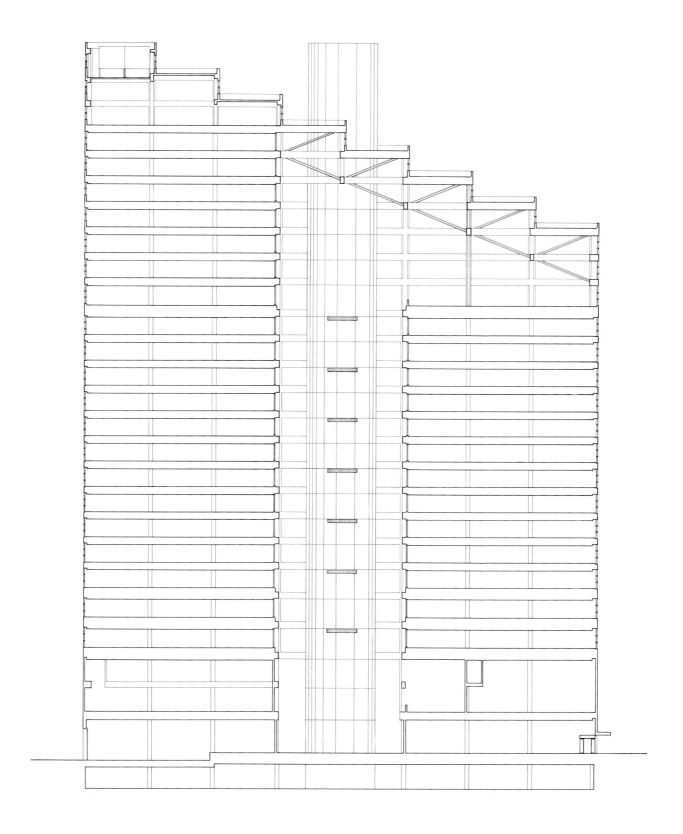

241

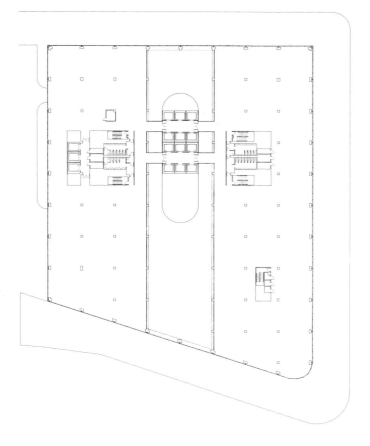

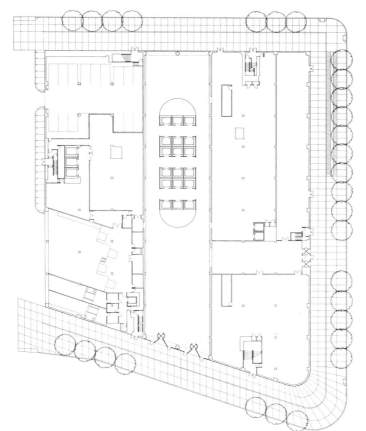

3. Plans (ground floor, typical floor).
4. View of the cafeteria and lounge area (model).

3. Grundrisse (Erdgeschoß, Normalgeschoß).
4. Blick in die Kantine und den Erholungsbereich.

30'

780 Third Avenue,
New York, New York

A 50-story commercial office tower, 780 Third Avenue is currently under construction between 48th and 49th Streets in Manhattan. The 470,000-square-foot tower, occupying a 22,092-square-foot site, is scheduled for completion in 1983.

Due to the building's unusual height-to-slenderness ratio, a concrete tube system was selected. The structure is braced diagonally and distributes the wind load equally among perimeter columns. The pattern of alternating red polished granite panels and grey-tinted insulating glass windows reveals the structural system. The interiors, as a result, are column-free and will provide flexible tenant space.

The design of the rectangular tower is in part a response to the New York City zoning resolution, which, prior to its amendment in 1982, allowed a building occupying 40 percent of its site to maximize the allowable floor area ratio. This stipulation permitted the design of a tall, slender tower – the floor plate is only 8,836 square feet, while the tower is over 550 feet tall.

At ground level, the plaza will be landscaped with trees, fountains, lights, and benches.

780 Third Avenue,
New York, New York

In einem besonders dicht bebauten Teil Manhattans an der Third Avenue zwischen der 48th und der 49th Street war ein Hochhaus mit Mietbüros zu planen. Die Architekten machten sich eine Bauvorschrift der Stadt New York zunutze, die einem Gebäude, dessen Grundfläche nicht mehr als 40% des Baugrundstücks einnimmt, eine maximale Geschoßflächenzahl zubilligt. Auf dem engen Grundstück ergab sich damit ein außergewöhnlich schlanker, 50geschossiger Turm mit etwa 43.700 m² Geschoßfläche. Bei einer Gebäudehöhe von über 167 m beträgt die Fläche eines Geschosses nur etwa 820 m².

Um diese Proportionen konstruktiv auf wirtschaftliche Weise zu bewältigen, wurde das Tragwerk als Betonrohr mit in die Rohrhülle integrierten, hinter den geschlossenen Fensterfeldern liegenden Diagonalgliedern ausgebildet. Die Grundrißfläche mit aus der Mitte gerücktem Kern blieb stützenfrei und ist flexibel unterteilbar. Das 1983 fertiggestellte Gebäude erhielt eine bündige Verkleidung aus poliertem, rotem Granit mit Öffnungen aus grau getöntem Isolierglas.

Auf Straßenniveau wurde eine mit Bäumen bepflanzte Plaza angelegt, die durch Brunnenanlagen, Beleuchtung und Sitzgelegenheiten eine städtische Ruhezone bildet.

1. The building in its urban context (photomontage).
2. Elevations (east, north, west, south).
3. Plan (typical floor).

1. Das Gebäude in seinem städtebaulichen Kontext (Photomontage).
2. Aufrisse (Ost, Nord, West, Süd).
3. Grundriß (Normalgeschoß).

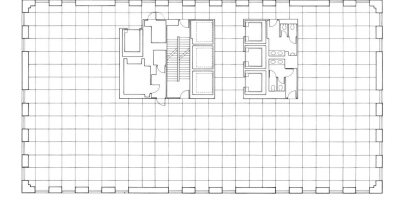

15'

Headquarters of
Alexander & Alexander,
New York, New York

The headquarters of this major insurance company occupies one floor in the Celanese Building on the Avenue of the Americas in midtown Manhattan. This interior design project, totalling 35,000 square feet, was completed in 1978. When Alexander & Alexander considered the decor of its corporate offices, the desire was to create a warm, personal environment for employees, clients and visitors. Art was considered crucial in achieving this, thus leading to the selection of nearly 100 separate pieces of art from around the world. On display in hallways, galleries, offices and rooms are works from America, Africa, India, China and other countries. The common idea in the selection of pieces was that most were created by people for actual use in their daily lives.
The Chairman of the Board's executive office is finished with teak floors and floor-to-ceiling lacquered screens at the windows. The interior walls are covered with handwoven linen framed in bronze. A mid-nineteenth century Kashmir shawl is the focal work of art. A contemporary desk with marble top and bronze base is positioned near an antique Oriental rug.
The bog oak conference table in the room adjacent to the president's office is trimmed with bronze blades and surrounded by eight chairs upholstered in suede. The floor is teak and the walls are of teak veneer and bronze-trimmed, handwoven linen. The artwork is highlighted by a lone star Mennonite quilt and a Chinese junk circa 1825-1850.
The executive dining room is a mixture of old and new. The glass and polished bronze dining table is flanked by twelve Queen Anne chairs. An unusual collection of artwork includes a red lacquer Thai teak bull and Yoruba twin figures. On one wall, again covered with handwoven linen, hang fifteen ceremonial weapons from the South Seas.

Hauptverwaltung der Firma
Alexander & Alexander,
New York, New York

Die Hauptverwaltung der Versicherungsgesellschaft Alexander & Alexander nimmt ein Geschoß mit etwa 3.300 m² Fläche im Celanese Building an der Avenue of the Americas im mittleren Manhattan ein. Die Einrichtung erfolgte 1978. Der Bauherr wollte seinen Mitarbeitern, Kunden und Besuchern eine einladende, individuelle Atmosphäre vermitteln, wozu ihm die Ausgestaltung der Räume mit Kunstwerken als ein besonders geeignetes Mittel erschien. So wurden in den Fluren, Warteräumen, Büros und Besprechungsräumen nahezu 100 Kunstwerke aus Amerika, Afrika, Indien, China und anderen Ländern ausgestellt. Der verbindende Leitgedanke bei ihrer Auswahl war, daß sie meist von Menschen für ihren unmittelbaren Gebrauch im täglichen Leben geschaffen worden sind.
Das Büro des Präsidenten der Gesellschaft erhielt einen Teakholzboden und als Sonnenschutz geschoßhohe, hochglanzlackierte Holzgitter anstelle von Vorhängen. Die Wandflächen sind mit handgewebtem Leinen bespannt und von Bronzewinkeln eingefaßt. Ein Schal aus Kaschmir, hergestellt in der Mitte des 19. Jahrhunderts, bildet den Blickpunkt dieses Raumes. Neben einem alten Orientteppich wurde ein moderner Schreibtisch mit einer Platte aus Marmor und einem Sockel aus Bronze aufgestellt.
Der Konferenztisch aus Mooreiche in dem Raum neben dem Büro des Präsidenten wurde mit Blattbronze beschlagen; die zugehörigen acht Stühle erhielten eine Wildlederpolsterung. Auch hier ist der Boden aus Teakholz. Die Wände haben ein Teakholzfurnier oder eine Bespannung aus handgewebtem Leinen, die auch hier mit Bronzewinkeln gefaßt wurde. Besonders ins Auge fallen in diesem Raum eine mennonitische Steppdecke und das Modell einer chinesischen Dschunke aus der ersten Hälfte des 19. Jahrhunderts.
Im Speiseraum der Firmenleitung wurden neue und alte Stilelemente miteinander vermischt. Der neue Eßtisch besteht aus Glas und polierter Bronze, die zwölf Sessel sind Originale im Queen-Anne-Stil. Zu den hier präsentierten Kunstwerken gehören neben einem rotlackierten thailändischen Bullen aus Teakholz und zwei Figuren der Yoruba fünfzehn an der Wand hängende Zeremonialwaffen aus der Südsee.

1. Plan.
2. Reception area.
3. President's office.
4. Executive dining room.

1. Grundriß.
2. Empfangsbereich.
3. Büro des Präsidenten der Gesellschaft.
4. Speiseraum für die leitenden Mitarbeiter.

30'

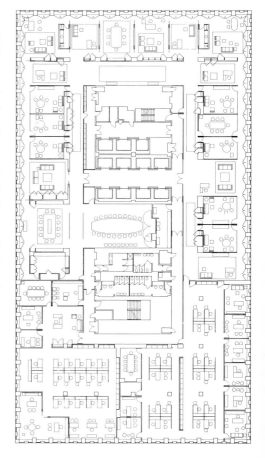

Headquarters of the
Continental Grain Company,
New York, New York

Since their move to midtown Manhattan in 1975, the Continental Grain Company headquarters has occupied 117,039 square feet on the 8th, 35th, and 48th through 50th floors of 277 Park Avenue. Perimeter offices on the typical floors vary from 10 feet by 15 feet, 15 feet by 15 feet to 15 feet by 20 feet. Each office affords a wide view of the city as well as a view of the interior reception gallery through floor-to-ceiling glass partitions. The executive 50th floor has nine offices, three conference rooms, a boardroom and an executive dining room.
Careful attention was given to the selection of materials, textures and colors. The floors are travertine, the core wall is covered in sisal trimmed in polished bronze, and the boardroom and dining room are enclosed in bronze tinted glass. Lacquered wood sun screens were chosen rather than conventional drapery. The elevator and office doors and structural columns are polished bronze and a polished bronze spiral staircase leads from the main reception area to the floor below. Works of art have been generously used to complement an atmosphere of subtle luxury. Modern etchings, aquatints, lithographs, and serigraphs, as well as paintings in oil and acrylic, tapestries and both primitive and modern sculptures are on view.

Hauptverwaltung der
Continental Grain Company,
New York, New York

Im Jahr 1975 bezog die Continental Grain Company das 8., 35., 48., 49. und 50. Geschoß mit einer Gesamtfläche von etwa 10.900 m² im Gebäude 277 Park Avenue im mittleren Manhattan. Die Größen der Einzelbüros entlang der Außenwände reichen von etwa 3,05 × 4,60 m über etwa 4,60 × 4,60 m bis etwa 4,60 × 6,10 m. Sie bieten einen weiten Blick über die Stadt; zugleich sind sie durch geschoßhohe Glastrennwände optisch mit den inneren Empfangszonen verbunden. Im 50. Geschoß ist die Firmenleitung mit neun Büroräumen, drei Besprechungsräumen, einem Konferenzsaal und einem Speiseraum untergebracht.
Größte Sorgfalt wurde der Materialwahl, der Oberflächenbehandlung und der Abstimmung der Farben gewidmet. Der Bodenbelag besteht aus Travertinplatten; die Wände des Kernbereichs wurden mit Sisal bespannt und die Kanten durch Winkel aus polierter Bronze gefaßt; der Konferenzsaal und der Speiseraum erhielten Trennwände aus bronzefarben getöntem Glas. Als Sonnenschutz dienen anstelle der üblichen Vorhänge hochglanzlackierte Holzgitter. Die Türen der Aufzüge und der Büroräume sowie die Stützen des Gebäudetragwerks wurden mit Tafeln aus polierter Bronze verkleidet. Aus polierter Bronze ist auch das Geländer der Wendeltreppe, die vom Empfangsbereich in das darunterliegende Geschoß führt.
Eine großzügige Ausstattung der Räume mit Kunstwerken trägt zusätzlich zu der anspruchsvollen Atmosphäre bei. Man findet hier moderne Radierungen, Tuschen, Lithographien und Serigraphien, Öl- und Acrylbilder, Wandteppiche sowie primitive und zeitgenössische Plastiken.

1. Plan (50th floor).
2. View of the reception area with spiral staircase leading to the floor below.

1. Grundriß (50. Geschoß).
2. Blick in den Empfangsbereich mit einer Wendeltreppe, die in das darunterliegende Geschoß führt.

30'

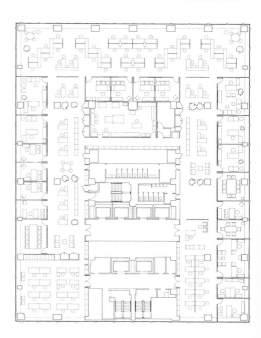

Executive Offices of
Swid/Cogan (GFI/Knoll)
New York, New York

This 3000-square-foot executive office atop Manhattan's glamorous Citicorp Center was designed for the two young entrepreneurial partners of GFI/Knoll. The space, which commands breathtaking views of uptown and downtown Manhattan, supports the two partners and two secretaries. The 54-foot square plan is oriented east to west maximizing the views. Two major spaces, a reception area and a large shared office for the two partners, are intriguingly divided and joined by round and square volumes. A clear glass door looks directly south to the summit of the Chrysler Tower. These volumes house a conference room, a lounge, a pantry and a lavatory/shower room. The design contrasts the subtle textures and tones of sand plaster and raw silk paneled walls with mirror polished stainless heads and bases. An acoustical off-white lacquered wood ceiling is incised with a grid, 1¼-inch square, disguising access panels for the flush incandescent downlights. The floor is a slipped parquet pattern of natural finish oak. The window wall columns, soffit, fascia and induction units are clad in white plastic laminate. The windows are fitted with narrow slat metal blinds.

The reception space is flanked by a 52-foot-long figured mahogany storage wall and two Pfister secretarial desks of the same wood. A classic grouping of pale suede Barcelona lounges rests above the 19th century Tabriz rug and in front of a colorful Helen Frankenthaler canvas.

In their office the partners share a 5-foot by 12-foot Pfister table and matching credenza, both of the same mahogany. Custom designed telephone pedestals and polished stainless clad keyboards and monitor rest beside and behind the executives, respectively. Silhouetted against the window wall is a grouping of Ming Aralias and Pleomele Referis in large terra-cotta pots. A brilliant Morris Louis canvas overlooks a casual grouping of suede and wool flannel upholstered Pfister lounges. Dotted in are lacquered mauve and khaki telephone drums and polished nickel floor lamps.

A sand plaster walled conference room lies beyond the solar bronze glass of the sliding door. The olive burl conference table is complemented with Brno chairs upholstered in a cotton cross bar weave. Custom engraved silver, china and crystal are stored in the credenza.

The executive bath with its polished black granite and mirrored cladding summarizes the clarity and classicism employed throughout this suite's design.

Chefbüros für
Swid/Cogan (GFI/Knoll)
New York, New York

Für die beiden jungen Firmeninhaber von GFI/Knoll war eine etwa 280 m² große Bürosuite mit quadratischem Grundriß an der Südwestecke des obersten Geschosses des bekannten Citicorp Center in Manhattan zu planen. Sie gliedert sich in zwei große zusammenhängende Bereiche, eine Empfangszone und den gemeinsamen Arbeitsraum der beiden Partner, sowie eine Zwischenzone mit kleinerem Aufenthaltsraum, Konferenzraum, Teeküche und Sanitärraum. Die Ganzglastür zwischen dem Empfangsbereich und dem Arbeitsraum der beiden Partner weist direkt auf die Spitze des Chrysler Tower.

Die durchlaufende, mattweiß lackierte Holzdecke hat ein etwa 32 × 32 mm messendes Raster mit darin eingepaßten Montageelementen für die bündig eingebaute Glühlampenbeleuchtung. Als Bodenbelag wurde ein Eichenparkett in Naturton gewählt, auf dem ein Täbris-Teppich aus dem 19. Jahrhundert liegt. Durch Profile aus hochglanzpoliertem, rostfreiem Stahl sind die mit naturfarbener Rohseide bespannten Wandflächen von Boden und Decke abgesetzt.

Alle Fensterflächen erhielten einen Blendschutz aus schmalen Metalljalousien, und die Verkleidungen der Fensterprofile sowie der Induktionsgeräte im Brüstungsbereich wurden mit Kunststoff furniert. Vor der Fensterwand im Arbeitszimmer stehen große Pflanzen in Töpfen aus Steinzeug. Im Empfangsbereich wurde eine über die ganze Raumlänge durchlaufende Schrankwand eingebaut, die mit stark gemasertem Mahagoni furniert ist. Auch die Arbeitstische der beiden Sekretärinnen und der gemeinsame, etwa 3,65 m lange und 1,50 m breite Arbeitstisch der beiden Partner wurden mit diesem Holz furniert. In Reichweite ihrer Arbeitsplätze haben die Partner frei stehende Telefonanlagen aus rostfreiem Stahl.

Die von Mies van der Rohe entworfenen Barcelona-Sessel im Eingangsbereich haben helle, genarbte Lederbezüge. Im Konferenzraum – den man vom Büro der Partner durch eine bronzefarben getönte Glastür mit Rahmen aus poliertem, rostfreiem Stahl unmittelbar erreichen kann – wurden ebenfalls Sitzmöbel von Mies van der Rohe verwendet, nämlich dessen Brünn-Stühle. Sie haben Baumwollbezüge, deren Quadratmuster die Deckenstruktur aufnimmt. Die Sanitärräume wurden mit poliertem schwarzem Granit und Spiegeln verkleidet.

Die insgesamt sehr frische und luxuriöse, dabei aber doch zurückhaltende Atmosphäre der Suite wird unterstrichen durch Bilder von Helen Frankenthaler und Morris Louis.

15'

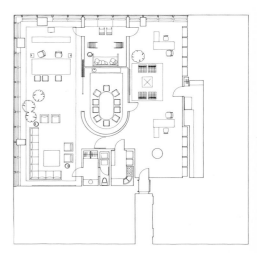

250

3, 4. Views of the partners' office.

3, 4. Blick in den Arbeitsraum der beiden Partner.

Vista International Hotel,
New York, New York

The Vista International Hotel at the World Trade Center in New York City was originally designed with 450 rooms in the late 1960's. A foundation and three levels were built before the owner's program was substantially increased due to the dynamic growth of the lower Manhattan market. When SOM became involved in 1978, their commission was to build an 825-room hotel on the pre-existing base. The 24-story steel frame building was completed in 1981.

The service level includes administrative offices, training facilities, and parking. Directly above, the lobby level, which is accessible from the street and the trade center concourse, includes check-in facilities, shops, and the ballroom. Off the trade center plaza, the plaza level contains the balance of the hotel's important public spaces: the business center with secretarial and communication services; two restaurants; and an expansive lounge. Because the hotel is located in a major financial district, a need for special facilities to serve an international investment community existed. While floors 4-19 contain guestrooms, the third floor is reserved for conference facilities with 12 conference rooms and a lounge, and floors 20-21 are used for the VIP Club. The Executive Fitness Center with a pool and racquetball courts occupy the top two levels.

In order to minimize the weight of the new structure, a steel frame rather than the originally planned concrete was selected. This enabled the engineers to increase the height of the hotel to 22 stories above the trade center plaza. Wind loading was also a problem as the hotel was constructed in one of the windiest places in the nation, and the solution required much heavier wind bracing than normally found in a 22-story building.

The first architect envisioned a dark anodized aluminum skin to match the other low-rise buildings in the complex. Given the increased bulk of the hotel, a light anodized skin, in the same design vocabulary as the two towers, was selected as more appropriate. Horizontal strips of glass and aluminum panels were used to contrast with the tower's vertically expressed skin, and to maintain the hotel's own architectural identity.

Vista International Hotel,
New York, New York

Das zum World Trade Center gehörende Vista International Hotel geht auf ein Ende der sechziger Jahre begonnenes 450-Betten-Hotel zurück. Man hatte bereits drei Geschosse hochgezogen, als der Bauherr auf Grund der dynamischen Marktentwicklung ein wesentlich erweitertes Programm vorlegte. Als SOM 1978 das Projekt übernahm, lautete ihr Auftrag auf den Bau eines 850-Betten-Hotels, für das die vorhandenen Bauteile übernommen werden mußten. Das 24geschossige Gebäude wurde 1981 fertiggestellt.

In den Geschossen der Sockelzone befinden sich die allgemeinen Einrichtungen des Hotels, darüber erhebt sich der langgestreckte, den städtebaulichen Vorgaben folgend abgeknickte Bettenturm. Im untersten Geschoß des Sockels liegen Verwaltungs- und Ausbildungsräume sowie Garagenplätze. Im Geschoß darüber sind die von der West Street und der Fußgängerebene des World Trade Center erschlossene Eingangshalle mit der Rezeption sowie Läden und Ballsaal untergebracht. Eine gegenüber dem Haupteingang liegende Wendeltreppe verbindet dieses Geschoß mit dem von der Plaza des World Trade Center erschlossenen Plazageschoß. Hier befinden sich Restaurants und Aufenthaltsräume. Im Geschoß darüber stehen den Gästen zwölf durch Schiebewände teilweise kombinierbare Konferenzräume zur Verfügung, die um eine zentral gelegene Halle mit Aufzuganschluß gruppiert sind. Oberhalb der Geschosse mit den Gästezimmern liegen im 20. und 21. Geschoß der VIP Vista Club und in zwei Geschossen darüber ein Fitneßzentrum mit einer Schwimmhalle und zwei Racketballhallen.

Wegen der auf ein niedriges Gebäude ausgelegten Fundamente wurde das Gebäude nicht, wie ursprünglich vorgesehen, aus Stahlbeton, sondern aus Stahl errichtet. Ein besonderes konstruktives Problem ergab sich aus den sehr hohen Windlasten – das Gebäude steht an einem der windreichsten Plätze der USA –, die zu wesentlich kräftigeren Versteifungen, als sie sonst bei einem Bau dieser Höhe üblich sind, führten.

Während der erste Architekt in Angleichung an die niedrigen Bauteile des Komplexes für die Außenhaut seinerzeit Elemente aus dunkel anodisiertem Aluminium vorgesehen hatte, wählte SOM angesichts der größeren Baumasse und einer geänderten Gebäudeform hierfür solche aus hell anodisiertem Aluminium. Die Fassade nimmt damit in Material und Farbe das Gestaltungsvokabular der beiden Hochhäuser des World Trade Center auf; entsprechend der abweichenden Nutzung und eigenen Identität des Hotels wurden die Außenwände jedoch horizontal gegliedert.

1. Site plan with typical hotel floor.
2. View of the Vista International Hotel with the World Trade Center across the Hudson River.

1. Lageplan mit Normalgeschoßgrundriß des Hotels.
2. Ansicht des Vista International Hotel mit dem World Trade Center über den Hudson River hinweg.

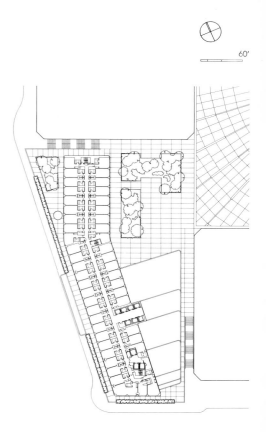

60'

254

3–5. Restaurants and lounges are located at the plaza level adjacent to the Trade Center Plaza. The "Greenhouse" restaurant, enclosed in a two-story glass structure, provides an outstanding dining environment.
6. The building is clad with a light anodized aluminum skin.

3–5. Auf der Platzebene neben dem Trade Center Plaza sind Restaurants und Eingangshallen angeordnet. Das Restaurant »Greenhouse« liegt in einer zweigeschossigen Glashalle, so daß der Speisesaal eine außergewöhnliche Atmosphäre ausstrahlt.
6. Das Gebäude wurde mit einer hellen Aluminiumhaut verkleidet.

Headquarters of
Texaco,
Harrison, New York

The Texaco corporate headquarters, completed in 1978, was built at a secluded location in a low-density residential neighborhood on the suburban fringe of New York City. The triangular 107-acre site is bordered by two expressways and a major street. The travertine clad, concrete building totals 1,156,000 square feet and can accommodate 2,100 employees. A terrace level houses mechanical equipment and personnel services, including a cafeteria, above which three office floors are stepped back around interior courtyards. A two-floor underground parking garage holds 1,500 cars.

The most important considerations in determining the conceptual design were the zoning restrictions, scale of the neighboring residential area, vehicular access and parking, and efforts to conserve both energy and the natural landscape. The solution was a single building centrally located on the site. The single building concept reduced the disturbance to the landscape, and the central location shielded the building from the neighboring community. Parking was located beneath and in front of the building; the roof deck was landscaped as a grassy forecourt containing a circular entrance drive. The long axis was positioned east-west in order to reduce the sun load on the tinted thermal glazing, which is also shielded by a 9-foot overhang. Floor-to-ceiling glazing is thus possible within the constraints of energy conservation, enabling the occupants to enjoy an unobstructed view of the natural landscape.

The interior terraced courtyards were planned for the enjoyment of the employees. Provision has also been made for the creation of a pond, a system of nature trails, and a dining area on the lawn outside the cafeteria.

Space planning was a major concern for the development of a program of 750,000 square feet of interior office space. A workstation concept evolved with four enclosed office types and five open area workstations. The workstations were developed into a flexible system for planning, the goal being to provide the client with a single open planning system that could be implemented without professional assistance in the future.

Hauptverwaltung der
Texaco,
Harrison, New York

Die 1978 fertiggestellte Hauptverwaltung der Texaco liegt in isolierter Lage am Rand des Großraums von New York und ist umgeben von locker gestreuter Villenbebauung. Das dreieckige, etwa 43 ha große Grundstück wird auf zwei Seiten von Autobahnen, auf der dritten von einer Anschlußstraße begrenzt. Die Entwurfskonzeption für die etwa 107.500 m² umfassende Bauanlage mit 2.100 Arbeitsplätzen mußte die behördlichen Bebauungsbeschränkungen und den Charakter der umliegenden Wohngegend ebenso berücksichtigen wie Gesichtspunkte der Energieeinsparung und der Schonung der anmutigen Landschaft.

Die Architekten ordneten die Baumasse in einem einzigen kompakten Gebäude in der Mitte des Geländes an. Damit wurde nur ein kleiner Teil des Grundstücks in Anspruch genommen und die Bebauung so weit wie möglich von dem umgebenden Wohngebiet abgesetzt, während der Ausblick von den Büros an klaren Tagen bis zum Empire State Building in Manhattan reicht. Zur Vermeidung großer Flächenparkplätze wurde dem Gebäude im Norden eine doppelgeschossige Tiefgarage mit 1.500 Stellplätzen vorgelagert, deren Dach begrünt wurde. Ein durchgehendes Untergeschoß, das südlich an diese Tiefgarage anschließt, nimmt Technikräume, einen Saal, die Gebäudeverwaltung und die Kantine auf. Darüber sind um einen Innenhof drei Bürogeschosse angeordnet, die nach oben terrassenartig zurückspringen.

Die Längsachse des Gebäudes wurde in Ost-West-Richtung gelegt, um die Sonneneinstrahlung auf die Fensterflächen aus getöntem Isolierglas gering zu halten. Ein Rückversatz der Glasfassaden um etwa 2,70 m bietet einen zusätzlichen Sonnenschutz. Durch diese Maßnahmen konnte man alle Geschosse ohne übermäßige Erhöhung der Kühllasten raumhoch verglasen.

Sowohl die terrassierten Innenhöfe als auch das umliegende Außengelände, das mit einem Wasserbecken, Spazierwegen und einer Speiseterrasse auf der Wiese vor der Kantine ausgestattet wurde, bietet den Beschäftigten eine intime, informelle Atmosphäre. Wesentliches Anliegen der Architekten war eine sorgfältige Einrichtungs- und Ausstattungsplanung der etwa 69.800 m² großen Büroflächen. Es wurden vier Einzelbüroraumtypen und fünf Typen von Arbeitsstationen für die Großräume entwickelt. Die Arbeitsstationen sind in ihrer Anordnung so leicht veränderbar, daß sie ohne Fachkräfte neu zusammengestellt werden können.

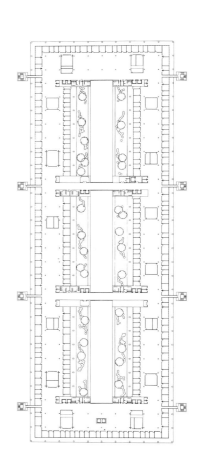

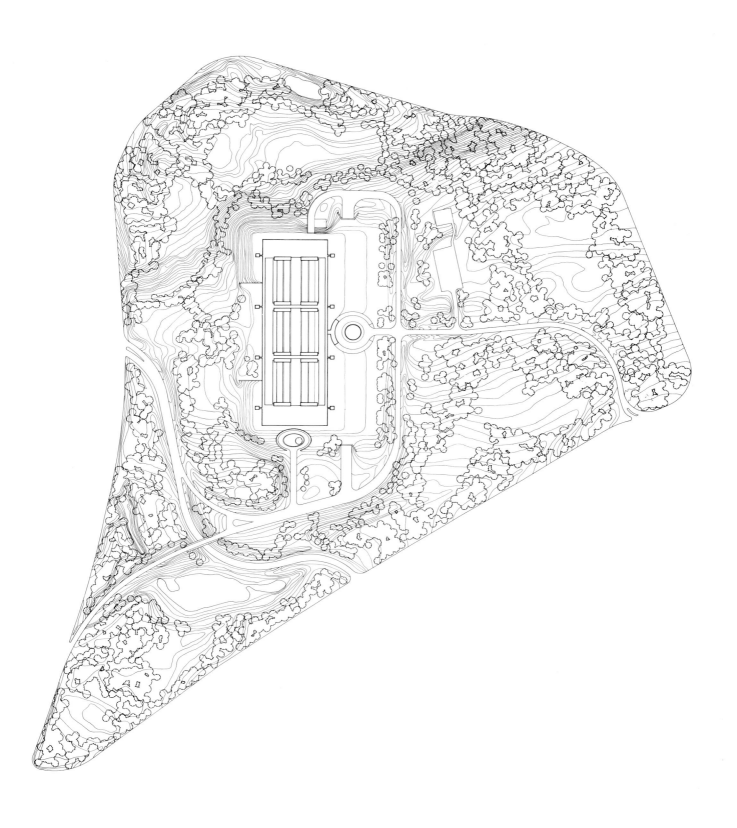

300'

3. Aerial view. The 107-acre site is bordered by two expressways and a major street.

3. Luftbild. Das etwa 43 ha große Grundstück wird von zwei Autobahnen und einer Hauptstraße begrenzt.

4. Office areas are oriented towards a series of interior courtyards which are extensively landscaped.

4. Die Büroflächen sind zu einer Reihe stark bepflanzter Innenhöfe hin orientiert.

Headquarters of the
General Electric Company,
Fairfield, Connecticut

General Electric's headquarters was built for 850 employees in two buildings on a 100-acre site in suburban Fairfield, Connecticut. Completed in 1974, the 851,224-square-foot complex is situated at the top of a slope rising steeply from the bordering Merritt Parkway. A primary consideration in siting the buildings was to reduce the visual impact on the neighboring residential area. This was accomplished by limiting the height to three floors above grade, dividing 470,000 square feet of office space into two structures conforming to the land contours, and locating the parking for 722 cars in connected concrete podia beneath the structures.

The main entrance is approached from a formal court between the podia, which are clad in precast concrete panels with a warm tone granite aggregate finish. Above, exposed steel trusses span 81 feet to form the main office structure. The fine detailing and smooth white paint of the trusses contrast with the rough surface below. Recessing the tinted thermal glazing emphasizes the depth of the 6½-foot trusses. The resulting sheltered terraces shade the interior and facilitate maintenance of the window wall. Air handling units above the exterior steel spandrels are connected to condenser-compressor units on the roof.

SOM conducted space planning studies and developed a new concept for the distribution of private and pool space. Both buildings are organized around interior courts to maximize the perimeter area needed for private offices. Interior work areas share the advantages of exterior offices with regard to size, lighting, and flexibility. Special furniture was designed to meet diverse requirements and accommodate an anticipated need for future departmental expansion or contraction.

Hauptverwaltung der
General Electric Company,
Fairfield, Connecticut

Die 1974 fertiggestellte, etwa 79.200 m² große und 850 Angestellte aufnehmende Hauptverwaltung der General Electric Company liegt auf einem etwa 40,5 ha großen Grundstück im äußersten Vorortgürtel von New York. Das Grundstück ist stark hügelig und wird im Norden von dem Merritt Parkway begrenzt, von dem aus es steil nach Süden ansteigt. Um die Beeinträchtigung der benachbarten Wohnbebauung so gering wie möglich zu halten, beschränkte man die Bauhöhe auf drei Geschosse über Geländeoberkante, teilte die Bürofläche von etwa 43.700 m² auf zwei Baukörper auf, die in Form und Länge an die Geländekonturen angepaßt sind, und brachte die 722 Parkplätze in den miteinander verbundenen Sockelgeschossen der beiden Gebäude unter.

Zwischen den beiden Sockelgeschossen entstand im Südosten ein Winkel, der den streng bepflanzten Eingangshof aufnimmt. Die Sockel wurden mit Waschbetonplatten verkleidet, die eine warme und rauhe, von Granitsplittern gebildete Oberfläche haben. Im Kontrast dazu wählte man für die beiden dreigeschossigen Bürobauten darüber ein kleinteilig detailliertes, weiß gestrichenes Stahlskelett mit einer Spannweite von etwa 24,70 m, hinter das die Wände aus dunklem Isolierglas weit zurückgesetzt sind. Durch die umlaufenden Terrassen wird die direkte Sonneneinstrahlung reduziert, die Wartung vereinfacht und die ungewöhnliche Dimension der fast 2 m hohen Träger unterstrichen. So vermitteln die in ihrer Anordnung spannungsvoll aufeinander bezogenen Baukörper einen klaren und einfachen, stark horizontalen Eindruck. Hinter den Trägern sind im Terrassenbereich Einzelklimageräte eingebaut, die mit zentralen Rückkühlwerken auf den Dächern in Verbindung stehen.

Ein großer Teil der Arbeitsplätze mußte in Einzelbüros untergebracht werden. Dem kommt einmal die Verteilung der Büroflächen auf zwei Baukörper entgegen, zum anderen erhielten die beiden Gebäude drei locker begrünte, quadratische Innenhöfe, an denen – wie an den meisten Außenseiten – abgeteilte Büroräume liegen. Für die innenliegenden Raumzonen entwickelten die Architekten ein neues Konzept großzügiger Raumaufteilung und als Konsequenz daraus ein eigenes Möblierungssystem. Die dort gelegenen Arbeitsplätze stehen denn auch denen an den Außenseiten in bezug auf Raumangebot, Beleuchtung und Flexibilität nicht nach.

1. Site plan.
2. The complex is situated at the top of a steeply rising slope.

1. Lageplan.
2. Die Anlage ist am oberen Rand eines steil ansteigenden Hanges angeordnet.

300'

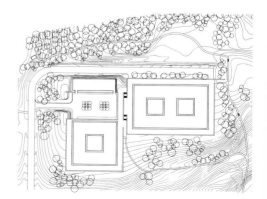

3. Plan (1st floor).
4. The long-span exterior steel structure was prefabricated. The fine detailing and smooth white paint of the trusses contrast with the textured surfaces below.

3. Grundriß (Erdgeschoß).
4. Das weitgespannte Stahlskelett wurde vorfabriziert. Die kleinteilige Detaillierung und der glatte weiße Anstrich der Stahlträger stehen in spannungsvollem Kontrast zu den grob strukturierten Oberflächen des darunterliegenden Sockelgeschosses.

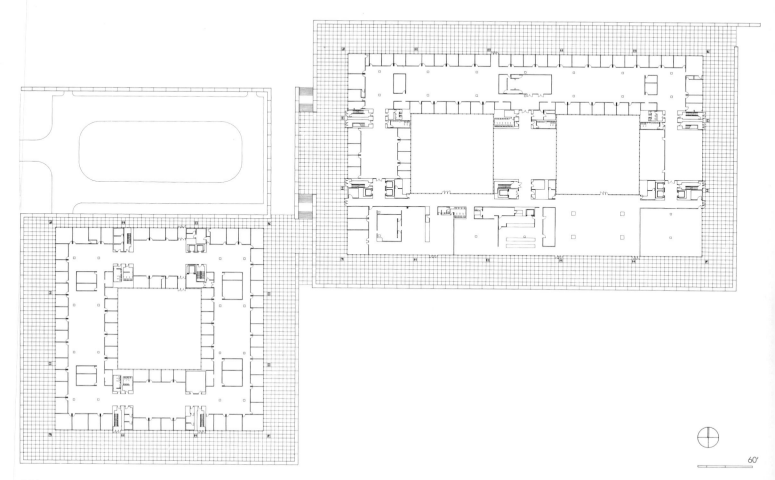

60'

Prudential at Princeton, Plainsboro, New Jersey

The Prudential Insurance Company commissioned SOM and Princeton University to study energy conservation in office buildings and to design a prototypical speculative office building that is low-cost and energy-efficient. The project is comprised of two three-story, 130,000-square-foot buildings, completed in 1983.

Set in a grove of deciduous trees where they are shaded from the low afternoon sun, the buildings are designed to capture the heat of the winter sun and block the summer sun. Both will maximize daylighting to reduce the electricity demand and cooling load. The control of daylight into exterior offices combined with interior "light slot" corridors will effectively daylight approximately 75 percent of the office space of each building. Atria will reduce the exposed perimeter office area.

The North Building, designed by SOM, utilizes an all glass exterior. To prevent heat loss, the exterior wall is constructed of two layers of glass separated by an 18-inch vertical plenum. Hot air collected in the south-facing atrium is ducted through underground concrete pipe that serves as mass thermal storage. When required, warm air is drawn from the mass thermal storage and directed into the double-layer exterior wall and then returned to the atrium. Direct sun entering through perimeter windows will be either bounced onto the ceiling for daylighting or rejected by thin-slat horizontal blinds in the double wall plenum. This will allow heat gain within the plenum to be vented off or captured. A fabric-covered ice pond will provide chilled water for cooling.

The South Building, designed by Princeton, is a solid-walled building where each facade is designed to respond to the solar conditions of each exposure. As a result, the windows on each elevation is differing to maximize winter heat gain and minimize summer heat gain, while still providing efficient daylighting. In the winter, the south wall becomes a huge solar collector. The atrium has skylights facing south that will warm the atrium; these large windows for daylighting can be built facing the atrium without winter heat loss. Passive architectural approaches dramatically reduce mechanical loads. The remaining demand is met by a high-efficiency ground water source heat pump system.

Prudential at Princeton, Plainsboro, New Jersey

Die Prudential Insurance Company beauftragte SOM und die Princeton University mit der Erstellung einer Studie über Möglichkeiten der Energieeinsparung bei Bürogebäuden und der Entwicklung eines Mietbürogebäudes, das sowohl billig als auch günstig im Energieverbrauch ist. Die Studien führten zu zwei dreigeschossigen, etwa 12.100 m² großen Gebäuden, die 1983 fertiggestellt wurden.

Die Bauten liegen in einem Hain von Laubbäumen, die sie im Sommer beschatten, und sind so entworfen, daß sie die Wintersonne einfangen, aber die Sommersonne abhalten. Bei beiden wird soweit wie möglich mit Tageslicht operiert, um den Stromverbrauch und die Kühllast zu reduzieren. Oberlichter über den Gängen tragen dazu bei, daß 75% der Büroflächen mit Tageslicht ausgeleuchtet werden. Glasüberdachte Innenhöfe reduzieren die Zahl der direkt an Außenwänden gelegenen Räume.

Der von SOM entworfene Nordbau hat eine ganz aus Glas bestehende Vorhangfassade. Um Wärmeverluste zu verhindern, bestehen die Außenwände aus zwei Schalen, die in einem Abstand von etwa 46 cm angeordnet sind. Das Atrium auf der Südseite wirkt im Winter als großer Sonnenkollektor, der von der niedrig stehenden Sonne aufgeheizt wird. An der Decke dieses Raumbereichs wird Warmluft abgesaugt, durch eine thermische Speichermasse unter das Gebäude geblasen und je nach Bedarf an den Nord-, Ost- und Westseiten wieder in den Zwischenraum der Außenwände eingeführt, um den Wärmeabfluß von den angrenzenden Büros nach außen auszugleichen. Automatisch betriebene Jalousien zwischen den beiden Schalen der Außenwände schränken zwar die Wärmeeinstrahlung und die Blendung ein, lassen jedoch einen großen Anteil des Tageslichtes passieren. Ein von einer Stoffmembran überdecktes, etwa 4,50 m tiefes Eisbecken liefert während der gesamten sommerlichen Kühlsaison aus dem im Winter angesammelten Schnee-Eis-Gemisch das Kühlwasser zur Raumkühlung.

Der südliche, von den Architekten der Universität geplante Bau hat vorwiegend geschlossene Steinfassaden. Die Fenster variieren bei diesem Bau in ihrer Größe entsprechend den verschiedenen Himmelsrichtungen, lassen aber in allen Fällen genügend Tageslicht in das Gebäude. Im Winter fungiert die Südwand als ein großer Sonnenkollektor. Das Atrium hat nach Süden ausgerichtete Oberlichter, die den Raum erwärmen, ohne daß sich im Winter ein Wärmeverlust ergibt. Der Energiebedarf wird zu einem großen Teil durch passiv wirkende Bauelemente sowie durch ein hochwirksames Wärmepumpensystem gedeckt.

1. Site plan with ground floor plan of the North Building.
2. General view of the South Building (to the left), designed by Princeton University architects, and the North Building (to the right), designed by SOM (model).

1. Lageplan mit Erdgeschoßgrundriß des Nordbaus.
2. Gesamtansicht (Modell). Links der von den Architekten der Princeton University entworfene Südbau, rechts der von SOM entworfene Nordbau.

Pages 268/269:
3–10. Miscellaneous diagrams illustrating the energy study.
11. South facade of the North Building (model). This building has double-layer all-glazed curtain walls. An atrium, located on the south side, acts as a large solar collector, heated by the low-angled sun.
12. North facade of the South Building (model).

Seiten 268/269:
3–10. Verschiedene Diagramme aus der Energiestudie.
11. Südseite des Nordbaus (Modell). Dieser Bau hat eine ganz aus Glas bestehende Vorhangfassade aus zwei Schalen. Ein Atrium auf der Südseite wirkt im Winter als großer Sonnenkollektor, der von der niedrig stehenden Sonne aufgeheizt wird.
12. Nordseite des Südbaus (Modell).

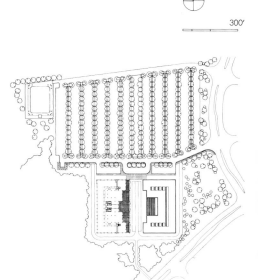

300'

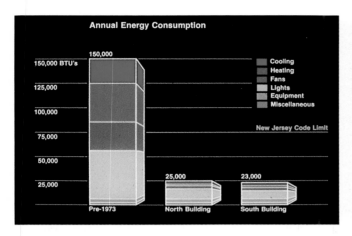

Annual Energy Consumption

150,000 BTU's — 150,000 — Pre-1973
125,000
100,000
75,000
50,000
25,000 — 25,000 North Building — 23,000 South Building

Legend: Cooling, Heating, Fans, Lights, Equipment, Miscellaneous

New Jersey Code Limit

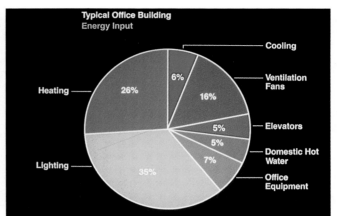

Typical Office Building
Energy Input

Cooling 6%
Ventilation Fans 16%
Elevators 5%
Domestic Hot Water 5%
Office Equipment 7%
Lighting 35%
Heating 26%

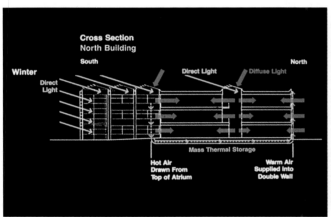

Cross Section
North Building

Winter
South — North
Direct Light
Diffuse Light

Mass Thermal Storage
Hot Air Drawn From Top of Atrium
Warm Air Supplied Into Double Wall

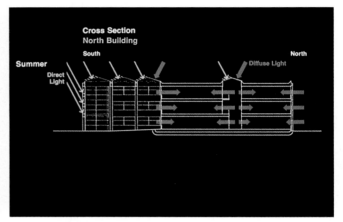

Cross Section
North Building

Summer
South — North
Direct Light
Diffuse Light

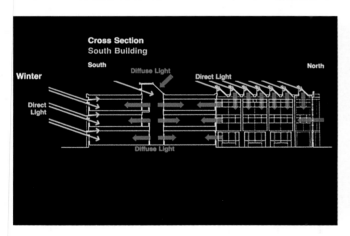

Cross Section
South Building

Winter
South — North
Direct Light
Diffuse Light

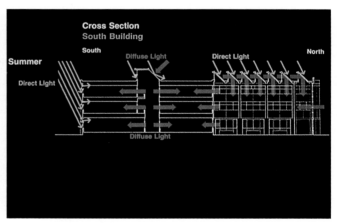

Cross Section
South Building

Summer
South — North
Direct Light
Diffuse Light

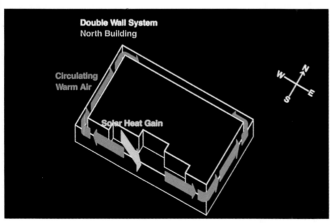

Double Wall System
North Building

Circulating Warm Air
Solar Heat Gain

W N E S

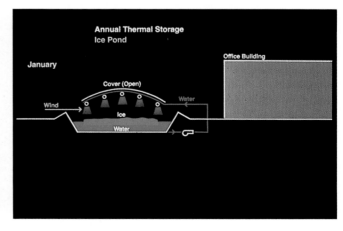

Annual Thermal Storage
Ice Pond

January
Cover (Open)
Wind
Water
Ice
Water
Office Building

**Administrative Building of the
Westinghouse Electric Corporation,
Churchill Borough, Pennsylvania**

The administrative office building, completed in 1974 for Westinghouse Electric Corporation, serves as a gateway for the entire Westinghouse complex of research and development buildings on a large rural site outside Pittsburgh, Pennsylvania. The central office structure was built to consolidate the administrative functions and personnel which had been located in separate departments of the existing buildings. Two significant factors influencing the design were the entry roadway bisecting the site and the client's desire to interconnect existing facilities on either side of the road.
Spanning the access road with a steel truss system at the center, the building marks the entrance to and becomes the focus of the research complex. Walkways join the administrative office building to the neighboring research facilities on either side. In addition, a previously isolated plaza has been integrated into the project and now serves as an employee entrance. The new three-story office building extends a full 320 feet in length. Its long, low silhouette skillfully reinforces the open character and topography of the surrounding meadowland.
Each of the three levels contains 26,300 square feet of office space. The sloping site allowed an employee cafeteria with panoramic views of the natural landscaping to be inserted below the office levels facing the entry side of the building. A pedestrian promenade on the first floor, cantilevered edges of the two upper floors, and bands of windows deeply recessed behind the spandrel planes emphasize the building's horizontal format. This image is further enhanced by a technically innovative continuous butt glazed system which eliminates exterior vertical mullions. An energy efficient building envelope with a low glass-to-window-wall ratio is permitted by the continuous bands of comparatively narrow fenestration.
Gray tinted solar glass and dark anodized aluminum panels with flush joints were chosen as cladding for the reinforced concrete structure, allowing the building to blend serenely with the natural colors of the surrounding landscape.

**Verwaltungsgebäude der
Westinghouse Electric Corporation,
Churchill Borough, Pennsylvania**

In der Nähe von Pittsburgh verfügt die Westinghouse Electric Corporation über ein großes Gelände mit verstreut liegenden Bauten, die der Forschung und Entwicklung dienen. Hier wurde 1974 zur Zusammenfassung aller Verwaltungsfunktionen ein zentrales Bürogebäude errichtet. Bis dahin waren die Verwaltungsabteilungen mit in den Forschungsgebäuden untergebracht und über das ganze Gelände verteilt. Bei der Planung mußte eine das Gelände durchschneidende Erschließungsstraße berücksichtigt und auf leichte Erweiterungsfähigkeit geachtet werden.
Der neue Verwaltungsbau hat drei Geschosse und eine Länge von etwa 97,50 m. Als zentraler Eingangsbau und Blickpunkt des Geländes überspannt er mit Stahlträgern mittig die Erschließungsstraße. Ein zuvor abseits gelegener Platz konnte durch den dorthin gelegten Personalzugang sinnvoll in die Anlage einbezogen werden und hat dadurch eine neue Funktion erhalten. Jede der drei Büroebenen hat eine Geschoßfläche von etwa 2.450 m². Durch das Auskragen der beiden Obergeschosse über das untere Stockwerk und weit hinter die Brüstungsebene zurückspringende Fensterbänder wird die horizontale Wirkung des Baukörpers unterstrichen.
Die Fassaden des Stahlbetonskelettbaus bestehen aus grau getöntem Sonnenschutzglas und dunkel anodisierten, bündig gestoßenen Aluminiumtafeln. Es wurde eine durchgehende Verglasung ohne außenliegende Vertikalsprossen gewählt, die den Horizontalcharakter des Gebäudes noch steigert.
Der Bau paßt sich mit seinen dunklen Oberflächen unauffällig in die umgebende Landschaft ein und setzt sich zugleich von den mit Sichtbetonelementen verkleideten älteren Bauten ab. Da die umlaufenden Fensterbänder relativ niedrig sind, entsteht ein für den Energieverbrauch günstiges Verhältnis von Glasflächen zu geschlossenen Fassadenteilen.

1. Plan (typical floor).
2. Site plan.

1. Grundriß (Normalgeschoß).
2. Lageplan.

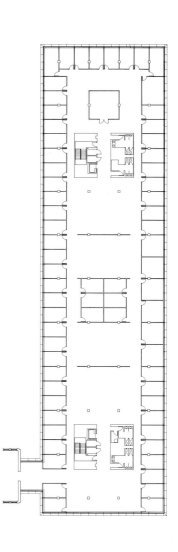

270

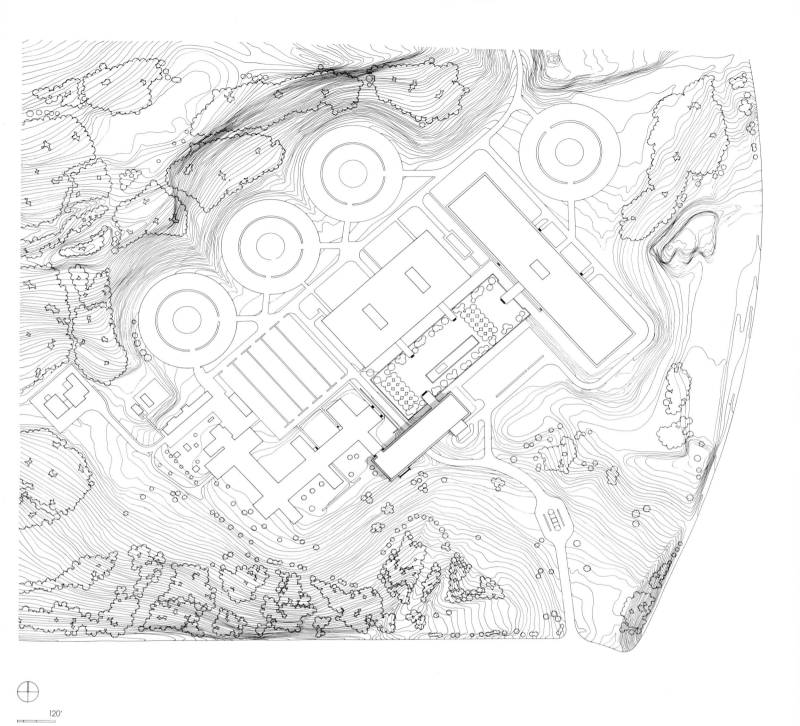

3, 4. Bands of windows are deeply recessed behind flush spandrel panels of dark anodized aluminum allowing the building to blend with the character of the surrounding landscape.

3, 4. Die Fensterbänder sind weit hinter die bündig gestoßenen Brüstungstafeln aus dunkel anodisiertem Aluminium zurückgesetzt, so daß der Bau sich gut in die flache Landschaft einfügt.

Sixty State Street,
Boston, Massachusetts

Located on an historically significant site in an area famed in America's past, the 38-story structure completed in 1978 was developed to provide over 800,000 square feet of premium rentable office and commercial retail space to the surrounding financial community. The design evolved an unusual shape on a setback location in order to lessen its high-rise impact on the quaint atmosphere of surrounding buildings and market areas.

Over 60 percent of the site has been developed for pedestrian use, highlighted by an elevated, landscaped terrace overlooking the surrounding historical area. Open plazas replace alleys and further encourage pedestrian traffic along celebrated walkways and the surrounding city streets. The tower has a distinctive, eleven-sided configuration influenced in part by the irregular shape of the site. The building's angular shape restores the visual line between Old State House and Faneuil Hall, the city's two most important landmarks, which had been obstructed by buildings previously occupying the site. The unusual floor plan also results in highly desirable office space, offering a potential for nine outside corner offices on each floor and a variety of unobstructed views of the harbor and surrounding cityscape. There are 31 office floors averaging 22,500 square feet each, as well as five smaller penthouse floors defined by a multi-tiered sloping roof. Three levels of underground parking accommodate 200 cars.

The all steel structural system consists of an exterior folded tube frame with moment-connected exterior columns spaced 10 feet on center, interconnected by deep spandrel beams which provide lateral load resistance for the tower. The steel columns are clad with Napolean Red granite set on triangular-shaped prefabricated steel strongbacks, between which are granite-clad spandrels and highly efficient dual pane reflective tinted glass. The reddish gray tone of the granite was chosen for its compatibility with the traditional red brick and old granite used throughout the area.

Plans for The Bay Club, a private luncheon club, were integrated into the design of the building, located on the 33rd and 34th floors. A two-story wall of glass and a terraced seating arrangement afford a spectacular view of the harbor from every table.

Sixty State Street,
Boston, Massachusetts

Das 1978 fertiggestellte Bürohochhaus wurde an einem geschichtlich bedeutsamen Platz im Bankenviertel von Boston errichtet. Als Teil der Sanierungsmaßnahmen um das Old State House, die Faneuil Hall und den Quincy Market erforderte die Bebauung an dieser Stelle besondere Rücksichtnahme auf die Umgebung. Entsprechend einer Empfehlung der Denkmalschutzbehörde wurde das 38geschossige Gebäude daher um etwa 50 m von der Faneuil Hall abgesetzt. Durch die abgewinkelte Grundrißform stellten die Architekten ferner eine frühere Sichtverbindung zwischen dem Old State House und der Faneuil Hall, die durch ein nunmehr abgerissenes Bauwerk lange Zeit verbaut gewesen war, wieder her. Zu der Fußgängerzone, die mehr als 60% der Grundstücksfläche einnimmt, gehört eine höher gelegene, begrünte Terrasse, von der aus man den umliegenden historischen Bereich überblickt. Das Hochhaus nimmt auf einer Fläche von etwa 74.400 m² Mietbüros und Geschäftsräume auf. Seine markante, elfseitige Grundrißform – eine Folge der städtebaulichen Rahmenbedingungen und des unregelmäßigen Grundstückszuschnitts – ergab günstige Zuschnitte für Büroaufteilungen und je Geschoß Raum für neun Eckbüros mit weitem Blick über Hafen und Stadt. Das Gebäude hat 31 Normalgeschosse mit einer Fläche von jeweils etwa 2.100 m² sowie unter einer schrägen Dachkonstruktion 5 kleinere Penthousegeschosse. Im 33. und 34. Geschoß ist ein privater Speiseklub untergebracht. Hier hat man von Sitzebenen verschiedener Höhe durch doppelgeschossige Glaswände einen großartigen Ausblick auf den Hafen.

Die als gefaltete Rohrhaut ausgebildeten Außenwände nehmen alle Querkräfte und die Vertikalkräfte der Außenzonen auf; die Stützen im Innenbereich des Turmes brauchen daher nur Vertikalkräfte abzuführen. Für die Außenwände wurde eine Stahlkonstruktion mit Stützen im Abstand von etwa 3 m und hohen Brüstungsträgern gewählt. In Abstimmung auf die Fassaden aus roten Ziegeln und Granit, die den umgebenden Baubestand kennzeichnen, erhielten die Außenwände des Neubaus eine Verkleidung aus napoleonrotem Granit, wobei die Platten an den Stützen auf dreieckigen Stahlprofilelementen aufsitzen. Die Fenster sind mit getönten und reflektierenden Doppelscheiben, die eine hohe Wärmedämmung aufweisen, verglast.

1. General view from the southwest.
2. Napoleon-red granite was chosen for compatibility with the traditional red brick and granite used throughout the area.

1. Gesamtansicht von Südwesten.
2. Zur Angleichung an die Bauten aus rotem Ziegelmauerwerk und Granit in diesem Teil der Stadt wurde das Hochhaus mit napoleonrotem Granit verkleidet.

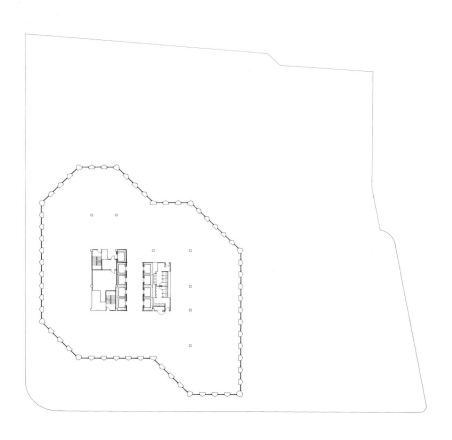

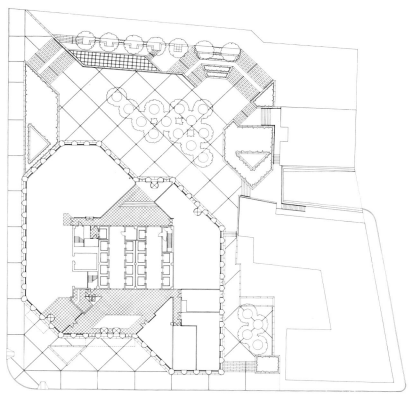

30'

3. Plans (ground level, typical floor).
4, 5. The angular shape of the building helps to restore the visual connection between the Old State House and Faneuil Hall, the city's two most important landmarks.

3. Grundrisse (Erdgeschoßebene, Normalgeschoß).
4, 5. Durch die abgewinkelte Form des Gebäudes wird die Sichtverbindung zwischen den beiden bedeutendsten Wahrzeichen der Stadt, dem Old State House und der Faneuil Hall, wiederhergestellt.

Harvard Square Station,
Cambridge, Massachusetts

As the first element in a four-mile "Red Line" rail transit extension program, the Harvard Square Station project included the design, demolition, and reconstruction of a grim, aging 1912 rail transit station as well as the even older, physically integrated bus transfer facility located within Harvard Square's street system.

A significant design factor of the project was the mandate by the City of Cambridge to provide continuous bus and rail transit service throughout the five-year construction period, while also providing continuous vehicular and pedestrian flows to the university and adjacent business establishments.

An intensive community participation program throughout design and construction has assured that transit service and traffic have been maintained and that the numerous, sometimes conflicting, interests of the Harvard Square area were heard and included in the design.

Principal architectural objectives of the surface restoration include a significant increase in attractive pedestrian areas by creating three major landscaped plazas, the extensive use of shrubs, ground cover, planters, benches, and brick crosswalks to improve the pedestrian quality of the Square and to control vehicular flows. The vaulted 1928 Harvard Square kiosk was restored as the Square's central newsstand. A new, low, glazed structure provides entry to the station's mezzanine.

Principal architectural features of the subway station include the use throughout of strong curvilinear forms deriving from bus and rail tunnel geometry; clear expressions of roof structure spanning the radial geometry of the station's spaces; the strict integration of station lighting into the roof structure to further reinforce the powerful, curving geometry; and the use of elegant but low-maintenance interior finishes. These include tiled wall surfaces with stainless steel enclosing columns and other structural elements. Textured brick and granite pavers cover all floor surfaces, also patterned to reinforce the station's curved spaces.

Harvard Square Station,
Cambridge, Massachusetts

Die Verlängerung der »Red Line« der U-Bahn nach Nordwesten machte den Bau eines neuen Bahnhofs unter dem Harvard Square und den angrenzenden Straßen notwendig, mit dem 1979 begonnen wurde. Im Zug dieser Maßnahme wird auch der dort bereits vorhandene unterirdische Busbahnhof renoviert und erweitert.

U-Bahn- und Busverkehr sowie Autoverkehr in beiden Fahrtrichtungen müssen während der etwa fünfjährigen Bauzeit aufrechterhalten werden. Weiterhin dürfen die Baumaßnahmen den Zugang zur Harvard University und zu den umliegenden Geschäften nicht beeinträchtigen.

Von einem neuen Bahnhofseingang aus, der ganz in der Nähe des alten Zugangs liegen wird, erreichen die Fahrgäste ein Verteilergeschoß. Von hier aus geht es über Rampen zu den Bahn- und Bussteigen weiter. Auch das Umsteigen zwischen Bussen und U-Bahn erfolgt auf dieser Ebene. Der Zugang soll weitgehend verglast werden, so daß Tageslicht bis auf das Podest der herabführenden Treppe fallen kann. Ein Teil des bestehenden unterirdischen Busbahnhofs liegt direkt unter den Fundamenten alter Geschäftsgebäude; hier wird der Tunnel belassen und renoviert. Unmittelbar nördlich der Verteilerhalle müssen die Zu- und Abfahrten jedoch verlegt werden, um Platz für die neuen Bahnsteige zu gewinnen. Einige der hierbei frei werdenden Tunnelräume liegen an der neuen Bushaltestelle auf der oberen Ebene des Untergrundbahnhofs und sollen in Verkaufsflächen verwandelt werden.

Der Bauherr forderte Ausbaumaterialien, die sehr niedrige Unterhaltskosten verursachen. Als vorherrschende Wandverkleidung kommen daher große Fliesen in einem zurückhaltenden Beige zur Verwendung. Zweifarbige Streifen aus roten und purpurroten Fliesenreihen gliedern die langen, weich geschwungenen Wandflächen und führen vom Eingang parallel zu den Rolltreppen hinunter über das Podest und durch die Verteilerhalle bis zu den Bahnsteigen. Der Großteil der Platzoberfläche des Harvard Square mußte für den Umbau entfernt werden. So ergab sich die einmalige Gelegenheit zu einer durchgreifenden Neugestaltung des Platzes und der Fußgängerflächen vom Holyoke Center über den Harvard Square bis zum Brattle Square und dem Elliott Square. Auch der als Flagstaff Park bekannte Bereich konnte in die Planung einbezogen werden.

1. Location map of the Boston-Cambridge metropolitan area. Key: 1 Harvard Square Station. 2. Train level (model). The station project includes the extension of an underground bus transfer facility. The sinuous forms of the station's spaces are derived from the required geometries of the merging bus and rail tunnels.

1. Übersichtsplan des Ballungsraumes Boston-Cambridge. Legende: 1 Harvard Square Station. 2. Bahnsteigebene (Modell). Das Projekt umfaßt auch die Erweiterung eines unterirdischen Busbahnhofs. Die geschwungenen Formen des Bahnhofs ergaben sich aus den notwendigen Radien der hier zusammenlaufenden Bus- und Bahntunnel.

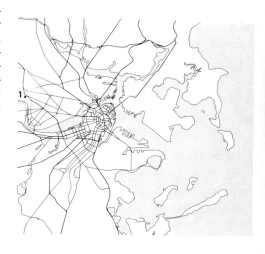

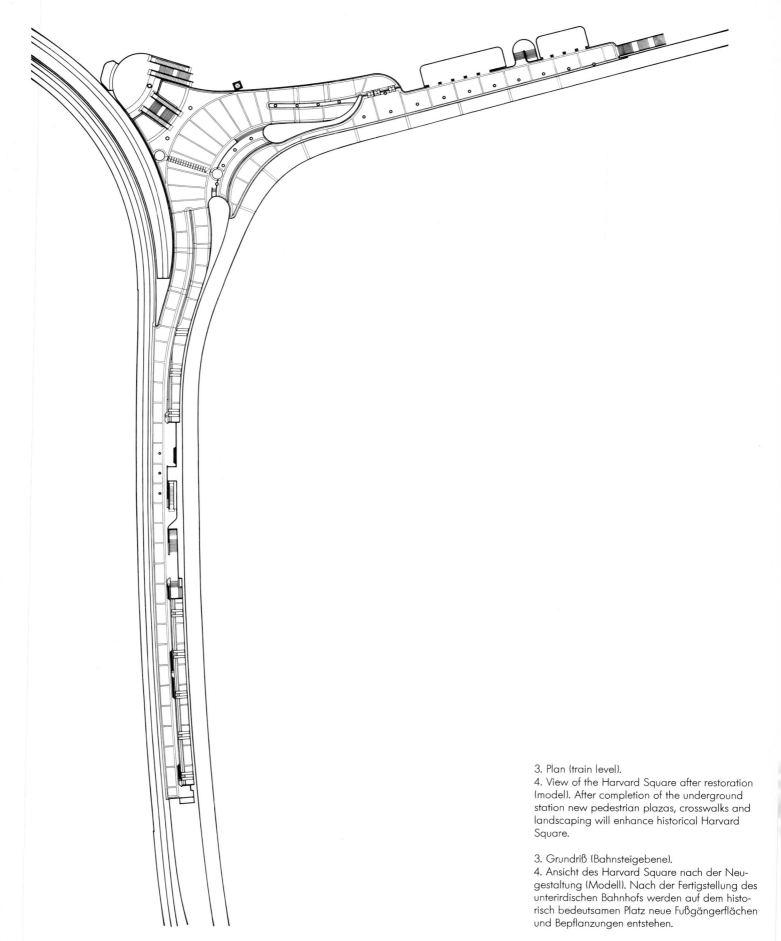

3. Plan (train level).
4. View of the Harvard Square after restoration (model). After completion of the underground station new pedestrian plazas, crosswalks and landscaping will enhance historical Harvard Square.

3. Grundriß (Bahnsteigebene).
4. Ansicht des Harvard Square nach der Neugestaltung (Modell). Nach der Fertigstellung des unterirdischen Bahnhofs werden auf dem historisch bedeutsamen Platz neue Fußgängerflächen und Bepflanzungen entstehen.

Plan for the
Capital Center,
Providence, Rhode Island

For three quarters of a century, the railroad tracks of Providence, Rhode Island, bisected the city's downtown. Located on a twenty foot high continuous embankment, the tracks presented a physical and visual barrier between McKim, Mead & White's classic State House to the north and the commercial core of the city to the south. In 1979, as part of a massive program to upgrade intercity rail travel on the east coast, the Federal Railroad Administration determined that the deteriorated tracks and bridges of Providence would be more costly to repair than to replace. City officials saw this as an opportunity not only to rebuild, but also to remove the railroad embankment and realign the tracks, achieving their longstanding goal of reuniting the downtown with the capital precinct. Sponsored by the Providence Foundation, the City, and the State of Rhode Island, the Capital Center Plan was commissioned to guide future development of the 60 acres of prime land newly opened up at the city's core by the proposed reconfiguration of the tracks.
Colonial and Federalist merchant houses on the east, the Victorian commercial core to the south, and the Beaux-Arts State House to the north were all testament to the city's enviable architectural heritage. Challenged by this context, the plan had to move and inconspicuously replace the railroad, screen a highway interchange, extend the downtown, honoring the view from the governor's window, all at the same time. The three roles of the city – commercial, historical and governmental – had to be acknowledged and functionally and aesthetically linked.
The thrust of the Plan is in the design of the public parks, waterways, and streets. These form a sequence of axial and symmetrical relationships reminiscent of a neoclassical past. Three streets extend from the existing city on axis with the State House dome. Future development will reinforce these corridors, making the streets important not only for the buildings they serve, but also for the views framed at either end. The new ground plane is tilted up toward the State House, allowing parking and the relocated railroad to be covered by a landscaped extension of the State House lawn. The Woonasquatucket River is widened into a water park, and old Union Station, endowed with a new terrace on the north, serves as portal and belvedere to the open space beyond. Private development is limited to the periphery of a cone-shaped apron focusing on the State House dome.

Plan für das
Capital Center,
Providence, Rhode Island

Das Zentrum von Providence, der Hauptstadt des Bundesstaates Rhode Island, wird überragt von der Kuppel des auf einer leichten Anhöhe gelegenen State House, das von McKim, Mead & White entworfen wurde. Diese städtebaulich bedeutsame Situation ist jedoch zur Zeit dadurch beeinträchtigt, daß das State House vom Geschäftszentrum der Stadt durch oberirdisch geführte Eisenbahngleise abgeschnitten ist. 1979 beschloß die Federal Railroad Administration, die Eisenbahntrasse zu verlagern, und SOM erhielt den Auftrag, für ein Areal von etwa 24,3 ha vor dem Kapitol ein Sanierungsprogramm zu erstellen und Bebauungsstudien anzufertigen. Dabei sollten auch die städtebaulichen Möglichkeiten genutzt werden, die der Lauf des unterhalb des Kapitolhügels gelegenen Woonasquatucket River bietet.
Das Projekt sieht vor, eine Abfolge von öffentlichen Grünanlagen und neuen Straßen unter Einbeziehung des Flusses durch axiale und symmetrische Beziehungen zum Kapitol an dessen beherrschende klassizistische Architektur anknüpfen zu lassen. Vom bestehenden Stadtbereich her sollen drei Straßen auf die Kuppel des Kapitols zuführen. Die Bebauung entlang dieser Achsen soll mit der Zeit deren städtebauliche Wirkung stärken und wichtige Sichtbeziehungen an ihren beiden Endpunkten entstehen lassen. Das gesamte Gelände soll angeschüttet werden, so daß es zum Kapitol hin leicht ansteigt und die neutrassierten Eisenbahnanlagen und Tiefparkebenen von der Erweiterung der Grünanlagen vor diesem historischen Bau überdeckt werden können. Der Fluß wird im Rahmen der Grünplanung zu einem Wasserpark ausgeweitet. Vor dem Gebäude der alten Union Station soll eine zum Fluß und zum Kapitol hin geöffnete Terrasse entstehen, so daß dieser Bau nach seiner Renovierung eine neue Bedeutung als städtebauliches Portal für die angrenzenden Freiflächen gewinnen kann. Private Bauvorhaben werden auf die Peripherie eines konisch zulaufenden Geländekeils beschränkt, der auf die Kuppel des Kapitols hin orientiert ist.
An den Straßen werden feste Baulinien und verbindliche Abstufungen der Bauhöhen vorgeschrieben, während die Grünanlagen locker übergreifen sollen. Ferner enthält der Plan detaillierte Aussagen über die Flächennutzung und die Verteilung der Parkplätze sowie über Fußgängerverbindungen und öffentliche Anlieferungsstraßen.

1. Site plan prior to station relocation. Key: 1 State House, 2 Union Station, 3 Woonasquatucket River.
2. General view of the Capital Center (model).
3. Site plan after station relocation.

1. Lageplan vor Verlegung des Bahnhofs. Legende: 1 State House, 2 Union Station, 3 Woonasquatucket River.
2. Gesamtansicht des Capital Center (Modell).
3. Lageplan nach Verlegung des Bahnhofs.

600'

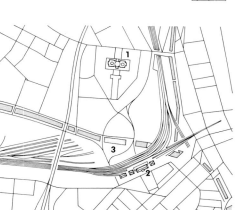

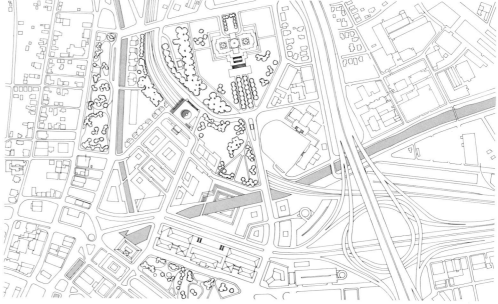

Providence Station,
Providence, Rhode Island

The need for a new railroad station in Providence was realized in 1979, when the decision was made to relocate the existing railroad embankment, a visual and physical barrier through the center of Rhode Island's state capital. The station plan evolved concurrently with Skidmore, Owings & Merrill's ambitious Capital Center Plan, guiding the expansion of the city's core. The new station is sited at the base of Smith Hill, 600 feet south of McKim, Mead & White's classic State House, and framed between two new streets radiating from the Capitol's dome. This prominent site demanded a solution respectful of the State House's preeminence, yet strong enough to establish an architectural standard for future development in the surrounding area when the station is completed in late 1984.

Like earlier railroad depots, Providence Station is designed to symbolize the culture of the people who will use it. While its clean, rational, and straightforward lines represent the functionalism and efficiency which characterize our modern society, traditional elements are not abandoned. A dome, symbol of the civic domain, proclaims the public use of the station and lends a classical richness reminiscent of the State House beyond. Columns along the north and south facades announce the status of the station as a public forum, and the station tower is functional and symbolic at the same time.

The station's position reinforces the sight lines between the downtown and the State House, as established in the Capital Center Plan. Within the station, the dome which caps the main waiting area serves to resolve the conflicting geometry between the exterior walls and the interior spaces, which are aligned with the angle of the curved tracks and platforms below. The circular motif of the dome is echoed in its oculus, repeated in the paving pattern in the waiting room, and reinforced by a grouping of four wooden benches.

Two parking levels for 400 cars are located below the plaza. An expansive landscape plan includes depressing and covering the tracks to the south of the State House and subtly regrading the area from the base of Smith Hill to the new station, serving to create a new, park-like extension of the magnificent State House lawn.

Providence Station,
Providence, Rhode Island

Zu Füßen des die Stadt beherrschenden Hügels mit dem State House von McKim, Mead & White, dem Kapitol des New-England-Staates Rhode Island, wurde 1982 mit dem Bau eines neuen Bahnhofsgebäudes begonnen. Der Bau wurde notwendig, weil die alte Eisenbahnlinie entsprechend dem Beschluß der Federal Railroad Administration um etwa 200 m nach Norden verschoben wird. Dort werden die Gleise in Tieflage, zum Teil offen, zum Teil unter neuer Bebauung und unter einem Parkgelände, verlaufen. Das neue Empfangsgebäude soll im Herbst 1984 fertiggestellt werden. Täglich werden rund 8.000 Pendler und Intercity-Passagiere diesen Bahnhof benutzen. Durch ein anziehendes Erscheinungsbild soll aber auch die weitere Öffentlichkeit angesprochen werden, damit die Benutzung der Bahn allgemein wieder attraktiver wird.

Das eingeschossige Gebäude ist nahezu quadratisch. An seiner Südwestecke steht ein weithin sichtbarer massiver Uhrenturm, der die bei Bahnhofsgebäuden von jeher gewohnte Rolle der Information und Orientierung übernimmt. Über diagonal angelegte Eingangshallen an den beiden parallel zu den Gleisen verlaufenden Straßenseiten gelangt man in einen quadratischen, von einer flachen Kuppel überwölbten Wartesaal, an dem Fahrkartenschalter, Reisebedarfsläden, Betriebsräume aller Art sowie die Abgänge auf die darunterliegenden Bahnsteige liegen.

An den Eingangsseiten wird der Fahrgast durch Dachvorsprünge, die von Doppelsäulenreihen getragen werden, vor der Witterung geschützt. Eine dreispurige Vorfahrt mit breiten Gehsteigen erleichtert das Ein- und Aussteigen am Bahnhofsvorplatz, unter dem in zwei Parkierungsebenen 400 Fahrzeuge Platz finden.

Die Architekten haben es verstanden, sowohl in der Gebäude- und Raumgestaltung als auch in den einzelnen Architekturelementen die Assoziation an das positive Erscheinungsbild alter Bahnhofsgebäude zu wecken. Zugleich gelang es ihnen, ein Gebäude zu schaffen, das sich, ohne seine Identität zu verlieren, der städtebaulichen Dominanz des State House unterordnet.

1. General view of the new railroad station looking towards the State House (model).
2. Plan (upper level).
3. Elevation.

1. Gesamtansicht des neuen Bahnhofsgebäudes in Richtung State House (Modell).
2. Grundriß (obere Ebene).
3. Aufriß.

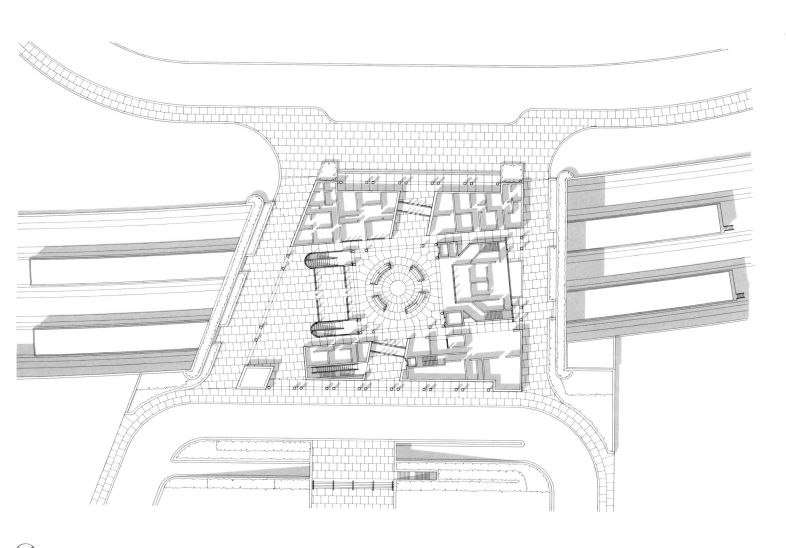

30'

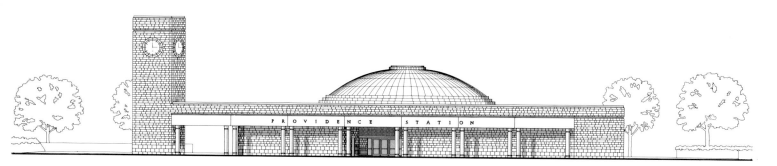

Reorganization of
The Mall,
Washington, D.C.

1. Location plan. Key: 1 Washington Mall, 2 Constitution Gardens.

1. Übersichtsplan. Legende: 1 Washington Mall, 2 Constitution Gardens.

In preparation for the 1976 Bicentennial celebration, the National Park Service commissioned Skidmore, Owings & Merrill to develop a circulation plan for the Washington Mall, based on the firm's master plan for the area completed ten years earlier. In order to limit automobile traffic in this great park, two streets which had flanked the central greensward, Washington and Adams Drives, were replaced with pedestrian walks, and the central axis of the Washington Mall was restored. The importance of the disciplines of simplicity and restraint were emphasized throughout the design of this site, which lies at the heart of America's national iconography.

The guiding philosophy of the design was to retain the appropriate dignity of the Mall while encouraging an increased level of visitor activity. Four major pathways were established, two bordering the central lawn and two under the existing elm plantations, extending for nearly a mile between the Capitol Reflecting Pool and the Washington Monument.

Compacted crushed stone was chosen as the walkway material because of the simple scale afforded by its even and jointless texture. The design acknowledges the use of this material in many formal applications in France, whose rich landscape tradition influenced not only Pierre L'Enfant, Washington's original planner, but the celebrated Senate Park Commission of 1901 as well. Samples from Versailles, the Tuileries, and the Bois de Boulogne were procured and tests conducted to achieve the installed walkways.

The street furniture is carefully organized under the canopy of the mature elm plantations to discreetly reinforce the formal edges while deferring to the grand axial views. Special care was taken to protect the shallow roots of the vulnerable existing elm trees that flank the walks adjacent to the National museums. The benches and light standards were chosen to reiterate traditional elements, and both were constructed anew with castings made for the head and base of the historic "Olmsted" light standard, relamped to extend the Mall's use into the evening hours. A special paint color, "Capital Brown", was specifically developed for all metal surfaces of the project. Traditional park information kiosks were provided near the entrances to the national museums, and new trash receptacles, bicycle racks and drinking fountains were also located throughout the area.

A second phase of the award-winning design, as yet unbuilt, includes the narrowing and decorative repaving of two streets adjacent to the national museums as well. At some future date, these streets may be reserved for tourmobiles and bicycles, thereby completing the effort to remove the automobile from this foremost National Park.

Umgestaltung der Grünanlagen
The Mall,
Washington, D.C.

Der vom Kapitol bis zum Washington Monument reichende östliche Teil der Mall wird von einer Reihe von Fahrstraßen durchzogen, die den Zusammenhang des ersten »Parks der Nation« immer wieder unterbrechen. Im Jahr 1976 wurden zwei dieser Fahrstraßen, der Washington Drive und der Adams Drive, die zentral in Längsrichtung der Mall verliefen, durch Fußwege ersetzt. Hiermit wurde der erste Schritt zur vollständigen Herausnahme des Fahrverkehrs aus der Mall getan. Für eine zweite Phase, in der der Madison Drive und der Jefferson Drive – die an den großen National-museen vorbeiführen – verengt, dekorativ gepflastert und auf den Verkehr mit Fahrrädern sowie Tourmobilen beschränkt werden sollen, haben die Architekten ihre Planung ebenfalls bereits abgeschlossen.

Anstelle des Washington Drive und des Adams Drive wurden auf einer Länge von etwa 1,6 km zwi-schen dem Wasserbecken vor dem Kapitol am einen Ende und dem Washington Monument am anderen Ende vier breite Fußwege neu angelegt, von denen zwei die Rasenfläche in der Mitte der Mall begrenzen und zwei unter den alten Ulmenreihen verlaufen.

Der Leitgedanke dabei war, unter Erhalt des anspruchsvollen Charakters der klassischen Mall mit entsprechender Kleinmaßstäblichkeit den Rahmen für eine stärkere Nutzung durch Besucher zu schaffen.

An diesem Ort, der für alle Amerikaner besonderen Symbolwert hat, war in erster Linie größte Zu-rückhaltung und Einfachheit geboten. Wesentlich für den Eindruck des Besuchers sind die axial ausgerichteten Fußwege aus verdichtetem Natursteinschotter sowie die Form und Anordnung der Straßenmöblierung.

Die Oberflächen der Wege wurden deshalb aus Natursteinschotter (vermischt mit Lehm, Sand und Wasser) hergestellt, weil sich dadurch eine kleinmaßstäbliche, gleichmäßige Struktur ohne Fugen ergibt, die sauber und fest ist und auch dem Charakter des Parks gemäß ist. Vorbilder für derartige Wege gibt es in vielen französischen Gärten, insbesondere in Versailles, in den Tuilerien sowie im Bois de Boulogne. Damit wurde an eine Tradition der Landschaftsarchitektur angeknüpft, von der nicht nur Pierre L'Enfant, der ursprüngliche Planer von Washington, ausgegangen war, sondern auch die vielgerühmte McMillan-Kommission im Jahr 1901. Vor der erneuten Anwendung in Wash-ington wurden Muster aus Frankreich untersucht und eine Reihe von Versuchen durchgeführt, um mit Sicherheit zu einem guten Ergebnis zu gelangen. Im Verlauf der beiden Wege, die an den Nationalmuseen vorüberführen, wurden die flachliegenden, empfindlichen Wurzeln der großen Ulmen durch Ringe von etwa 5 m Durchmesser, die mit Lehm eingefaßt und mit baltischem Efeu be-pflanzt wurden, geschützt. Ein konzentrischer Ring mit noch größerem Durchmesser, der bündig in die Wegeoberfläche eingelassen wurde, ermöglicht es, im Fall besonderer Trockenperioden die Baumwurzeln künstlich zu bewässern.

Die Straßenmöblierung, betont in zurückhaltender Form die geometrischen Einfassungen, ordnet sich jedoch dem Durchblick unter dem Blätterdach der großen Ulmenreihen unter. Sowohl für die Bänke als auch für die Kandelaber wurden Abgüsse alter Vorbilder gewählt, um die Verbindung mit der Tradition an diesem historisch so bedeutungsvollen Ort zu wahren. Kopf und Sockel der Kande-laber stammen von alten Leuchten des Landschaftsarchitekten Olmsted. Die Papierkörbe wurden in Abstimmung auf ihren besonderen Aufstellungsort neu entworfen. Alle Metalloberflächen sind in einem speziellen »Kapitol-Braun« gestrichen.

In der Nachbarschaft der Museen wurden Informationsstände sowie Fahrradständer und Trink-brunnen aufgestellt, und das Joseph Henry Monument beim Eingang zum Gebäude der Smithson-ian Institution erhielt neue Stufen, die in Form und Farbgebung an alte Vorbilder aus der Umgebung des Kapitols anknüpfen.

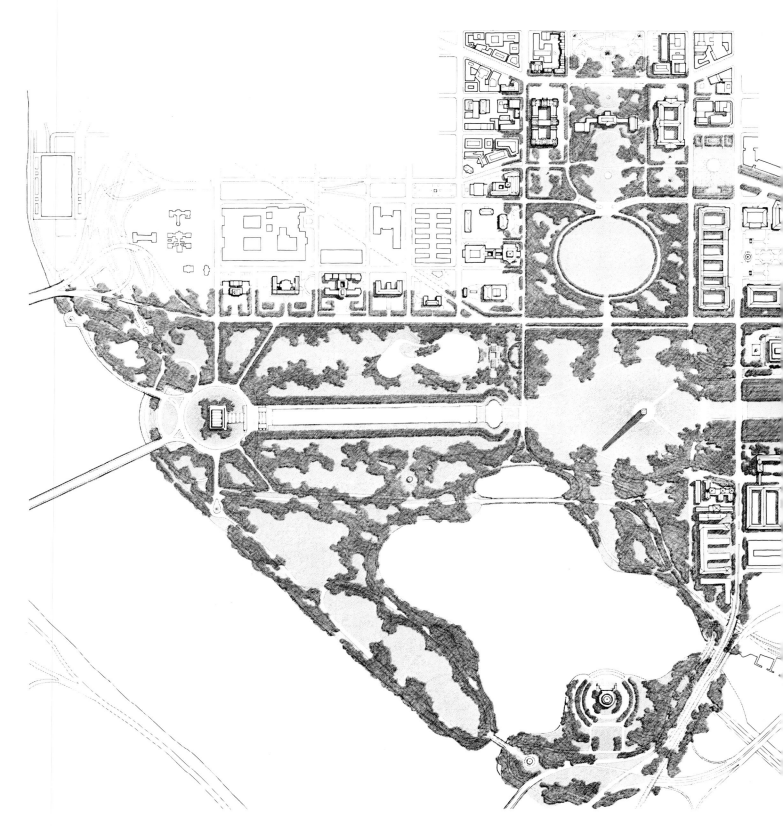

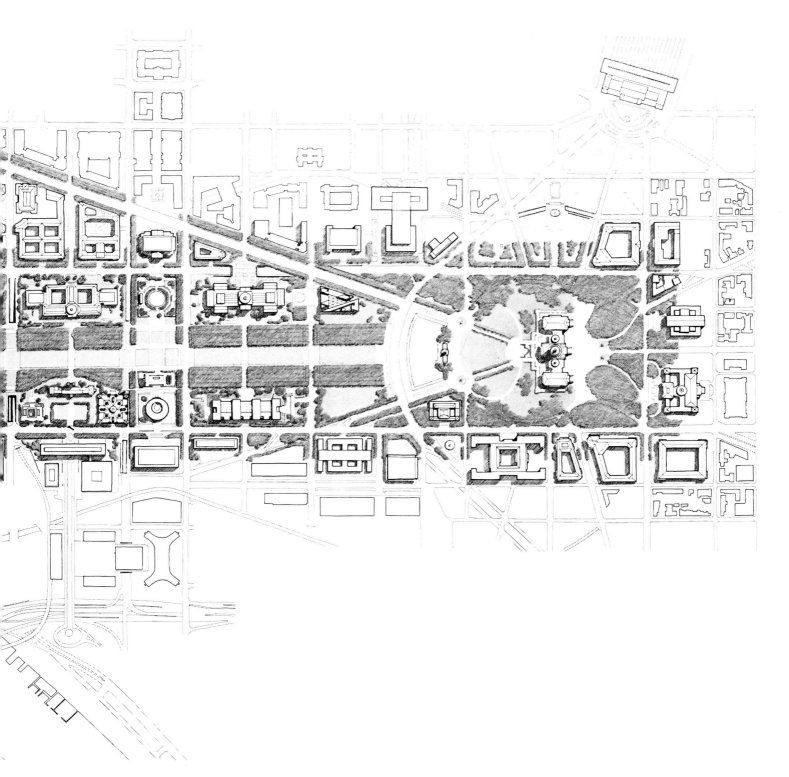

Constitution Gardens,
Washington, D.C.

Constitution Gardens, completed in 1976, carries forward the goal of the National Park Service to reclaim the Washington Mall in the heart of the nation's capital as a pedestrian-oriented urban park. While the eastern half of the Mall was being constructed, Skidmore, Owings & Merrill's attention was again turned to the western half – a treeless site between Constitution Avenue and the Lincoln Memorial Reflecting Pool, occupied only by Navy Department buildings which had been constructed fifty years earlier to "temporarily" house World War I personnel.

After the removal of these barracks-like structures, an informal wooded park was developed on the 52-acre site. In keeping with the character of the rest of West Potomac Park surrounding the Lincoln Memorial, Constitution Gardens provides an urban oasis, sheltering pedestrians, tourists, and bicyclists from the heavy traffic of Constitution Avenue. A floor plane of softly contoured meadows is shaded by a canopy of trees as it slopes gently to meet the curving shoreline of an irregularly shaped, six-acre lake. A network of paths meanders in the shade following the contour lines. The design, deliberately executed as a "stage" for future activities, features paths which open into tree-encircled areas, providing a natural setting for modest garden structures and a variety of events. The site has been chosen as the appropriate setting for two new memorials, with the Vietnam Veterans Memorial located on the west in a meadowed area, and the Memorial to the 56 Signers of the Declaration of Independence on an island in the center of the lake.

The same sturdy Dutch elms that line the Reflecting Pool border the park on the south. From inside the park, the visitor can catch glimpses of the Washington Monument and the Smithsonian Institution buildings to the east and of the Lincoln Memorial to the west. Special care in both grading and the selection of plant materials was taken by SOM's architects and landscape designers, with Arnold Associates as consultant. Maples, beech, oak, gum, and tulip trees predominate, and graceful willows characterize the lake's central island, reached by a footbridge leading from the shore. At the eastern end of Constitution Gardens, a natural plaza on one of the highest points will be the future site of a visitor's pavilion, offering information, rest and refreshment facilities, and featuring tables along the terraces which step down to the water's edge.

Constitution Gardens,
Washington, D.C.

Auf der westlichen Seite der vom Kapitol zum Washington Monument und weiter zum Lincoln Memorial verlaufenden Mall befanden sich zwischen der Constitution Avenue und dem langgezogenen Wasserbecken vor dem Lincoln Memorial seit dem Ersten Weltkrieg »provisorische« Gebäude des Marineministeriums. Ziel des National Park Service war es seit langem, wie andere Bereiche auch diesen Teil der Mall wieder dem Fußgänger zugänglich zu machen und in eine Parkanlage mit urbanem Charakter umzuwandeln. Anläßlich der Zweihundertjahrfeier der USA im Jahr 1976 konnte diese Absicht dann endlich verwirklicht werden.

Das etwa 21 ha große Gelände war baumlos und wurde in Anlehnung an den West Potomac Park, der im Süden anschließt und das Lincoln Memorial umgibt, in eine frei gestaltete Grünanlage umgewandelt. Die verkehrsreiche Constitution Avenue tritt für den Parkbesucher nicht mehr in Erscheinung, ermöglicht dem vorbeifahrenden Autofahrer jedoch Einblicke in den Grünraum. Die wesentliche Blickbeziehung des neuen Parks ist die zum Obelisken des Washington Monument; daneben gibt es Durchblicke zum Lincoln Memorial im Westen und zu den Gebäuden der Smithsonian Institution im Osten.

Eine sanfte, leicht modellierte, in freien Formen gestaltete, fast romantische Landschaft bildet den Hintergrund für vielfältige Freizeiteinrichtungen. Rasenflächen mit weichen Konturen, die von einem dichten Blätterdach beschattet werden, fallen leicht zum Ufer eines unregelmäßig geformten Sees ab. Durch die Baumgruppen schlängelt sich, den Geländekonturen folgend, ein Netz von Rad- und Fußwegen, die hier und da von Bäumen gesäumte Freiflächen streifen. Ein kleiner Fußgängersteig führt vom Ufer zu einer mit Weiden bestandenen Insel inmitten des künstlichen Sees.

In dem Park fanden auch zwei neue Denkmäler ihren Platz: auf einer Wiese im westlichen Teil das Vietnam Veterans Memorial und auf der Insel das Memorial to the 56 Signers of the Declaration of Independence.

1. Location plan. Key: 1 Washington Mall, 2 Constitution Gardens.
2. Aerial view of the Constitution Gardens towards the Lincoln Memorial.

1. Übersichtsplan. Legende: 1 Washington Mall, 2 Constitution Gardens.
2. Luftaufnahme der Constitution Gardens in Richtung Lincoln Memorial.

3–5. An undulating, informal and almost romantic landscape was created. Softly contoured meadows slope gently to meet the curving shoreline of an irregularly shaped lake.

3–5. Es wurde eine bewegte, lockere, fast romantische Landschaft geschaffen. Rasenflächen mit weichen Konturen fallen leicht zum Ufer eines unregelmäßig geformten Sees ab.

Kuwait Chancery
in Washington, D.C.

The Kuwait Chancery in Washington, located at the International Center, was completed in 1982. The building provides office space for 68 employees on three floors, including offices for cultural, military and educational activities. A 50-seat auditorium with audio-visual capabilities, a catering kitchen, guest restroom facilities, and an apartment for the resident engineer are in the first basement. Parking is available for 43 cars, 39 below grade and 4 on grade; a ramp from a loop road provides access to the garage and a covered off-street loading berth.

The two upper floors are supported by steel trusses cantilevering from two structural steel cores anchored at opposing corners. Suspended clear frameless glazing is used to enclose the entrance level. The second and third levels are glazed with insulating green-tinted frameless glass and spandrel panels with interior aluminum mullions. The building exterior is clad with stainless steel panels. Grey granite covers terrace and subgrade walls and the interior and exterior entrance level pavement.

In strong contrast to the smooth, high polish of the Chancery exterior, the interior is a colorful, highly decorative, vibrant space. The rotated square concept common to Islamic design is used to generate both building form and interior decorative motifs. A faceted skylight above the main reception hall refracts light with a prismatic effect across brightly painted walls. Enhancing the filtration of light, open wooden screens partition the ground floor space. Colorful marbles intricately inlaid in a geometric pattern contrast with grey granite paving. A rotated square fountain is the central decorative element of this space. Visitors and employees enjoy wide views of the surrounding area through expansive glass walls.

Gesandtschaft des Kuwait
in Washington, D.C.

Die im International Center gelegene Gesandtschaft des Kuwait in Washington wurde 1982 fertiggestellt. Das Gebäude, in dem auch die Abteilungen für kulturelle, militärische und erzieherische Angelegenheiten untergebracht sind, bietet in den drei oberen Geschossen 68 Arbeitsplätze. Im 1. Untergeschoß befinden sich ein Auditorium mit 50 Plätzen, eine Küche, Erfrischungsräume für Gäste sowie die Wohnung des Hausmeisters; das 2. Untergeschoß nimmt eine Tiefgarage mit 39 Stellplätzen auf, zu denen noch 4 Stellplätze an der Vorfahrt hinzukommen. Die Rampe, die von der an das Grundstück grenzenden Ringstraße zu der Tiefgarage führt, erschließt auch einen Anlieferungsplatz.

Die beiden Obergeschosse werden von Stahlfachwerkbindern getragen, die auf zwei sich gegenüber liegenden Kernzonen an den Ecken des quadratischen Grundrisses aufliegen und von dort auskragen. Die erhöht liegende Eingangsebene ist sprossenlos mit großen Klarglasscheiben verglast, während in den beiden Obergeschossen grün getöntes Isolierglas in rahmenloser Konstruktion und Brüstungspaneele mit nach innen gekehrten Aluminiumrahmen zur Ausführung kamen. Alle geschlossenen Fassadenflächen wurden mit Elementen aus rostfreiem Stahl verkleidet.

Die äußere Gestalt des eleganten, in seiner Fassadendurchbildung nur zweigeschossig und dadurch im Maßstab kleiner wirkenden Kubus ist kristallin-einfach. Demgegenüber erinnern im Inneren farbige, abstrakt-dekorative Elemente an die islamische Tradition des Kuwait. Grundmotiv ist das um seine Achse gedrehte Quadrat, das im Islam häufig vorkommt und sowohl die Gebäudeform als auch die Ausgestaltung bestimmt. Man betritt das Erdgeschoß an der Eingangsseite übereck, also in der Diagonalen, die auch die formale Gestaltung der Terrasse und des großen Innenhofs für die Empfänge der Gesandtschaft bestimmt. Dieser Hof ist im Erdgeschoß quadratisch und in den beiden Bürogeschossen darüber sechzehneckig mit etwa der Hälfte der Fläche, die er im Erdgeschoß einnimmt. Durch ein vielseitig gefaltetes Oberlicht ergibt sich auf den mit starken Farben bemalten Wänden ein vibrierender prismatischer Effekt. Wie die Wände sind auch die geometrischen Einlegearbeiten aus Marmor in kräftigen Farben ausgeführt, womit sie in Kontrast zu dem Bodenbelag aus grauem Granit stehen. Aus der verglasten Halle des Erdgeschosses bietet sich ein weiter Blick über die umgebende Landschaft.

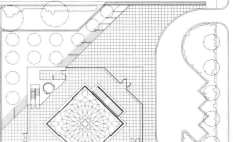

30'

3. Section.
4. View of the interior courtyard. A faceted sky-light refracts light with a prismatic effect across brightly painted walls. Colorful marbles intricately inlaid in a geometric pattern contrast with grey granite paving.

3. Schnitt.
4. Blick in den gedeckten Innenhof. Ein Oberlicht mit vielfach gebrochener Form läßt das Licht mit prismatischem Effekt auf die mit starken Farben bemalten Wände fallen. Geometrische Einlegearbeiten aus farbigem Marmor stehen in Kontrast zu dem Bodenbelag aus grauem Granit.

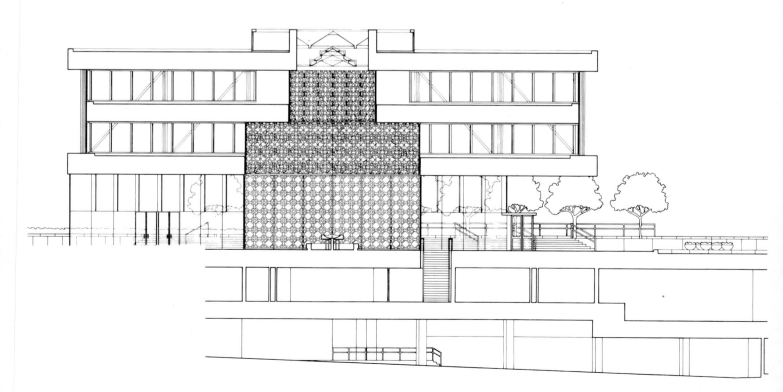

Georgia-Pacific Center,
Atlanta, Georgia

The Georgia-Pacific Corporation world headquarters in downtown Atlanta was completed in 1982. At 52 stories, the 1,360,000-square-foot tower is one of the largest and tallest building in the southeastern United States. Georgia-Pacific Center rises above a landscaped plaza at the intersection of Peachtree and Houston Streets, and borders Margaret Mitchell Square.

The building fills its site to respect the openness of the square. Its stepped profile is a design response to the site and the varied heights of surrounding buildings. Another major design response occurs in plan, with the west facade set at a 60-degree angle in order to relate the tower to the intersection of the major streets. The stepped profile is also a way of combining the economic advantages of a conventional elevator system with the range of smaller floor areas required by the Atlanta market. A range of floor sizes was desired, from about 28,000 square feet for Georgia-Pacific's floors in the lower portion of the building to 24,000 square feet, 20,000 square feet and 17,000 square feet for tenant floors in the upper portions.

Structurally, the building is a modified tube with columns closely spaced at 10-foot intervals around the perimeter. Three sides are connected by stiff spandrel beams and completed by a truss on the east wall. A 7-foot square window is placed in each 10-foot bay. The perimeter tube and the core act together through connecting floor members to resist wind stresses.

Mechanical equipment rooms with direct access to outside air are located on each floor. The air/water system has variable air volume for interior space and a fan coil system for the perimeter. The energy efficient lighting system is based on the building's 5-foot by 5-foot planning module. The fixture itself delivers task levels of lighting only in task areas, with reduced or ambient levels in circulation, reception or lounge areas.

The Georgia-Pacific Center includes a low-rise building for a computer center, 250-seat auditorium, conference rooms, a restaurant, a cafeteria, and shops. A health club and jogging track are located on the roof of the garage, which provides parking for more than 700 cars.

Georgia-Pacific Center,
Atlanta, Georgia

Der im Zentrum von Atlanta gelegene und die Hauptverwaltung der Georgia-Pacific Corporation aufnehmende Büroturm wurde 1982 fertiggestellt. Mit 52 Geschossen und einer Bruttogeschoßfläche von etwa 126.500 m² ist er einer der höchsten und zugleich größten Bauten im Südosten der USA. Er erhebt sich über einer begrünten Plaza an der Kreuzung zwischen der Peachtree Street und der Houston Street und bildet damit eine der Begrenzungen des Margaret Mitchell Square.

Die Rücksichtnahme auf den offenen Platz, die Höhenentwicklung der Nachbarbebauung, die Tatsache, daß in Atlanta nur relativ kleine Büroflächen vermietbar sind, und die wirtschaftliche Ausnutzung des Aufzugsystems führten dazu, das Gebäude nach oben in mehreren Stufen zurückspringen zu lassen. Auf Grund der Lage des Grundstücks an zwei Straßen, die sich in einem Winkel von 60° kreuzen, ergab sich zudem eine entsprechende Winkelabweichung der Westfassade. Der Bauherr nimmt selbst nur die unteren, etwa 2.600 m² großen Geschosse des Turmes in Anspruch, während die oberen Geschosse, die etwa 2.200 m², 1.850 m² und 1.600 m² groß sind, vermietet wurden.

Das Stahltragwerk des Turmes ist eine modifizierte Rohrkonstruktion mit einem Stützenabstand von etwa 3 m an den drei durchlaufenden Außenseiten. Diese drei Gebäudeseiten bilden eine steife Rohrhaut, die durch ein System von Aussteifungsträgern auf der abgetreppten vierten Seite ergänzt wird. Jedes Stützenfeld enthält ein quadratisches Fenster von etwa 2,10 m Seitenlänge. Die Außenwände sind mit dem Kern durch die Decken biegesteif verbunden, so daß die Windkräfte nach dem Prinzip des Doppelrohrs abgetragen werden.

Jedes Geschoß ist mit eigenen Heiz- und Kühlaggregaten ausgestattet. Die dezentrale Versorgung und der damit verbundene Wegfall von Vertikalschächten für die Luftführung hatten erhebliche Einsparungen zur Folge. Das Beleuchtungssystem basiert in seinen Abmessungen auf dem Ausbauraster von etwa 1,50 × 1,50 m. Die Leuchtenelemente liefern eine hohe Beleuchtungsstärke nur in den Arbeitsbereichen, während in den Verkehrs- und den sonstigen Nebenzonen die Beleuchtungsstärke reduziert ist.

In Verbindung mit dem Büroturm wurden auch zwei niedrige Nebengebäude errichtet. In dem einen sind die Computerzentrale, ein Konferenzsaal mit 250 Plätzen, Besprechungsräume, ein Restaurant, eine Kantine und Läden untergebracht, in dem anderen eine Hochgarage für etwa 700 Wagen sowie ein Fitneßzentrum mit Joggingbahn.

1. Section.
2. The building profile is a design response to the site and the varied heights of the surrounding buildings.

1. Schnitt.
2. Die Gebäudeform wurde mit Rücksicht auf Lage und Zuschnitt des Baugrundstücks sowie die verschiedenen Höhen der umliegenden Bauten entwickelt.

3. Plans (ground level, typical floor).
4. Elevation.

3. Grundrisse (Erdgeschoßebene, Normalgeschoß).
4. Aufriß.

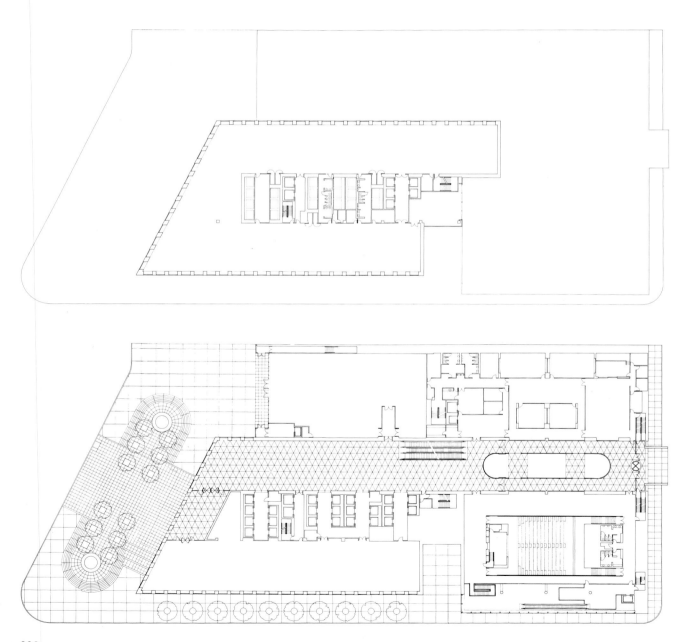

30'

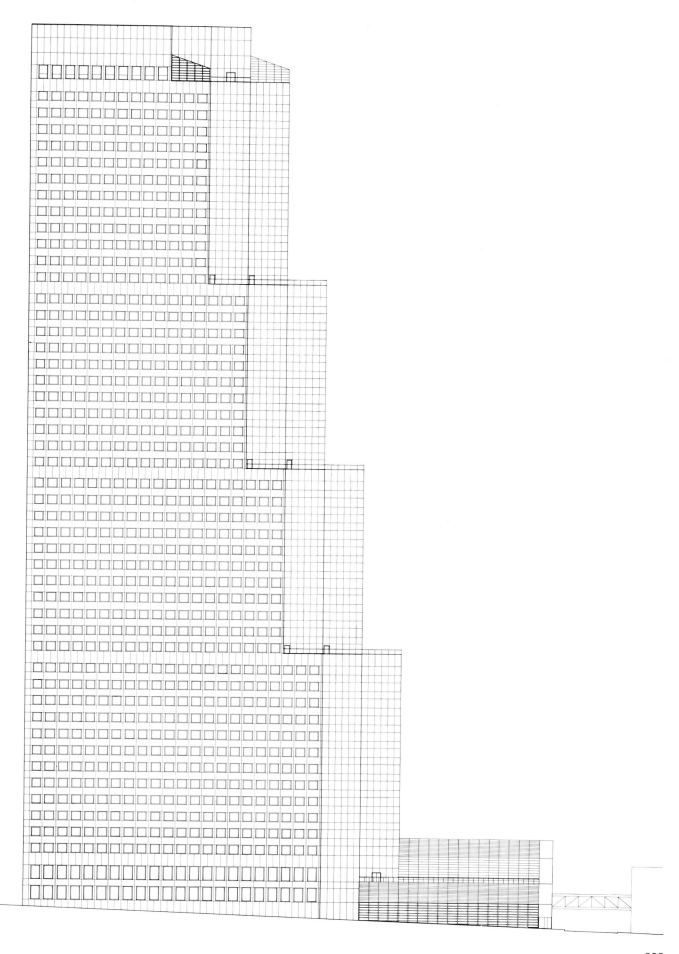

**Interterra,
Miami, Florida**

This multi-use complex completed in 1982 is located on a 95,000-square-foot site bounded by Brickell Avenue, SE 13th Street, and Miami Avenue. The complex consists of a 220,000-square-foot, 18-story office tower and a five-story garage containing 622 cars. A retail concourse is located below the 35,000-square-foot plaza. The tower is clad with a silver-blue reflective glass curtain wall with black resinous aluminum mullions. The east and west facades are recessed, allowing for more perimeter office space. Natural ventilation is provided for the smoke-proof stair towers located within the deeply cut facade. The garage is enclosed by 4-inch by 4-inch black anodized aluminum grillwork, which establishes a consistent architectural treatment for all elevations. Between the tower and the garage, exterior elevators clad in black resinous panels serve the garage floors, retail level, and office tower lobby. The plaza is extensively landscaped with trees and flower beds and contains public seating.
The structural system for the office tower is a combination of cast-in-place reinforced concrete and precast, pre-stressed concrete construction. The floor system is a composite deck of precast, pre-stressed joists and a cast-in-place 4½-inch-thick lightweight concrete slab. The garage structure is of reinforced concrete.

**Interterra,
Miami, Florida**

Der 1982 fertiggestellte Komplex liegt auf einem etwa 8.800 m² großen Grundstück, das von der Brickell Avenue, der SE 13th Street und der Miami Avenue gesäumt wird. Er besteht aus einem 18ge-schossigen Büroturm mit einer Bruttogeschoßfläche von etwa 20.500 m², einer fünfgeschossigen Garage mit 622 Stellplätzen und einer Ladenstraße unter einer etwa 3.300 m² großen Plaza. Der Turm ist mit einer Vorhangwand aus silberblau reflektierendem Glas in schwarzen Aluminiumrah-men verkleidet. Die Ost- und Westfassaden sind eingezogen, um mehr Bürofläche an Außenwän-den zu erhalten. Im Einschnitt der Westfassade liegen zwei natürlich belüftete Treppenhäuser. Die Garage ist mit einem Gitterwerk aus schwarz anodisiertem Aluminium mit einer Maschenweite von etwa 10 × 10 cm umgeben, so daß alle Fassaden in übereinstimmender Weise behandelt sind. Zwi-schen der Garage und dem Turm liegen mit schwarzen Paneelen verkleidete Aufzüge, die die Garagengeschosse, die Ladenstraße und die Halle des Turmes bedienen. Auf der Plaza finden sich Bäume, Blumenbeete und Sitzgelegenheiten.
Als Tragwerkssystem für den Turm wurde eine Mischkonstruktion aus Ortbeton und vorgespannten Fertigteilen gewählt. Die Decken bestehen aus vorgespannten Fertigbalken und an Ort und Stelle gegossenen, etwa 11,5 cm dicken Leichtbetonplatten. Auch die Garage hat ein Tragwerk aus Beton.

1. View of the tower from the east.
2. Plan (ground level).

1. Ansicht des Hochhauses von Osten.
2. Grundriß (Erdgeschoßebene).

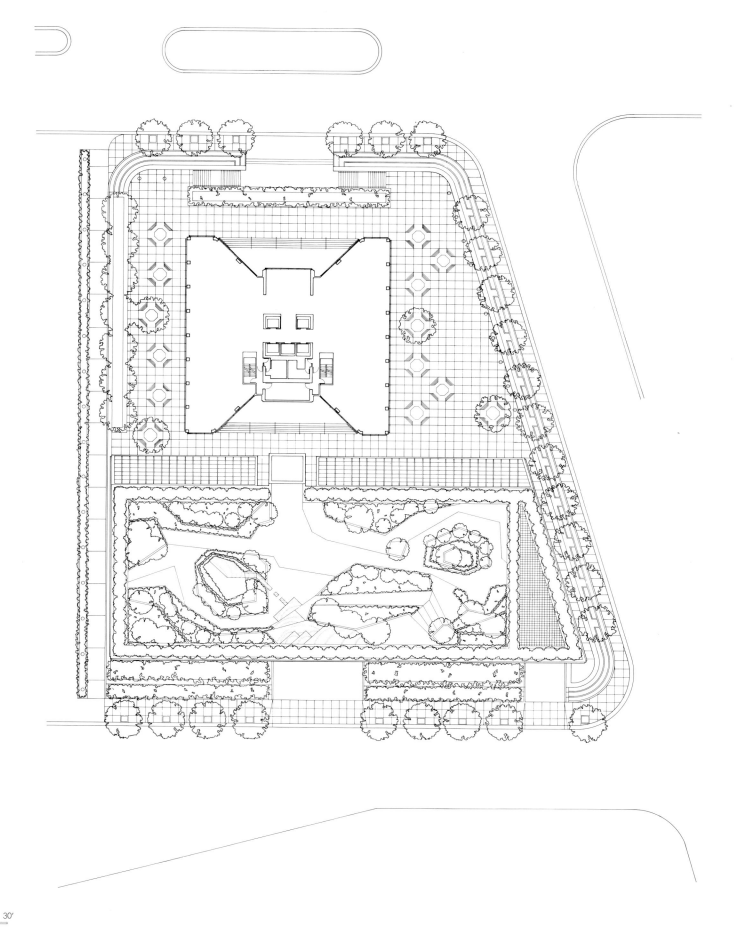

30'

Southeast Financial Center,
Miami, Florida

The new headquarters of the Southeast Bank is scheduled for completion in 1983. It consists of three elements: a 55-story office tower containing 1.2 million square feet of space fronting on Biscayne Boulevard, a separate 17-story annex containing the banking hall, 12 levels of parking, a retail arcade and an athletic club, with a large landscaped open-air court beneath a roof spanning between the buildings.
The tower is a composite tube frame rising on a basically rectangular plan. The southeast corner of the building steps back in a series of bays turning away from a near neighbor and orienting to the park and the bay.
Both buildings are clad in a white, thermal finished granite. The tower elevations have a grid overlay of black polished granite strips into which a large window is introduced, it divided in turn into four equal lights, all framed in white and glazed with silver reflecting glass, creating an elaborate pattern of squares within squares. The annex employs the same materials (except for glass) in a different manner, incorporating pierced openings to facilitate garage ventilation.
Both the tower lobby and the banking hall in the second building are elevated one floor above the plaza level. On this plaza, pedestrian traffic is generated throughout the development, along attractively appointed retail space accessible from the southeast 3rd Avenue side. A glazed bridge connects the tower lobby and the banking hall above the plaza.
The plaza is roofed by a white steel space frame 12 stories above its surface. It is paved in a pattern of stones and tiles, shaded by royal palms, and is to be furnished with benches, tables and chairs, and other accoutrements of a public space.

Southeast Financial Center,
Miami, Florida

Die im Bau befindliche neue Hauptverwaltung der Southeast Bank besteht aus drei Elementen: einem 55geschossigen Büroturm mit etwa 112.000 m² Fläche am Biscayne Boulevard, einem 17geschossigen Annex mit einer großen Bankhalle, 12 Parkgeschossen, einem Sportklub und einer Ladenstraße sowie einer großen überdachten Plaza zwischen diesen beiden Bauten.
Der Büroturm stellt eine Rohrkonstruktion dar, die auf einem rechteckigen Grundriß aufgebaut ist. An der dem Bay Front Park zugekehrten Südostecke hat das Gebäude eine Reihe von sägezahnähnlichen Rücksprüngen, so daß außer einem dreieckigen Platz auch eine große Zahl der begehrten Eckbüros mit Ausblick nach mehreren Seiten entstand. Die Auflösung der Südostecke des Turmes in kleinteilige Elemente wird durch eine Fassadenverkleidung mit quadratischen Feldern aus hellem Granit im Wechsel mit Streifen aus poliertem, schwarzem Granit und Öffnungen aus silberfarben reflektierendem Glas unterstrichen. Ein Spiel von Quadraten innerhalb von Quadraten ergibt sich durch die Vierteilung der über die volle Geschoßhöhe reichenden und besonders breiten Fenster durch weiße Sprossen. Für die Verkleidung der stark horizontal gegliederten, ruhigen Fassaden des Annexes wurde heller Granit derselben Art wie am Hochhaus gewählt.
Sowohl die Eingangshalle des Büroturms als auch die mit dieser durch eine verglaste Brücke verbundene Bankhalle im Annex sind um ein Geschoß über das Plazaniveau angehoben, so daß der Fußgängerverkehr zwischen den Läden und Restaurants auf dieser Ebene nicht gestört wird.
Das Dach der Plaza besteht aus einem weiß gestrichenen Raumfachwerk, das zwischen den Büroturm und den Annex gespannt ist. Als Belag für den Boden der Plaza wählte man Naturstein und Fliesen. Dicht gepflanzte Königspalmen werden diesem mit Bänken, Tischen und Stühlen sowie anderem Straßenmobiliar ausgestatteten öffentlichen Platz Schatten spenden.

1. View of the landscaped open-air court between the office tower and the 17-story annex (model).
2. Axonometric view of the open-air court. Shaded by clusters of royal palms this is the focal point of the project.

1. Blick auf den mit einem verglasten Raumfachwerk überdeckten und bepflanzten Freilufthof zwischen dem Bürohochhaus und dem 17geschossigen Annex (Modell).
2. Axonometrie des Freilufthofs. Der von Königspalmen beschattete Platz bildet den Hauptanziehungspunkt der Anlage.

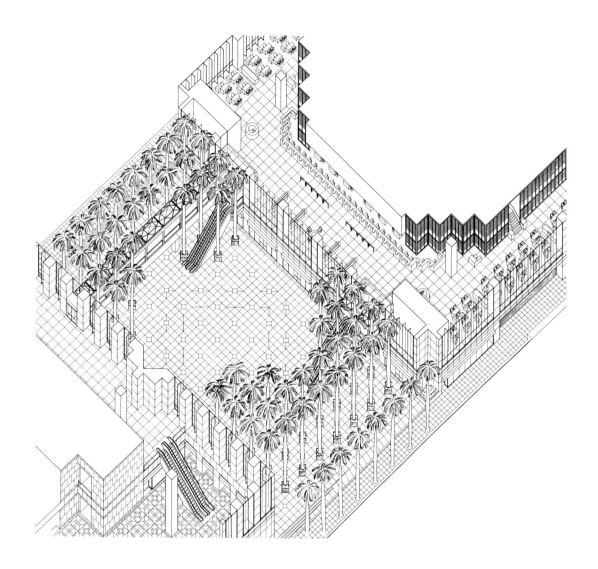

3. Plans (ground level, roof).
4. View of the complex from the Bay Front Park
(model).

3. Grundrisse (Erdgeschoßebene, Dach).
4. Ansicht der Anlage vom Bay Front Park aus
(Modell).

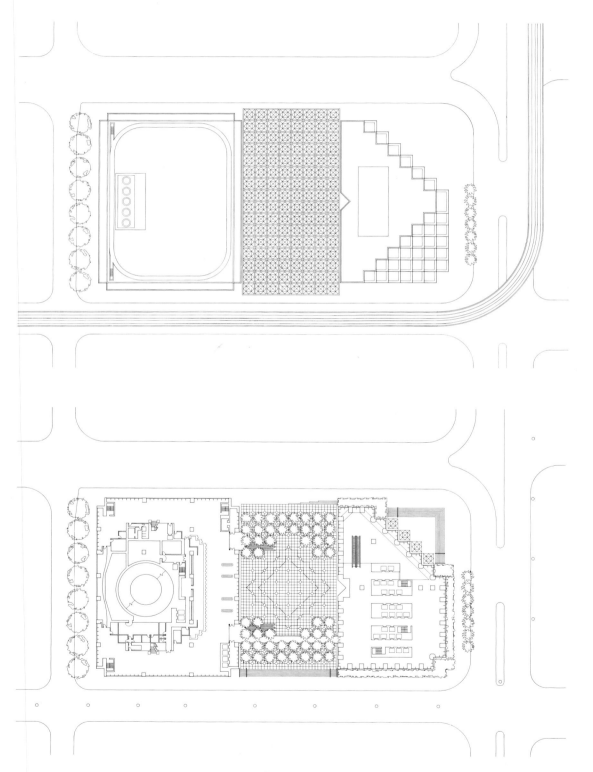

60'

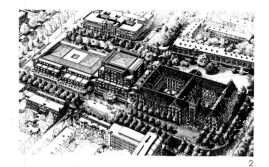

2

Das Ausland

In den siebziger Jahren gelang es SOM, bedeutende Architektur- und Planungsaufträge auf verschiedenen Kontinenten zu erhalten – oft in Ländern, die einen schnellen Industrialisierungs- und Verstädterungsprozeß durchmachen. Bei jedem dieser Projekte ergab sich von neuem eine Diskussion über das Streben der modernen Architektur nach Allgemeingültigkeit. Sollten die Architekten universale, mechanistische Formen vorschlagen – die sich durch Originalität und Modernität auszeichnen –, oder sollten sie einheimische Formen aufgreifen und nach landesüblichen Antworten auf Klima und Topographie suchen? Ist es SOM gelungen, diese Fragen bei ihrem großartigen Haj Terminal in Dschidda, bei der Hauptverwaltung der Royal Dutch Shell in Den Haag [2] oder bei der amerikanischen Botschaft in Moskau [3] zu lösen?

In einem Jahrzehnt, in dem die Ölkrise des Jahres 1973 Zweifel an einer von Energiequellen abhängigen Umwelt auslöste, schickte SOM junge Entwurfsarchitekten in vorindustrielle Länder, in denen es weder moderne Bautechniken noch moderne gesellschaftliche Strukturen gab. In den Planungen dieser Architekten für die Universität in Heluan südlich von Kairo [4] und die Universität Kebangsaan in Sabah, Ostmalaysia [5, 6] zeigt sich ihr Bemühen um die Ableitung ihrer Formensprache aus landesüblichen Techniken. Im Gegensatz zu dem weltmännischen europäischen Bauherrn, der sich ein modernes, mit Kunstwerken ausgestattetes Büro in Paris wünschte und von SOM in der elegantesten, an der Park Avenue in New York heimischen Art bedient wurde, hegten Regierungsvertreter in wirtschaftlich im Aufstieg befindlichen Ländern oft Zweifel, ob westliche Gestaltungsvorstellungen und Techniken nicht die gewohnten sozialen und kulturellen Strukturen zerstören würden. Das früher von SOM geplante Gebäude der Banque Lambert [7] war eine hervorragende Lösung für Brüssel, aber in Ägypten, dem Iran oder Malaysia waren weder die Technik noch die Wirtschaftsstruktur für einen solchen Bau vorhanden.

Bei SOM herrschte keineswegs eine einheitliche Auffassung über die Frage der angemessenen Architektur in Entwicklungsländern. Die Vorschläge reichen von einer an landesübliche Themen anknüpfenden Formensprache bis hin zu Manifesten eines kraftvollem Neuerungsgeistes. Bei den Bauten der Banco de Occidente in Guatemala-Stadt [8] schufen Bruce Graham und Adrian Smith vom Chicagoer Büro aus Licht, Farbe und Textur Räume mit fein abgestimmtem Maßstab und mit einfachen, einheimischen Bauformen, die an Luis Barragan erinnern. Im Gegensatz dazu stellt die von Gordon Bunshaft, Partner im New Yorker Büro, entworfene National Commercial Bank in Dschidda [9] ein großes, dreieckiges Prisma dar, das von einem zentralen, offenen Schacht und von Höfen durchbrochen wird. So

3

4

5

6

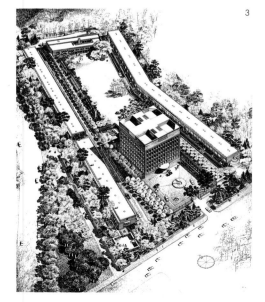

7

International

In the 1970's, as now, SOM won important architectural and urban design commissions on several continents where nations are undergoing rapid industrialization and urbanization. Each project stirred debate over modern architecture's quest for universality. Should architects propose universal, mechanistic forms, memorable for originality and modernity, or should they catch indigenous themes and native responses to climate and terrain? Did SOM resolve that debate in their marvelous Haj Terminal at Jeddah, Royal Dutch Shell Petroleum Company Headquarters in the Hague [2], or the U.S. Embassy in Moscow [3]? In a decade when the 1973 oil crisis provoked doubts about energy-dependent environment, SOM sent young designers to preindustrial nations where neither building technologies nor social patterns were familiar. Their plans for Helwan University, south of Cairo [4], and Kebangsaan University in Sabah, East Malaysia [5, 6], reveal their efforts at evolving form from native technologies. In contrast to the urbane continental client who wanted a modern, art-filled Parisian office and won SOM's most elegant Park Avenue response, governmental leaders in economically ascendant nations often worried whether western aesthetics and technology would disrupt traditional social and cultural patterns. SOM's earlier Banque Lambert [7] was wonderful for Brussels, but Egypt, Iran and Malaysia had neither the technology nor corporate structure ready for it.

SOM was by no means united on the question of architecture for developing nations. Proposed forms ranged from expressions of indigenous themes to declarations of bold inventions. For the Banco de Occidente buildings in Guatemala City [8], SOM/Chicago partners Bruce Graham and Adrian Smith modelled light, color and texture within gently scaled spaces and elemental, vernacular forms reminiscent of Luis Barragan. In contrast, the National Commercial Bank of Jeddah [9], proposed by SOM/New York partner Gordon Bunshaft, is a tall triangular prism pierced by a central well and courtyards. However much the prismatic frame may reduce glare and dissipate heat, it is original, and its abutting circular garage and adjoining banking hall lack Islamic or Saudian reference. Is such new universal configuration wanted, and does it announce Saudi Arabia's emancipation, or only private ambitions that may be transitory? It can of course be argued that such an avowedly modern, universal form is desirable. If an agrarian or nomadic nation strikes riches and overnight acquires airplanes, microwave antennas, telephones, television, computers, and modern medicine, why should it not celebrate its arrival and ascendancy in original symbols? If they are exquisite, even daring and brilliant, they may set goals and summon pride.

8

9

1. Skyline of Jeddah, Saudi Arabia.
2. Addition to the headquarters of Royal Dutch Shell, The Hague, The Netherlands.
3. United States Embassy, Moscow, USSR.
4. Helwan University, Helwan, Egypt.
5, 6. Kebangsaan University, Sabah, East Malaysia.
7. Banque Lambert, Brussels, Belgium.
8. Montufar branch of the Banco di Occidente, Guatemala City, Guatemala.
9. National Commercial Bank, Jeddah, Saudi Arabia.

313

10

11

sehr auch dieser prismatische Bau Schutz vor Licht und Hitze bieten mag, so stellt er doch eine originäre Form dar, und auch die angrenzende Hochgarage sowie die Bankhalle sind nicht aus islamischer oder saudischer Überlieferung hergeleitet.

Man kann natürlich der Meinung sein, daß eine solche bewußt moderne, universale Form erstrebenswert ist. Wenn schon ein auf Landwirtschaft oder Nomadentum gegründetes Land zu Reichtum kommt und sich über Nacht Flugzeuge, Mikrowellenantennen, Telephon, Fernsehen, Datenverarbeitungsanlagen und die moderne Medizin aneignet – warum sollte man die Einführung und den Einfluß dieser Errungenschaften nicht mit den zugehörigen baulichen Symbolen feiern? Wenn diese auserlesen – ja sogar wagemutig und brillant – sind, können sie Ziele setzen und Stolz auslösen. Überdies haben die neuzeitlichen internationalen Finanzgesellschaften keine lokalen Bezüge. Der Wirtschaftskonzern ist eine übernationale Erscheinung, und Michael McCarthy, Partner im New Yorker Büro, vermittelt mit den neuartigen, originellen Bauformen des Al-Jaber-Komplexes [10] diese Tatsache seinen kuwaitischen Bauherren. Eine ähnliche Wirkung geht von den SOM-Projekten in Mexiko und Kanada aus. Für die Hauptverwaltung der Grupo Alfa südlich von Monterrey in Mexiko [11] plante SOM gewölbte Hallen und umschlossene Gärten. Das vom New Yorker Büro geplante First Canadian Center in Calgary [12] besteht aus zwei hohen Bürotürmen, die durch einen dreieckigen Pavillonbau mit drei Geschossen für die Bank of Montreal verbunden sind.

Welche Botschaften sollen in einer fremden Kultur aufgenommen werden? Sollen die Architekten angesichts dessen, daß in Rijad nur noch Überreste einer aus Lehmziegeln erbauten Festung bestehen und die Beduinen keine Tradition ortsfester Architektur besitzen, für das Bauen in Saudi-Arabien moderne Ausdrucksmöglichkeiten finden, oder sollen sie sich Varianten der viktorianischen Villen und der Beaux-Arts-Banken in Dschidda einfallen lassen; sollen sie mit Motiven des maurischen Baustils in Spanien aufwarten oder sich an die Architektur von Berberdörfern in Nordafrika anlehnen? Oder genügt es vielleicht, wenn man die Gebäude nach westlicher Art plant und lediglich ortsansässige Handwerker beschäftigt sowie Dekorationen hinzufügt – wie die Fahnen aus gebatiktem Stoff in der ansonsten neutralen Halle des Hotels Lanka Oberoi in Sri Lanka [13]?

Besonders in Nordafrika und im Nahen Osten stieß SOM auf die Herausforderung regionaler Traditionen. Die Bauherren dort benötigten oft Hilfe bei der Aufstellung von Bauprogrammen für Krankenhäuser und Universitäten. Walter Netsch, Partner im Chicagoer Büro, brachte das algerische Ministerium für höhere Erziehung und wissenschaftliche Forschung dazu, amerikanische Berater in Erziehungsfragen zu

12

10. Kuwait Markets Group – Ahmed Al Jaber Street Commercial Center, Kuwait City, Kuwait.
11. Headquarters of the Grupo Industrial Alfa, Monterrey, Mexico.
12. First Canadian Centre, Calgary, Canada.
13. Lanka Oberoi Hotel, Colombo, Sri Lanka.
14, 15. University of Tizi-Ouzou, Tizi-Ouzou, Algeria.

14

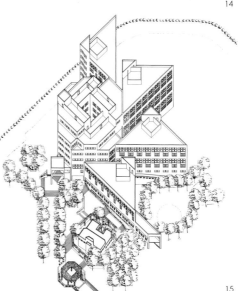
15

Then, too, some aspiring nations may be more ready than others to import both social change and an architecture that hastens the change. Moreover, there is nothing local about the modern international financial corporation. The commercial corporation is universal, and, with innovative, distinctive forms, SOM/New York partner Michael McCarthy conveys that message in the Al Jaber Commercial Complex [10] for his Kuwaiti clients. A similar message is sent by SOM's Mexican and Canadian projects. For the Grupo Alfa in Mexico, SOM proposed vaulted halls and internal gardens for its headquarters south of Monterrey [11]. Acknowledging the Energy Belt alliance in western Canada, SOM/New York's First Canadian Centre in Calgary [12] consists of two tall towers joined by a triangular three-story pavilion for the Bank of Montreal.

What messages in a foreign culture should be heard? If Riyadh has only remnants of a mud brick fort and the Bedouin has no heritage of permanent architecture, should architects invent modern forms for Saudi Arabia or spring variations on Jeddah's Victorian villas and Beaux Arts banks, capture themes from Spain's Islamic architecture and recall Berber villages in North Africa or mosques in Iran? Or will it suffice to design western structures and add local crafts and ornament, like the batik banners suspended within SOM's otherwise universal Lanka Oberoi hotel lobby in Sri Lanka [13]? Downtown Casablanca and Beirut sadly show the result of feckless modernism. Deciding that such insensitivities are intolerable, SOM's partners sought for more.

Where SOM met regional challenges was in North Africa and the Middle East. There, clients often needed help in organizing the programs for hospitals and universities. SOM/Chicago partner Walter Netsch encouraged the Algerian Ministry of Higher Education and Scientific Research to retain American educational consultants. The resulting University of Tizi-Ouzou [14, 15] arranges technical disciplines around four courtyards, each offering specialized libraries, classrooms and laboratories. A second Algerian campus, the University of Blida, assigns fifteen fields of study to four specialized colleges, with university-owned student housing and a separate site for Blida's Teaching Hospital.

For Helwan University in Egypt, SOM/Chicago's Netsch and DeStefano developed sequences of courtyard and building that reflect a set of principles SOM had developed. Foremost was the goal of solving each project's problem in its broadest urban implications. A second was to combine residential space with work places in culturally relevant ways. A third was to find means to reduce dependency on electricity and emphasize natural means for modifying temperature and gaining ventilation. A fourth principle was to use local materials and manpower and modularize mass produced units so that labor intensive,

13

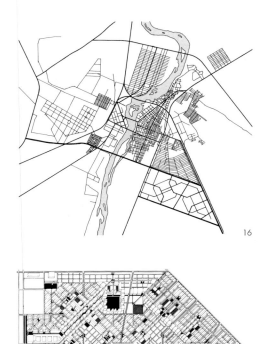

16

17

beschäftigen. Bei der Universität in Tizi-Ouzou [14, 15], einem Ergebnis dieser Zusammenarbeit, sind die technischen Disziplinen um vier Innenhöfe herum angeordnet, an denen jeweils Spezialbibliotheken, Hörsäle und Labors liegen. Bei einem zweiten Campus, dem der Universität in Blida, sind fünfzehn Fachbereiche vier spezialisierten Kollegzentren zugeordnet; hinzukommen Studentenwohnanlagen und ein auf einem eigenen Grundstück geplantes Lehrkrankenhaus.

Für die Universität in Heluan entwickelte Netsch zusammen mit seinem Chicagoer Kollegen Abfolgen von Höfen und Gebäuden, die eine Reihe von SOM befolgter Grundregeln widerspiegeln: An erster Stelle steht die Regel, die besonderen Probleme jedes Projektes in ihren weitesten städtebaulichen Zusammenhängen zu lösen. Die zweite Regel ist die, Wohnungen und Arbeitsstätten in einer der jeweiligen Kultur entsprechenden Weise zu verbinden. Die dritte besteht in der Suche nach Möglichkeiten zur Verringerung der Abhängigkeit vom elektrischen Strom und zur Anwendung natürlicher Mittel für Temperaturregelung und Belüftung. Die vierte fordert den Rückgriff auf Baustoffe und Arbeitskräfte des Landes sowie die Standardisierung vorgefertigter Einheiten, so daß Angehörige arbeitsintensiver, nichtmechanisierter Gesellschaften die Montage durchführen können. Die fünfte beinhaltet die Anerkennung der privaten Sphäre und die liebevolle Einbeziehung von Wasser, Schatten und Schutzdächern. Die sechste Regel schließlich ist die, öffentliche Wege und Freiräume reichhaltig auszugestalten.

Diese sechs Grundregeln dienten als Leitfaden für die städtebaulichen Planungen von SOM in den Wüstenregionen des Nahen Ostens, wo die Regierungen zusammen mit petrochemischen Industrieanlagen neue Städte und Häfen gründeten. Auf ebenem, baumlosem Gelände angesiedelt, von Wasserarmut, plötzlichen Überschwemmungen und heißen Winden bedroht, lastet auf diesen Städten die Sonnenhitze, die jeden Tag unterteilt in Arbeit und Schule am Morgen, Ruhezeit zu Hause über Mittag, wieder Arbeit am Spätnachmittag und Mußestunden in der Öffentlichkeit am Abend. Dazu kommen weitere Einschnitte durch häufige religiöse Übungen. Diese Gesichtspunkte des Zeitablaufs, des Klimas, der Bodenbeschaffenheit und des kulturellen Lebens kristallisierten sich 1975 bei Diskussionen in Schiras heraus, als die SOM-Partner Goldstein, DeStefano und Khan mit der Mandala Collaborative aus Teheran bei der Planung wichtiger islamischer Städte zusammenarbeiteten.

In der ölreichen iranischen Provinz Chusistan, wo sich fünf große Flüsse vereinigen und in den Persischen Golf fließen, plante das SOM-Büro in San Francisco die Neue Stadt Jondi Shapur [16, 17], deren Generalplan 1976 zum Modellvorhaben für Wohnungsbauprojekte der iranischen Regierung erklärt wurde. Ebenso plante das Büro in San Francisco – im weiteren Verlauf

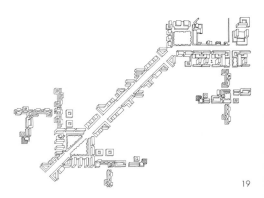

18

19

16, 17. Jondi Shapour New Town, Jondi Shapour, Iran.
18, 19. Bandar Shapour New Town, Bandar Shapour, Iran.
20. Yanbu New Town, Yanbu, Saudi Arabia.
21. King Abdul Aziz University, Makkah, Saudi Arabia.
22. Haj Terminal, King Abdul Aziz International Airport, Jeddah, Saudi Arabia.

316

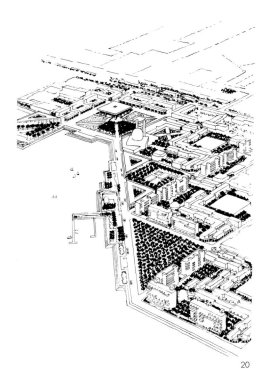

20

nonmechanized societies could assemble them. The fifth was to recognize privacies and celebrate any special reverences for water, shade and canopy, and the sixth was to enrich public ways and sanctuaries.

Those six principles guided SOM's town planning in the Middle East's desert regions where governments started new towns to support petrochemical plants and ports. Occupying flat, treeless sites and threatened by scarce water, flash floods, and searing winds, such towns feel the sun's heat, which divides each day into work and school at dawn, middays at home, late afternoons at work and evenings at public leisure, with further intervals marked by frequent religious worship. Those features of time, climate, terrain and culture emerged in SOM's discussions at Shiraz in 1975 when SOM partners Goldstein, DeStefano and Khan joined Teheran's Mandala Collaborative in planning important Iranian towns.

In Iran's Khuzestan, the oil-rich province where five great rivers converge and flow into the Persian Gulf, SOM/San Francisco planned a new perimetal community, Jondi Shapour [16, 17], whose master plan in 1976 was endorsed as a model for Iranian government-sponsored housing. SOM/San Francisco, later augmented by SOM/Chicago, also planned a new town on a flat plain near Bandar Shapour [18, 19]. Selecting a site distant from Bandar Shapour's refineries and petrochemical industries, the urban designers proposed a lake and reservoir and brought precious water in open irrigation canals along the major boulevard and subsidiary roads within urban districts. Paths radiating from the bazaar lead to nodes and intersections, which are the principal locations for religious, medical, educational and governmental buildings.

SOM's work in the Middle East culminated in large planning projects in Saudi Arabia. For the new petrochemical town on the Red Sea south of Yanbu [20], SOM/San Francisco laid an orthogonal grid on the port's curved shoreline and assigned a triangular site to the town center. For Umm Al-Qura University, formerly called the King Abdul Aziz University, near Makkah [21], SOM/Chicago, led by partners Roger Seitz and Fazlur Khan, proposed a campus that embodies many features of the historic Islamic "madrassa". While neither Yanbu's new town nor the university will be built to SOM's plans, the most important of SOM's Saudi Arabian projects, the Haj Terminal at Jeddah [22], was completed and has drawn international acclaim. Initially, the Haj Terminal project was undertaken by SOM/New York partner Gordon Wildermuth who had led the team designing the Jeddah Airport since 1975. Soon, however, the Haj Terminal enlisted Gordon Bunshaft, Raul de Armas, Roy Allen and John Winkler in New York and then engaged Chicago's Fazlur Khan and Parambir Gujral who probed structure and energy in membrane and tensile structures. It is a re-

21

22

mit Unterstützung des Chicagoer Büros – eine Neue Stadt auf einer großen Ebene bei Bandar Shapur [18, 19]. Die Architekten schlugen die Anlage eines Sees vor und wollten das kostbare Wasser über offene Bewässerungskanäle an der baumbestandenen Hauptstraße und an den Nebenstraßen in den Wohnvierteln entlangleiten. Von dem Basar ausgehende Fußwege sollten zu Knotenpunkten und Kreuzungen führen, die als bevorzugte Orte für Moscheen, medizinische Einrichtungen und Regierungsgebäude vorgesehen waren.

Die Tätigkeit von SOM im Nahen Osten erreichte mit großen Projekten in Saudi-Arabien ihren bisherigen Höhepunkt. Bei der Planung der auf petrochemischer Industrie gegründeten Neuen Stadt Yanbu am Roten Meer [20] legte das Büro in San Francisco ein rechteckiges Raster über das unregelmäßige Küstengelände und wies der Stadtmitte ein dreieckiges Grundstück zu. Für die Umm Al-Qura University (früher King Abdul Aziz University) bei Mekka [21] sah das Chicagoer Büro unter Leitung der Partner Fazlur Khan und Roger Seitz eine Hochschulanlage vor, die viele Eigenschaften der traditionellen islamischen »Madrassa« beinhaltet. Während aber weder die Neue Stadt Yanbu noch diese Universität entsprechend den Planungen von SOM ausgeführt werden, vollendete SOM kürzlich den Haj Terminal in Dschidda [22] als bedeutendstes Werk des Büros in Saudi-Arabien und fand damit weltweite Anerkennung. Zunächst lag das Projekt in Händen von Gordon Wildermuth, Partner im New Yorker Büro, der seit 1975 die Entwurfsgruppe für den Flugplatz von Dschidda leitete. Dann befaßten sich auch seine New Yorker Kollegen Gordon Bunshaft, Raul de Armas und Roy Allen mit dem Terminal. Schließlich wurden Fazlur Khan und Parambir Gujral vom Chicagoer Büro hinzugezogen. Auf Grund der aufeinander abgestimmten Arbeit der Büros in Chicago und New York entwickelten sich Bauform und Technik mit zwingender Logik.

Als zeltartige Stadt in der Wüste ist der Haj Terminal ein altes Symbol, das Eingangsportal zum Islam, das mit modernen Mitteln geschaffen wurde. Es ist der Vorstellung von Architekten entsprungen, die ihr ganzes Bemühen darauf richteten, Technologie mit baukünstlerischer Einsicht zu verbinden. Mit einer Formensprache, die weder universalem Modernismus noch ortsgebundenem Konservatismus entsprang, tritt das Gebäude den Beweis dafür an, daß die moderne Technologie im Dienst einheimischer kultureller Werte eine großartige Integrationskraft zu vermitteln vermag.

markable feat of collaboration and advanced SOM's interoffice strength.

A tented city in the desert, the Haj Terminal is an ancient symbol, the gateway to Islam, achieved by modern artistry. It was imagined by architects who did not withhold their best efforts at wedding technology to aesthetic insight. Neither a universal modernism nor a local traditionalism, the Haj Terminal proves that modern technology may have magnificent integrity while serving indigenous cultural themes.

Headquarters of the
Banco de Occidente,
Guatemala City, Guatemala

In 1978 three buildings were completed in Guatemala City for Banco de Occidente, one of the oldest banking institutions in Guatemala: the three-story headquarters in the ancient city center and two smaller suburban branch banks. Architectural continuity was sought for all locations through the use of indigenous colors, similar effects of light and shadow, and repetitive use of textures and materials. In contrast to the typical approach to local reconstruction projects, the architects consciously reinforced the buildings' relationship to the Guatemalan context by using only locally available construction materials and adopting local architectural concepts, such as open courtyards, terraces, gardens, fountains and trellises. Because of frequent local power failures, the buildings are designed to function without artificial illumination. Heating and cooling systems are omitted from the buildings, and all three poured-in-place reinforced concrete structures are designed to resist Zone 3 earthquake forces.
The headquarters provides maximum teller and public contact areas on level 1; executive offices, board room and semi-public contact on level 2; and an employee lounge and non-public functions at level 3. Major design elements are exterior walls predominantly of opaque stucco, an interior/exterior courtyard, and a two-story banking room with a translucent fabric roof to allow soft natural light to enter the hall. A stone base at street level provides a durable surface to withstand high pedestrian traffic and vandalism. Terrace openings to the north and setback openings on the west control light, and operable wood louvers modulate ventilation.

Hauptsitz der
Banco de Occidente,
Guatemala-Stadt, Guatemala

Für eine der ältesten Banken in Guatemala wurden 1978 in Guatemala-Stadt drei neue Gebäude errichtet: der dreigeschossige Hauptsitz im alten Stadtzentrum und zwei kleinere Filialen in Vorstädten. Für die verschiedenen Bauten wurde durch die Verwendung miteinander verwandter, in dieser Region gebräuchlicher Farben, durch ähnliche Licht- und Schatteneffekte und durch sich wiederholende Oberflächen und Baumaterialien ein einheitlicher Charakter angestrebt. Im Gegensatz zu der üblichen Praxis legten die Architekten Wert darauf, die Gebäude in den guatemaltekischen Kontext einzubinden, indem sie nur landesübliche Baumaterialien verwendeten und auch landesübliche Architekturelemente übernahmen, wie offene Höfe, Terrassen, Gärten, Brunnen und Pergolen. Wegen der häufigen Stromausfälle wurden die Gebäude so konzipiert, daß sie auch ohne künstliche Beleuchtung benutzt werden können; auf Heizung und Klimaanlagen wurde überhaupt verzichtet. In allen drei Fällen besteht das Tragwerk, das den in der Erdbebenzone 3 auftretenden seismischen Kräften zu widerstehen vermag, aus Stahlbeton.
Beim Hauptsitz der Bank liegen im Erdgeschoß eine große Bankhalle mit den Büros für starken Publikumsverkehr, im 1. Obergeschoß Direktionsräume, Sitzungssaal und Büros mit geringerem Publikumsverkehr und im 2. Obergeschoß die übrigen Büros und ein Aufenthaltsraum für die Mitarbeiter. Wesentliche Gestaltungselemente sind die rauhen Putzflächen der Außenwände, ein großer Hof und eine zwei Geschosse einnehmende Bankhalle, bei der das von oben einfallende Licht durch ein transluzentes Textilmaterial gedämpft wird. Da in diesem Bereich der Stadt lebhafter Fußgängerverkehr herrscht, erhielt das Gebäude im Erdgeschoß zum Schutz gegen mutwillige Zerstörungen eine bis auf Augenhöhe reichende Verkleidung aus Naturstein. Die Belichtung erfolgt auf der Nordseite über Terrassen und auf der Westseite über tiefe Einschnitte in der Wand; die Belüftung läßt sich über verstellbare Holzjalousien regulieren.

1. Plan (ground floor).
2, 3. Interior views.

1. Grundriß (Erdgeschoß).
2, 3. Innenansichten.

Pages 322/323:
4, 6. Exterior views.
5. View of the courtyard.

Seiten 322/323:
4, 6. Außenansichten.
5. Blick in den Innenhof.

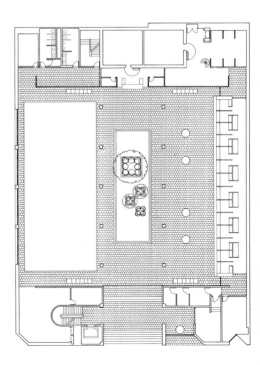

Montufar Branch of the Banco de Occidente, Guatemala City, Guatemala

The 4,500-square-foot Montufar branch is a small, eight-teller facility located on property with existing party walls on all sides. The facility is accessible from two points through existing shopping centers. Skylights were designed to provide natural light and ventilation with minimal direct sunlight on work surfaces. Each skylight uses concrete block louvers for ventilation. A large skylit courtyard with reflecting pool is used to increase the sense of openness and strengthen the illusion of interior as exterior space.

Zweigstelle Montufar der Banco de Occidente, Guatemala-Stadt, Guatemala

Die kleine Filiale der Banco de Occidente in einer Vorstadt von Guatemala-Stadt ist mit acht Schaltern ausgestattet und hat eine Fläche von etwa 420 m². Sie wurde auf einem Grundstück errichtet, das allseits von den Brandwänden angrenzender Gebäude umgeben ist. Es gibt zwei Zugänge, zu denen man über benachbarte Einkaufsmärkte gelangt. Die Oberlichter wurden so angeordnet, daß die direkte Sonneneinstrahlung auf den Arbeitsflächen so gering wie möglich ist. Jedes Oberlicht ist mit Lamellen aus Betonstein zur natürlichen Be- und Entlüftung ausgestattet. Um den Eindruck der Abgeschlossenheit zu mildern und die Illusion eines Freiraums zu erzeugen, wurde ein großer, von oben belichteter Innenhof mit einem spiegelnden Wasserbecken vorgesehen.

1. Plan (ground floor).
2. Skylights provide natural light and ventilation with minimal direct sunlight.

1. Grundriß (Erdgeschoß).
2. Oberlichter sorgen bei minimaler direkter Sonneneinstrahlung für natürliche Belichtung und Belüftung.

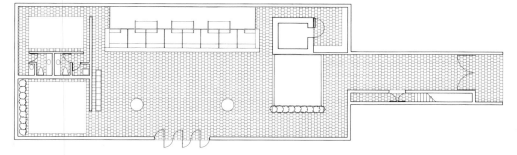

15'

3, 4. Indigenous colors and materials, combined with subtled effects of light and shadow, reinforce the building's relationship to the Guatemalan context.

3, 4. Durch den Gebrauch von landesüblichen Farben und Baustoffen in Verbindung mit subtilen Licht- und Schattenwirkungen wird die Einbindung des Gebäudes in den guatemaltekischen Kontext unterstrichen.

Headquarters of the Grupo Industrial Alfa, Monterrey, Mexico

1–3. General views (model).
4. Plan (main level) and section.

1–3. Gesamtansichten (Modell).
4. Grundriß (Hauptgeschoß) und Schnitt.

The new headquarters complex of Grupo Industrial Alfa, completed in 1982, is constructed on a large 25-acre wooded site at the foot of the Sierra Madre Oriental Mountains about 9.5 miles south of the Monterrey city center. The relative infrequency of automobile traffic, the density of natural vegetation on the site and the magnificent views combine to inspire a feeling of quiet serenity.

The location of the site and the shape of the two-story complex are the result of programmatic requirements and a desire to incorporate the undisturbed natural setting and mountain views.

The basic elements of the 195,000-square-foot building program are a general office building, a large auditorium and cafeteria, and the executive offices. The components, varying in height and elevation, are united by a barrel-vaulted galleria, which dominates the building complex in both its height and form.

Exterior vertical and horizontal sunscreening devices, which vary with the different orientations, are used throughout the building. The exterior walls of the concrete structure have a stucco finish with punched windows glazed in clear glass. The use of planted courtyards, formal open courts, and a garden court shaded by a high trellis over the cafeteria recall the Mexican tradition of landscape design.

The formal vocabulary of the exterior facades was developed with two primary concerns in mind. The first was to express the interior organization of private versus public spaces, while the second was to respond to the problem of light penetration into the interior zones.

The use of Mexican materials in the form of terra-cotta pavers, stuccoed concrete and wood serves to create an overall sense of warmth and texture in the spaces.

Hauptverwaltung der Grupo Industrial Alfa, Monterrey, Mexiko

Der 1982 fertiggestellte Komplex der Hauptverwaltung der Grupo Industrial Alfa wurde auf einem etwa 10 ha großen, bewaldeten Grundstück errichtet, das 15 km südlich des Stadtzentrums von Monterrey am Fuß der Sierra Madre Oriental liegt. Das ruhige, vom Verkehr kaum berührte Gelände vermittelt mit seiner dichten, natürlichen Vegetation und seinem großartigen Ausblick ein Gefühl friedlicher Abgeschiedenheit.

Anordnung und Gliederung der zweigeschossigen Baugruppe ergaben sich sowohl aus dem Funktionsablauf als auch aus dem Wunsch, die ursprüngliche Umgebung und die Aussicht auf die Berge angemessen zu berücksichtigen.

Die Hauptelemente der etwa 18.000 m² großen Anlage sind der Bereich der allgemeinen Verwaltung, ein Auditorium, die Kantine und der Bereich der Geschäftsleitung. Zusammengebunden wurden die in Höhe und Fassadengliederung verschieden geformten Bauteile durch eine tonnengewölbte Galerie, die den Komplex sowohl durch seine Höhe als auch durch seine Form beherrscht.

Der Komplex ist ringsum mit vertikalen und horizontalen, mit den Himmelsrichtungen wechselnden Sonnenschutzeinrichtungen ausgestattet. Die äußeren Wände der aus Stahlbeton errichteten Baugruppe wurden verputzt; die in tiefen Laibungen sitzenden Fenster bestehen aus Klarglas. In formal strengen, offenen Höfen und einem durch eine Pergola beschatteten Gartenhof über der Kantine wird an die mexikanische Tradition der bewachsenen Patios angeknüpft.

Die Wahl des Formenvokabulars für die äußere Erscheinung entsprang zum einen dem Wunsch, die innere Differenzierung in private und öffentliche Bereiche auch außen sichtbar zu machen, zum anderen der Notwendigkeit, das Innere vor direktem Sonnenlicht zu schützen.

Der weitgehende Gebrauch typisch mexikanischer Materialien wie Bodenfliesen aus Terrakotta, verputzter Beton und Holz trug dazu bei, dem Bau ein spezifisches Kolorit zu geben.

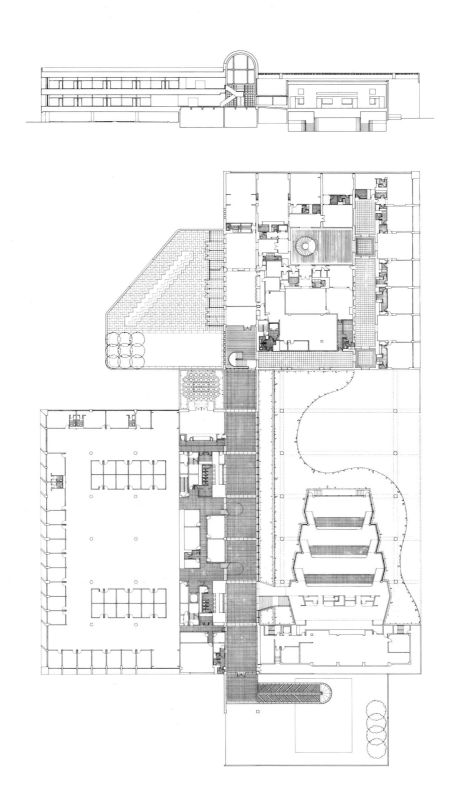

60'

First Canadian Centre,
Calgary, Alberta, Canada

The 2,000,000-square-foot First Canadian Centre, under construction on an L-shaped site in downtown Calgary, is scheduled for completion in 1985. This complex will completely fill its 2.18-acre site, with a banking pavilion occupying the corner.

The banking pavilion, a soaring cathedral-like space, rises under uneven slopes to a 10-story peak. Inset between the towers, it is the complex's focal point, connecting three levels of public space. The completely glazed pavilion is a steel frame structure faced with white granite. From the cold outdoors, tenants and visitors enter a climate-controlled, light and airy hall warmed by red granite floors and walls.

The taller tower rises 64 stories, cutting back at the 42nd floor, while the shorter 43-story tower cuts back at the 22nd floor. At the lower levels, the plan is in the shape of a large parallelogram with truncated corners; the upper level plan is halved at a 45 degree angle. This configuration produced varying floor sizes to suit the needs of both large and small companies. The interior spaces are designed for an open office plan and optimize perimeter space for private offices. Sloped, grey-tinted, insulated glass roofs double as exterior walls for the uppermost floors, creating three dimensional spaces in the sky. These floors can be cut back to create a mezzanine level at four locations within the towers. Below grade space contains two levels of parking for 165 cars and loading facilities.

The structural system for the towers is based on a tube-in-tube concept involving an exterior reinforced concrete-framed tube and an interior shear wall core tube. The 64-story tower is a composite concrete tube-in-tube system with a long-span steel truss floor system, while the 43-story tower is an all concrete system. The exterior column spacing for the 43-story tower was modified to make the tube grid more responsive to table form construction for the concrete floors.

The pre-assembled cladding system for the towers consolidates in one pre-cast concrete sandwich panel the white Sardinian polished granite finish material (with joints sealed), building insulation, metal flashing, window frames, slightly reflective silvery blue window glazing, and window cleaning tracks.

First Canadian Centre,
Calgary, Alberta, Kanada

Das First Canadian Centre, das 1985 fertiggestellt sein wird, hat eine Bruttogeschoßfläche von etwa 186.000 m² und nimmt ein etwa 8.800 m² großes Grundstück im Zentrum von Calgary ein. Die Anlage umfaßt zwei Hochhäuser mit 64 und 43 Geschossen und einen die Grundstücksecke ausfüllenden Bankpavillon.

Der 10 Geschosse hoch aufsteigende, wie eine Kathedrale wirkende Bankpavillon ist der Mittelpunkt des ganzen Komplexes und bindet drei Geschosse mit öffentlichen Einrichtungen zusammen. Der vollständig verglaste Bau hat ein mit weißem Granit verkleidetes Stahltragwerk. Im kalten kanadischen Klima bietet er Mietern und Besuchern einen witterungsgeschützten, hellen und luftigen Treffpunkt.

Beide Türme sind in Anpassung an die Grundstücksform im Grundriß ein Parallelogramm mit abgeschnittenen Ecken, von dem jedoch jeweils nur eine Hälfte bis zur vollen Höhe durchläuft, während die andere auf mittlerer Höhe mit einem abgeschrägten Glasdach endet. Dadurch ergaben sich unterschiedliche Geschoßgrößen, was für die Vermietbarkeit von Vorteil ist. Da die Gebäudekerne jeweils in Grundrißmitte liegen, treten sie in den oberen Bereichen vor den dort geschlossenen seitlichen Außenwänden in Erscheinung. Von den oberen Geschoßebenen aus, die hinter den Schrägen aus grau getöntem Glas liegen, bieten sich Ausblicke nach allen Seiten über die Stadt und auf die umliegenden Berge. Unter dem Straßenniveau können auf zwei Garagenebenen 165 Wagen abgestellt werden.

Als Tragwerkssystem für die beiden Türme wurde eine Rohr-in-Rohr-Konstruktion mit der Außenwand als äußerem und dem Kern als innerem Rohr gewählt. Bei dem 64geschossigem Turm bestehen die beiden Rohre aus Beton und die Träger aus Stahl, während der 43geschossige Turm eine reine Betonkonstruktion darstellt. Die Achsabstände der äußeren Stützen wurden beim niedrigeren Turm in Anpassung an das Tragverhalten der Betondecken modifiziert.

Von besonderem Interesse sind die vollkommen vorgefertigten und im Werk eingeglasten Fassadenelemente, die jeweils zwei Fensterfelder in Geschoßhöhe umfassen und für deren Außenhaut weißer, polierter Granit aus Sardinien mit Fensteröffnungen aus silberblau reflektierendem Glas gewählt wurde.

1. General view (photomontage).
2. Plans (ground level, typical floor).

1. Gesamtansicht (Photomontage).
2. Grundrisse (Erdgeschoß, Normalgeschoß).

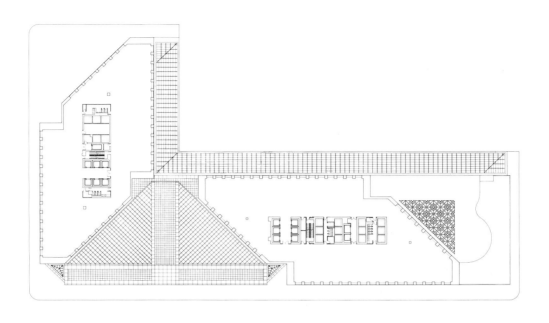

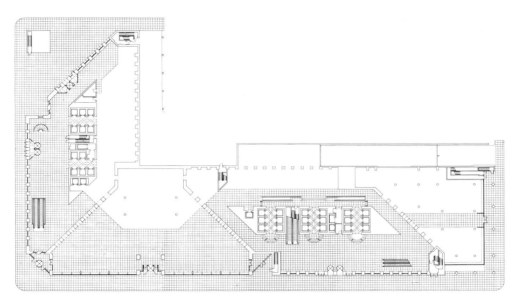

30'

Agnelli Suite,
Paris, France

This executive suite, completed in 1976, occupies the top floor of the 44-story Tour Fiat office tower in the La Défense section of Paris.

Colors and materials for this 7,400-square-foot interiors project were selected to complement an existing private art collection. Travertine walls and floors of the main reception gallery are punctuated by polished stainless steel covering doors and columns. The gallery is reached by a round private elevator from the floor below. Two large offices, a conference room, a board room, and secretarial space are located on one side of the gallery. Partitions separate these rooms from the main gallery, allowing perimeter circulation. On the opposite side of the gallery are a dining room, kitchen, bedroom, bath, and sauna, in addition to small support offices. In the dining room, leather and stainless steel chairs surround a stainless steel and glass dining table. The two large private offices are furnished with desks of English oak burl and stainless steel, and leather and stainless steel chairs. The couches are upholstered with handwoven materials and handwoven light wool rugs cover teak floors. Lacquered wood sunscreens open to reveal sweeping views over the city.

Agnelli-Suite
Paris, Frankreich

Diese 1976 fertiggestellte, etwa 700 m² große Chefsuite nimmt das oberste Geschoß des 44geschossigen Tour Fiat im Neubaugebiet La Défense ein. Sie umfaßt zwei Direktionsbüros, einen Empfangsraum mit Sekretariat, einen kleinen und einen großen Konferenzraum, einen Speiseraum mit Küche, mehrere kleinere Büros, ein Schlafzimmer mit Bad sowie eine Galerie als Eingangsbereich und zur Nutzung bei gesellschaftlichen Anlässen.

Farben und Oberflächen wurden sorgfältig auf die Kunstsammlung des Bauherrn abgestimmt. Die Wandoberflächen und die Böden in der Galerie bestehen aus Travertinplatten. Der frei stehende Aufzugsschacht wurde ebenso wie die runden Stützen des Tragwerks und die Türen zu den Büroräumen mit Tafeln aus hochglanzpoliertem, rostfreiem Stahl verkleidet. Alle an den Außenwänden gelegenen Räume des eigentlichen Direktionsbereiches erhielten einen Riemenboden aus Teakholz, auf dem leichte, handgewebte Teppiche aus Wolle liegen. Die Tische und Stühle haben Gestelle aus rostfreiem Stahl. Für den Tisch im Speiseraum wurde eine Platte aus Glas gewählt, die Platten der Arbeitstische in den Direktionsbüros bestehen aus englischer Eiche. Die Sofas sind mit handgewebten Stoffen bezogen. Die Stelle von Vorhängen nehmen raumhohe, lackierte Holzgitter ein.

1. Plan.
2. Executive dining room.

1. Grundriß.
2. Speiseraum für leitende Mitarbeiter.

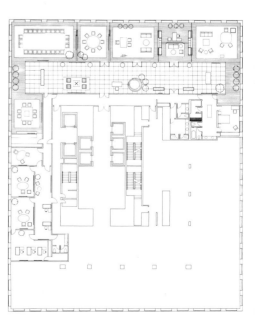

3, 4. In the reception gallery travertine walls and floors are contrasted by polished stainless steel, covering doors and columns.

3, 4. In der Empfangsgalerie kontrastieren Wand- und Bodenflächen aus Travertin mit Tür- und Stützenverkleidungen aus rostfreiem Stahl.

**Addition to the Headquarters of
Royal Dutch Shell,
The Hague, The Netherlands**

Scheduled to begin construction in 1983, the new central office building for the Shell Petroleum Company will contain approximately 300,000 square feet of space on an 86,000 square-foot site adjacent to the existing headquarters in The Hague. The surrounding context consists of three-to-four-story residential blocks, a prominent point across from the site being occupied by a three-story office building designed by the Dutch architect Berlage during the 20's. Height limitations for the site have been established by the authorities with the intention of safeguarding the predominately low-rise residential character of the area.
In keeping with European traditions the client provided program requirements for office space consisting of typically small offices each with a window for natural light, and offices for the managing directors with associated meeting and dining facilities. The old neighboring office building was to be integrated as a functioning part with the new additions while maintaining its significant historical image.
The program requirements for all offices to have natural light resulted in a design concept grouping office space around several interior courts. This continues the scheme of the old headquarters which has two open courts; however, the new solution provides for enclosed skylit atria. Adjacent to the old offices, the new headquarters building is a square, eight-story block with a major central atrium to which a four-story low-rise element with two atria is linked on the other side. The new structures are made to appear smaller than they really are by varied external massing and step-backs. Responding to the neighborhood character, traditional brick will be used for the exterior with granite cladding the first floor base to underline the horizontal impression of the new buildings.

**Erweiterung der Hauptverwaltung der
Royal Dutch Shell,
Den Haag, Niederlande**

Für das neue, etwa 28.000 m² große Bürogebäude der Royal Dutch Shell, mit dessen Bau 1983 begonnen wurde, stand ein etwa 8.000 m² großes Grundstück direkt neben dem bestehenden Gebäude zur Verfügung. Die Umgebung besteht aus drei- bis viergeschossigen Wohnbauten; an prominenter Stelle gegenüber dem Grundstück liegt ein dreigeschossiges Bürogebäude des niederländischen Architekten Berlage aus den zwanziger Jahren. Die Höhenentwicklung auf dem Grundstück ist durch Vorschriften, die den von der Wohnbebauung geprägten Charakter des Gebietes sichern sollen, eingeschränkt.
Das Raumprogramm beinhaltet sowohl Normalbüros – die entsprechend den in Europa vorherrschenden Vorstellungen als kleine Einzelräume mit natürlicher Belichtung auszubilden sind – als auch Direktionsbüros mit Besprechungs- und Speiseräumen. Der Altbau sollte unter Erhaltung seines markanten Charakters in die Anlage eingebunden werden.
Aus der Forderung nach Einzelbüros mit natürlicher Belichtung ergab sich die Anordnung der Nutzflächen um mehrere Innenhöfe. Damit wird an das Bebauungsschema der alten Hauptverwaltung mit ihren beiden offenen Höfen angeknüpft; die neuen Höfe sind jedoch als Atrien mit Glasdach konzipiert. Unmittelbar an den Altbau schließt sich ein quadratischer, achtgeschossiger Baukörper mit großem, zentralen Atrium an, gefolgt auf der dem Altbau gegenüber liegenden Seite von einem viergeschossigen Bau mit zwei Atrien. Die neuen Baukörper erhalten durch abgestufte Fassaden mit Vor- und Rücksprüngen eine starke Gliederung und erscheinen dadurch kleiner und niedriger, als sie wirklich sind. In Anpassung an die umgebende Bebauung wählte man eine Fassade aus Klinkermauerwerk mit einem den horizontalen Charakter betonenden Erdgeschoßsockel aus weißem Granit.

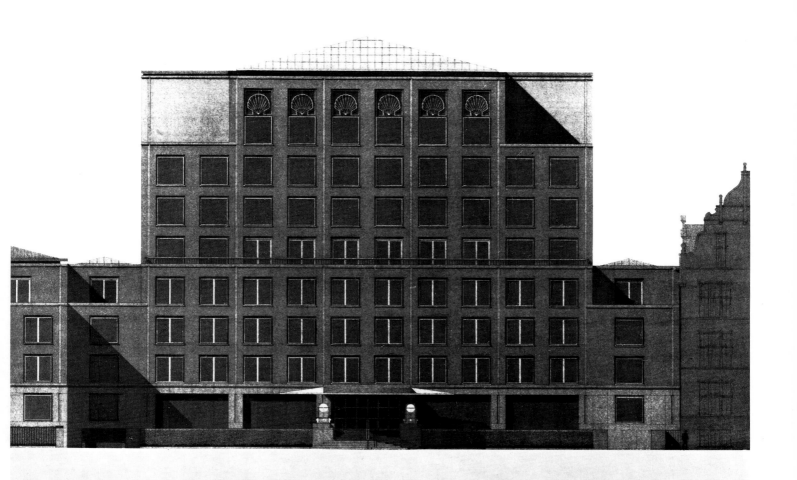

1. Elevation rendering of the eight-story building element.

1. Aufrißdarstellung des achtgeschossigen Bauteils.

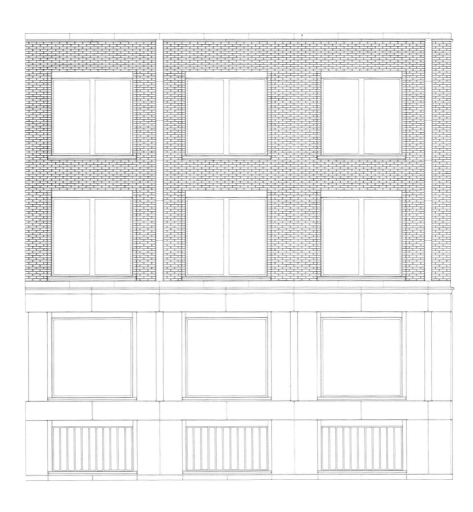

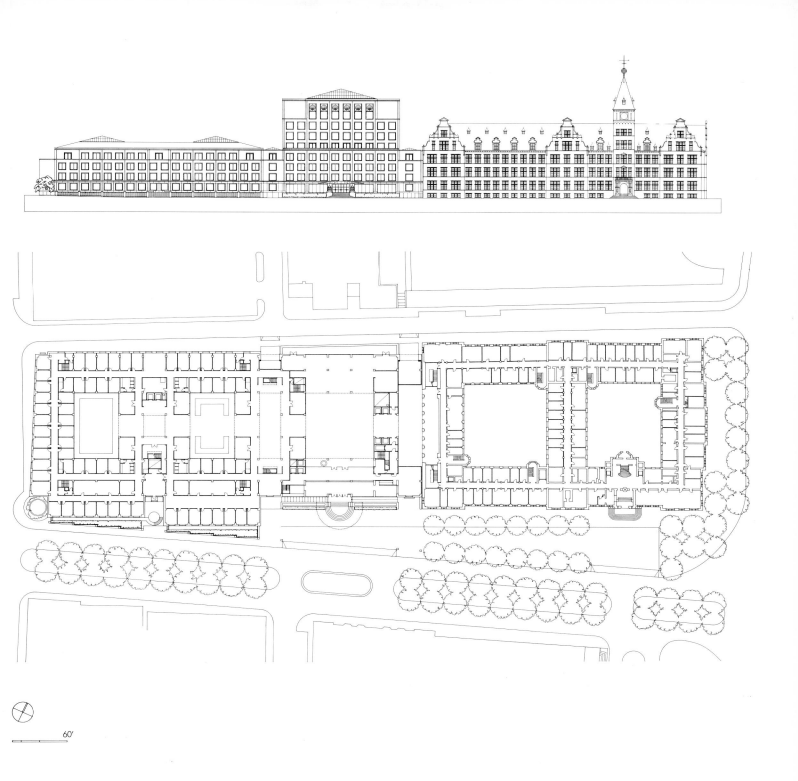

3. Plan (ground floor) and elevation.

3. Grundriß (Erdgeschoß) und Ansicht.

United States Embassy,
Moscow, USSR

On a site of 10.5 acres in Metropolitan Moscow the proposed United States Embassy will provide 633,000 square feet of enclosed space with offices, service and community facilities as well as 146 staff apartments. The site is generally rectangular in shape but has a gentle slope to the west. The housing consists of three- and four-story terraces along the long east and west sides of the site, providing each unit with individual access and identity as well as with favorable morning and afternoon sun exposure. The housing thus serves as enclosures for a large central common – the focus and unifying space for the whole complex. Whereas the top surface of this green common is used for recreational and social activities, numerous service and community facilities including a gymnasium, theater, commissary and medical center, along with parking are located below. There will be ample depth and strong enough structure to support extensive landscaping, including large trees.

Due to the natural slope of the site the lower level facilities are accessible and obtain daylight at the western edge of the common. Located at the south end, the eight-story square office block bounds the common space. An equally square forecourt, the size of the building plan, will link the main entry to public access from Devyatinsky Avenue. At the opposite end of the common is the school with its playground directed south towards the greensward and full sunlight. There will be a secondary entrance to the complex on this side.

The common in the center of the complex essentially is an outdoor living room for the whole community with an unbroken surface of grass and large trees introduced in carefully placed groupings, shrubs lining the edges. The space is large enough for casual ballgames at one end and for mothers walking or permabulating their babies simultaneously at the other end. At its east and west edges the common is bounded by wide walkways, the western one being at the lower level due to the natural slope of the site. Both of these walkways are sized to accept cars under special circumstances or at occasional emergencies – like moving household goods, service vehicles and guest parking in the evening.

Botschaft der Vereinigten Staaten,
Moskau, UdSSR

Für die geplanten neuen Gebäude der amerikanischen Botschaft in Moskau steht ein Baugrundstück von etwa 4,25 ha im Herzen der Stadt zur Verfügung. Auf einer Gesamtfläche von etwa 59.000 m² sind Büros, Service- und Gemeinschaftseinrichtungen sowie 146 Wohnungen für Botschaftsangehörige vorgesehen. Das Grundstück fällt nach Westen hin leicht ab.

Die Wohnungen sind in schmalen, drei- bis viergeschossigen Reihenhauszeilen an der Ost- und der Westseite des Grundstücks angeordnet. Bei dieser Lage hat jede Wohnung ihren eigenen Zugang und ist leicht zu identifizieren; auch die Besonnung ist vormittags wie nachmittags günstig. Die beiden Zeilen bilden zugleich die seitlichen Begrenzungen für einen großen, zentral gelegenen Freiraum, auf den sich die gesamte Anlage orientiert und dessen Gestaltung die Architekten größtes Gewicht beimaßen. Dieser Hof ist als Erholungs- und Freizeitgelände durchgehend begrünt. Darunter liegen auf der gesamten Fläche sowohl alle Service- und Gemeinschaftseinrichtungen wie Sporthalle, Theater, Hausverwaltung und Gesundheitszentrum als auch die Garagenplätze. Um die Bepflanzung des Hofes mit größeren Bäumen zu ermöglichen, sind die Humusschicht und die Deckenkonstruktion entsprechend hoch ausgebildet.

Durch das Gefälle des Baugeländes erhalten die unteren Räume auf der Westseite des Hofes natürliches Licht und sind hier direkt zugänglich. Am Südende wird der Freiraum von dem achtgeschossigen, quadratischen Bürogebäude der Botschaft flankiert, dessen Haupteingang über einen abgeschlossenen, ebenfalls quadratischen Vorhof gleicher Größe von der Straße aus zu erreichen ist. An der gegenüber liegenden Schmalseite des Hofes liegt die Schule mit ihrem zum Grünbereich im Süden hin orientierten Pausenhof. An dieser Seite des Grundstücks ist ein zweiter Eingang zur Botschaftsanlage vorgesehen.

Die Grünanlage im Zentrum ist groß genug, um gleichzeitig gelegentliche Ballspiele an einem Ende und das Spazierengehen von Müttern mit ihren Kleinkindern am anderen Ende zu erlauben. Längsseitig wird der Hof von breiten Wegen flankiert, von denen der auf der Westseite gelegene wegen des Gefälles, das das Baugrundstück hat, um eine Geschoßebene tiefer liegt. Falls es besondere Umstände – wie Umzüge, Anlieferungen und Veranstaltungen – erfordern, können auf diesen Wegen auch Kraftfahrzeuge abgestellt werden.

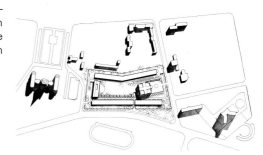

3. Plans (lower level, street level, upper level).
4. South elevation of the office block.

3. Grundrisse (untere Ebene, Straßenebene, obere Ebene).
4. Aufriß der Südseite des Bürogebäudes.

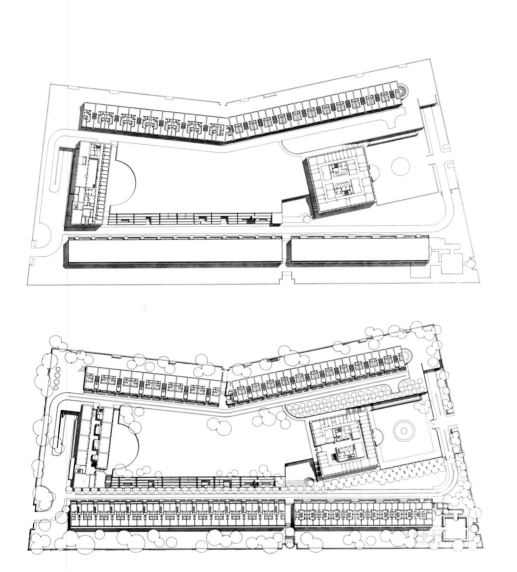

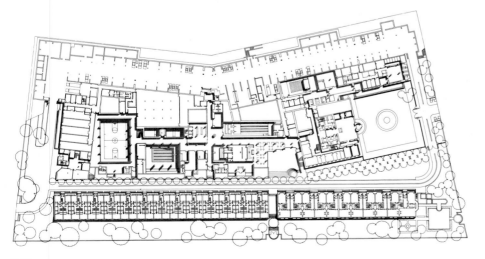

120'

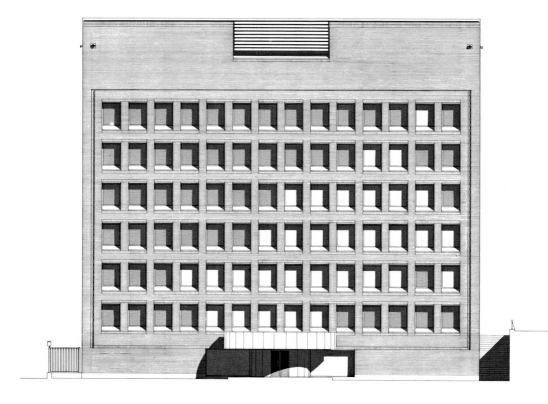

Teaching Hospital and Housing Communities at the University of Blida, Blida, Algeria

On a fanning alluvial plain at the foothills of the Atlas Mountains southwest of Algiers, the University of Blida will serve 10,000 students. The master plan for its teaching hospital, to be completed in 1986, is designed to permit shared use of services and equipment often duplicated in a departmentally organized hospital.

The core hospital consists of diagnostic and surgery blocks, outpatient clinics and bedcare units. Major medical services are located in the diagnostic block. Teaching departments are assigned to outpatient modules and sited directly opposite those diagnostic services to which they most relate. Bedcare units, located between the diagnostic and surgery blocks, have pedestrian bridges and ramps to both service areas.

The hospital will also include a service block, dental clinic and special care units. The service block, parallel to the diagnostic block, houses central linen and food services for the entire complex. The psychiatric and infectious disease wards, physically isolated from the core hospital, each include autonomous diagnostic and outpatient services.

Departmental disciplines are accommodated along double-loaded corridors in each leg of the outpatient modules. Central desks at the apex of each angle serve two corridors of physicians' offices and ECO rooms. Thirty-seat lecture halls linking two modules are used for advanced training in specialized fields. These lecture halls and the general classroom building are at the northern edge of the complex, adjacent to the main university campus.

Pinwheel bedcare units are designed to minimize staff and support space requirements. Bed units are arranged so as to segregate views into men's and women's wards. Small courtyards, formed by the building geometry, can be used as waiting areas for family members. The main entry court, formed by the angled diagnostic and surgery blocks, is also a terraced garden waiting area with small shops and tea rooms.

At the southern end of the 80-acre site, the infectious disease ward is fully isolated. Interior, uncontaminated staff circulation supplements the patient walkway system between bedcare units, diagnostic services and physicians' offices.

The diagonally sited buildings step down the modest slope of the site. To increase their seismic stability, each long block is designed as a series of small, structurally independent elements with expansion joints and exterior service towers. The teaching hospital complex, as the entire university, uses Algerian materials, in-situ concrete frames and masonry infill. Buildings' widths allow for cross ventilation with operable, wooden-frame windows.

The three housing communities, each for 2,000 students, were designed to encourage social interaction at a village scale. Each student suite consists of six double sleeping rooms of 100 square feet grouped around a central living room and sharing common toilet and shower rooms. Exterior entry stairs lead to shared covered balconies off the living areas. A concern for efficient ventilation and sunscreening resulted in the development of an octagonal module, formed by paired sleeping rooms, which became the basic design element.

Within the walled enclosure, each men's or women's community follows one of three basic configurations. Blocks containing student suites and common activity facilities are situated in response to individual site conditions, internal circulation patterns and social groupings. Further emphasizing the community sense at different scales, a hierarchy of outdoor spaces reaches from a central activity area to large landscaped courts and small courtyards among the housing clusters. Common activity centers are located near the main entrance to each community and differ from the housing clusters by their rectilinear geometry. They include a restaurant, library and multi-purpose auditorium, meeting and activity rooms, as well as an infirmary and shops.

In all communities, native materials such as locally fabricated wooden-frame operable windows and decorative tile sills will be used. The stucco facades will be painted in a variety of colors. SOM has also designed three student housing complexes for the university in Annaba, 300 miles further east. Three variations of the housing unit combined with several activity space arrangements give each 20-acre site a unique character.

1. Location map of Algeria. Key: 1 Blida, 2 Algiers, 3 Tizi-Ouzo, 4 Annaba, 5 Mediterranean Sea, 6 Atlantic Ocean.

1. Übersichtsplan von Algerien. Legende: 1 Blida, 2 Algier, 3 Tizi-Ouzou, 4 Annaba, 5 Mittelmeer, 6 Atlantik.

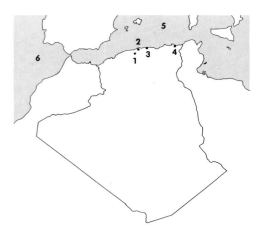

Lehrkrankenhaus und Wohnanlagen der Universität Blida, Blida, Algerien

Die Universität der Stadt Blida, die am Rand der Vorberge des Atlas südwestlich von Algier liegt, wird einmal Ausbildungsstätten für 10.000 Studenten bieten.

Die Gesamtplanung des Lehrkrankenhauses, das 1986 fertiggestellt werden soll, basiert darauf, die in einem streng nach Abteilungen gegliederten Krankenhaus oft mehrfach vorhandenen Einrichtungen und Geräte hier zusammenzufassen und gemeinsam zu nutzen.

Das Krankenhaus besteht in seinem Kern aus den Blöcken für die diagnostische und die chirurgische Abteilung, den Stationen für ambulante Behandlung und den Pflegeeinheiten. Die Lehreinrichtungen sind den Stationen für ambulante Behandlung angegliedert und liegen genau gegenüber den diagnostischen Fachabteilungen, zu denen sie in der engsten Beziehung stehen. Die Bettenhäuser befinden sich zwischen den Blöcken für die diagnostische und die chirurgische Abteilung und sind mit beiden über Brücken verbunden.

Weitere Bestandteile des Krankenhauses sind ein Serviceblock, eine Zahnklinik und medizinische Sonderabteilungen. Der Serviceblock, der parallel zum Block für die diagnostische Abteilung angeordnet ist, versorgt mit seiner Wäscherei und seiner Küche das gesamte Krankenhaus. Die Abteilungen für Psychiatrie und Infektionskrankheiten, die vom Kern des Krankenhauses räumlich getrennt sind, enthalten jeweils eigene diagnostische Einrichtungen und auch eigene Stationen für ambulante Behandlung.

Die Einheiten für ambulante Behandlung werden durch Mittelflure erschlossen. Von zentralen Schaltern an der Spitze der Flügel können mit einem Minimum an Personal jeweils zwei Korridore überwacht werden. Zu jeder der vier Einheiten gehört ein Hörsaal für Fortgeschrittenenkurse in Spezialdisziplinen. Sowohl diese Hörsäle als auch der allgemeine Unterrichtsbau liegen am nördlichen Rand der Anlage.

Auch die windmühlenförmigen Bettenhäuser wurden auf den Betrieb mit einem Minimum an Personal und Nebeneinrichtungen hin geplant. Die Stationen wurden so gestaltet, daß zwischen Männerstationen und Frauenstationen keine Blickverbindung besteht. Durch die Gebäudeform ergaben sich kleine Innenhöfe, die als Wartezonen für Familienangehörige dienen. Auch der Hof vor dem Haupteingang in der Spitze zwischen den Blöcken für die diagnostische und die chirurgische Abteilung ist als eine solche Wartezone ausgebildet.

Die Infektionsabteilung liegt am südlichsten Punkt des etwa 32,5 ha großen Geländes. Ein nicht kontaminiertes Wegenetz für das Personal ergänzt hier das System der Patientenwege.

Die diagonal verlaufenden Bauteile folgen stufenweise dem leichten Gefälle des Geländes. Um die Erdbebensicherheit zu erhöhen, besteht jedes der langgestreckten Gebäude aus einer Reihe von kleinen, konstruktiv unabhängigen und voneinander durch Dehnfugen getrennten Einzelelementen mit frei davorgesetzten Servicetürmen. Wie die übrigen Bauten der Universität wird auch das Lehrkrankenhaus aus algerischen Baustoffen errichtet. Alle Gebäude sind Ortbetonskelettkonstruktionen mit Mauerwerksausfachung. Die geringen Gebäudetiefen lassen Querlüftung mit beweglichen Fensterflügeln zu.

Ziel bei der Planung der drei Wohnanlagen, die jeweils 2.000 Studenten aufnehmen werden, war es, durch einen dörflichen Maßstab die soziale Interaktion zu fördern. Jede Wohneinheit besteht aus sechs etwa 9,5 m² großen Doppelschlafzimmern, einem zentral gelegenen Gemeinschaftswohnraum sowie Toiletten und Duschen. Außenliegende Zugangstreppen führen zu gemeinschaftlich genutzten, gedeckten Balkons, die den Wohnräumen vorgelagert sind. Auf ausreichende Lüftungsmöglichkeiten und guten Sonnenschutz wurde besonderer Wert gelegt. Aus diesen Forderungen ergab sich als durchgehendes Entwurfselement ein aus paarweise zusammengefaßten Doppelzimmern bestehender Grundmodul.

Die mauerumschlossenen und nach Geschlechtern getrennten Wohnanlagen folgen drei verschiedenen Formfigurationen, die aus den jeweiligen topographischen Gegebenheiten, internen Verkehrsbeziehungen und sozialen Gruppierungen abgeleitet wurden. Zur Stärkung des Gemeinschaftsgeistes bemühte man sich um ein breites Angebot an Freiräumen, das von einer zentral gelegenen Erholungsfläche über große begrünte Höfe bis zu kleinmaßstäblichen Innenhöfen bei den Wohneinheiten reicht. Am Eingang der einzelnen Wohnanlagen wurden jeweils die übergeordneten Einrichtungen wie Restaurant, Bibliothek, Mehrzweckhalle, Gruppenräume, Apotheke und Läden zusammengefaßt. Von den Wohneinheiten unterscheiden sich diese Bereiche durch ihre rechtwinkelige Form.

Alle Wohnanlagen werden mit heimischen Materialien und Bauelementen errichtet, darunter Holzfenster mit zu öffnenden Flügeln und Fensterbänke aus dekorativen Fliesen. Die Putzfassaden werden in verschiedenen Farbtönen gestrichen.

Von SOM stammt auch der Entwurf von drei studentischen Wohnanlagen für die Universität in Annaba, das etwa 480 km weiter östlich liegt. Drei Varianten der Hauseinheit, kombiniert mit verschiedenen Anordnungen der Gemeinschaftseinrichtungen, geben den etwa 8 ha großen Wohnanlagen jeweils einen unverwechselbaren Charakter.

2. Site plan of the University of Blida. Key:
A academic departments and support facilities,
B housing community no. 1, C teaching hospital;
1 academic pavilion, 2 outpatient services,
3 diagnostic block, 4 registration and main entry,
5 main courtyard, 6 bedcare units, 7 surgery
block, 8 administration/dental block, 9 department head offices, 10 psychiatric ward, 11 service
block, 12 infectious diseases.

2. Lageplan der Universität Blida. Legende:
A akademische Fachbereiche mit Nebenanlagen,
B Wohnanlage Nr. 1, C Lehrkrankenhaus, 1 akade-
mischer Pavillon, 2 Ambulanz, 3 diagnostische
Abteilung, 4 Aufnahme und Haupteingang,
5 Haupthof, 6 Bettenstationen, 7 chirurgische
Abteilung, 8 Verwaltungsbereich und zahnärzt-
liche Abteilung, 9 Büros der Abteilungsleiter,
10 psychiatrische Abteilung, 11 Serviceblock, 12 Infektionsabteilung.

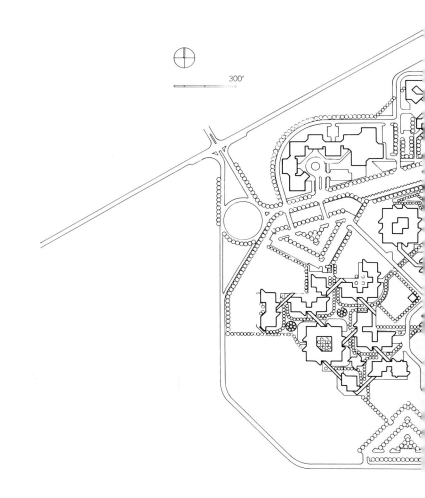

300'

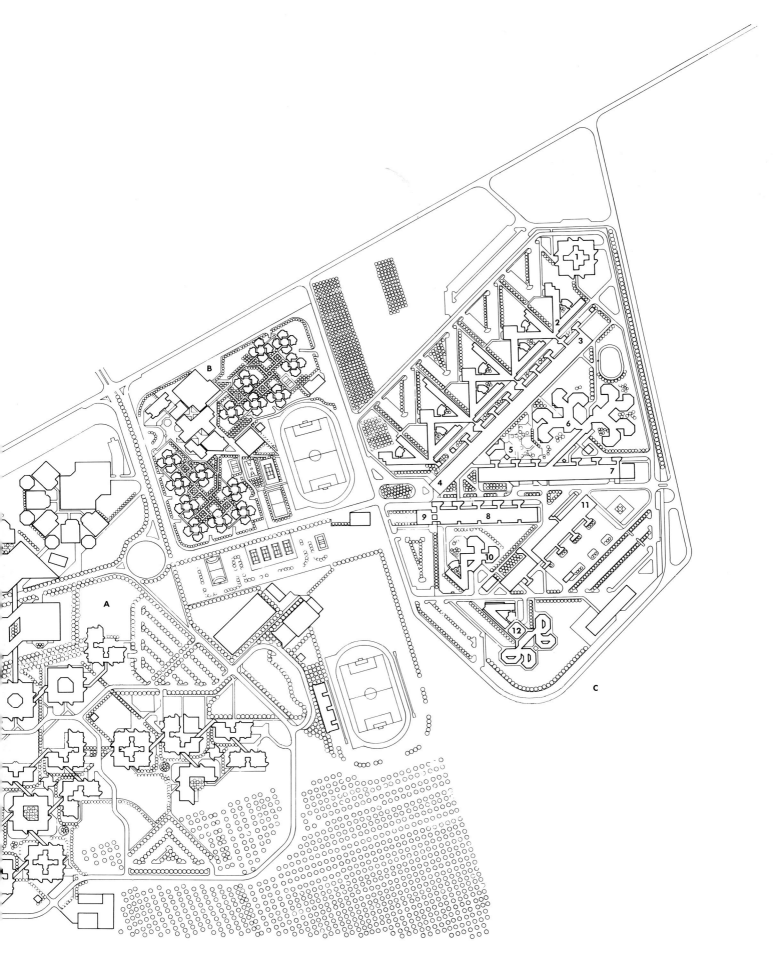

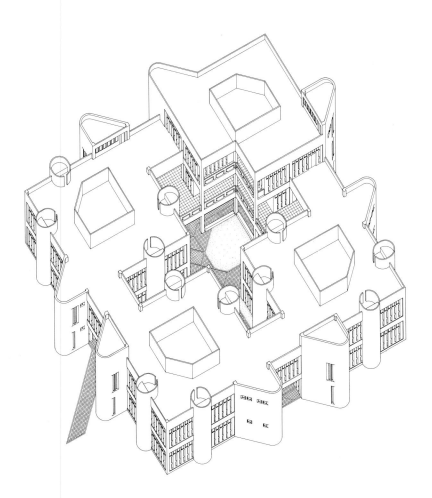

3. Axonometric view of a typical academic pavilion.
4. Site plan of an academic department.

3. Axonometrie eines akademischen Pavillons.
4. Lageplan eines akademischen Fachbereichs.

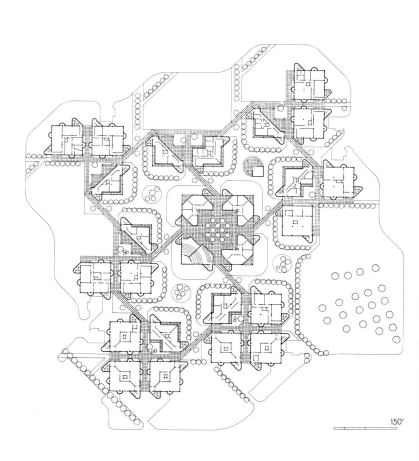

150'

5. Axonometric view of a typical housing cluster.
6. Plan of a typical housing cluster.

5. Axonometrie einer Wohneinheit.
6. Grundriß einer Wohneinheit.

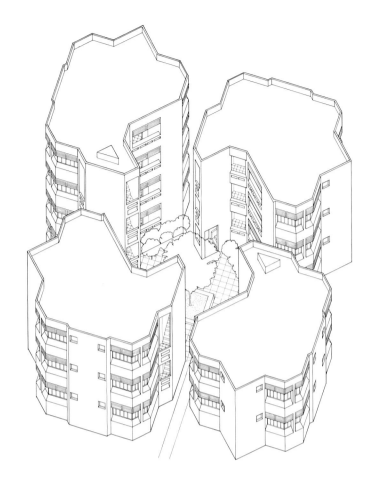

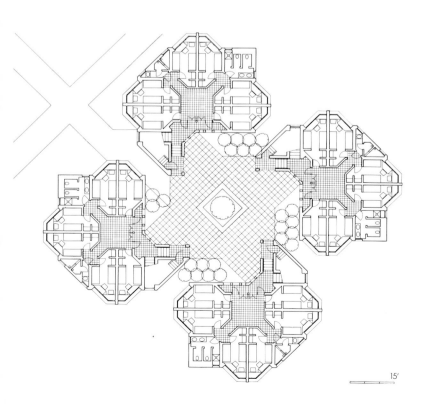

15'

349

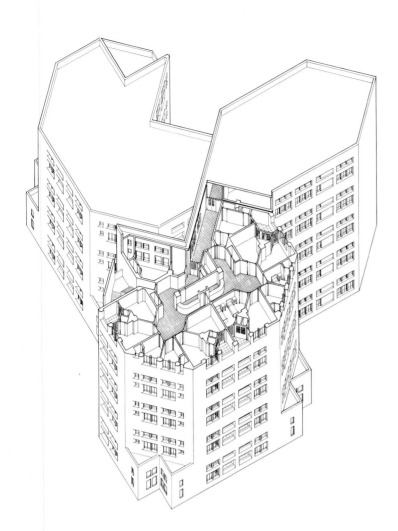

7. Axonometric view of a bedcare cluster.
8. Plan of a bedcare unit.

7. Axonometrie einer Betteneinheit.
8. Grundriß des Bettenbereichs.

30'

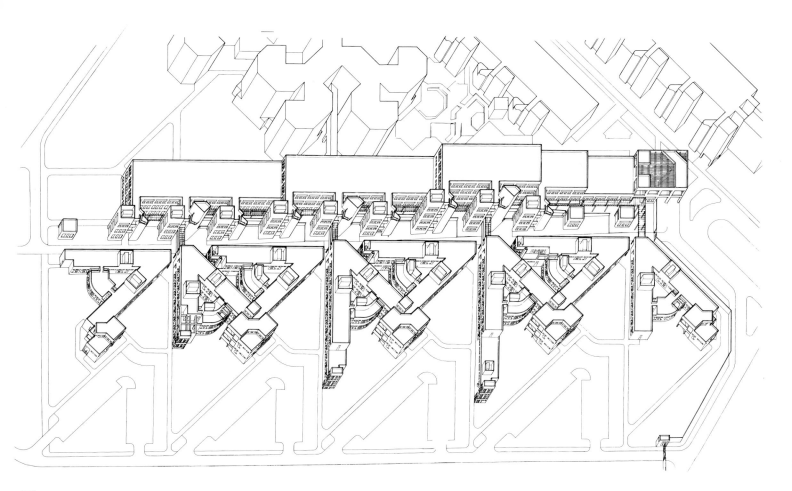

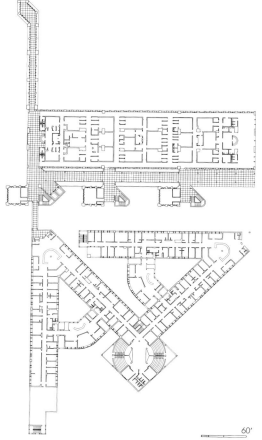

9. Axonometric view of the diagnostic block and the outpatient services.
10. Partial plan (second floor) of the diagnostic block and the outpatient services.

9. Axonometrie des diagnostischen Blocks und der Ambulanz.
10. Teilgrundriß (2. Geschoß) des diagnostischen Blocks und der Ambulanz.

60'

University of Tizi-Ouzou,
Tizi-Ouzou, Algeria

Construction is scheduled to begin in 1983 on the 197-acre site of the University of Tizi-Ouzou, 60 miles east of Algiers. When completed, the university will have an area of nearly 1,000,000 square feet. Technical and engineering programs will be offered to 6,400 students who will reach the campus by bus or from the student housing complex to the north. The north-south entry spine, bordered by an L-shaped administration building, leads to an entry court with a student union and cultural complex which contains an auditorium and a series of fine and performing arts studios. The geometry of this complex is symmetrically repeated to the southwest in the first of four reading rooms which form a pinwheel around the central library. Beyond, a central plaza will be an informal garden with landscaped walkways and coffee houses. Bordering the plaza to the east is the student restaurant. Four dining areas and a faculty dining hall surround a central kitchen.

Academic zones extend to the north and south of the garden plaza. General education facilities are closest to the core. Housing paired disciplines, repetitive academic clusters step up the sloping valley. The southernmost cluster, devoted to electrical and civil engineering, abuts workshops and laboratories for heavy machinery. The forestry and exact sciences cluster to the northern end is surrounded by workshops, laboratories and greenhouses. A smaller laboratory group serves the two central clusters.

Each academic cluster comprises classrooms, lecture halls, departmental libraries, laboratories and offices. Shared facilities line opposite sides of a central octagonal courtyard. The repetitive arrangement allows economical grading of terraces at one-level increments. The low, two- to five-story buildings are structurally independent for greater seismic stability.

Conventional Algerian building techniques and components are used extensively in the in-situ concrete structures with masonry infill and stucco cladding.

Universität Tizi-Ouzou,
Tizi-Ouzou, Algerien

Die neue Universität von Tizi-Ouzou, das etwa 100 km südöstlich von Algier liegt, soll ab 1983 auf einem etwa 80 ha großen Gelände errichtet werden. Nach Fertigstellung wird sie ein Raumangebot von etwa 93.000 m² haben. Das Lehrangebot für etwa 6.400 Studenten wird vorwiegend die technischen und ingenieurwissenschaftlichen Disziplinen umfassen. Für die Studenten, die aus der Stadt oder von den nördlich gelegenen Studentenheimen kommen, ist die Hochschulstadt mit dem Bus zu erreichen. Ihr Weg führt von der Haltestelle entlang einer Nord-Süd-Achse, an der das abgewinkelte Verwaltungsgebäude der Universität liegt, auf einen Eingangshof. An diesen Hof grenzt das Studenten- und Kulturzentrum, das ein Auditorium und eine Reihe von Studios für bildende und darstellende Künste enthält. Unmittelbar südwestlich wiederholt sich die Geometrie dieser Anlage symmetrisch in der Form des ersten von vier Lesesälen, die sich windradartig um die Zentralbibliothek legen. Es folgt der als lockerer Garten gestaltete Hauptplatz der Universität. An der Ostseite dieses Platzes liegt die Mensa mit vier Studentenspeisesälen und einem Speisesaal für das Lehrpersonal, die sich alle um eine zentrale Küche gruppieren.

Nach Norden und Süden schließen an den begrünten Hauptplatz die eigentlichen akademischen Bereiche an; dem Platz am nächsten sollen die Einrichtungen für Studenten in den beiden ersten Studienjahren errichtet werden. In sich wiederholenden Baugruppen, die in Höhenstufen dem nach Süden hin ansteigenden Tal folgen, werden die Fachabteilungen jeweils paarweise untergebracht. Die südlichste dieser Gruppen wird die Abteilungen Bauingenieurwesen und Elektrotechnik aufnehmen; sie ist umgeben von Winkelbauten mit Werkstätten und Labors für die Arbeit an größeren Maschinen. In ähnlicher Form legen sich um die nördlichste Gruppe am entgegengesetzten Ende der Universität – die der Forstkunde und den Naturwissenschaften dienen soll – Labors, Werkstätten und Gewächshäuser, während die beiden zentral gelegenen Unterrichtsgruppen von einem kleineren Laborbereich begleitet werden.

Die Baugruppen der akademischen Bereiche umfassen Unterrichtsräume, Hörsäle, Teilbibliotheken und Labors sowie Büros. An einem achteckigen Hof liegen einander die von den beiden Fachbereichen einer Baueinheit gemeinsam genutzten Einrichtungen gegenüber. Die Gleichartigkeit dieser Gruppen ermöglicht eine wirtschaftliche Lösung für die Terrassierung um jeweils ein Geschoß entsprechend dem Geländeverlauf. Außerdem ergeben sich dadurch kleine, zwei- bis fünfgeschossige Baukörper, die als konstruktiv unabhängige Einheiten erdbebensicherer sind.

Soweit es möglich ist, werden überall algerische Baustoffe und Baumethoden verwendet. Die Gebäude sollen als leicht herstellbare, wirtschaftliche Skelettbauten aus Ortbeton mit Mauerwerkausfachung und Putzfassaden errichtet werden.

1. General view (model).
2. Site plan. Key: 1 gymnasium and swimming pool, 2 administration, 3 library, 4 restaurant, 5 teaching cluster.

1. Gesamtansicht (Modell).
2. Lageplan. Legende: 1 Sporthalle und Schwimmhalle, 2 Verwaltung, 3 Bibliothek, 4 Mensa, 5 Unterrichtscluster.

300'

353

3. Axonometric view of a teaching cluster.

3. Axonometrie eines Unterrichtsclusters.

4. Axonometric view of the library.

4. Axonometrie der Bibliothek.

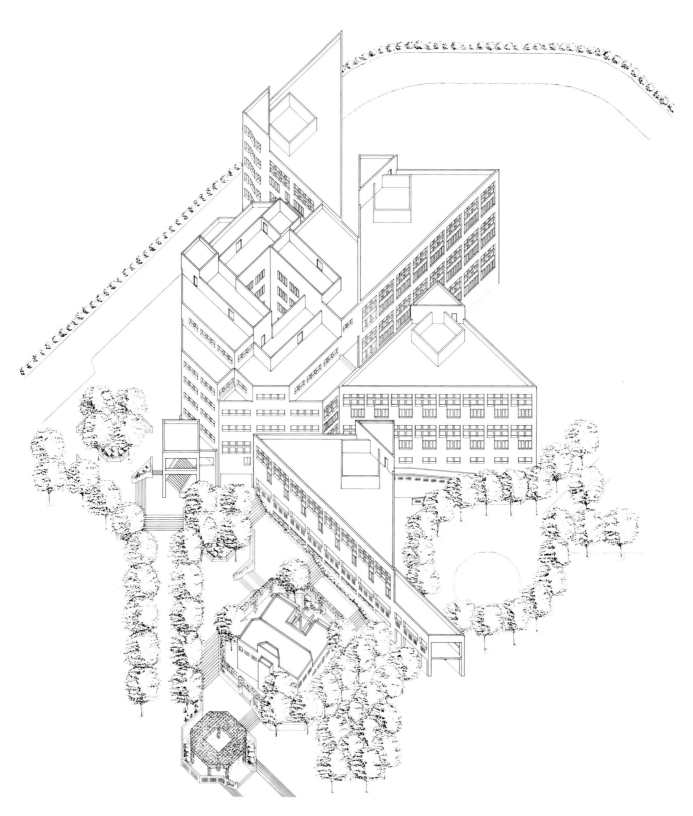

**Kuwait Markets Group – Ahmed Al Jaber Street
Commercial Complex,
Kuwait City, Kuwait**

The complex will incorporate a three-story retail base with parking for 1,319 cars, an indoor public park, and two 20-story office towers in a 838,700-square-foot development. The complex will be situated in an area which will be an extension of the main commercial and financial districts and will front a major thoroughfare which terminates in one of the royal palaces.

This project establishes a precedent for the innovative and efficient use of land in the central business district of a city where, typical of most urban areas, land is both scarce and very expensive. It is the first occasion in Kuwait City where the municipality and a private investment group have agreed to cooperate in the development of a large-scale commercial project. The project maximizes the potential of the site and provides a generous mix of uses in addition to creating a garden oasis for the inhabitants of a harsh, desert climate.

To shade tenants from direct sunlight, travertine sun screens with flush travertine louvers set at a 45-degree angle within the screen portals will form the southeast and southwest facades of the office towers. Green tinted, slightly reflective glass with stainless steel mullions will allow light in through the curving wall of the northern facade and allow an unobstructed view of the Persian Gulf. The commercial activity of Ahmed Al Jaber Street will be enhanced by small shops opening onto the street under an arcade which links three public entrances. The parking structure at the rear will create a definite edge for the complex and reinforce the orientation toward the major thoroughfare. As design development proceeds, other issues will be addressed. For example, the area to the rear of the complex is currently vacant. Should this area be developed, the scheme could be modified to include storefronts, and pedestrian as well as vehicular entrances at the ground level.

The public space will be covered by a long vault between two anchoring domes. Slightly reflective clear glass overlaps tinted green glass arches in the vault and concentric rings in the domes to restrict the heat of the sun while allowing light in. The totally air-conditioned environment will be landscaped with extensive gardens, pools, and fountains. Pedestrian bridges and elevators connect the parking and shopping levels.

**Kuwait Markets Group – Ahmed Al Jaber Street
Commercial Complex,
Kuwait City, Kuwait**

Für ein langgestrecktes Areal an der Ahmed Al Jaber Street in Kuwait City machten die Architekten einen Bebauungsvorschlag, der auf einer Fläche von etwa 78.000 m² ein dreigeschossiges Einkaufszentrum sowie zwei gleichartige, jeweils 20geschossige Hochhäuser vorsieht. Im 1. Untergeschoß, im Erdgeschoß und auf einer Mezzaninebene sollen Läden und Geschäfte liegen. Erschlossen wird dieser Bereich, der sich über das gesamte Grundstück erstreckt, durch ein zentral angeordnetes, vollklimatisiertes Atrium mit einem durchlaufenden Glastonnendach. An den beiden Enden des Atriums liegen Rundplätze, die von großen Glaskuppeln mit Sonnenschutzeinrichtungen überdacht werden.

In der großzügigen Fußgängerzone soll es ausgedehnte Grünanlagen, Wasserbecken mit Brunnen, Verbindungsstege und Aufzüge mit verglasten Kabinen geben. Auch die unteren Geschosse der Bürotürme sind in den Atriumbereich integriert. In ihrer Orientierung sind diese Hochhäuser, deren Grundriß jeweils aus einem Dreieck mit vorgelagertem Kreissegment gebildet werden, auf die Sonneneinstrahlung abgestimmt. Während die Nordseiten Vorhangwände aus grün getöntem, leicht reflektierendem Glas erhalten sollen, durch die das Licht direkt einfällt, plant man, vor die Fensteröffnungen auf den Südost- und Südwestseiten Sonnenschutzelemente aus Travertin zu setzen.

Auf der gesamten Länge der Ahmed Al Jaber Street sind schattenspendende Arkaden vorgesehen. Sie sind den Läden vorgelagert und sollen die drei öffentlichen Hauptzugänge zum Atrium verbinden. Neben der Tiefgarage ist auch ein oberirdisches Parkhaus als Abschluß der Bebauung an der südöstlichen Grundstücksgrenze geplant, das von einer bestehenden Nebenstraße aus Zugang hat.

1. General view of the complex (model).
2. Plan (ground level).

1. Gesamtansicht der Anlage (Modell).
2. Grundriß (Erdgeschoß).

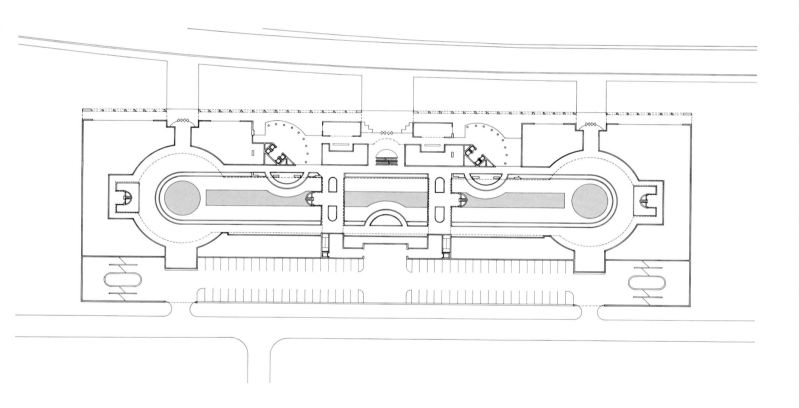

3. Section through the three-story retail base and elevation of the towers.
4. View of the complex from the north (model). Green tinted, slightly reflective glass with stainless steel mullions will allow light in through the curving wall of the northern facades of the towers.
5. Aerial view of the complex (model). The central public space will be covered by a long vault between two anchoring domes.

3. Schnitt durch den dreigeschossigen Sockelbau mit Läden und Aufriß der beiden Bürotürme.
4. Ansicht der Anlage von Norden (Modell). Auf den gekrümmten Nordseiten der Bürotürme fällt das Licht durch grün getöntes, leicht reflektierendes Glas in Rahmen aus rostfreiem Stahl ein.
5. Luftansicht der Anlage (Modell). Der zentrale öffentliche Raum wird von einer langen Glastonne überwölbt, die an ihren beiden Enden von Rundkuppeln eingefaßt ist.

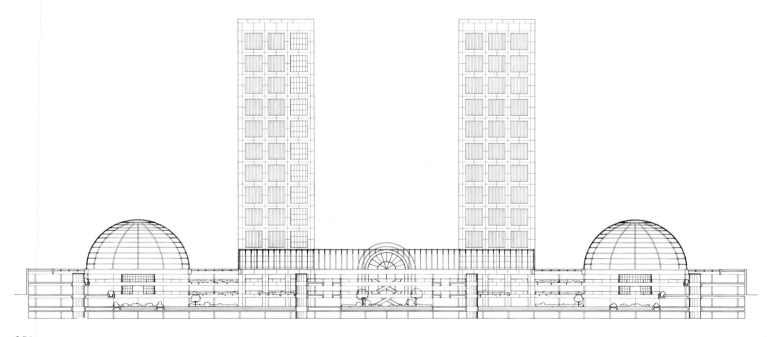

Bandar Shapour New Town,
Bandar Shapour, Iran

The SOM master plan and development plan for the New Town of Bandar Shapour were executed between 1974 and 1976, in joint venture with the Mandala Collaborative of Tehran. They provide guiding principles and implementation mechanisms for a community of approximately 200,000 to support a planned port expansion and new petrochemical complex to be built on the shores of the nearby Persian Gulf. The site is on the southern bank of the Harrahi River near the existing town. The first planning stage established the master plan which is a management tool describing the socio-economic goals of the new town. It also identifies required land uses and proposes design principles which combine traditional Persian and modern town planning concepts. The new town is envisioned by the plan as a modern, industrial city which maintains continuity with traditional design sensitivities developed over centuries of building in the Persian countryside.

The development plan addresses the first phase of construction for an initial population of 50,000 and serves as an operational document for the provision of housing and community facilities. It is primarily a package of controls, performance standards and design guidelines which are to remain effective through the entire development period.

Of critical importance to both plans is the integration of local and traditional values with contemporary modes of town building. In summary, these values include compact structures sited to provide maximum protection from the desert sun clustered to create networks of walkways providing shade and water as well as access to places of gathering and recreation. In addition, the plan introduces innovative, modern concepts to deal with contemporary needs such as transportation, energy conservation and waste treatment. Residential neighborhoods are made particularly responsive to the unique cultural aspects of Islamic life. Privacy has been maintained even in the densest areas.

Neue Stadt Bandar Shapur,
Bandar Shapur, Iran

In Zusammenarbeit mit der Mandala Collaborative aus Teheran erstellten die Architekten zwischen 1974 und 1976 zwei Planstudien für eine Neue Stadt bei Bandar Shapur im Iran. Hier sollte in Zusammenhang mit einer geplanten Hafenerweiterung und einer neuen petrochemischen Anlage am nahe gelegenen Persischen Golf eine Stadt für 200.000 Einwohner entstehen. Als Standort war ein Gelände am Südufer des Harrahi-Flusses in Aussicht genommen worden.

Zunächst wurde ein Generalplan für die Erstellung der ganzen Stadt verfaßt. Darin sind die sozioökonomischen Zielvorstellungen und die erforderlichen Flächennutzungen und Bauwerke umrissen. Außerdem wurden Leitlinien zur Schaffung eines ausgewogenen Gemeinwesens mit einem Zusammenspiel von traditionellen und modernen Stadtplanungskonzepten entwickelt.

Der Entwicklungsplan beschäftigt sich mit einem ersten Bauabschnitt für 50.000 Einwohner und sollte als Ausführungsgrundlage für die Bereitstellung von Wohnungen und Gemeinschaftseinrichtungen in den ersten Jahren der jungen Stadt dienen. Im wesentlichen sind in diesem Planwerk Entwicklungskontrollen, Anwendungsmaßstäbe und Gestaltungsvorschriften niedergelegt, die während der gesamten Wachstumsperiode der Stadt bestimmend sein sollten.

Entscheidende Entwurfsaufgabe war die Verbindung lokaler Traditionen mit modernen Stadtbauverfahren. Die Anpassung an die extremen klimatischen Verhältnisse wurde durch den Rückgriff auf Bauweisen und Bauformen in den alten Dörfern dieses Gebietes versucht. Eine kompakte Bauweise mit schattigen Wegen und Wasser, die größtmöglichen Schutz vor der Wüstenhitze bietet, verbindet sich mit neuartigen Verkehrs-, Energieversorgungs- und Abfallbeseitigungsmethoden. Die Wohnviertel sind in ihrer Anlage den speziellen kulturellen Merkmalen der islamischen Welt angepaßt, wobei der Sicherung der Privatsphäre auch in den dichtesten Gebieten eine besondere Aufmerksamkeit geschenkt wurde.

1. Regional map. Key: 1 New Town, 2 Bandar Shapour, 3 Persian Gulf, 4 flood detention, 5 Ahwaz-Bandar Shapour highway.
2. Aerial view of the New Town looking south.

1. Übersichtsplan. Legende: 1 Neue Stadt, 2 Bandar Shapur, 3 Persischer Golf, 4 Hochwasserrückhaltebecken, 5 Straße von Ahwas nach Bandar Shapur.
2. Luftansicht der Neuen Stadt in Richtung Süden.

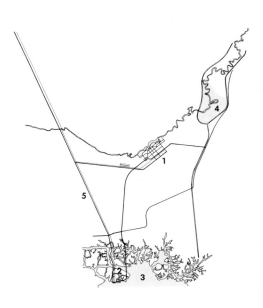

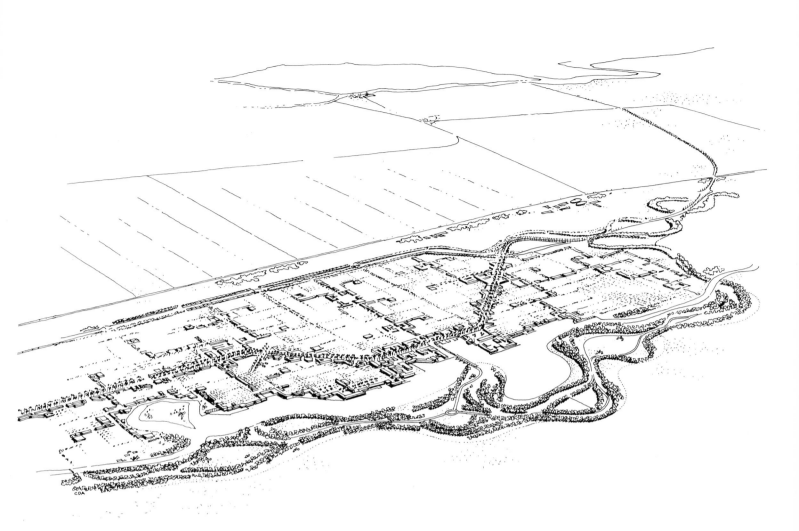

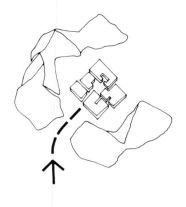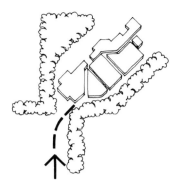

Regional gateway
Natural elements traditionally form regional gateway (left).
In New Town, natural plant forms are used to create a sense of arrival (right).

Tor zur Region
Das Tor zur Region wird traditionell von natürlichen Elementen gebildet (links).
In der Neuen Stadt vermitteln natürliche Formen der Bepflanzung ein Gefühl des Ankommens (rechts).

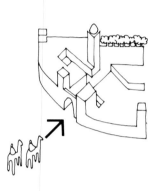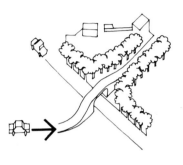

Town gateway
Traditional town gate (left).
Elevated entry road establishes vista point prior to arrival in New Town (right).

Tor zur Stadt
Traditionelles Stadttor (links).
Eine hochgelegene Zufahrtsstraße bietet vor der Ankunft in der Neuen Stadt einen Aussichtspunkt (rechts).

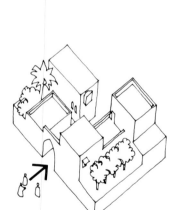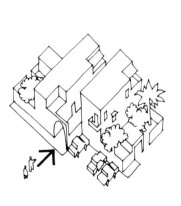

Neighborhood gateway
Mahlelleh of Persian city is defined by walls and gateways (left).
New Town residential clusters are articulated by walls and gateways to denote zones of pedestrian and vehicular movement (right).

Tor zum Stadtviertel
Das Mahlelleh der alten persischen Stadt ist von Mauern mit Zugangswegen gekennzeichnet (links).
Die Wohngruppen der Neuen Stadt sind durch Mauern und Zugänge, die Verkehrsbereiche für Fußgänger und Fahrzeuge ausgrenzen, voneinander abgehoben.

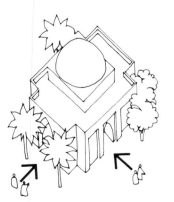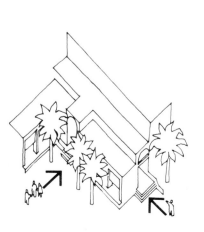

Building gateway
Traditional emphasis on gateway in Persian building (left).
New Town built form has similar emphasis on point of entry (right).

Tor zum Gebäude
In traditioneller Art betonter Zugang zu einem alten persischen Gebäude (links).
In den Bauformen der Neuen Stadt zeigt sich eine ähnliche Betonung der Eingangssituation (rechts).

3. Design principles combine traditional Persian
and modern town planning concepts.
4. View of the main boulevard leading to the
town center.

3. In den Gestaltungsrichtlinien sind persische Traditionen mit neuzeitlichen Grundsätzen der Stadt-
planung vereint.
4. Blick auf den zur Stadtmitte führenden Haupt-
boulevard.

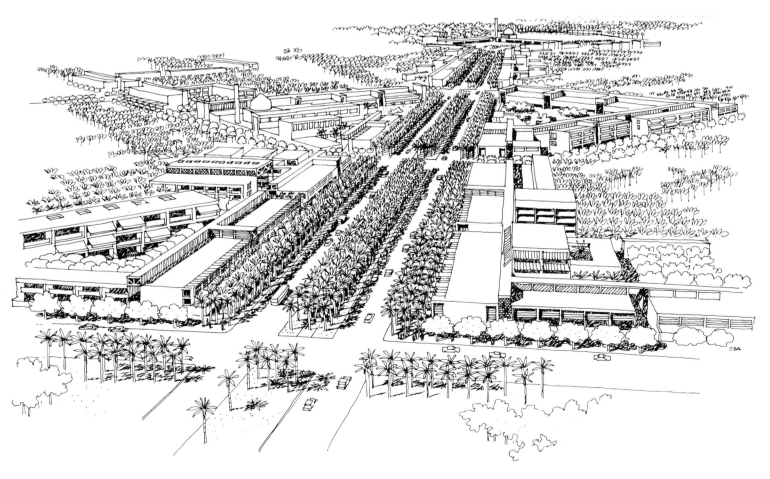

King Abdul Aziz University,
Makkah, Saudi Arabia

The proposed site for the university is in a relatively flat valley surrounded by low, barren mountains west of the Holy City of Makkah. Conceived as a meeting place for scholars throughout the Islamic world, the academic setting was designed to reflect the social, cultural and historical patterns of Saudi Arabian traditions. The overall development calls for a student population of 10,000 men and 5,000 women, with future expansion for an additional 50 percent.

The essential relationships of major campus components reflect a commitment to the traditional separation of male and female students. There are effectively two campuses. The internal relationships of each campus reflect similar principles of organization but, with the exception of administrative functions, each operates as a distinct entity. No allowance for either academic or social contact among students or faculty members of opposite sexes has been provided.

The Makkah-Jeddah Road separates the site into two distinct areas. All academic and administrative functions, single student residences, student services, and physical support facilities are located north of the road; also included are housing for married students and single and married faculty and staff. The site south of the Makkah-Jeddah Road will support a housing community containing 2,400 dwelling units and includes a number of commercial and service support facilities. In order to maintain traditional social values, the general form and texture of the communities is intended to incorporate characteristics of established Islamic urban settlements.

The master plan, completed in 1978, incorporates a low-rise, high-density configuration of tightly clustered buildings. The desire for easy, comfortable pedestrian movement underlies the creation of spaces among buildings and limits distances between component elements, resulting in a compact overall geometry.

A building form using thermal mass was developed to respond to the extreme climatic conditions prevalent in Makkah. Housing units were designed to maximize night ventilation. Courtyard elements maximize air ventilation and add daylight to interior spaces. Coupled with the thermal mass, this produces free cooling for a substantial portion of the year.

King Abdul Aziz University,
Mekka, Saudi-Arabien

Das Gelände für den neuen Campus der Universität liegt in einem relativ flachen, von niedrigen, unbewachsenen Bergen umgebenen Tal westlich von Mekka. Mit der Verlagerung der kleinen alten Universität aus der Stadt soll eines der führenden wissenschaftlichen Zentren der islamischen Welt entstehen. Der Campus ist zunächst auf 10.000 Studenten und 5.000 Studentinnen ausgelegt; durch eine spätere Erweiterung läßt sich die Kapazität noch einmal um 50% steigern.

Ausgehend von der durch die Tradition vorgegebenen Trennung der Geschlechter besteht die Anlage aus zwei funktional und räumlich geschiedenen Komplexen, die zwar gemeinsam verwaltet werden, im übrigen jedoch als selbständige Einheiten operieren. Es gibt sowohl unter den Studenten als auch unter den Lehrern keinerlei akademischen und sozialen Kontakt zwischen Männern und Frauen.

Auf dem Areal nördlich der das Tal durchschneidenden Straße Mekka–Dschidda sind neben allen akademischen Einrichtungen und der zentralen Verwaltung die Wohnheime für alleinstehende Studenten mit den zugehörigen Nebenanlagen vorgesehen. Weiterhin soll dort eine gewisse Anzahl von Wohnungen für verheiratete Studenten sowie für Mitglieder des Lehrkörpers und andere Hochschulbedienstete untergebracht werden. Südlich der Straße sollen 2.400 Wohneinheiten mit Läden und Serviceeinrichtungen entstehen. Mit Rücksicht auf die überkommenen sozialen Vorstellungen sollen die allgemeine Form und Textur der Wohnbereiche an Merkmale traditioneller islamischer Siedlungen anknüpfen.

Der 1978 fertiggestellte Generalplan der Architekten sieht stark verdichtete, niedrige Gebäudegruppen in geometrischer Gestaltung vor. Die Dimensionen der Platzfolgen und die Entfernungen zwischen den Gebäuden sind auf die Belange des Fußgängers abgestellt.

Um den in Mekka herrschenden extremen klimatischen Bedingungen zu begegnen, wurde eine Bauform gewählt, bei der große thermische Massen zur Verwendung kommen. Die Hauseinheiten wurden so gestaltet, daß eine optimale Lüftung während der Nacht gewährleistet ist. Im Verein mit der hohen thermischen Speicherfähigkeit der Gebäude erreicht man so für einen beträchtlichen Teil des Jahres eine kostenlose Kühlung.

1. Location plan of Makkah. Key: 1 existing university, 2 new campus.
2. Plan of the women's university.

1. Übersichtsplan von Mekka. Legende: 1 bestehende Universität, 2 neues Universitätsgelände.
2. Grundriß der Frauenuniversität.

Pages 366/367:
3. Partial view of the campus (model).

Seiten 366/367:
3. Teilansicht des Universitätsgeländes (Modell).

Pages 368/369:
4. Axonometric view of a courtyard building in the women's university.

Seiten 368/369:
4. Axonometrie eines Hofgebäudes in der Frauenuniversität.

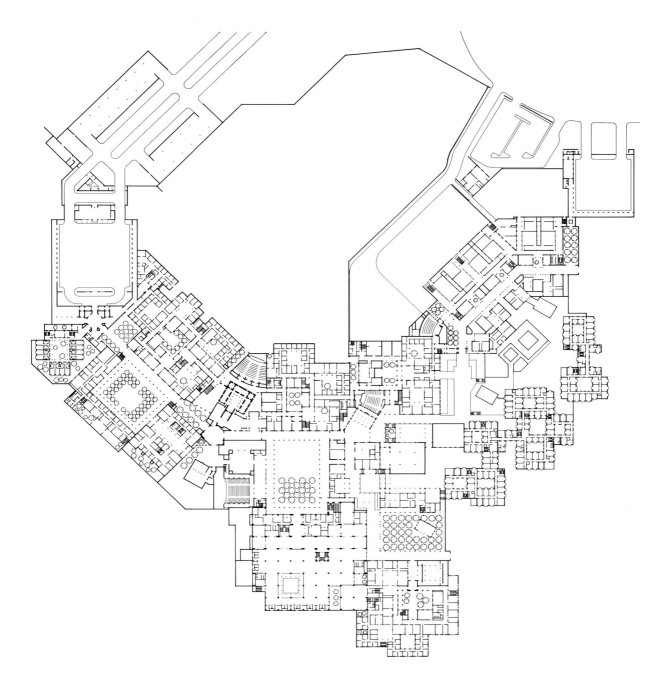

120'

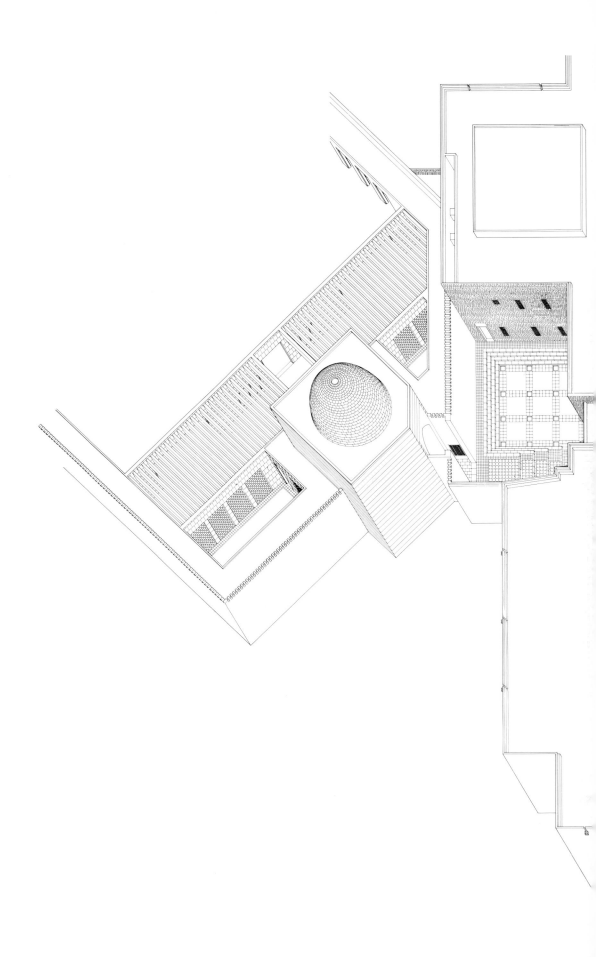

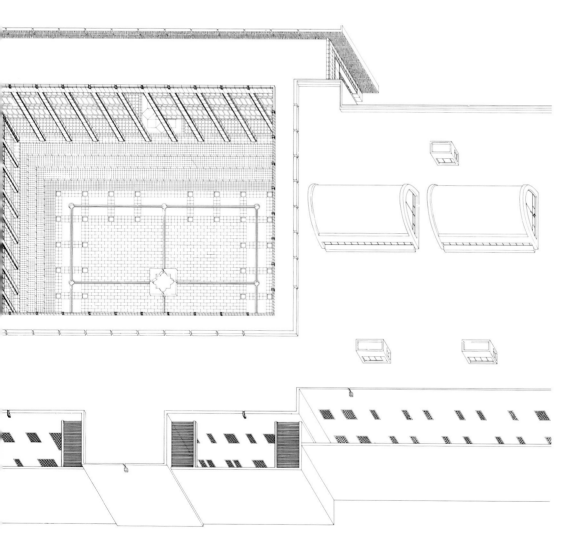

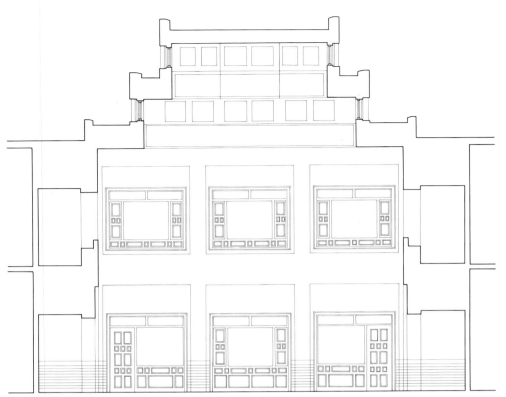

5. Section through a typical faculty court in the women's university.
6. Plan of the reception court in the women's university.
7. Courtyard portals in the women's university.
8. Ornamental tile patterns.

5. Schnitt durch einen Fachbereichshof in der Frauenuniversität.
6. Grundriß des Zugangshofes der Frauenuniversität.
7. Hofportale in der Frauenuniversität.
8. Dekorative Fliesenmuster.

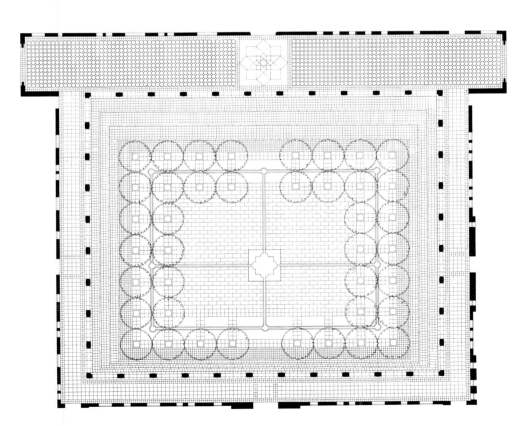

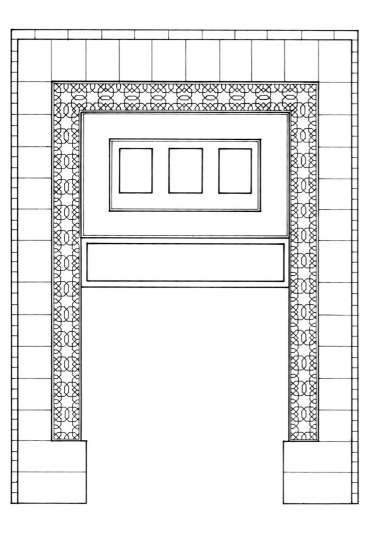

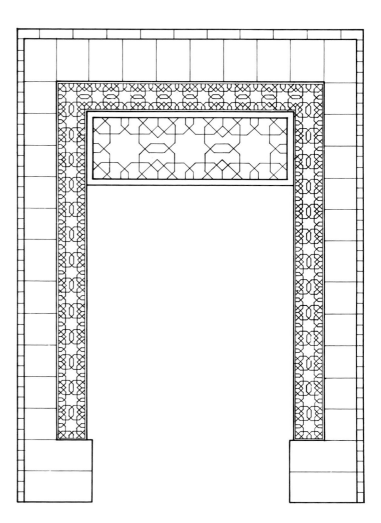

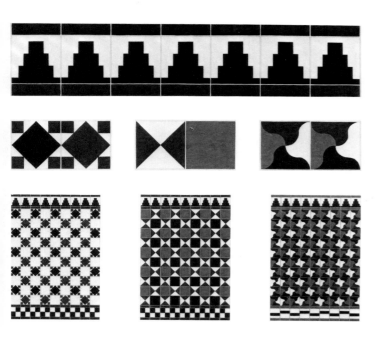

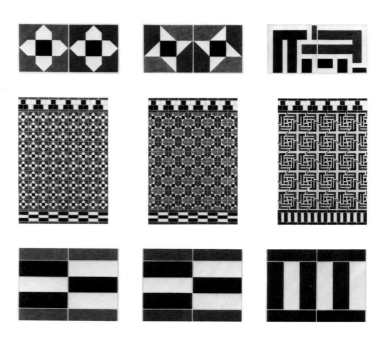

371

Yanbu New Town,
Yanbu, Saudi Arabia

The SOM master plan for the New Town of Yanbu creates a strong framework that uses interchangeable modules and building prototypes. This framework permits program flexibility and change as well as insuring an impression of completeness at any point in the thirty year construction period.

The new town is to be built on a 13,580-acre site on the Red Sea five miles south of the existing town of Yanbu. The primary employment base for the projected 150,000 population is petrochemical production and shipping.

Initial development is to occur blockwise from the town center with the first residential unit and the center being mutually supportive. Community social services are distributed throughout the town. By contrast, mosques, shops, health clinics and schools are clustered within residential neighborhoods.

The central planning concept provides a clearly defined physical framework which respects two overriding concerns. First, the climate of the region is extremely harsh and, second, the cultural heritage of future inhabitants will be unusually complex. People of widely ranging backgrounds must live side by side in a desert setting. The plan's major concepts are to respect multiple cultural backgrounds, promote privacy between residential units and provide protection from the desert sun. The physical design concept creates shade at every opportunity as well as privacy between neighborhood districts and individual buildings.

Residential areas are composed of modular housing types which include single-family units, villas, townhouses and walk-up apartments. The largest percentage of neighborhoods are developed at the lowest densities. The town center is the highest density area with buildings at a height of four stories. Arterials to the town center are lined with three- and four-story apartment clusters.

The Yanbu plan is a comprehensive one which addresses management problems and the unpredictable nature of future populations as well as physical form. The use of prototypes and modular units is an aid in communicating its essential urban design intentions to the many groups who will participate in its implementation.

Neue Stadt Yanbu,
Yanbu, Saudi-Arabien

Die Planung für die etwa 8 km südlich des alten Yanbu vorgesehene Neue Stadt, die mit der Petrochemie als Lebensgrundlage in 30 Jahren auf etwa 150.000 Einwohner anwachsen soll, mußte auf zwei besondere Voraussetzungen Rücksicht nehmen. Einmal ist das Klima dieser Region höchst unwirtlich, und zum anderen sind die kulturelle Herkunft und die darauf beruhenden Ansprüche der zu erwartenden Bevölkerung ungemein vielschichtig.

Im Plan werden alle Bereiche des Lebens einer Stadtgemeinschaft erfaßt, von der Arbeit über Sozial- und Freizeiteinrichtungen und die Religionspflege bis hin zu den Verkehrssystemen und dem Wohnen. Für die Anordnung von Schulen, Parks und Ladenzonen war die bequeme Erreichbarkeit zu Fuß ausschlaggebend. Das Straßensystem ist auf klare und einfache Orientierbarkeit sowie eine im allgemeinen unmittelbare Erschließung aller Bereiche mit öffentlichen und privaten Verkehrsmitteln ausgerichtet. Es gibt nur wenige Wohnsammelstraßen, und die Durchgangsstraßen verlaufen in großen Abständen, um den Fußgänger vom Fahrverkehr fernzuhalten. Für die Gestaltung der Wohnbauten waren in erster Linie der Schutz vor der heißen Wüstensonne und die Sicherung der Privatsphäre maßgebend.

Die Architekten befaßten sich auch mit den organisatorischen Schwierigkeiten, die in einem sehr kurzfristig zu verwirklichenden Bauprogramm und einer nicht vorhersehbaren Bevölkerungsstruktur liegen. Mit auswechselbaren Grundelementen und Gebäudeprototypen wurde versucht, die Anpassungsfähigkeit an veränderte Programme und eine stufenweise Realisierung sicherzustellen. Die Arbeit mit Prototypen erleichtert überdies die Darstellung der wesentlichen städtebaulichen Absichten des Plans gegenüber den vielen Bevölkerungsgruppen, die an seiner Durchführung mitwirken sollen.

1. Regional map. Key: 1 Yanbu New Town, 2 Yanbu, 3 Red Sea, 4 airport, 5 Yanbu-Jeddah highway, 6 industry.
2. General view of Yanbu New Town towards the town center.

1. Übersichtsplan. Legende: 1 Neue Stadt, 2 Yanbu, 3 Rotes Meer, 4 Flughafen, 5 Straße von Yanbu nach Dschidda, 6 Industriegebiet.
2. Gesamtansicht der Neuen Stadt Yanbu in Richtung Stadtmitte.

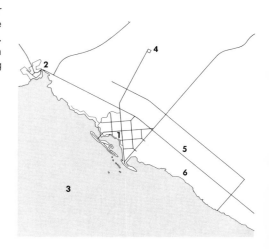

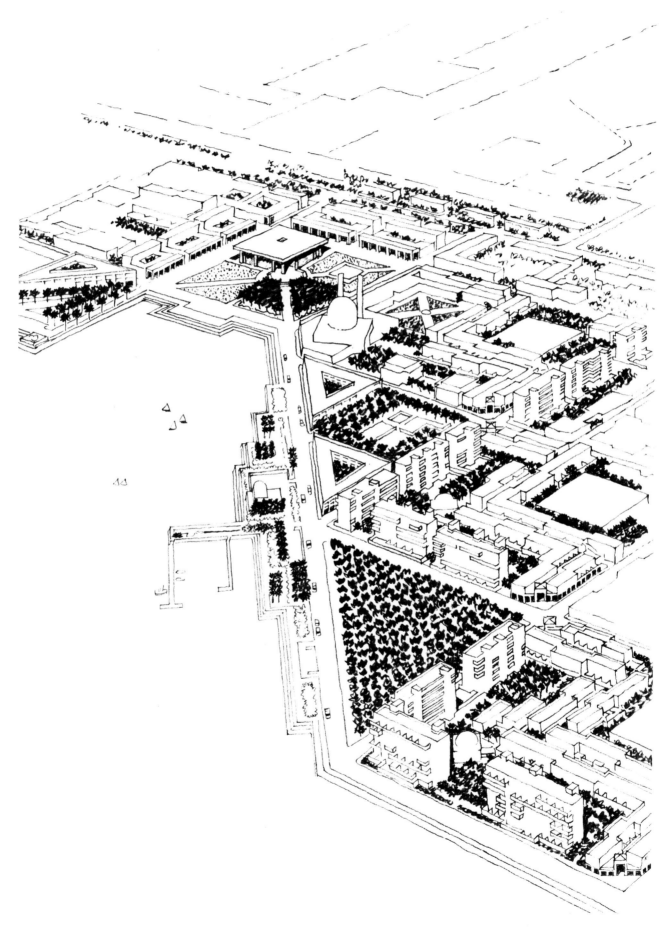

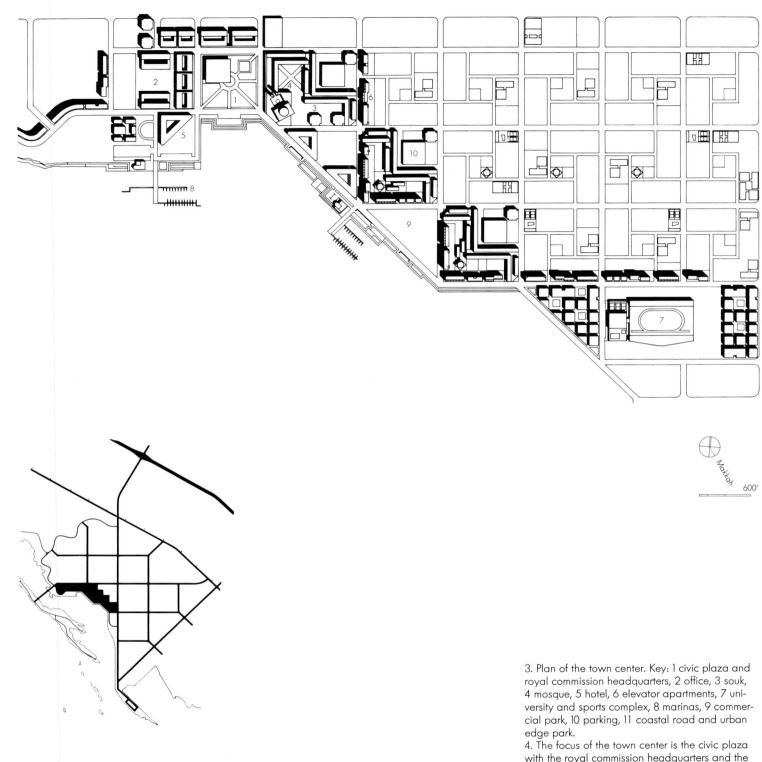

3. Plan of the town center. Key: 1 civic plaza and royal commission headquarters, 2 office, 3 souk, 4 mosque, 5 hotel, 6 elevator apartments, 7 university and sports complex, 8 marinas, 9 commercial park, 10 parking, 11 coastal road and urban edge park.
4. The focus of the town center is the civic plaza with the royal commission headquarters and the main mosque.

3. Plan der Stadtmitte. Legende: 1 öffentlicher Platz und Hauptverwaltung der königlichen Kommission, 2 Bürogebäude, 3 Suk, 4 Moschee, 5 Hotel, 6 hohe Wohngebäude, 7 Universität und Sportanlagen, 8 Yachthafen, 9 Gewerbegebiet, 10 Parkplätze, 11 Küstenstraße und Park am Stadtrand.
4. Den Blickpunkt in der Stadtmitte bildet der öffentliche Platz mit dem Gebäude der königlichen Kommission und der Hauptmoschee.

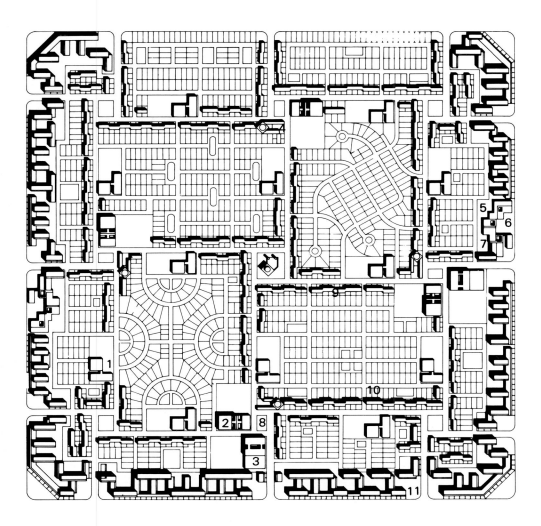

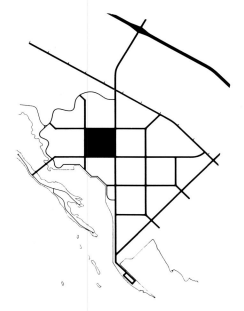

Makkah

600'

5. Plan of a residential module. Key: 1 elementary school, 2 intermediate school, 3 secondary school, 4 mosque and commercial, 5 arterial commercial, 6 municipal services (clinic/social welfare), 7 cultural center, 8 major open space, 9 villas, 10 townhouses, 11 walk-up apartments.
6. View into a residential neighborhood.

5. Plan eines Wohnquartiers. Legende: 1 Grundschule, 2 weiterführende Schule, 3 Oberschule, 4 Moschee und Geschäfte, 5 Hauptgeschäftsbereich, 6 öffentliche Einrichtungen (Krankenhaus, Sozialstation), 7 Kulturzentrum, 8 Freiraum, 9 Einzelhäuser, 10 Reihenhäuser, 11 höhere Apartmenthäuser.
6. Blick in ein Wohnviertel.

National Commercial Bank, Jeddah, Saudi Arabia

Traditionally, buildings in Saudi Arabia have spread out, but the irregular site and the desire to take advantage of spectacular views of the historic old city and the Red Sea led to the design of a high-rise structure. The 600,000-square-foot, 27-story triangular bank is flanked by a helical, 160,000-square-foot parking garage for 400 cars. Currently under construction on a 126,700-square-foot site between the old city and the sea, the project is scheduled for completion in 1983.

Instead of individual windows in the tower's outer travertine enclosure, colossal openings will allow views from and light into the interior across three landscaped courts that alternate position on two sides of the triangular shaft. Each of the resulting V-shaped floors of 18,000 square feet will thus be shielded from the direct effects of sun and wind, while a central wall that extends from the skylight of the first floor banking hall through the roof will allow accumulated heat to rise out of the courts. In developing this form, SOM has incorporated at least two indigenous traditions: the principle of ventilation and – more importantly – the principle of turning the building inward. The office floors overlook the old city to the southeast through two seven-story openings and the Red Sea to the north through a nine-story opening.

Executives occupying the top floor where windows are recessed behind a sheltering arcade will have views in all directions. The chairman's suite, including the central boardroom, will occupy the entire south side of the building.

At ground level, the public banking hall will be a grand space. White and green marble floors repeat the pattern of the coffered concrete ceiling 30 feet above. A level for an auditorium, cafeteria, lounge and other common facilities will surround the lowest of the courts recessed into the steel tower. A core for elevators, stairs, toilets and other services has been placed at the third side of the triangular tower, allowing for flexible office space.

National Commercial Bank, Dschidda, Saudi-Arabien

Obgleich Saudi-Arabien traditionell ein Land der Flachbauten ist, entschied man sich hier wegen des Grundstückszuschnitts und des großartigen Ausblicks über die Stadt und das Rote Meer für ein Hochhaus. Der 27geschossige, dreieckige Turm mit einer Fläche von etwa 56.000 m² wird von einer runden Garage mit 400 Stellplätzen gesäumt; das Grundstück hat eine Größe von etwa 11.800 m² und liegt zwischen der Altstadt und dem Meer. Die Fertigstellung des Komplexes ist für 1983 geplant.

Der Bautradition in den islamischen Ländern folgend, kehrt sich das mit Travertin verkleidete Stahlbetongebäude nach innen und wendet sich so von Sonne und Hitze ab. Alle Büroräume sind auf dreieckige Höfe hin orientiert, die aus dem Baukörper des Turmes ausgeschnitten sind. Zwei der Höfe sind sieben Geschosse hoch und öffnen sich zur Stadt hin; der dritte, auf mittlerer Höhe gelegene Hof erstreckt sich über neun Geschosse und kehrt sich dem Meer zu. Im Grundriß ergaben sich durch diese Höfe zwei relativ schmale, V-förmig zusammenlaufende Flügel mit etwa 1.700 m² großen Geschoßflächen. Die drei Innenhöfe überlappen sich in Gebäudemitte. Dadurch entstand ein Licht- und Luftschacht, der die gesamte Gebäudehöhe durchläuft und die Hitze aus den Höfen durch natürliche Zirkulation nach oben abführt.

Das oberste, ganz umlaufende Bürogeschoß, in dem die Direktion untergebracht ist, öffnet sich auf allen Seiten über schützende Arkaden direkt nach außen. Die Suite des Vorsitzenden der Bank nimmt zusammen mit dem zentralen Sitzungssaal die gesamte Südseite des Gebäudes ein.

Alle Aufzüge, Treppen und Sanitärräume sind zusammen mit anderen Nebeneinrichtungen in einem Doppelkern vor der dritten, nicht von Innenhöfen durchbrochenen Dreiecksseite des Turmes untergebracht, so daß die Büroflächen ohne vorgegebene Bindungen frei unterteilbar bleiben. Zugleich konnte so auch die Bankhalle im Erdgeschoß, die sich über die gesamte Grundrißfläche des Dreiecks erstreckt, von störenden Einbauten freigehalten werden. Entsprechend ihrer Größe erhielt dieses Geschoß eine Höhe von etwa 9 m. Die Halle wird von einer Betonkassettendecke mit einem sich aus der Grundrißform ergebenden Dreiecksraster überspannt, das sich im Muster des Bodenbelags aus grünem Marmor wiederholt. Über der Hallenmitte öffnet sich ein Oberlicht zu dem Schacht, der die Innenhöfe vertikal verbindet.

1. Plan (typical floor).
2. General view (model).

1. Grundriß (Normalgeschoß).
2. Gesamtansicht (Modell).

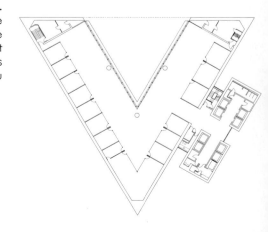

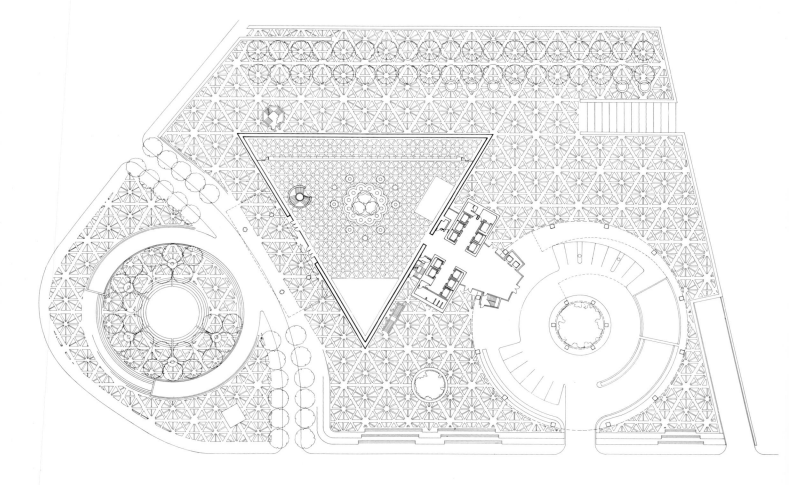

3. Plan (ground level).
4. Section.

3. Grundriß (Erdgeschoßebene).
4. Schnitt.

60'

380

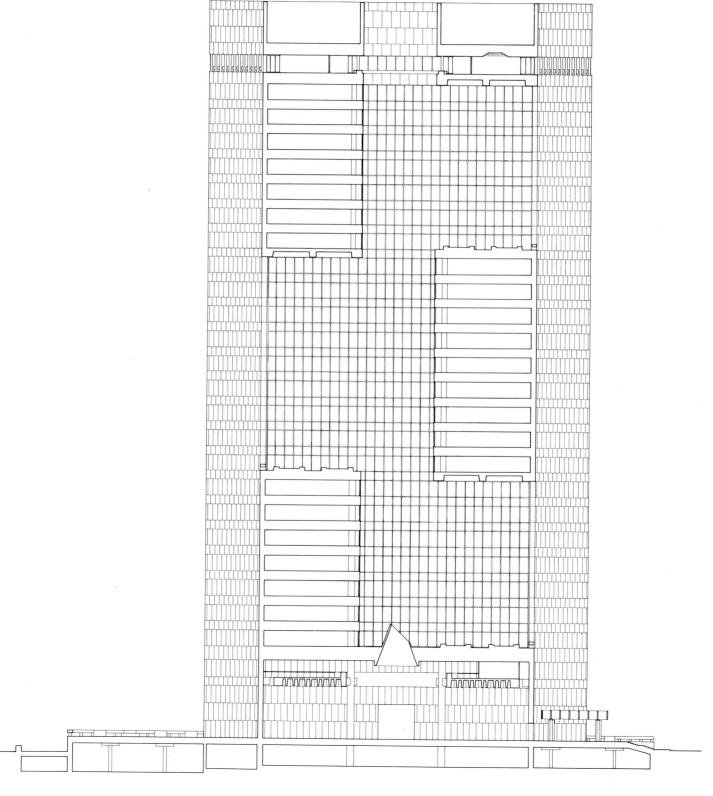

Haj Terminal,
King Abdul Aziz International Airport,
Jeddah, Saudi Arabia

The Haj Terminal at the King Abdul Aziz International Airport in Jeddah is located approximately 43.5 miles west of the Holy City of Makkah. Since Jeddah is the only large commercial city in close proximity to Makkah, all air traffic bound for Makkah arrives in Jeddah and proceeds by land transportation from Jeddah to Makkah. Normal airport facilities are capable of handling this traffic during most of the year; however, approximately once a year, vast numbers of Moslem pilgrims from all over the world travel to Makkah to participate in the Haj pilgrimage. The Haj activity takes place within about a six week period resulting in unusually high air traffic for this rather short period of time. Since the public facilities at the new airport were designed to handle only the normal flow of domestic and international air traffic, a separate terminal facility was required to process the Haj pilgrims.

The Haj Terminal design program required the facility to handle a large volume of people with highly diversified needs over a short period of time. It is projected that this facility will process approximately 950,000 pilgrims during the Haj by the year 1985. It is estimated that the terminal complex will need to accommodate 50,000 pilgrims at one time for periods up to 18 hours during arrival and 80,000 pilgrims for periods up to 36 hours during departure. This time is required in order to transfer between air and land transportation. Therefore, appropriate space, determined to be approximately 5,400,000 square feet, must be created which is adaptable and flexible to the Hajiis' needs.

In response to these requirements, a scheme was developed which provided for a linear terminal building adjacent to the aircraft parking aprons and a large, sheltered support complex adjacent to the terminal building. This scheme provided for minimum walking distance for the pilgrims from the planes to the air-conditioned terminal where all formal processing and baggage handling is accomplished. The pilgrims then proceed into the naturally ventilated support area where they will organize for travel by land to Makkah. Because of the rather severe environment in Jeddah, the support complex must be protected from the sun by a roof covering.

As it may take as many as 18 hours for the pilgrim to conclude the necessary preparations for the Haj, great care has been taken in the design of the support area to make the pilgrim's time in the area as pleasant as possible. Under each module, facilities are located for the pilgrim to rest, sleep and acquire both prepared foods or food which the pilgrim himself may prepare. In addition, many washing and toilet facilities have been provided in each module as well as offices providing banking, postal, airline, bus and taxi, and general information support services.

There are 210 semi-conical Teflon-coated Fiberglas roof units contained within a total of ten modules. Five modules located on each side of the central spine entry road cover a total area of approximately 105 acres. A single module contains 21 semi-conical fabric roof units stretched and formed by 32 radial cables. The modules are supported by 45-meter-high steel pylons located on a square 45-meter grid. The columns taper from 2.50 meters at their base to 1.00 meter at the top. In each module, steel cables radiate from the top of the columns to a 3.96-meters diameter central steel tension ring to which are attached the steel radial cables. The inherent long-span characteristics of steel cable structures allow for the spacing of columns to be far enough apart to give not only a very open feeling to the large support area but to allow for maximum flexibility in planning for the various support buildings located within the support area.

The form and height of the fabric roof units promote circulation of air from the open side of the support area up to and through the open steel tension ring located at the top of the roof unit. Mechanical fan towers placed intermittently between the columns enhance air circulation. Acoustical problems created by the many thousands of pilgrims located beneath the fabric roof are also diminished due to roof height and material. The fabric roofs provide shelter from intense desert heat. Because the fabric has a low heat transmission, it allows the sun to cast a warm light over the support area; at night, it will become a great reflective surface as pylon-mounted uplights bounce light from the roof to the ground below. Located under the landscaped central mall, two large exhaust fans for each module draw off exhaust fumes of the buses.

1. Location plan of the airport. Key: 1 Haj Terminal, 2 North Terminal, 3 South Terminal, 4 royal reception area, 5 maintenance, 6 operations, 7 administration, 8 Red Sea.

1. Übersichtsplan des Flughafens. Legende: 1 Haj Terminal, 2 Nordterminal, 3 Südterminal, 4 königliches Empfangsgebäude, 5 Unterhaltseinrichtungen, 6 Betriebsanlagen, 7 Verwaltung, 8 Rotes Meer.

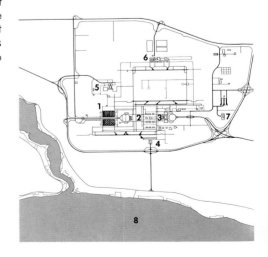

2. Location plan of the Haj Terminal. Key: 1 apron,
2 vehicle loading, 3 buses and taxis.

2. Übersichtsplan des Haj Terminal. Legende:
1 Flugsteig, 2 Be- und Entladezone für Fahrzeuge,
3 Autobusse und Taxis.

Haj Terminal, King Abdul Aziz International Airport, Dschidda, Saudi-Arabien

Der King Abdul Aziz International Airport liegt etwa 70 km westlich der heiligen Stadt Mekka, die alljährlich während der »Haddsch« von Hunderttausenden von Pilgern besucht wird. Da Dschidda die einzige größere Stadt in der Nähe von Mekka ist, landen und starten hier alle mit dem Flugzeug reisenden Pilger. Die sich über ungefähr sechs Wochen erstreckende Haddsch hat daher auf dem Flughafen von Dschidda einen unerhört starken Anstieg des Verkehrs zur Folge, der von den normalen Einrichtungen nicht mehr bewältigt werden konnte und einen eigenen Terminal für die Pilger erforderlich machte.

Bei der Planung für den 1982 fertiggestellten Haj Terminal war davon auszugehen, daß hier innerhalb kurzer Zeit eine große Anzahl von Menschen mit höchst unterschiedlichen Bedürfnissen zu versorgen sind. Für das Jahr 1985 rechnet man während der Haddsch-Periode mit etwa 950.000 Pilgern, die das Flugzeug benutzen. Danach werden sich hier zur gleichen Zeit etwa 50.000 ankommende beziehungsweise 80.000 abfliegende Pilger aufhalten, und zwar bis zu 18 Stunden nach der Ankunft und sogar bis zu 36 Stunden vor dem Abflug. Aus diesen Zahlen ergab sich ein Flächenbedarf von etwa 500.000 m².

Der Haj Terminal besteht aus zwei gleichen Teilen mit einer Größe von jeweils etwa 315 × 685 m, die durch eine breite Grünzone, in der auch die Verkehrsanbindungen liegen, getrennt sind. An den beiden Längsseiten befinden sich die Auf- und Abgänge zu den Flugzeugen und die Abfertigungseinrichtungen. Der Grundmodul der riesigen Dachkonstruktion besteht aus einem Raster von etwa 45 × 45 m. Jeweils 21 dieser Einheiten sind zu einer Gruppe zusammengefaßt, und fünf mit ihren Längsseiten gereihte Gruppen bilden eine der Hälften. An den beiden Längsseiten des Gesamtkomplexes – zugleich den Kopfseiten der Gruppen – sind insgesamt 20 Positionen für Großflugzeuge vorhanden. Nach Verlassen ihres Flugzeugs begeben sich die Pilger auf die Obergeschoßebene des längsseitig durchlaufenden, frei in die erste Modulreihe eingestellten, klimatisierten Empfangsgebäudes und unterziehen sich dort den üblichen Einreise- und Gesundheitsformalitäten, bevor sie über eine flach geneigte Rampe ihr Gepäck und die Zollabfertigung erreichen. Nach Verlassen der Abfertigungseinrichtungen finden sie sich schließlich in dem riesigen Wartebereich.

Die Überdachung hat in erster Linie die Aufgabe, die Pilger vor der Wüstenhitze zu schützen, da mit Regen ja kaum zu rechnen ist. Die jeweils ein Rasterfeld einnehmenden Zeltkuppeln bestehen aus etwa 1 mm dickem, mit Teflon beschichtetem Glasfasergewebe. Das Gewebe, das drei Viertel der Wärmestrahlung der Sonne abhält, läßt diffuses Licht mit warmem Ton einfallen und vermittelt einen ständigen Kontakt zur Außenwelt. Nachts werden die Hallen indirekt beleuchtet, indem die Zeltunterseiten das Licht der an frei stehenden Pylonen befestigten Strahler auf die Bodenflächen reflektieren.

Die Form der Dachkonstruktion wurde nicht allein auf Grund statischer Überlegungen gewählt – eine Reihung in der Mitte gestützter Zelte wäre wirtschaftlicher gewesen –, sondern auch im Hinblick auf ihren Symbolwert. Sie soll Erinnerungen an die traditionellen Nomadenzelte wecken, wie sie früher Pilger auf dem Landweg durch die Wüste benutzten: Aus der Luft glaubt der Ankommende, sich einem Feld solcher Zelte zu nähern. Die 210 halbkonischen Zeltkuppeln hängen an 45 m hohen Stahlrohrmasten, die auf dem 45-m-Grundrißraster stehen. Von einem Querschnitt von 2,50 m am Boden verjüngen sich diese Masten auf 1,00 m an der Spitze. Die 21 Dacheinheiten einer Gruppe werden jeweils durch 32 Radialkabel, die von den Stützenköpfen ausgehen, verspannt und bilden eine konstruktive Einheit in der Art eines statisch vielfach unbestimmten Durchlaufsystems. Alle Zeltkuppeln einer Gruppe mußten gleichzeitig hochgezogen und verspannt werden. Zur Aufnahme der Spannkräfte und Windlasten sind die äußeren beiden Mastenreihen einer Gruppe an den Ecken zu Viererereinheiten und dazwischen zu Doppeleinheiten verbunden. Die Zeltunterseiten reichen an den Masten bis auf eine Höhe von etwa 20 m über dem Boden herab; den höchsten Punkt erreichen die Felder in der Mitte mit einem Stahlspannring von 3,96 m Durchmesser, der 35 m über dem Boden liegt. An diesem Stahlring laufen die Radialkabel von den Mastspitzen zusammen.

Die durch die Stahlseilkonstruktion möglichen Stützweiten vermitteln nicht nur einen großzügigen, weiträumigen Eindruck in den Wartezonen, sondern boten auch ein Höchstmaß an planerischer Freiheit bei der Anordnung der von der Dachkonstruktion unabhängigen Einbauten. Querschnitt und Höhe der Zeltkuppeln führen zu einer höchst erwünschten Luftzirkulation von den Wartebereichen durch die offenen Spannringe in Feldmitte ins Freie. Außerdem haben Form, Höhe und Material der Kuppeln günstige akustische Bedingungen zur Folge, was bei der großen Zahl von Menschen, die sich gleichzeitig darunter aufhalten, von außerordentlicher Bedeutung ist. Großer Wert wurde auf eine freundliche und ansprechende Ausgestaltung der Wartezonen gelegt. Der Reisende findet sowohl Ruhe- und Schlafgelegenheiten als auch Restaurants und Läden für Lebensmittel. Außerdem stehen ihm Waschgelegenheiten und Toiletten sowie Bankfilialen, Postämter, Luftfahrtbüros und allgemeine Informationseinrichtungen zur Verfügung.

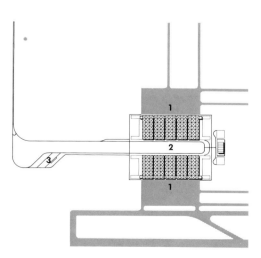

3, 4. The tents, pylons, cables, and tension rings
were designed as a single component and repli-
cated to create the final complex. The tent design
was described and drawn by the computer.

3, 4. Die Zeltdächer, Masten, Zugkabel und
Spannringe sind gleichartige Grundelemente, die
für den Bau der Gesamtanlage in entsprechender
Zahl vervielfältigt wurden. Die Zeltform wurde von
einem Computer berechnet und gezeichnet.

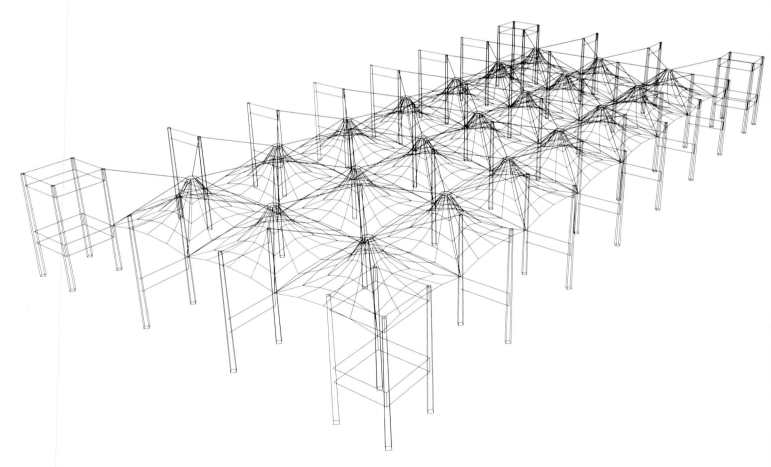

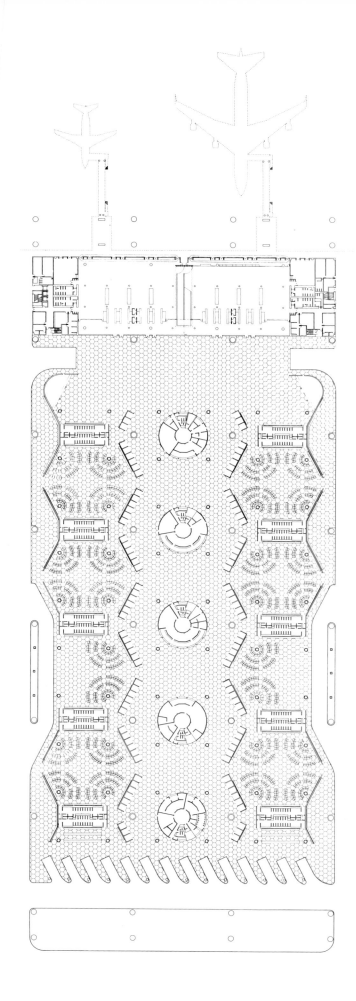

5. Plan of one of the ten modules.
6. Twenty wide-body aircraft gate positions – two at the short side of each module – are available.

5. Grundriß eines der zehn Gebäudeteile.
6. Es gibt zwanzig Parkpositionen für Großraumflugzeuge – jeweils zwei an der kürzeren Seite jedes Gebäudeteils.

Pages 388–391:
7–25. The Haj Terminal not only fulfills the requirements of its functional program, but also provides a moving and uplifting experience to the pilgrims as they set foot on the soil of the holy land of Islam.

Seiten 388–391:
7–25. Der Haj Terminal erfüllt nicht nur Forderungen rein funktionaler Art, sondern vermittelt den Pilgern mit dem Betreten des heiligen Landes des Islams zugleich auch ein eindrucksvolles und erhebendes emotionales Erlebnis.

Photo Credits · Photonachweis

10 (1)	Ronald Moore	52 (1)	Bob Hollingsworth
10 (2)	Jim Hedrich/Hedrich-Blessing	53 (2)	Bob Hollingsworth
10 (3)	Wolfgang Hoyt/ESTO	55 (4)	Bob Hollingsworth
11 (4)	Ezra Stoller/ESTO	61 (4)	Bob Hollingsworth
11 (5)	Howard N. Kaplan/HNK	63 (6)	Bob Hollingsworth
12 (6)	Ezra Stoller/ESTO	69 (3)	Jane Lidz
12 (7)	Ezra Stoller/ESTO	70 (4)	Jane Lidz
12 (8)	Ezra Stoller/ESTO	70 (5)	Jane Lidz
13 (9)	Hedrich-Blessing	71 (6)	Jane Lidz
13 (10)	Ezra Stoller/ESTO	71 (7)	Jane Lidz
14 (11)	Stewart's, Inc.	72 (1)	Jane Lidz
14 (12)	Orlando R. Cabanban	73 (2)	Jane Lidz
14 (13)	Bob Hollingsworth	75 (2)	Wes Thompson
15 (14)	Howard N. Kaplan/HNK Architectural Photography	75 (3)	Wes Thompson
		77 (5)	Wes Thompson
15 (15)	Bob Hollingsworth	80 (2)	Wayne Thom Associates
15 (16)	Merrick/Hedrich-Blessing	80 (3)	Wayne Thom Associates
16 (17)	Wolfgang Hoyt/ESTO	80 (4)	Wayne Thom Associates
16 (18)	Orlando R. Cabanban	80 (5)	Wayne Thom Associates
17 (19)	Bob Hollingsworth	81 (6)	Wes Thompson
17 (20)	Wayne Thom Associates	83 (2)	Ronald Moore
17 (21)	Merrick/Hedrich-Blessing	88 (1)	Wayne Thom Associates
18 (22)	Howard N. Kaplan/HNK	90 (1)	Jaime Ardiles-Arce
18 (23)	Greg Hursley/Hursley & Lark	93 (4)	Jaime Ardiles-Arce
19 (24)	Orlando R. Cabanban	94 (5)	Jaime Ardiles-Arce
19 (25)	Wolfgang Hoyt/ESTO	95 (6)	Jaime Ardiles-Arce
19 (26)	Mak Takahashi	97 (2)	James Lemkin
22 (33)	Wolfgang Hoyt/ESTO	98 (3–14)	Bruce Forster, Thomas J. Houha/SOM Lawrence Hudetz
23 (24)	Bob Hollingsworth	99 (15)	Bruce Forster
24/25 (1)	Wayne Thom Associates	100/101 (1)	Bill Engdahl/Hedrich-Blessing
26 (4)	Mak Takahashi	102 (2)	Merrick/Hedrich-Blessing
26 (5)	R. Wenkam	102 (3)	Hedrich-Blessing
27 (11)	Marley Baer	103 (4)	Orlando R. Cobanban
27 (12)	Bruce Forster	103 (5)	Guy Arnold
27 (14)	Wes Thompson	103 (6)	Hedrich-Blessing
28 (15)	Ezra Stoller/ESTO	103 (7)	Lewellyn Studio
28 (16)	Mak Takahashi	104 (8)	Balthazar Korab
28 (17)	Mak Takahashi	104 (9)	Ezra Stoller/ESTO
28 (18)	Mak Takahashi	105 (10)	Bill Engdahl/Hedrich-Blessing
28 (19)	Jeremiah O. Bragstad	105 (11)	Ezra Stoller/ESTO
29 (20)	Sunderland Aerial Photographers	105 (12)	Steve Grubman
29 (21)	Ezra Stoller/ESTO	105 (13)	Ezra Stoller/ESTO
29 (22)	Mak Takahashi	106 (14)	Ezra Stoller/ESTO
29 (23)	Bob Hollingsworth	106 (15)	Merrick/Hedrich-Blessing
29 (24)	R. Wenkam	106 (16)	Ezra Stoller/ESTO
30 (25)	Wayne Thom Associates	106 (17)	Balthazar Korab
30 (26)	Ronald Moore	107 (19)	Orlando R. Cabanban
30 (27)	Wayne Thom Associates	107 (20)	Merrick/Hedrich-Blessing
30 (28)	Jeremiah O. Bragstad	107 (21)	Orlando R. Cabanban
30 (30)	Gerald Ratto	107 (22)	Orlando R. Cabanban
31 (31)	Bob Hollingsworth	108 (23)	Nick Wheeler
31 (32)	Gerald Ratto	108 (24)	Hedrich-Blessing
31 (33)	Bob Hollingsworth	108 (25)	Merrick/Hedrich-Blessing
31 (34)	Bob Hollingsworth	108 (26)	Ezra Stoller/ESTO
32 (35)	Jane Lidz	108 (27)	Balthazar Korab
32 (37)	Jane Lidz	108 (28)	Wolfgang Hoyt/ESTO
33 (38)	Bob Hollingsworth	109 (29)	Harr/Hedrich-Blessing
33 (39)	Bob Hollingsworth	109 (30)	Greg Murphey
34 (1)	Bob Hollingsworth	109 (31)	Orlando R. Cabanban
35 (2)	Jaime Ardiles-Arce	111 (2)	Merrick/Hedrich-Blessing
37 (4)	Bob Hollingsworth	113 (4)	Merrick/Hedrich-Blessing
39 (2)	Bob Hollingsworth	113 (5)	Merrick/Hedrich-Blessing
41 (4)	Bob Hollingsworth	114 (1)	Wolfgang Hoyt/ESTO
43 (2)	Bob Hollingsworth	115 (2)	Wolfgang Hoyt/ESTO
45 (4)	Bob Hollingsworth	121 (3)	Jim Hedrich/Hedrich-Blessing
45 (5)	Bob Hollingsworth	121 (4)	Jim Hedrich/Hedrich-Blessing
47 (7)	Bob Hollingsworth	123 (1)	Harr/Hedrich-Blessing
49 (2)	Gerald Ratto	124 (2)	Howard N. Kaplan/HNK
49 (3)	Gerald Ratto	126 (4)	Howard N. Kaplan/HNK
		126 (5)	Bill Engdahl/Hedrich-Blessing

127 (6)	Guy Arnold	230 (11)	Steve Rosenthal	314 (11)	Orlando R. Cabanban
129 (2)	Bill Hedrich/Hedrich-Blessing	231 (13)	Wolfgang Hoyt/ESTO	314 (12)	Jack Horner
133 (4)	Ezra Stoller/ESTO	231 (14)	Warren Jagger	315 (13)	Thomas J. Houha/SOM
134/135 (5)	Steve Grubman	231 (15)	Wolfgang Hoyt/ESTO	315 (14)	Orlando R. Cabanban
137 (2)	Ezra Stoller/ESTO	231 (16)	Wolfgang Hoyt/ESTO	317 (21)	Howard N. Kaplan/HNK
139 (4)	Ezra Stoller/ESTO	232 (17)	Paul Stevenson Oles, AIA	317 (22)	Jay Langlois/Owens-Corning Fiberglas
139 (5)	Ezra Stoller/ESTO	232 (18)	Helmut Jacoby	321 (2)	Nick Wheeler
140/141 (6)	Ezra Stoller/ESTO	232 (19)	Wolfgang Hoyt/ESTO	321 (3)	Nick Wheeler
144 (3)	Ezra Stoller/ESTO	232 (20)	Steve Rosenthal	322 (4)	Nick Wheeler
144 (4)	Ezra Stoller/ESTO	232 (21)	Nick Wheeler	322 (5)	Nick Wheeler
145 (5)	Ezra Stoller/ESTO	232 (22)	Wolfgang Hoyt/ESTO	323 (6)	Nick Wheeler
146/147 (6)	Ezra Stoller/ESTO	233 (23)	Harr/Hedrich-Blessing	325 (2)	Nick Wheeler
148 (1)	Merrick/Hedrich-Blessing	233 (24)	Wolfgang Hoyt/ESTO	326 (3)	Nick Wheeler
149 (2)	Merrick/Hedrich-Blessing	233 (25)	Jack Horner	327 (4)	Nick Wheeler
153 (2)	Hedrich-Blessing	234 (26)	Wolfgang Hoyt/ESTO	328 (1)	Orlando R. Cabanban
155 (4)	Merrick/Hedrich-Blessing	234 (27)	Wolfgang Hoyt/ESTO	328 (2)	Orlando R. Cabanban
157 (2)	Balthasar Korab	235 (28)	Wolfgang Hoyt/ESTO	328 (3)	Orlando R. Cabanban
159 (4)	Balthazar Korab	235 (29)	Wolfgang Hoyt/ESTO	330 (1)	Jack Horner
162 (2)	Hedrich-Blessing	237 (2)	Wolfgang Hoyt/ESTO	333 (2)	Jaime Ardiles-Arce
164 (5)	Hedrich-Blessing	239 (4)	Wolfgang Hoyt/ESTO	334 (3)	Jaime Ardiles-Arce
165 (6)	Hedrich-Blessing	240 (1)	Wolfgang Hoyt/ESTO	335 (4)	Jaime Ardiles-Arce
167 (2)	Ezra Stoller/ESTO	243 (4)	Wolfgang Hoyt/ESTO	353 (1)	Orlando R. Cabanban
169 (4)	Ezra Stoller/ESTO	244 (1)	Jack Horner	356 (1)	Wolfgang Hoyt/ESTO
170 (1)	Orlando R. Cabanban	247 (2)	Jaime Ardiles-Arce	359 (4)	Wolfgang Hoyt/ESTO
173 (4)	Orlando R. Cabanban	247 (3)	Jaime Ardiles-Arce	359 (5)	Wolfgang Hoyt/ESTO
173 (5)	Orlando R. Cabanban	247 (4)	Jaime Ardiles-Arce	366/367 (3)	Howard N. Kaplan/HNK
175 (2)	Sadin/Karant Photography	249 (2)	Ezra Stoller/ESTO	379 (2)	Ezra Stoller/ESTO
176/177 (3)	Sadin/Karant Photography	251 (2)	Jaime Ardiles-Arce	385 (4)	Jay Langlois/Owens-Corning Fiberglas
179 (2)	Wolfgang Hoyt/ESTO	252 (3)	Jaime Ardiles-Arce	387 (6)	Jay Langlois/Owens-Corning Fiberglas
179 (3)	Wolfgang Hoyt/ESTO	253 (4)	Jaime Ardiles-Arce	388/389 (7–24)	Jay Langlois/Owens-Corning Fiberglas
181 (2)	Merrick/Hedrich-Blessing	255 (2)	Wolfgang Hoyt/ESTO	390/391 (25)	Jay Langlois/Owens-Corning Fiberglas
183 (4)	Paul Warchol/ESTO	256 (3)	Wolfgang Hoyt/ESTO		
185 (2)	Balthazar Korab	256 (4)	Wolfgang Hoyt/ESTO		
187 (4)	Balthazar Korab	256 (5)	Wolfgang Hoyt/ESTO		
188/189 (1)	Joe C. Aker	257 (6)	Wolfgang Hoyt/ESTO		
190 (2)	Ezra Stoller/ESTO	260 (3)	Jack Horner		
190 (3)	Ezra Stoller/ESTO	261 (4)	Wolfgang Hoyt/ESTO		
190 (4)	Ezra Stoller/ESTO	263 (2)	Ezra Stoller/ESTO		
191 (5)	Stewart's, Inc.	265 (4)	Ezra Stoller/ESTO		
191 (6)	Ezra Stoller/ESTO	267 (2)	Wolfgang Hoyt/ESTO		
191 (7)	Ezra Stoller/ESTO	269 (11)	Wolfgang Hoyt/ESTO		
191 (8)	Jeremiah O. Bragstad	269 (12)	Wolfgang Hoyt/ESTO		
192 (9)	Orlando R. Cabanban	272 (3)	Ezra Stoller/ESTO		
192 (10)	Orlando R. Cabanban	273 (4)	Ezra Stoller/ESTO		
192 (11)	Orlando R. Cabanban	274 (1)	Nick Wheeler		
192 (12)	Harr/Hedrich-Blessing	275 (2)	Nick Wheeler		
193 (14)	Peter Aaron/ESTO	277 (4)	Harr/Hedrich-Blessing		
193 (15)	Greg Hursley/Hursley & Lark	277 (5)	Gorchev & Gorchev		
194 (18)	Joe C. Aker	279 (2)	Steve Rosenthal		
194 (19)	Joe C. Aker	281 (4)	Steve Rosenthal		
197 (2)	Hursley/Lark/Hursley	283 (2)	Warren Jagger		
199 (4)	Wes Thompson	284 (1)	Warren Jagger		
201 (2)	Joe C. Aker	290 (3)	Wolfgang Hoyt/ESTO		
203 (4)	Joe C. Aker	291 (4)	Wolfgang Hoyt/ESTO		
203 (5)	Joe C. Aker	291 (5)	Wolfgang Hoyt/ESTO		
204 (1)	Joe C. Aker	291 (6)	Wolfgang Hoyt/ESTO		
207 (4)	Joe C. Aker	293 (2)	Harlan Hambright		
209 (2)	Gerald Ratto	294 (3)	Wolfgang Hoyt/ESTO		
213 (2)	Joe C. Aker	295 (4)	Wolfgang Hoyt/ESTO		
222 (1)	Orlando R. Cabanban	295 (5)	Michael Fisher/ESTO		
225 (4)	Orlando R. Cabanban	297 (2)	Wolfgang Hoyt/ESTO		
226/227 (1)	Erich Locker	299 (4)	Wolfgang Hoyt/ESTO		
228 (2)	Wolfgang Hoyt/ESTO	301 (2)	Wolfgang Hoyt/ESTO		
228 (3)	Ezra Stoller/ESTO	304 (1)	Wolfgang Hoyt/ESTO		
228 (4)	Ezra Stoller/ESTO	306 (1)	Harr/Hedrich-Blessing		
228 (5)	Union Carbide Corporation	309 (4)	Harr/Hedrich-Blessing		
229 (6)	Ezra Stoller/ESTO	312 (5)	Jim Hedrich/Hedrich-Blessing		
229 (7)	Ezra Stoller/ESTO	313 (7)	Ezra Stoller/ESTO		
229 (8)	Ezra Stoller/ESTO	313 (8)	Nick Wheeler		
229 (9)	Joseph W. Molitor	313 (9)	Ezra Stoller/ESTO		
230 (10)	Steve Rosenthal	314 (10)	Wolfgang Hoyt/ESTO		